GLOBAL MARKET BRIEFINGS

INVESTORS' GUIDE TO THE
UNITED KINGDOM

CONSULTANT EDITOR:
JONATHAN REUVID

PUBLISHED IN ASSOCIATION WITH:

**KOGAN
PAGE**

London and Sterling, VA

The views expressed in this book are those of the authors, and are not necessarily the same as those of UK Trade & Investment.

Publisher's note
Every possible effort has been made to ensure that the information contained in this book is accurate at the time of going to press, and the publishers and authors cannot accept responsibility for any errors or omissions, however caused. No responsibility for loss or damage occasioned to any person acting, or refraining from action, as a result of the material in this publication can be accepted by the editor, the publisher or any of the authors.

First published in Great Britain and the United States in 2005 by Kogan Page Limited

120 Pentonville Road
London N1 9JN
United Kingdom
www.kogan-page.co.uk

22883 Quicksilver Drive
Sterling VA 20166-2012
USA

© Kogan Page, Jonathan Reuvid and the individual contributors, 2005

ISBN 0 7494 4224 7

British Library Cataloguing-in-Publication Data

A CIP record for this book is available from the British Library.

Library of Congress Cataloging-in-Publication Data

Investors' guide to the United Kingdom / editor, Jonathan Reuvid.
    p. cm.
Includes index.
ISBN 0-7494-4224-7
    1. Investments--Great Britain. 2. Industries--Great Britain. 3. New business enterprises--Law and legislation--Great Britain. 4. Great Britain--Economic conditions--1997– I. Reuvid, Jonathan.
HG5432.I618 2004
330.941--dc22
                                    2004017688

Typeset by Saxon Graphics Ltd, Derby
Printed and bound in Great Britain by Thanet Press Ltd, Margate

Editor's Note

About this book

This book contains an outline of the major legal, taxation and commercial issues that will need to be considered by an overseas individual or company proposing to do business in England and Wales. The contents of many of the legal and taxation chapters of this book apply equally to Scotland and Northern Ireland. However, the law in Scotland and Northern Ireland can differ in varying degrees from that in England and Wales. In addition, court procedures and remedies are substantially different. In this Guide, all references to the United Kingdom and to United Kingdom law are references to England and Wales and the law in England and Wales only, except where the text otherwise requires. If an overseas person is considering doing business in Scotland or Northern Ireland, then legal advice should be sought from persons qualified to practice in those areas.

This book is intended to provide a summary of the basic legal and taxation provisions only and should not be relied on as providing legal advice. It is certainly not a legal textbook and makes no pretence that it is exhaustive on any subject referred to. Anyone considering doing business in the United Kingdom should obtain professional advice relating to their specific investment or activity and to the applicability of the relevant legislation to the particular facts. The law is as stated on 1 March 2004.

For potential inward investors seeking to study all these factors in their business decision process, this book is designed to provide an understanding of start-up considerations in the United Kingdom (Part 4) and the corporate and personal legal regulatory environment (Part 5). Parts 1 and 2 are intended to impart a working knowledge of key investment sectors and specific industry sectors of opportunity in which investors may wish to engage. Part 6 is a compendium of information about England's 10 regions and Northern Ireland, Scotland and Wales. Further contacts relating to the industry sectors and the contributors to the book are detailed in the Appendices.

Contents

Foreword   *ix*
Mike O'Brien, Minister for International Trade and Investment

List of Contributors   *xi*

Part 1 Economic Overview

1.1 The UK Economy and Investment Environment   3
     Jonathan Reuvid and UK Trade & Investment
1.2 The UK and the European Union   9
     Jonathan Reuvid

Part 2 Principal Investment Sectors

2.1 The Stock Exchange Main Market   15
     Robert Coe, Wilder Coe
2.2 AIM – The Alternative Investment Market of the London Stock
     Exchange   22
     AIM
2.3 The UK Commercial Property Market: Future Trends   30
     Dr Nigel Almond and Dr Sotiris Tsolacos, Jones Lang LaSalle
2.4 UK Commercial Property Investment   46
     Dr Nigel Almond and Dr Sotiris Tsolacos, Jones Lang LaSalle
2.5 Agricultural and Residential Property   62
     Richard Binning and Richard Donnell, FPD Savills
2.6 Mergers and Acquisitions and Joint Ventures   71
     Sara Bradbury, David Kent, Daniel Rosenberg and Paul Webb,
     Inward Investment Group, Taylor Wessing
2.7 Private Equity and Venture Capital   86
     Professor Colin Mason, Strathclyde University
2.8 Technology and Innovation – the Cambridge Phenomenon   107
     Alan Barrell and Mark Littlewood, Library House, Cambridge
2.9 Art and Collectibles   119
     James Goodwin

Part 3 Industry Sectors of Opportunity

3.1 The Automotive Industry   133
     Mark Norcliffe, Society of Motor Manufacturers and Traders

3.2   Biotechnology   142
       Jeanette Walker, ERBI
3.3   Chemical Industries   153
       Neil Harvey, International Trade and Sector Groups, Chemical
       Industries Association
3.4   Creative Industries   160
       Jonathan Reuvid
3.5   Electronics Sector   170
       Jonathan Reuvid
3.6   Electronic Commerce   175
       BT eLocations
3.7   Financial Services   181
       Kevin Smith, AWS Structured Finance
3.8   Food and Drink   186
       Jonathan Reuvid
3.9   Gaming   193
       David Kent, Inward Investment Group, Taylor Wessing
3.10   Pharmaceuticals   199
       Lilly
3.11   Renewable Energy   204
       Allan Taylor, Renewables UK
3.12   Software   219
       Charles Ward, Intellect UK
3.13   Telecommunications   227
       BT eLocations
3.14   Utilities   234
       Neil Gould, Powergen

Part 4 Investment and Start-up Considerations

4.1   Legal Overview for Inward Investors   241
       David Kent, Inward Investment Group, Taylor Wessing
4.2   Grants and Incentives within EU Parameters   255
       Siegfried Doetjes, PNO-j4b
4.3   Development and Business Support Agencies   262
       Jonathan Reuvid and the Small Business Service (SBS)
4.4   Business Risk   275
       Norman Cowan, Wilder Coe
4.5   Company Formation – Methods and Legal Implications   279
       Ian Saunders, Artaius Ltd
4.6   Commercial Banking Services   288
       Jonathan Reuvid and HSBC
4.7   Finance for Companies   295
       Jonathan Reuvid and HSBC

4.8   Financial Reporting and Accounting   303
      Michael Bordoley with Jitendra Pattani, Wilder Coe
4.9   Business Taxation   312
      Bob Tranter, Wilder Coe
4.10 Taxation Planning   324
      Bob Tranter, Wilder Coe
4.11 Outsourcing   332
      Alfred Levy, Artaius Ltd
4.12 Relocation Issues   337
      Stephen Heath and Johan Taft, SPB[3]

Part 5 Corporate and Personal Legal Environment

5.1   Protection of Intellectual Property (Brand Protection)   343
      Christopher Benson, Chris Jeffrey, David Kent and Jason Rawkins,
      Inward Investment Group, Taylor Wessing
5.2   Employment, Pensions and Stock Options   360
      Paul Callaghan, Michael Porter, Fleur Benns and David Kent,
      Inward Investment Group, Taylor Wessing
5.3   Immigration into the United Kingdom   374
      Gavin Jones and David Kent, Inward Investment Group, Taylor
      Wessing
5.4   Taxation for Foreign Nationals   382
      Tim Cook, Wilder Coe
5.5   Regulation of Financial Services   392
      Richard Millar, Eversheds
5.6   Money Laundering Regulations   399
      Mark Saunders, Wilder Coe
5.7   Environmental Issues   404
      Alison Askwith and David Kent, Inward Investment Group, Taylor
      Wessing

Part 6 UK Regional Options

6.1   North East England   415
      One North East
      6.1.1 Gateshead   432
      6.1.2 Newcastle   436
6.2   North West England   442
      Northwest Development Agency
6.3   Yorkshire and Humber   448
      Yorkshire Forward
      6.3.1 Barnsley   456
      6.3.2 Doncaster   464

6.4	West Midlands	468
	West Midlands Development Agency	
6.5	East Midlands	475
	East Midlands Development Agency	
	6.5.1 Leicester and Leicestershire	479
	6.5.2 Nottingham	482
6.6	East of England	486
	Invest East of England	
6.7	London	490
	London First Centre (LFC)	
	6.7.1 Thames Gateway	510
	Gateway to London	
6.8	South East England	516
	South East England Development Agency (SEEDA)	
6.9	South West England	522
	South West England Development Agency	
	6.9.1 Swindon	527
6.10	Northern Ireland	535
	Invest Northern Ireland	
6.11	Scotland	544
	Scottish Enterprise	
6.12	Wales	556
	Welsh Development Agency	
	Appendix 1 Contributors' Contact Details	*569*
	Appendix 2 Industry Sector Websites	*575*
	Appendix 3 Key Government Agencies	*581*
	Index	*585*
	Index of Advertisers	*594*

Foreword

I am delighted to have been asked to write this foreword to the *Investors' Guide to the United Kingdom*. Cross-border investment can be a powerful stimulant for economic prosperity. Countries and companies can both take lasting benefit from the exchanges of ideas, skills and technologies that come from successful investment projects.

This government is committed to maintaining the UK as Europe's top destination for inward investment and warmly welcomes international companies and individual entrepreneurs to establish operations, partnerships or joint ventures here.

Our powerful combination of a business friendly and stable economy, strong IT and telecommunications infrastructure and a skilled, flexible workforce are very persuasive reasons for us to remain Europe's most attractive investment location.

In fact the high quality of our skills and services makes us the leading European location for high value investment sectors, including; automotive, software, electronics, pharmaceuticals, financial services and telecommunications.

We have a long tradition as a trading nation and have continued to make the UK ever more open to trade and investment and able to respond to the increasingly competitive and fast changing global economy.

The UK is a great place in which to do business and it is no coincidence that the UK is getting the largest share of investment into Europe while enjoying its longest unbroken period of economic growth for over two hundred years.

UK Trade & Investment's Inward Investment Group, their partner agencies in the English regions, Scotland, Wales and Northern Ireland and investment officers in British Embassies and Consulates overseas are all well placed to show how the UK could become a key element in your global business strategy.

You can find out more about the UK as a business location from the UK Trade & Investment website www.uktradeinvest.gov.uk.

Mike O'Brien
Minister for International Trade and Investment

List of Contributors

Dr Nigel Almond is Senior Researcher at Jones Lang LaSalle, specializing in UK commercial real estate markets.

Alison Askwith is a Partner at Taylor Wessing and a member of the Inward Investment Group, specializing in environmental issues.

Alan Barrell is a Founder Partner of Library House, the Cambridge research centre and networking hub.

Fleur Benns is a Senior Associate at Taylor Wessing, specializing in employee benefits and share options.

Christopher Benson is a Senior Associate at Taylor Wessing, and a member of the Inward Investment Group, specializing in intellectual property rights.

Richard Binning is an Associate at the Oxford office of FPD Savills, specializing in farm sales.

Michael Bordoley is a Partner at Wilder Coe Chartered Accountants.

Sara Bradbury is a Senior Associate in the Inward Investment Group at Taylor Wessing, specializing in mergers, acquisitions and joint ventures.

Paul Callaghan is a Senior Associate at Taylor Wessing, specializing in employment law.

Robert Coe is Senior Partner at Wilder Coe Chartered Accountants.

Tim Cook is a Taxation Partner at Wilder Coe.

Norman Cowan is Head of Business Recovery at Wilder Coe.

Siegfried Doetjes is Managing Director of PNO-j4b Consulting Ltd.

Richard Donnell is Head of UK Residential Research and a Director of FPD Savills.

James Goodwin MA, MBA, is a freelance art and business consultant, affiliated with Sotheby's.

Neil Gould is SME Manager, Powergen.

Neil Harvey is Manager, International Trade and Sector Groups, Chemical Industries Association.

Stephen Heath is Managing Director of SPB[3], the relocation specialists.

Chris Jeffery is a Senior Associate at Taylor Wessing and a member of the Inward Investment Group, specializing in intellectual property rights.

Gavin Jones is a Senior Associate in the Inward Investment Group of Taylor Wessing, specializing in immigration issues.

David Kent is a Partner and the Head of the Inward Investment Group at Taylor Wessing.

Alfred Levy is Managing Director of Artaius Ltd, providers of business outsource solutions.

Mark Littlewood is Business Development Director of Library House, the Cambridge buy-side research house and networking hub.

Professor Colin Mason is Professor of Entrepreneurship at Hunter School of Entrepreneurship, University of Strathclyde.

Richard Millar is a consultant at Eversheds LLP, specializing in the regulation of financial services.

Mark Norcliffe is Head of the International Department at the Society of Motor Manufacturers and Traders (SMMT).

Jitendra Pattani is a Partner at Wilder Coe Chartered Accountants.

Michael Porter is a Senior Associate at Taylor Wessing, specializing in pensions law.

Jason Rawkins is a Partner at Taylor Wessing and a specialist in intellectual property rights.

Jonathan Reuvid is a Kogan Page author and consultant editor and the senior editor of *Global Market Briefings*.

Daniel Rosenberg is a Partner at Taylor Wessing, specializing in mergers, acquisitions and joint ventures.

Ian Saunders is Managing Director of Artaius Company Services Ltd, which specializes in company formation and management services.

Mark Saunders is a Partner at Wilder Coe Chartered Accountants. Wilder Coe are appointed representatives of Integra International® an interactive global network of local independent accounting and consulting firms dedicated to exchanging information and advising growing businesses and professionals.

Kevin Smith is an international financial consultant and Managing Director of AWS Structured Finance Ltd.

Johan Taft is a Director of SPB[3], the relocation specialists.

Allan Taylor is Industry Sponsorship Manager at Renewables UK, a section of the Department of Trade and Industry.

Bob Tranter is a Taxation Partner at Wilder Coe, Chartered Accountants.

Dr Sotiris Tsolacos is Associate Director and Acting Head of UK Research at Jones Lang LaSalle, London.

Jeanette Walker is Director of Business Development, ERBI.

Charles Ward is Marketing Director of Intellect UK.

Paul Webb is a Partner at Taylor Wessing, specializing in mergers, acquisitions and joint ventures with the Inward Investment Group.

Part 1

Economic Overview

1.1

The UK Economy and Investment Environment

Jonathan Reuvid and UK Trade & Investment

With its population of just over 60 million (July 2003 estimate), the United Kingdom is part of the world's largest trading entity, the European Union (EU), whose population has now been enlarged to 456 million since 1 May 2004 following the accession of 10 new members to the previous Western European grouping of 15 states. However, the United Kingdom is also a major market and economy in itself and has the lowest barriers to inward foreign investment in the industrialized world, according to a June 2003 report of the Organisation for Economic Co-operation and Development.

Table 1.1.1 UK major macro-economic indicators (%)

	1999	2000	2001	2002	2003	2004(e)	2005(f)
Economic Growth	2.8	3.8	2.1	1.6	2.2	3.1	2.7
Consumer Spending (% change)	4.4	4.6	3.1	3.4	2.5	3.8	2.5
Investment (% change)	2.2	4.8	3.6	(2.6)	(0.5)	5.2	4.1
Inflation (CPI)	1.7	0.8	1.2	1.3	1.4	1.5	1.8
Unemployment Rate	6.0	5.5	5.1	5.2	5.0	4.8	4.8
Short-term Interest Rate	5.4	6.1	5.0	4.0	3.6	4.5	5.6
Public Sector Balance/GDP	1.1	3.9	0.7	(1.5)	(2.9)	(2.9)	(2.9)
National Debt/GDP	55.8	55.6	50.4	52.0	53.5	55.0	55.0
Export (% change)	4.3	9.4	2.5	(0.9)	(0.9)	4.2	8.7
Imports (% change)	7.9	9.1	4.5	3.6	1.1	7.5	9.3
Current Account Balance, as % of GDP	(2.3)	(2.1)	(1.8)	(1.8)	(2.7)	(2.3)	(2.7)

Note: (e) Estimate (f) forecast.
Source: Coface www.trading-safely.com 3 September 2004.

The UK economy in brief

The vital statistics of the UK economy are recorded in Table 1.1.1 and illustrate its favourable current performance in comparison with the other US$3 trillion economies of Western Europe and many other EU members.

Growth
GDP growth in the United Kingdom in 2003 was 2.2 per cent, signalling recovery from the effects of the global downturn, and is forecast to rise above 3 per cent for 2004. The economy is expected to return to trend in 2005.

Interest rates
The Bank of England's Monetary Policy Committee reduced the interest base rate to 3.5 per cent in July 2003, bringing long-term interest rates, which had been below 6 per cent for over two years, to their lowest rates since the 1960s. Under the present government, the Bank of England has independence to set interest rates to meet the government's maximum inflation target of 2.5 per cent. In 2004, the Bank Committee raised the base rate progressively as a measure to dampen increasing consumer debt and inflationary pressures, aggravated by the threat of escalating oil prices.

Inflation
UK inflation remains below the OECD and EU average and the longest period of sustained, low inflation since the 1960s is forecast to continue. The EU15 average CPI rate was 1.5 per cent in March compared with 1.1 per cent in the United Kingdom. In fact, the UK inflation rate has been continuously among the lowest in the EU since the start of 2000. In manufacturing, output prices have been at an annual rate of around 2 per cent while input prices for materials and fuels have risen rather faster at over 3 per cent.

Unemployment
Since 1997 the United Kingdom's long-term unemployment rate has fallen by 75 per cent, with youth unemployment at only 20 per cent of its pre-1997 level. The present unemployment rate of around 5 per cent is significantly lower than the current EU average of 8.8 per cent and is the lowest among the G7 nations.

Foreign trade
The United Kingdom runs a deficit on current account, which is forecast to rise to 2.3 per cent for 2004. The strong pound sterling was

a factor in the 0.9 per cent fall in exports and 1.1 per cent increase in imports during 2003; both exports and imports continue to rise.

Public finances
The government's accelerated programmes to speed up improvements in education, transport and health services have impacted public current expenditure and generated a budget deficit since 2001, which reached 2.9 per cent of GDP in 2003 and is expected to remain the same in 2004. The deficit is therefore below the Maastricht Treaty criterion level for euro entry and compares favourably with both France and Germany, the two largest economies in the Eurozone.

The inward investment environment

The underlying strength of the UK economy is an important factor in its popularity as an investment location. Although services, particularly banking, insurance and business services, account for the largest proportion of GDP, manufacturing industry remains important. In particular, higher value-added sectors like chemicals, pharmaceuticals, aviation, automobile engines, software, IT services and electronics have been developing rapidly.

Agriculture is highly mechanized, intensive and efficient by European standards, producing about 60 per cent of the nation's food requirements with only 1 per cent of the labour force. The United Kingdom retains large reserves of coal, natural gas and oil so that energy production accounts for 10 per cent of GDP and holds one of the highest shares among industrialized nations.

With its diverse economy, the United Kingdom remains the fourth largest trading nation, accounting for 5 per cent of world trade in goods and services (World Trade Organization, 2002). On forecast growth trends, the UK economy is expected to overtake that of Germany by 2025.

Inward investment data
According to the UNCTAD, *World Investment Report 2003*, the United Kingdom is the second largest recipient of overseas direct investment (ODI) after the United States. The United Kingdom holds 22 per cent of the stock of EU inward investment and 9 per cent of the worldwide stock of ODI valued at US$2,623.9 billion (excluding Belgium and Luxembourg). For the year 2003–04 a total of 811 successful inward investment projects were recorded by UK Trade & Investment, generating 25,463 new jobs. The projects are analysed by investing country in Table 1.1.2.

In 2004 KPMG analysed cost advantages/disadvantages of eleven countries relative to the United States in a 10-month research

Table 1.1.2   UK inward investment projects by investing country (2003/04)

	Projects	New jobs
US	314	10,668
France	54	1,318
Japan	52	2,344
Canada	51	562
Germany	49	2,876
Irish Republic	30	1,126
Norway	30	314
India	28	646
Sweden	24	417
China	23	324
Rest of EU	69	2,462
Rest of the World	87	2,406
Total	811	25,463

Source: UK Trade & Investment

programme that measured the combined impact of 27 significant cost components in 98 cities. The basis for comparison was the after-tax cost of start-up and operation for 17 specific businesses over a 10-year time horizon and the findings were published in its *Competitive Alternatives Report*. The United Kingdom was judged to be the most competitive in Europe, both in terms of business costs advantage (2.4 per cent) and manufacturing costs (2.5 per cent). Italy was the second most competitive country on business costs and Luxembourg on manufacturing costs. The Netherlands and Germany were found to suffer considerable cost disadvantages against the United States.

Benefits of the United Kingdom for inward investors

There are four main reasons why the United Kingdom is the most favoured inward investment location in Europe and attracts around 40 per cent of Japanese, US and Asian investment into the EU:

- The United Kingdom has a skilled, well-motivated and adaptable workforce of 28 million and high standards of education with a strong emphasis on vocational education and training. Labour market regulations in the United Kingdom, including working hours, are the most flexible in Europe, and staffing costs are highly competitive. In the past two decades the government has addressed the structural imbalances of the economy by greatly reducing public ownership and, until recently, containing the growth of the social welfare programmes.

- The United Kingdom has a strong science and technology base with world-class design, research and development disciplines. Many UK universities and scientific institutes are taking part in collaborative research projects with businesses.

- The business environment is focused on providing the right conditions for companies of all sizes to grow in the United Kingdom, and innovate and compete in global markets. Financial incentives are available for companies setting up in certain areas of the United Kingdom. More generally, the United Kingdom has the lowest main corporation tax rate of any major industrialized country, and there are no additional local taxes on profits.

- In terms of infrastructure, the United Kingdom has the lowest utilities costs in the EU and a telecommunications industry that is among the world's most advanced. The United Kingdom's integrated transport network provides fast, low-cost delivery throughout Europe. Every location in the United Kingdom is within 100 miles of a container port. The Channel Tunnel links the United Kingdom by road and rail to the rest of Europe, bringing both Paris and Brussels only three hours from London by rail.

Further reading

UK Inward Investment 2003–2004, an annual report by UK Trade & Investment, available at www.uktradeinvest.gov.uk.

If you want to sell overseas, **UK TRADE & INVESTMENT** can help.

We're the government organisation that provides advice and support to businesses in the UK who are trading abroad or thinking about it.

We have a network of experts in over 200 locations worldwide and throughout the UK who can offer you fast, authoritative market intelligence, free sales leads and advice on the local rules and regulations.

Whatever the size of your business, we're here to help so you can make a success of trading overseas.

To take your business further, faster, call 020 7215 8000 or visit www.uktradeinvest.gov.uk

1.2

The United Kingdom and the European Union

Jonathan Reuvid

The EU is now the most important market for UK exporters, accounting for around two-thirds of the United Kingdom's foreign trade. The ratio represents a dramatic change in the United Kingdom's economy from 1972, the date of its passing of the European Communities Act, when most of its markets were beyond Europe, mainly the Commonwealth countries of Australia, New Zealand, Canada, West and East Africa and the Caribbean. This transformation in the orientation of the UK economy is the direct result of EU membership and the resultant changes to the way in which the United Kingdom does business have been far-reaching.

EU law

In terms of trade, commercial regulations and most areas of the law, in particular competition law, the United Kingdom is bound by EU law, which prevails over UK law and takes the following four forms:

- Treaties that are binding on member states and EU institutions.

- Regulations also binding on all member states that do not require any implementation or adoption by national parliaments.

- Directives that are binding but leave a member state to choose how the required result will be achieved. In the United Kingdom, the alternative methods are an Act of Parliament or delegated legislation.

- Decisions of the European Court of Justice of the Communities, which are binding on the highest courts of member states (the House of Lords in the case of the United Kingdom) in their entirety.

Areas of regulation in which the United Kingdom does not conform to EU law or practice are taxation and labour law where the government negotiated exclusions in the Maastricht Treaty.

EU grants, incentives and business support

UK investment incentives and regional support programmes are tailored within EU parameters and the programmes administered from Brussels by the European Commission. The range of various schemes available to inward UK investors and programme rules are complex. Chapters 4.2 and 4.3 provide outline descriptions and some insight into the complexities.

The Eurozone

The United Kingdom has not joined the European Monetary Union (EMU), which came into being with effect from 1 January 1999. The forebodings for the impact on sterling and the UK economy expressed at the time have not been realized. UK importers and exporters have learnt to trade in the euro as a matter of routine, and the City of London retains its domination of financial markets despite fears that the centre of gravity would move to Frankfurt.

Only Denmark, Sweden and the United Kingdom of the then EU15 have held back from the Eurozone for the time being. Both Denmark and Sweden have rejected the euro through national referenda. The UK Chancellor of the Exchequer has established criteria for judging whether the UK economy is sufficiently aligned to the Eurozone before joining and a referendum is expected some time after the next General Election.

In fact, the relatively good performance of the UK economy has complicated the case for joining the Eurozone. Public opinion polls continue to show a majority of Britons opposed to the EMU and the outcome of a referendum is uncertain.

The EU constitution

Of more immediate concern is the outcome of current negotiations between member states on the adoption of a European Constitution that would involve closer political and administrative ties and raise issues of sovereignty. The government has identified specific issues, such as taxation, on which it will not accept EU harmonization. Other member states, in particular Poland and Spain, hold firm views on other issues such as the structure and voting rights in a more integrated community. The UK government has confirmed that there will be a national referendum if a constitution is agreed shortly by the Meeting of Ministers, which could be held towards the end of 2005. Once again, the outcome of such a poll is highly uncertain.

Part 2

Principal Investment Sectors

2.1

The Stock Exchange Main Market

Robert Coe, Wilder Coe

Introduction

The London Stock Exchange has been helping to finance companies and provide a market for their shares for over 200 years. Many successful privately owned companies will ultimately reach a stage in their development where they will need to consider whether to list their shares on a public market.

Admission

A two-stage admission process applies to companies that want to have their securities admitted to the London Stock Exchange's Main Market for listed securities. The securities need to be admitted to the Official List by the UK Listing Authority (UKLA), a division of the Financial Services Authority, and admitted to trading by the London Stock Exchange. Once both processes are complete, the securities are officially listed on the London Stock Exchange.

The Main Market is the London Stock Exchange's principal market for listed companies from the United Kingdom and overseas. It currently includes approximately 1,800 UK companies and 400 overseas companies.

Within the Main Market two subsidiary groupings exist: 1) techMark, which groups together innovative technology companies listed on the main market enhancing their visibility and profile (launched in November 1999 techMark has 235 companies from 23 different sub-sectors); and 2) techMark Medi Science, a specialist market that groups together pioneering health care companies listed on the Main Market. Launched in 2001 it includes 47 companies.

Separately from the Main Market, the London Stock Exchange operates the Alternative Investment Market (AIM), which is a global market for young and growing companies. Launched in 1995 it has been specifically developed to meet the needs of companies not yet mature enough to join the Main Market. Over 700 companies from the United Kingdom and overseas are currently quoted on AIM.

Advantage and disadvantages

The advantages and disadvantages of seeking a listing are as follows:

Advantages

- access to capital for growth;
- providing a market for your company's shares;
- employee commitment;
- ability to take advantage of acquisition opportunities;
- higher public profile;
- reassurance for customers and suppliers.

Disadvantages

- susceptibility to market conditions;
- potential loss of control;
- disclosure requirements and ongoing reporting;
- loss of privacy;
- costs and fees;
- management time;
- directors' responsibilities and restrictions.

Regulatory requirements

The UKLA's listing rules set the specific regulatory requirements that have to be met to be allowed to list on the Main Market. In addition to meeting the UKLA's requirements for granting officially listed status, an applicant to the London Stock Exchange needs to be admitted to trading on the Main Market. The Exchange has a set of straightforward admission and disclosure standards that will help a company to gain admission to the Main Market. The regulatory requirements are as follows:

- The company must be incorporated under UK law as a public limited company.

- The company must normally have published or filed audited accounts covering a three-year period.

- The company should have an independent trading and revenue earning record covering the same period.

- The company directors must show they have the appropriate collective experience and expertise to run all areas of the business.

- The company must be able to show it has enough working capital for its current needs for at least the next 12 months.

- Once the company is listed, at least 25 per cent of its shares should be in public hands.

- A company listing its shares on the market must have a total market capitalization of not less than £700,000 and would normally be expected to have a market capitalization much larger than this figure.

The company must demonstrate that it complies with the Corporate Governance requirements as set out in the Combined Code. Corporate Governance refers to the way a company conducts itself and structures its top management. The main current benchmark for best practice is the Combined Code issued by the Higgs Committee.

In its role as the UKLA, the Financial Services Authority has a legal obligation to oversee the listing process, and to ensure that its rules are met. This duty involves the UKLA in reviewing and approving the prospectus or listing particulars. This document, which will be passed to the UKLA by an applying company's sponsors (namely its corporate adviser), primarily contains information on the company and its business and must satisfy the UKLA's listing rules to ensure that only companies meeting the conditions for listing come to the Main Market.

Ways to market

Depending upon the nature of a company's business and its capital requirements it may choose one of three different ways in which to come to the Main Market:

- Public offer. In this case, the sponsor will offer a company's shares to private and/or institutional investors. The sponsor will also usually arrange for the offer to be underwritten, meaning that any shares not bought will be purchased by institutions that have agreed to do so for a fee.

- Placing. This method involves offering the shares to a selected base of institutional investors. This allows the company to raise capital but with lower costs and greater freedom in terms of how it is done.

- Introduction. This is where a company joins the market without raising capital and is therefore often the least expensive and most straightforward way to join the market. Generally, a company can use this method if over 25 per cent of its shares are in public hands and there is already a fair spread of shareholders.

Costs of listing

Coming to the Main Market is a major investment for any business. A listing on the Main Market is likely to cost a company at least £500,000 in professional fees. This figure can rise significantly for a sizeable listing especially when the factors such as underwriting fees are taken into account.

Flotation timetable

For a Main Market, listing the process is generally expected to take between 12 and 24 weeks depending upon the size, complexity and method of flotation.

Continuing obligations

The continuing obligations of the UKLA require all listed companies to fulfil two aims: 1) to ensure the timely disclosure of all relevant information; and 2) the equal treatment of all shareholders.

The company has an obligation to notify the market of any information that would be likely to lead to a substantial movement in the price of its shares – for example, new developments in its activity that are not public knowledge, any changes in the company's financial condition, the performance of its business or in its expectation of its performance. For all listed companies the fundamental rule is that they must notify the market as soon as possible of any price-sensitive information that might be a significant change in the company's financial position or outlook or a major new development.

Directors' responsibilities

The directors of a newly listed company will have accepted legal responsibility for the information their company published during the flotation process.

Dealing restrictions in the model code

All directors of a listed company have to comply with a range of restrictions on their share dealing activities. These are grouped together in the model code, which is designed to prevent people with unpublished price-sensitive information from dealing on the basis of this information and thereby gaining an advantage over other shareholders.

Report and accounts

All listed companies must publish their annual report and accounts including an audited financial statement no later than six months after the end of the financial year. The company also has to prepare unaudited half-yearly figures within four months of the end of its half-year. Failure to comply with these timescales will result in the company having the listing of its shares suspended.

Transaction and document disclosure

Many types of transactions must be disclosed and for some, such as a major acquisition or disposal, shareholder approval is required in advance for the deal to go ahead. As a rule of thumb, the larger or more significant the transaction the greater the disclosure requirements imposed on the company.

The OFEX market

The OFEX market was created to establish London as the principal financial community with a clearly defined 'three tier' market place for companies looking to progress upwards from OFEX to AIM to the official list (Main Market).

The OFEX market commenced in October 1995 and is operated by OFEX plc, which in turn is regulated by the Financial Services Authority. The OFEX market differs from AIM and the Main Market in that the latter two are regulated by the London Stock Exchange, while the former is regulated by an independent company. OFEX is therefore not a recognized investment exchange as defined by the Financial Services and Markets Act 2000, and securities traded on OFEX are defined as unlisted and unquoted and are not traded on-exchange. It was created specifically to provide a market in its shares for smaller, immature companies seeking the advantages of a public listing.

The OFEX market provides the same considerable benefits to a company as any public market place. The choice of appropriate market place will depend upon the size and funding requirements of the company concerned. Some of the main reasons for using OFEX include:

- To raise equity-based finance from private and institutional investors.

- To provide shareholders with a way of buying and selling their shares.

- To allow the company to provide the visibility and transparency of price and share transactions for its shareholders.

- To have an independently valued share price.

- To create a visible profile for the company, allowing it to broaden its shareholder base and generate awareness of its company's products and services. OFEX can be used to introduce overseas investors to UK businesses.

- Shares traded on OFEX are defined as unlisted and unquoted and therefore overseas investors in UK businesses may be eligible to benefit from certain types of UK tax relief.

- Using OFEX as the first step towards growing the business and moving to a more senior secondary market in due course.

How OFEX works

The OFEX market provides a trading platform for the securities of its client companies. Any company looking to join the OFEX market must make an application to do so via a Corporate Adviser member. The Corporate Adviser member will make the application to OFEX on behalf of the company and must him- or herself be regulated by the Financial Services Authority. In addition, a company seeking an OFEX quotation will have to retain the services of a Financial Services Authority-regulated UK stockbroker through whom dealings in the company's shares will have to be transacted.

Admission to OFEX
The criteria for admission to OFEX are not the same as those set by the UK Listing Authority, and OFEX traded securities are not considered to be listed. OFEX does not give any warranty to investors regarding securities traded on OFEX and their value or prospects nor the suitability of an investment in such companies.

Continuing obligation
Issuers of securities using OFEX must abide by the OFEX Rule Book, which sets out the continuing obligation rules. If an issuer breaches the Rule Book there is the possibility that the securities will be suspended from trading on the OFEX market.

Market supervision

There is no maximum or minimum size of company that is entitled to make an application to OFEX nor does it matter whether a company is a public limited company or a private limited company. However, if the company wishes to raise capital, public limited company status is a requirement. There is no requirement for a defined trading history although the information disclosure requirements on a start-up business will be more onerous than on more mature companies.

General requirement

The company making an application for its securities to join OFEX must do so through a Corporate Adviser who is both a member of OFEX and regulated by the Financial Services Authority. The application consists of various forms that need to be completed and which must be accompanied by supporting documentation. The type of supporting documentation depends upon whether the company is established, a start-up and/or raising capital. The requirements to provide information both when a company joins the OFEX market or intends completing a transaction, whether it be the acquisition of a company or the raising of fresh capital, is generally far less onerous than for an equivalent transaction on the London Stock Exchange.

Costs

When a company joins the OFEX market it will incur an application fee of £5,000 (exclusive of VAT) and an annual fee that is charged on a sliding scale dependent on the market capitalization of the company.

The OFEX market is normally used by smaller companies and fundraisings tend to be for lesser amounts, normally between £500,000 and £1 million. Costs of these fundraisings can normally be expected to be in the region of £100,000 to £200,000.

AIM – The Alternative Investment Market of the London Stock Exchange

AIM

Introduction

The Alternative Investment Market (AIM) for smaller, growing companies was launched in June 1995 by the London Stock Exchange. Unlike other growth markets, AIM is designed both for domestic and overseas companies across all industry sectors, not just technology companies.

AIM is by far the most successful of the European growth markets attracting almost 60 per cent of all Western European IPOs (Initial Public Offerings) in 2003. At the end of 2003 there were 754 companies quoted on AIM including 66 IPOs for the year.

AIM is operated, regulated and promoted by the London Stock Exchange and its rules have been tailored to suit the unique requirements of growing businesses. Its flexibility has meant that it has succeeded in attracting a wide range of companies, from young and venture capital-backed businesses to longer-established concerns. Similarly, AIM companies cover a broad range of activities, from leading-edge technology to distribution, oil and gas, restaurants and leisure.

Last year the London Stock Exchange introduced a fast-track admissions procedure to AIM for companies already quoted on certain other international markets. To date over ten overseas companies have joined AIM using this route, saving money and time by avoiding the need to produce a new admission document.

The continuing success of AIM in recent difficult market conditions reflects the quality of its regulation and the flexibility of its structure. A new dedicated AIM management team set up by the London Stock Exchange in early 2004 demonstrates their ongoing commitment to AIM.

Admission

Since its inception AIM's guiding principle has been to create a regulatory environment that is especially designed to meet the needs of smaller companies. By offering a more flexible approach than other markets the AIM admission process with its Nomad system (see next section) has been designed to ensure proper quality control of prospective AIM companies while maintaining its attractiveness to a diverse range of enterprising companies.

There are fewer suitability criteria for admission to AIM than on other markets. Specifically, AIM requirements include:

- no minimum shares required in public hands;

- no trading record requirement;

- no minimum market capitalization;

- no restrictions on the transferability of the company's shares;

- no requirement to be incorporated in the United Kingdom;

- no requirement to re-state any historic accounts.

As with any quotation on a stock exchange, AIM companies are obliged to issue regular trading statements once they have joined and although price-sensitive information must be disclosed, the AIM rules do not require formal quarterly reporting. Best practice in Corporate Governance is strongly advised.

As a result of its flexible admissions procedure AIM attracts younger growth companies that frequently have shorter trading histories. While potential returns may be high, AIM companies may also be higher risk. However, to ensure the running of an orderly market, companies joining AIM must comply with key legislation. Each company applying to AIM must:

- appoint a Stock Exchange-approved Nominated Adviser (Nomad);

- appoint a broker – a securities house that is a member of the London Stock Exchange (that can be the same firm as the Nominated Adviser);

- have no restrictions on the free transferability of shares;

- prepare an admission document – including all relevant information on the company and its activities – including financial information and any projections, together with details of all directors.

An AIM company will be required to produce an AIM admission document unless it has also been traded on a Designated Market (see Designated Market section below). The AIM admission process itself is very straightforward with the Nominated Advisers (Nomads) acting as the principal quality controllers for the market. In the normal course of business, when a Nominated Adviser declares to the London Stock Exchange that in its opinion a company is appropriate for AIM, the London Stock Exchange will admit the company to AIM three days later.

During the three-day period, the London Stock Exchange will set up the necessary trading systems and notify various interested internal and external parties (such as market makers and index compilers) about a company's imminent admission.

The AIM rules

Like the admissions process, the AIM rules are tailored to the needs of smaller, growing, companies. There are 43 clear and short rules and nine schedules, which are drafted in non-technical language and are intended to be easily understood. Before a company can join AIM it must submit a declaration confirming that it will adhere to them.

Once admitted to AIM, companies are required to disclose certain matters on an ongoing basis, such as major contracts, the appointment of directors and any price-sensitive matters. Any failure to make proper disclosures is treated severely by the London Stock Exchange. The rules are available on the AIM section of the London Stock Exchange's website with definitions and guidance notes.

The role of the Nominated Adviser (Nomad) and broker

Key to AIM's flexible regulatory regime are the Nominated Advisers or Nomads. It is an absolute requirement that every AIM company has a Nomad from the London Stock Exchange's approved register, as well as a broker.

The role of the Nomad

A Nomad is a firm of experienced corporate finance professionals approved by the London Stock Exchange, whose role is to:

- assess whether a company is appropriate for the AIM market;
- support a company's initial application;
- explain the AIM rules to the company's board;
- help a company meet AIM rules/requirements on a continuing basis.

The Nomad's main task is to assess the suitability of a potential new applicant seeking to float on AIM. In effect, the Nomad will project manage the complete flotation process. The Nomad will coordinate the financial due diligence carried out by suitably qualified accountants (not the company's auditors) and legal due diligence by appropriate lawyers. If the company operates in a specific industry sector an additional specialist report may be commissioned to support the company strategy. The due diligence process is intended to be exhaustive, and will put a high demand on senior management's time.

A Nomad will also ensure that company directors are aware of their responsibilities and obligations under AIM rules. Nomads will approve any admission document, prospectus or circular issued by an AIM company. However, a company's directors are ultimately responsible for compliance with AIM's regulations, including the accuracy of the information in its admission document.

After admission, the Nomad must remain available at all times to help and guide its companies on the application of the AIM rules whenever they need its advice. Conversely, an AIM company must seek advice from its Nominated Adviser whenever its advice is required.

Nomads have an overriding responsibility to protect the reputation and integrity of the market, which means that they should use all reasonable endeavours to seek to ensure that the companies for which they act conduct themselves in ways befitting companies that have their securities traded on a public market. Nomads effectively stake their reputations on the quality of the companies they support.

Nomads are vetted and authorized by the London Stock Exchange and are subject to regular reviews by the Exchange. Nomads may be censured or removed from the register if they fail to act with proper skill and care in warranting that companies are appropriate for a flotation. If a Nomad is dismissed or resigns, trading in that company's shares is suspended until a replacement is appointed.

At present, there are over 72 authorized Nomads, from both the United Kingdom and overseas, whose details are available on the AIM section of the London Stock Exchange's website.

The role of the broker

An AIM broker will advise on the various methods of flotation, capital raising and timing of the initial float. The broker will be a securities house that is a member of the London Stock Exchange and they will work with the Nomad in respect of any fundraisings. The broker can be the same firm as the Nomad but the firm will need to have procedures in place to avoid any conflict of interest. The broker will play an important role in bringing buyers and sellers of shares together, and making a success both of the flotation and trading in the market after flotation.

AIM Designated Markets – companies traded on other markets

In May 2003, the London Stock Exchange introduced AIM Designated Markets, a streamlined admission route for companies that have already been admitted to other major international markets. The Designated Markets are the Australian Stock Exchange, Euronext, Deutsche Börse, JSE Securities Exchange, South Africa, Nasdaq, NYSE, Stockholmsbörsen, Swiss Exchange, Toronto Stock Exchange and the UKLA Official List.

Provided that a company has been admitted to the main board of any of these markets for at least 18 months it can apply to be admitted to AIM without having to publish an admission document. Instead of producing an admission document, companies are required to provide a range of information by way of an announcement 20 business days before the date of its expected admission. The announcement must include, among other requirements, details of the business of the company, its intended strategy post-admission and its financial situation. A company wishing to join AIM from a Designated Market will still require a Nomad to warrant that it is appropriate for AIM.

Benefits and key considerations of an AIM flotation

Many of the advantages and disadvantages of AIM are endemic to any stock exchange quotation, but it is important for each potential entrant to evaluate thoroughly the appropriateness of joining a public market and specifically of joining AIM:

Advantages

- Flexible entry requirements. AIM's rules are specifically designed to be brief and straightforward and the admissions process is simplified by the Nomad regulatory process.

- Access to capital. Since its launch in 1995 AIM has helped companies raise over £10.5 billion through an initial share placing and through further share issues.

- A higher company profile. AIM quotation confers greater visibility and prestige. AIM has seen increasing interest from institutional investors with share trading doubling in 2003.

- A possible first step towards the senior market. Many companies use AIM as a stepping stone to a full listing on the London Stock Exchange.

- Increased opportunities to make acquisitions. An AIM flotation can provide access to funds for growth and a company can use shares as currency for acquisitions.

- Employee benefits. A quotation provides an opportunity to offer employees a valuable reward through share option packages.

- An opportunity to create a market for the company's shares and widen its shareholder base. AIM can provide the opportunity to bring in new shareholders or provide an exit route for founder share-holders and other stakeholders.

- Tax benefits. There is a range of tax benefits associated with AIM (see website for details).

Disadvantages

- Disclosure requirements and ongoing reporting. Although vital to ensure confidence in the market there are strict requirements on the disclosure of information. Regular reporting can add to the cost of being on a public market and the responsibilities of directors.

- Vulnerability to irrational share movements in the market. A company's share price is not determined by its own performance alone. The share price can be affected by the general state of the economy or particular developments in industry sectors.

- Increased scrutiny. Companies joining a market are not only subjected to an initial scrutiny by potential investors and analysts, but also on an ongoing basis after joining the market.

- Impact on management time and costs. The process of flotation can be demanding on management time. Provisions need to be made to manage the flotation process, while at the same time, still meeting the demands of running the day-to-day business.

Investor attitudes

Although there are no official requirements of profitability or length of trading for coming to AIM, companies seeking to raise funds are likely to find that investors may take a different view. Investors will look at a range of elements when assessing companies quoted on AIM. Longer trading records and an indication of profitability are favourable. However, as in all fundraising operations, the key element in making a company's shares saleable to investors is the quality and integrity of management. The Nominated Adviser will need to be sure that the nucleus of a strong management team is in place and if necessary a company may appoint non-executive directors to strengthen the team. The investment community has been known to look at the experience of the management team and a sound business plan in lieu of trading records.

Recent new issues and outlook

Table 2.2.1 below shows the 162 newcomers to AIM in 2003 broken down by industry sector.

Table 2.2.1   New issue investments by sector – Jan–Dec 2003

Sector	No of New Issues	Value of Investments (£m)
Mining	17	44.66
Oil & Gas	5	27.82
Chemicals	3	5.88
Construction & Building Materials	6	10.30
Forestry & Paper	1	2.00
Steel & Other Metals	1	0.00
Aerospace & Defence	1	1.65
Diversified Industrials	0	0.00
Electronic & Electrical Equipment	6	27.50
Engineering & Machinery	4	2.40
Automobiles	5	1.78
Housing Goods & Textiles	7	0.00
Beverages	0	0.00
Food Producers & Processors	4	11.42
Health	6	32.37
Personal Care & Household Products	1	0.00
Pharmaceuticals & Biotechnology	5	14.47
Tobacco	0	0.00
General Retailers	3	0.35
Leisure & Hotels	10	267.86

continued opposite

Sector	No of New Issues	Value of Investments (£m)
Media & Entertainment	12	43.78
Support Services	10	53.02
Transport	4	3.16
Food & Drug Retailers	0	0.00
Telecommunication Services	3	2.21
Electricity	0	0.00
Utilities – Other	1	388.97
Banks	0	0.00
Insurance	2	0.80
Life Assurance	0	0.00
Investment Companies	1	0.00
Real Estate	5	7.61
Speciality & Other Finance	17	61.59
Investment Entities	4	50.72
Information Technology Hardware	4	11.37
Software & Computer Services	14	17.77
Total Equities	162	1,091. 43

The table indicates that there was a revival of investment interest in software companies, mirroring an appetite for technology-based companies in the overall market. However, the bulk of activity continued to be in more traditional industries such as mining and oil and gas. Leisure and entertainment featured strongly. However, the bulk of the institutional involvement was in the companies that moved from the Main Market to AIM.

Outlook

Equity markets throughout the world experienced two years of tough trading, especially for smaller companies. However, signs of improving conditions emerged at the end of 2003, which saw increased activities in further issues and IPOs, and it is hoped that the increased flow of new companies coming to AIM will be sustained through 2004 with improving valuations and liquidity.

AIM is not only the most international European growth market but also the largest by market capitalization, having considerably more companies listed than all of the other growth markets in Europe combined. It is well placed to take advantage of any prolonged upturn in equity market conditions.

Updated information on recent and forthcoming admissions, trading statistics, company announcements, Nominated Advisers, conferences and events is available on the Exchange's website: www.londonstockexchange.com.

2.3

The UK Commercial Property Market: Future Trends

Dr Nigel Almond and Dr Sotiris Tsolacos, Jones Lang LaSalle, London

Background

Property market size

Commercial real estate plays an important role in the UK economy, providing a significant (£87 billion) contribution to total output, representing nearly 10 per cent of UK GDP as at 2002. Of course, this underestimates its true importance, as buildings accommodate the United Kingdom's business activity base.

At the end of 2002, the total value of the commercial property in the United Kingdom was estimated to be worth £446 billion, with residential property adding a further £2,800 billion. Over half of the commercial real estate is owned for investment purposes, with the remainder owner-occupied by both individual companies, and to a lesser degree, the government.

Figures from the *Commercial Floorspace Survey* published by the Office of the Deputy Prime Minister (ODPM), in conjunction with the Valuation Office Agency (VOA) and University College London (UCL) show that in 2003 there was 591 million square metres of commercial floorspace in England and Wales of which nearly two-thirds was in factories and warehouses, with retail accounting for 19 per cent and offices 15 per cent (see Table 2.3.1). Retail is further split between different uses, with the majority of properties (80 per cent) classified as shops, and the remainder as financial services and food and drink outlets.

Table 2.3.1   Non-domestic premises in England and Wales 2003

	No of Properties	Floorspace (000s sq m)
Retail Premises	564,536	111,853
of which: Shops	448,059	90,883
Financial Services	45,595	6,457
Food & Drink	57,460	7,462
Other	13,422	7,051
Offices	319,285	98,025
Factories	265,273	229,567
Warehouses	201,098	151,744
Total	1,350,192	591,189

Source: ODPM, VOA, UCL

There is a wide variation in the spread of space across the United Kingdom, with the greatest amount located in the North West and Merseyside, although Greater London has a high proportion of office and retail space. The overall stock of offices in Greater London totals 28.5 million square metres, of which 19 million square metres (67 per cent) is in the core West End, City and Docklands sub-markets.

Structure of the industry

The UK property industry comprises many professions and organizations, with different disciplines providing advice on a range of activities. Firms engaging in surveying, agency, real estate consultancy and service provision activities represent the backbone of the industry. There are, of course, other players involved in real estate, including financial institutions, planning companies, legal firms and architectural practices, which are regulated by separate organizations and rules. In the United Kingdom the main body representing the surveying profession is the Royal Institution of Chartered Surveyors (RICS), which ensures standards are maintained. Table 2.3.2 provides a brief summary of the key players in the market place.

Table 2.3.2   Key players in the UK property market

Player	Role
Real Estate Consultancy Firms	These firms, ranging from the multinational firms such as Jones Lang LaSalle, CBRE and others to small independent organizations are the backbone of the profession. These firms provide advice to a variety of organizations on the sale, acquisition and disposal of space. They are involved in the valuation and management of real estate and provide investment advice and strategy work for the major pension funds and other institutional investors. Firms also provide holistic advice to major corporate organizations in terms of their occupational requirements and strategies. This advice is backed up by research-based work supplied either in-house or through independent providers. Some of the larger firms also have in-house teams of auctioneers, planners and building surveyors.
Auctioneers	Auctioneers, who are surveyors themselves, deal with the sale of property via auctions, as opposed to the traditional method of private treaty. Auctions are generally used for the sale of secondary property, especially smaller lot sizes (though not always) to private individuals and property companies.
Planners	Planners oversee and determine applications within their respective areas. They are, however, also employed within firms of surveyors in advising developers and other parties in the submission and appeals to planning applications.
Property Research Organizations	In recent years there has been an increase in the number of independent research organizations providing both advice on specific aspects and investment, but also in the provision of market-based data.
Solicitors	Solicitors provide a range of services including advice on transactions, leases, litigation and on the structural form of property investment vehicles.

continued overleaf

Player	Role
Banks	Banks (high street, investment and merchant) and building societies provide the funding to investors for the acquisition and development of schemes.
Insurance & Pension Funds	Insurance and pension funds are key investors in commercial real estate and employ significant teams in the management of these portfolios. This is not restricted to UK firms – a significant number of overseas funds also invest in the United Kingdom.
Property Companies	Property companies, both listed and private, are major players in the market, holding land for development opportunities or investment purposes. Given the discount to net asset value, many property companies have de-listed and gone private in recent years.
Private Individuals	In recent years private individuals have become significant players in the market, investing and trading in property. While a significant number invest in secondary lower-value lot sizes, in recent years they have also become owners of more substantial assets.
Construction Companies	Construction companies are important to developers undertaking the construction and fit-out of buildings. Some construction firms may also hold property.

Source: Adapted from Brett, M (1997) Property & money, *Estates Gazette*, London

Leasing structure in the United Kingdom

The United Kingdom has a distinctive leasing system that both overseas occupiers and investors need to understand. In contrast to owning property outright, firms may choose to lease their premises, for which a number of different products are on offer, particularly within the office market. Leasing products vary, and include fully serviced offices on short-term contracts to traditional space on longer-term contracts. Some firms may also wish to outsource space needs to a specialist provider, for example, Land Securities Trillium or Mapeley. When seeking to secure premises in the United Kingdom it is always appropriate to seek advice from a professionally qualified surveyor. The following sections outline the various characteristics of the traditional institutional lease in the United Kingdom.

Lease length

Traditionally, an occupier will enter into a lease that will be subject to the legislative framework, which may provide rights for renewal, or other obligations, expressed or otherwise by law. The length of lease will be a matter for negotiation, or could be restricted on the assignment of a lease. In recent years the average length of a typical institutional-style lease has fallen from under 20 years to below 15 years. Lease lengths are typically longer for retail property as retailers traditionally seek longer leases particularly in order to recoup the cost of their fit-out. Figure 2.3.1 highlights the change in lease lengths over time for the main sectors.

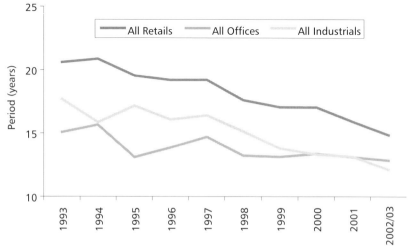

Figure 2.3.1   Changes in lease length for the main sectors (1993–2003)
Source: IPD/BPF

In taking a lease for a long time, occupiers need to be aware of the possible restrictions that may arise should they seek to assign a lease. The Landlord and Tenant (Covenants) Act 1995 led to a change in rules regarding 'privity of contract'. For leases entered into before this Act, the obligations between the original property owner and tenant remain enforceable even if the lease has been transferred or assigned. Leases entered into after this Act was introduced are not subject to this restriction, releasing the tenant from any future obligations on the transfer or assignment of the lease. Of course, there may be restrictions placed in the terms of the lease in respect of, for example, the financial standing of the tenant.

Rent review

Leases will contain provision for rent reviews, the period and nature of review being set out in the terms of the lease as agreed between the property owner and tenant. Traditionally, rent reviews in the United Kingdom will be every five years to the then open market value, subject to an upwards-only clause, preventing the rent from falling below the passing rent (should rents have fallen). The rent at review will be subject to negotiation between the two parties with reference to rents recently agreed (comparables) for similar premises in the open market.

Sometimes the lease will have another basis on which the rent will be reviewed. This could be that rents are reviewed by a fixed percentage, to a certain sum, or are set to rise by the then rate of inflation, possibly with a cap or collar to restrict the level of increase. The exact nature of the review will be specified in the lease.

Repairing obligations

The general obligation to repair is placed on the tenant to undertake, or pay for (often in the case of a multi-tenanted building by way of a service charge) all necessary repairs, even if these pre-date the lease. This is typically referred to as an FRI (Full Repairing and Insuring) lease. Special provisions can be incorporated into the lease that may limit the obligations to keep the property in its initial condition at the time the lease is granted, and a special Schedule of Condition can be attached to the lease. In some limited circumstances the lease may limit repairs to the interior of the property, with the property owner undertaking the external repairs, otherwise referred to as IRI (Internal Repairing and Insuring) lease.

Incentives and other obligations

Some leases may contain additional provisions such as the inclusion of a break clause in which one or both of the parties is able to determine the lease at a certain point in time and subject to any penalties agreed between the parties. There may also be a time period specified by which the parties must serve their notice to break the lease.

In addition to break options, a lease may contain other incentives such as a rent-free period. This is often provided for a short period, say three to six months, to allow the tenant to undertake fit-out works, although at times when leasing activity is slow the level of rent-free may increase dependent on the negotiations.

At the time of signing the lease, the property owner may require the tenant to provide a deposit covering rent for a certain period of time. A guarantee may also be required against the obligations for the term of the lease, which may be enforced even if a business fails.

Lease reform

In April 2003, the government in conjunction with various professional bodies representing the property profession produced a voluntary code of practice aimed at providing greater flexibility in the leasing market.

The aim is to provide not only shorter leases, but also alternative review conditions compared with the traditional upwards-only review clause, and provide for other incentives such as greater use of break clauses. At the time of writing, the review process was still ongoing, with the government reiterating its intention to introduce legislation should the profession fail to be seen to provide greater flexibility.

In addition to the cost of renting and professional fees, occupiers will also have a liability to other occupational and leasing costs, including taxation and running/maintenance charges.

Taxation, management and transaction costs

On taking a lease (or even acquiring premises freehold) stamp duty will be payable on the transfer of the property. The freehold rates are outlined in Table 2.3.3. As of 1 December 2003 new rates came into force for leases, with the rate set at a 1 per cent of the net present value of the rental stream, discounted at a rate of 3.5 per cent. An individual will be exempt from liability where the net present value of the income stream is below £150,000. Further, there are exemptions if a property lies within a ward designated as being of 2,000 areas of multiple deprivation. Further details on stamp duty are available at www.inlandrevenue.gov.uk, and the current rates are set out in Table 2.3.3. It is recommended that professional advice be sought with regard to the tax implications, including value-added tax.

Table 2.3.3   Stamp duty rates (as at December 2003)

Value Band	Rate
Up to £60,000	0
£60,000, no more than £250,000	1%
£250,000, no more than £500,000	3%
Over £500,000	4%

Source: Inland Revenue

There are also further ongoing costs. Occupiers are required to pay business rates to provide a contribution to the provision of local services. In simple terms, the rates payable are based as follows: (rateable value × multiplier) less any relief. The multiplier, known as the uniform business rate, is set by the rating authorities and increases by the rate of inflation each year. The rateable value is also subject to a five-year review, the last list being introduced in 2000. More specific information on the level of rates, relief, exemptions and reviews can be obtained from the Valuation Office Agency (www.voa.gov.uk).

Specific running costs on the property (service charges) will also be payable and will vary depending on the location, size and age of building. The provision of air-conditioning will also have an impact. Table 2.3.4 provides an outline of the likely costs (per square metre) based on both air-conditioned and non-air-conditioned buildings in various locations of the United Kingdom. In recent years service charge costs have risen above the rate of inflation with maintenance, insurance and security charges adding to the increase.

Table 2.3.4   Office occupancy costs 2001

	Air-conditioned	**Non-air-conditioned**
London – City	64.48	49.51
London – West End	64.15	55.97
Greater London	56.40	31.75
South	50.48	26.59
North	36.71	30.46
Scotland	42.41	32.29
UK Average	56.19	39.72

Note: Units: £s per square metre.
Source: Jones Lang LaSalle, *Office Oscar* 2002

A further factor that occupiers may wish to consider is the potential impact of the accountancy standards FRS12, which are likely to be introduced in 2005, requiring companies to list leasehold liabilities on the balance sheet. This could act as a driver towards shorter leases.

The structure of UK property investment

Investor categories

The investment market comprises a number of players ranging from the traditional institutional investor to the private individual. The institutions are the dominant players and include life, general insurance and pension funds. These include both those based in the United Kingdom, but also in Europe, the United States and other countries. Examples include Grosvenor, Scottish Widows and Legal and General. In addition, there are a number of property companies (quoted and private) that are not only involved in development, but also hold property for investment purposes. Examples of these include Land Securities, British Land, Hammerson, Slough Estates and Quintain. In addition to these core groups of investors there are also a number of private (high net worth) individuals and other indirect property investment vehicles, such as limited partnerships and property unit trusts, which have holdings in commercial real estate.

Estimating the total level of investment in commercial property is not easy; the chart in Figure 2.3.2 is taken from the 2003 *IPD Digest* showing estimates based on a number of combined sources of data equating to £245 billion worth of investment, around 55 per cent of the total level of investment.

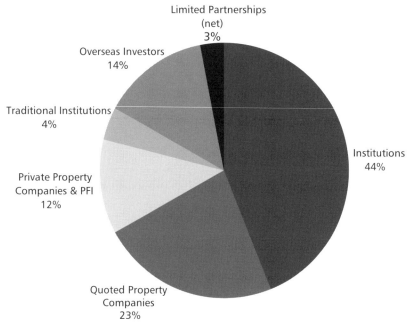

Figure 2.3.2 Major property investors – end 2002
Source: DTZ, IPD, ONS, UBS Warburg

Of the investments held by institutions, including insurance funds, pension funds and investment trusts (as measured by National Statistics) these totalled £89.7 billion at the end of 2002 (5.4 per cent of total assets).

One particular trend in recent years has been the significant increase in activity from private individuals within the property market, especially for secondary property acquired in the auction room. This activity has been driven by a number of factors, including the performance of alternative assets such as equities, the low cost of finance and improved fundability of real estate, increased knowledge and the diversification benefits of holding real estate.

The chart in Figure 2.3.3 shows the historical trend in activity within the auction room based on a four-quarter moving average to eliminate the seasonal levels of activity. It is clear that since late 1999, when private individuals started to enter the market, the level of turnover has increased dramatically from £156 million in the first quarter of 2000 to £311 million by the fourth quarter of 2003. This has been mirrored in the private treaty market where the proportion of acquisitions by private investors (both by value and number) has risen from circa 3 per cent in 1999 to over 10 per cent in both 2002 and 2003 (source: Propertydata).

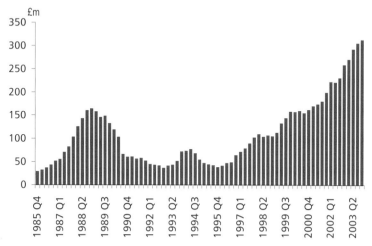

Figure 2.3.3   Auction room activity (1985–2003)
Source: Jones Lang LaSalle/IPD ARAS

This shift can be partially attributed to the low cost of finance and fundability of property, in which the level of returns measured by the yield is greater than the cost of finance as charted in Figure 2.3.4.

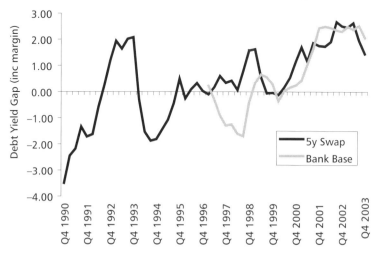

Figure 2.3.4   Debt yield gap (1990–2003)
Source: Jones Lang LaSalle/IPD; Bloomberg

Readings above the zero line suggest that property yield (the initial return) is higher than the cost of borrowing. In this graph the cost of borrowing is measured by 1) the bank's base rate and 2) the five-year swap rate. The difference between the property and cost of finance, the debt yield gap, has steadily increased since 2000. As the chart shows, even accounting for a margin of risk over the cost of finance (be this the bank base rate or swap rate) there are still positive returns to be gained from investing in real estate.

Property lending

The level of lending to real estate has also increased significantly since the mid-1990s, reflecting not only the demand from individuals and institutional investors at a time of strong investment performance, but also the willingness of banks and other financial institutions to lend. Figure 2.3.5 shows the level of lending based on figures from the Bank of England, in which the total amount outstanding to real estate topped over £100 billion by the end of the fourth quarter of 2003. This compares to £41 billion at the time of the last peak. Figures from the Bank of England do not cover the whole market, and exclude securitizations, conduit lending, lending by building societies and offshore loans. Including this data, the total amount outstanding is estimated to be closer to £130 billion. In 2003, it is evident that the increase in lending is slowing, with the proportion of lending to real estate compared to total debt in the market levelling at just under 9 per cent, below the peak of over 10 per cent in the last cycle.

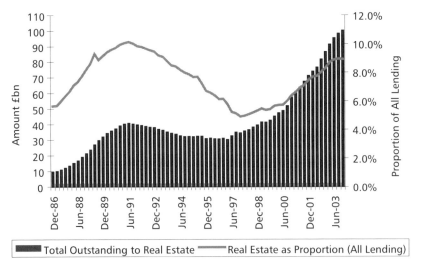

Figure 2.3.5   Bank lending to real estate
Source: Bank of England

Property investment products

The main sectors in the occupier market and in investors' portfolios are offices, retail and industrials. Offices are often located and clustered within the main towns and cities, although more recently there has been a trend towards out of town business parks. Retail is split into a number of sectors. These include standard shops, shopping centres and retail warehouses. The latter are retail units based on retail parks and include DIY operators (for example, Homebase and B&Q), electrical outlets (Comet and Currys) and more recently some high street names such as Next and Marks & Spencer. Industrial premises include a variety of types, ranging from standard industrial and manufacturing units to distribution warehouses and high-tech accommodation, which often includes an element of office accommodation. Although trends in these sectors are determined by different influences, aspects of property environment such as leasing and availability of performance indicators are common to all sectors.

An investor has a number of options to enter the UK property investment market. They range from directly owning a building to indirect (securitized or non-securitized vehicles). Market conditions and other parameters such as the investors' objectives and the portfolio structure require that the investor seeks professional advice to identify the most appropriate option for entering the UK market. A brief description of the main options is given in Table 2.3.5.

Table 2.3.5   Investment options

Direct Investment	
Property Owner	Direct ownership of buildings. Liquidity problems (unable to sell the property fast with no impact on selling price) are highlighted but as the holding horizon lengthens and portfolio is reviewed regularly, liquidity risks are reduced. Investor can purchase directly but auction is also an option for investment requiring smaller capital outlays (say less than £15m).
Indirect Securitized Vehicles	
Property Shares	Shares of property developers and property investment companies. They help create a diversified portfolio at low cost but prices affected by general stock market trends and exhibit greater volatility than direct investments. They usually trade at a discount to net asset value (similar to real estate investment trusts in the United States), which has led many firms to go private in the United Kingdom.

continued over

Property Bonds and Commercial Mortgages Backed Securities	Securitization of loans/income streams. They create a liquid and tradeable property-backed asset. An appealing feature is that they transfer credit risk to lenders and they are rated by S&P (Standard and Poor's). Future streams of revenues are rather weak and a criticism relates to unrealistic assessments of mortgage lending values and being not so liquid.

Other Indirect Vehicles

Property Unit Trusts (PUTs)	Twenty-seven funds that hold a wide mix of properties or specialize in a particular sector. Usually managed by insurance companies or they can be listed. HSBC has made a secondary market. PUTs are closest to offering a truly tax effective investment vehicle with low initial capital outlay and achieving diversification. However, unit holders are exposed to falling markets. Because demand for investment in property is derived largely from more sophisticated investors the majority of property unit trusts are unauthorized, providing less regulation, and therefore greater flexibility in the operation of the fund.
Property Limited Partnerships	Legal entity with two or more partners with limited liability. The taxation regime is similar to that for partnerships. There is no tax relief for the interest paid on monies borrowed to invest in an investment Limited Partnership. Limited Partnerships are not taxed but partners are. They facilitate access to specific property assets such as shopping centres, factory outlet centres, residential and leisure investment, which require specialist and intensive management, with limited liability. Property Limited Partnerships can be less liquid than buildings and there is no established secondary market for Limited Partnership shares. Moreover, there is no agreement on the method of valuing Limited Partnership shares.
Property Derivatives	Forward contracts: purchase or sale of instrument, the price of which is linked to the IPD (Investment Property Databank) indices of property values at the current price, with delivery and settlement at a specified date. Swap: exchange of one vehicle for another to change the maturity, quality or mix of assets.

In December 2003, the Chancellor of the Exchequer announced that the UK government is to issue a consultation document from the instruction of a REIT (Real Estate Investment Trust) style investment in the United Kingdom. A REIT is an income-distributing tax transparent vehicle that bears no tax on incomes or gains provided it meets pre-agreed distribution levels. The nature of the vehicle is not yet known, but it should allow investment in both commercial and residential real estate. If the vehicle receives the go-ahead it is unlikely to be introduced until 2005 at the earliest.

Performance indicators and market transparency

There is a wealth of indicators for property performance in the United Kingdom that investors can monitor to gauge performance by property sector and region. The availability of these indicators and data facilitates the construction of benchmarks against which investors assess the performance of their funds.

The main database is that of the Investment Property Databank (IPD), which compiles a wide range of property performance data (www.ipdindex.co.uk). At December 2002 IPD covered 11,500 properties with a total value of £102.8 billion, which is about two-thirds of the total investments of UK institutions and listed property companies.

The frequency of the main performance indicators outlined in Table 2.3.6 depend on the particular indicator but most of them are available annually, semi-annually and quarterly. A good number of them are produced monthly. Obviously, as frequency increases, the samples upon which these indicators are based become smaller. These indicators cover both the main sector and sub-sectors.

Table 2.3.6   Performance indicators

Indicator	Definitions/Description	Sources
Estimated Rental Values (ERVs)	Valuation or appraisal estimates of the rent that a property might reasonably be expected to command in the open market at the valuation date reflecting the terms of any existing lease. Series related both to prime and secondary properties.	IPD, and real estate consultancy firms.
Market Rents	Rents achieved and achievable in the open market.	Jones Lang LaSalle 50 Centres, selected real estate consultancy firms.

continued overleaf

Indicator	Definitions/Description	Sources
Income Return	Net income receivable per time period expressed as a percentage of the capital value over the period. Net income is rent passing excluding management costs, ground rent and other irrecoverable expenditure.	IPD, selected real estate consultancy firms.
Capital Growth	The increase in values net of capital expenditure as a percentage of the initial capital value.	IPD, real estate consultancy firms.
Total Returns	A measure of investment return showing overall performance of the portfolio; it is the summation of capital value growth and net income return.	IPD, real estate consultancy firms.
Income Returns, Capital Growth and Total Returns by Style	Total returns produced by style for growth and value properties; the sample of properties is split into high- and low-yielding property.	Jones Lang LaSalle.
Initial Yield	Rent passing (net of ground rent) as a percentage of the capital value. Refers to both prime and secondary properties.	IPD, real estate consultancy firms.
Equivalent Yield	Discount rate that equates the future income flows to the current capital value; both prime and secondary properties are covered.	IPD, real estate consultancy firms.
Yield Impact	Indicates impact on capital values due to changes in equivalent yield in standing investments.	IPD, real estate consultancy firms.
Rent Void	Rental value in vacant tenancies divided by current income in all tenancies.	IPD, real estate consultancy firms.
Demand (Take-up, Supply, Absorption), Vacancy, Completions	Indicators to monitor the demand for commercial space, the availability of space by different building grade, expected completions, building starts. This information is available to local markets.	Real estate consultancy firms.

References

Brett, M (1997) Property & money, *Estates Gazette*, London

Commercial and Industrial Floorspace and Rateable Value Statistics 2003 in England & Wales, November 2003, ODPM

Freemans Guide to the Property Industry (2000) Freemans Publishing

Understanding Commercial Property Investment; A Guide for Financial Advisers (2003) Seven Dials Consulting (and sponsored by IPF, RICS and BPF)

2.4

UK Commercial Property Investment

Dr Nigel Almond and Dr Sotiris Tsolacos, Jones Lang LaSalle

Occupier markets

Occupier activity in the commercial real estate market is monitored through real estate practice firms and other bodies. The latter include specific providers of data, for example, *Estates Gazette* and *Focus* by way of subscription to services, with various other real estate consultants undertaking their own monitoring, which is often published in market monitoring reports. These publications are often published free of charge and are accessed via individual websites. In addition, the RICS (Royal Institution of Chartered Surveyors) also produces a

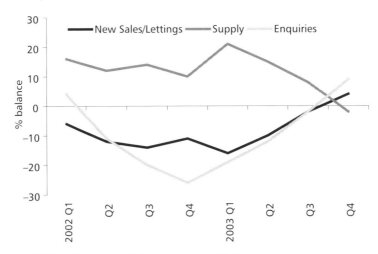

Figure 2.4.1   Commercial property activity
Source: RICS

number of reports, including a quarterly commercial market survey based on its members in England and Wales.

Figure 2.4.1 highlights recent changes in the market place for commercial real estate overall. Activity is represented by the balance of surveyors reporting a rise in activity minus those reporting a fall. As the chart shows there has been a steady improvement in new sales and lettings during 2003, with a positive balance reporting an increase in the final quarter of 2003. In contrast, available supply registered a fall, providing positive news, especially given the current over-supply of office space. Enquiries also improved, providing evidence that sales and lettings should pick up further in due course.

The most widely monitored market is that of the London office market, which is subject to cyclical movements in demand and supply, with a consequent impact for rents. Figure 2.4.2 shows the changes in take-up and vacancy rates since 1984, and clearly depicts the late 1980s' and 1990s' booms and the subsequent falls in the markets, with vacancy levels moving in the opposite directions.

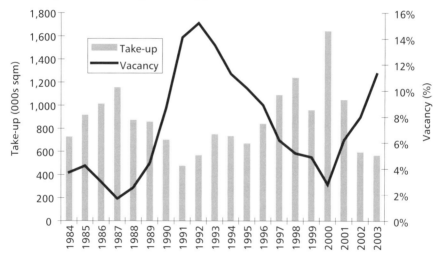

Figure 2.4.2   Central London take-up and vacancy
Source: Jones Lang LaSalle

Unlike the early 1990s, when a significant level of development activity pushed the vacancy rate to about 15 per cent, the late 1990s' boom saw a third of the level of speculative construction compared with the previous boom. This is partly a result of greater caution, but also the high number of pre-lets on vacant sites to occupiers, especially in the Docklands area to the east of London. As a consequence, vacancy levels have not risen as high as in the previous market cycle. Nevertheless, there remains a significant level of space surplus, much of which this time round is being released by occupiers rather than traditional investors. As the market outlook improves and firms start to recruit, the hope is that they will review their space needs, withdraw space from the market and reoccupy.

The movements in demand and supply are also reflected in rental movements, which are discussed later in this chapter. As mentioned earlier, investors seek to maintain headline rental levels to protect the value of their assets, and therefore movements in incentives and lease flexibility can provide early indications on market movements. Table 2.4.1 compares changes in lease lengths and incentives for all property sectors over the past two years based on data recorded by the RICS, and shows how lease lengths have generally decreased, while incentives have increased, although dissipating in recent quarters.

Table 2.4.1 Reported change in lease length and inducements

	% Balance of Surveyors Reporting a Change in:	
	Lease length over past year	Value of inducements over past quarter
2002 Q1	−13	18
2002 Q2	−9	12
2002 Q3	−16	21
2002 Q4	−25	29
2003 Q1	−26	29
2003 Q2	−23	35
2003 Q3	−18	26
2003 Q4	−20	15

Source: RICS

The economy and the property market

The relationship between the economy and the property market

The UK real estate market is closely linked with economic activity; therefore, understanding the behaviour of the economy and its future performance is important to those involved in both the investment and leasing markets. Figure 2.4.3 shows a strong relationship between the variation in employment growth in Central London and the amount of office space firms demand. A measure of the closeness of a relationship is the correlation coefficient. A value of 1 signifies a perfect relationship. The value of 0.77 obtained for employment and office take-up represents a strong relationship. Of course, firms may hoard available space or use it more intensively as their employment requirements change. But the strength of the relationship signifies the linkages between business activity and employment variation and demand (take-up) for office space.

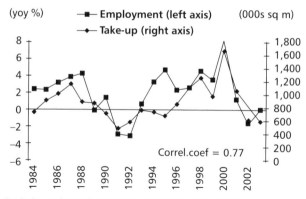

(yoy %)   ■ Employment (left axis)   (000s sq m)
           ◆ Take-up (right axis)

Note: Employment refers to employment in financial, business services and public administration in Greater London.

Figure 2.4.3   Central London office market: employment growth and demand (take-up)
Source: Jones Lang LaSalle, Experian Business Strategies (employment date)

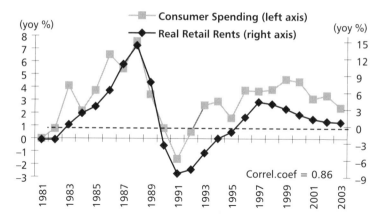

Figure 2.4.4   UK retail property market: consumer spending and retail rents
Source: IPD, ONS

Retail rents, understandably, show a close relationship with consumer spending growth. As consumers increase their spending, so the profitability of retailers and the ability to pay higher rents increases. The relationship is very strong (the correlation coefficient takes a value of 0.86). In Figure 2.4.4, we can observe that the slowdown in consumer spending growth in the last few years is mirrored in a similar trend exhibited by retail rent growth.

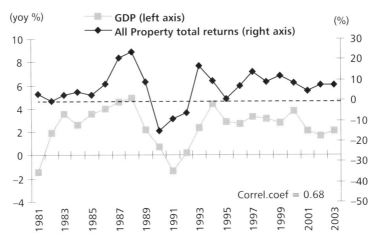

Figure 2.4.5 UK – all property: GDP and total returns
Source: IPD, ONS

Total returns (a combination of the income from property and the change in its price) is closely related to GDP growth. The recession of the early 1990s resulted in negative returns from property. As a consequence, investors lost confidence in the property market. In the recent global downturn, unlike the stock markets, the property sector performed well, offering investors steady returns. This performance, charted in Figure 2.4.5, has reinstated confidence in the sector.

Understanding the relationships between the property market and the economy is important for assessing market trends and for providing forecasts for performance by sector and geographical market.

Outlook for the economy

Whereas the United States and a number of European countries, including France and Germany, have all suffered technical recessions, GDP growth in the United Kingdom has held up and remained positive throughout the period 2001 to 2003. The slowing in GDP growth and the significant fall in employment growth in the financial and business services sector have impacted on the office markets, especially within London and the South East, which were so heavily dominated by companies related to the equities and technology sectors. In contrast, continued retail spending has meant the performance of the retail sector has held up relatively well.

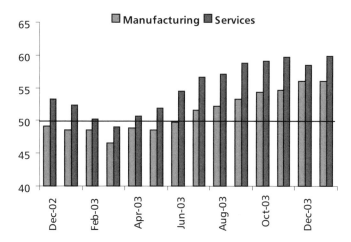

Figure 2.4.6   Business activity levels
Note: Readings over 50 indicate expansion.
Source: Chartered Institute for Purchasing and Supply (CIPS)

Positive news about the economy is conveyed by influential surveys. The CIPS (Chartered Institute of Purchasing and Supply) survey clearly shows that both the manufacturing and service sectors continue to expand. Business activity in the service sector seems to have stabilized. Similarly, in the manufacturing sector, business activity levels are steady following strong expansion in the last quarter of 2003, as illustrated in Figure 2.4.6. The value of these surveys is that they provide more timely information of business activity and are not subject to revisions to the same degree as economic data.

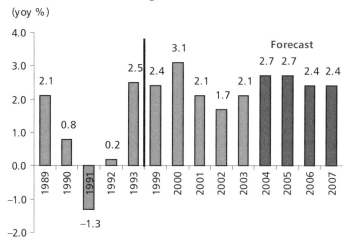

Figure 2.4.7   Gross Domestic Product (GDP) growth in the United Kingdom
Source: ONS, HM Treasury Survey of Independent Forecasts

Further, economic forecasts now suggest that the UK economy enters a period of stronger economic growth (2004–05) compared with the previous three years (2001–03). The average of forecasts produced by independent organizations and monitored by the Treasury, reproduced as Figure 2.4.7, suggests growth at 2.7 per cent per annum in the next two years. A cooling off is subsequently predicted, reflecting the fact that the slack in the economy is being absorbed and economic policy is aiming to keep close to trend (around 2.5 per cent).

In the next few years the rebound in fixed investment, which comprises business investment, construction of dwellings and government spending, will drive economic recovery in the United Kingdom. In particular, government spending has been strong and provided a cushion against recessionary risks in the global downturn of 2001–03. Government spending rose by over 20 per cent in 2003 and it is expected to rise by about 30 per cent in 2004 and a further 10 per cent in 2005.

Business investment (about 11.5 per cent of GDP as at 2002) is also forecast to recover. Net rates of return (profitability) have stabilized and improved in some sectors. This should bring an improvement in business investment. Recovery in the equities market could also give a boost. However, business investment tends to lag GDP growth as firms test the resilience of the economy before they increase investment spending.

Of course, private consumption remains a key contributor to GDP growth despite the lower growth rates predicted for the next few years. It is forecast that the contribution of consumer spending to the annual GDP growth rates (of 2.7 per cent) in 2004 and 2005 will be 1 per cent. The improvement in the external environment is also seen as another key contributor to growth. Exports are expected to rebound strongly in 2004, posting growth of 4 per cent compared with an expected fall of 1.7 per cent in 2003. However, at the same time, imports rise, which is a leakage from national income. Overall however, net trade (which is exports minus imports) is not expected to subtract from GDP growth as was the case in 2002 and 2003.

The recovery is not risk-free. According to the National Institute, a boost to households' financial wealth is expected in the short term from better-performing equity, concern that partly underpinned the recent rises in interest rates. The Treasury estimates that with personal debt at historically high levels, consumers' appetite for further increases in borrowing is likely to recede and less mortgage equity withdrawal is expected, although the impact of the latter on consumption is not clear. A reduction in personal consumption would impact on the retail sector. Nevertheless, latest forecasts show consumption growth of 2.6 per cent in 2004 compared with 2.4 per cent in 2003.

We do not see any risks to consumer spending growth and economic recovery arising from households being unable to service their debts. The labour market is strong with high employment levels and continuous earnings growth. The high levels of employment largely underpinned the strength of both the housing market and consumer spending growth in the last few years. The historically low interest rates were of course another major factor.

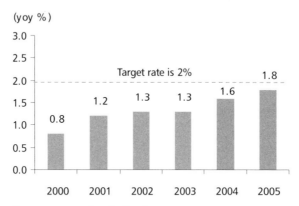

Figure 2.4.8   Consumer price inflation
Source: Concensus forecasts

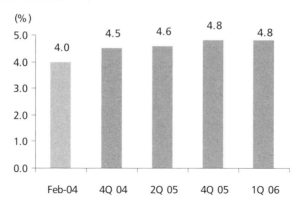

Figure 2.4.9   Market expectations of the Bank's official interest rate
Source: Bank of England

As the economic growth rate accelerates, interest rates are expected to rise. However, interest rate rises should not exceed 5 per cent in the next two years, as inflation does not pose a risk. The economic expansion in the United Kingdom is not predicted to be inflationary. Inflation (consumer price index) is forecast to remain below the 2 per cent target rate. Forecasts of consumer price inflation and the Bank of England official interest rate are given in the two bar charts, Figure 2.4.8 and Figure 2.4.9.

Useful economic data sources

Given the linkages between the economy and property market activity the availability of data and access to information describing economic activity is essential for investors. In the United Kingdom there is a vast array of economic data published on the UK economy throughout the year, including both official data provided by the Office of National Statistics, together with other survey-based data provided by various representative and trades bodies, including most notably the Confederation of British Industry (CBI) and the Chartered Institute of Purchasing Supply (CIPS). These databases cover the economy at the national, regional and local levels.

Table 2.4.2 summarizes a number of key pieces of survey data, which are important in understanding the performance of the economy, both immediately and in the future. Much of this data is freely available for current periods, although some historical time-series data are only available by subscription. All official UK statistics are currently available free of charge.

Table 2.4.2   UK sources of economic data

Data	Comment	Released	Provider	Internet Link
Economic Growth (GDP)	Size and growth of economy and its component sectors.	Quarterly	National Statistics	www.statistics.gov.uk
Industrial Production	Index of production showing output in various production/ manufacturing industries.	Monthly	National Statistics	www.statistics.gov.uk
Interest Rate	Current bank base rate and background to rate decision.	Monthly	Bank of England	www.bankofengland.co.uk
Retail Sales	Level of sales.	Monthly	National Statistics	www.statistics.gov.uk
Labour Market	Levels of employment, unemployment and earnings at UK and regional level.	Monthly	National Statistics	www.statistics.gov.uk
Swap Rates	Finance rates often used on loans for real estate.	Daily	Financial Times	www.ft.com
Inflation	Current rate of inflation and contributory factors.	Monthly	National Statistics	www.statistics.gov.uk
Inflation Outlook	Inflation report, providing the current outlook for inflation and the UK economy.	Quarterly	Bank of England	www.bankofengland.co.uk

continued overleaf

Data	Comment	Released	Provider	Internet Link
Treasury Forecasts	Independent forecasts of various economic data over two and four years.	Monthly	HM Treasury	www.hm-treasury.gov.uk
Business Sentiment	Survey data on business activity, including output and employment, for the manufacturing and service sectors.	Monthly	Chartered Institute of Purchasing and Supply	www.cips.org
Business Sentiment	Survey data on manufacturing, retail and financial services sectors.	Monthly and Quarterly	Confederation of British Industry	www.cbi.org.uk
Consumer Confidence	Indicator of confidence on a range of measures.	Monthly	Martin Hamblin GFK	www.martinhamblin-gfk.com
Business Activity	Survey data on orders, employment, capacity utilization, cashflows.	Quarterly	British Chambers of Commerce	www.britishchambers.org.uk
Financial Stability	Review of the financial stability of the UK economy.	Bi-annual	Bank of England	www.bankofengland.co.uk

Future performance of the UK property investment market

Performance forecasts

As illustrated in the previous section, the strong relationship between property market performance and the economy allows us to forecast the former. Indicative outputs of such forecasting work are presented in this section.

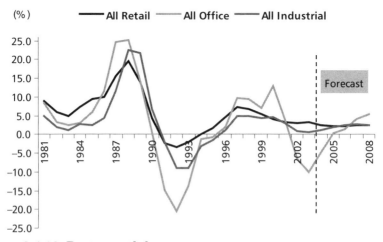

Figure 2.4.10 Rent growth by sector
Source: Jones Lang LaSalle (Dec 2003 forecasts); IPD (data)

Figure 2.4.10 shows rent forecasts by broad sector in the United Kingdom as a whole. It also illustrates the past volatility of rents. In the recession of the early 1990s, all sectors experienced falling rents with the more pronounced falls in the office sector. In the recent downturn it was only the office sector that saw negative rental growth but not as severe as previously. Rental growth in retail and industrials is expected to stabilize for the next few years and rise just above inflation. Rents in the office sector are expected to strengthen from 2005 onwards. The risk from negative rental growth is very small in the next three to four years.

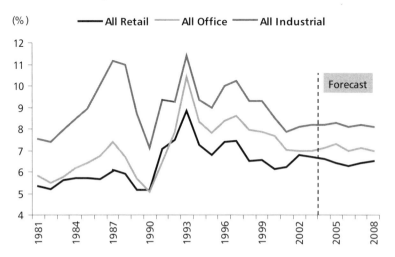

Figure 2.4.11   Income returns by broad sector
Source: Jones Lang LaSalle (Dec 2003 forecasts); IPD (data)

Income returns, especially in the industrial sector, are considered an advantage for property investment. As Figure 2.4.11 illustrates, income returns reached a high in 1993 but since then they have been falling. We forecast that income returns will stabilize moving forward, hence maintaining this advantageous feature of property assets.

Capital growth is the most volatile performance component of property. This volatility has been reduced since 1993, reflecting lower volatility in rental growth and interest rates (which feed into equivalent yields). As Figure 2.4.12 shows, capital values (prices) of office buildings fell in 2002 and 2003 and are not expected to increase until 2005. The other sectors will broadly see small variations in capital values but will remain positive. Adding these forecasts to the income return forecasts we expect property to deliver annual total returns around 8.7 per cent in the next five years.

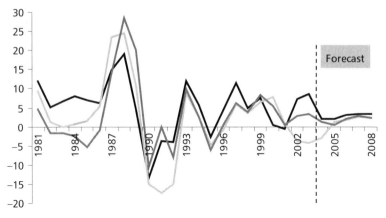

Figure 2.4.12   Capital value growth by broad sector
Source: Jones Lang LaSalle (Dec 2003 forecasts); IPD (data)

Future investment trends

A notable trend in property investment in the United Kingdom is the decreasing share of investment in land and property as a percentage of overall holdings that began in the early 1980s and appears to be bottoming out now (see Figure 2.4.13), although it is early days to make such an assessment.

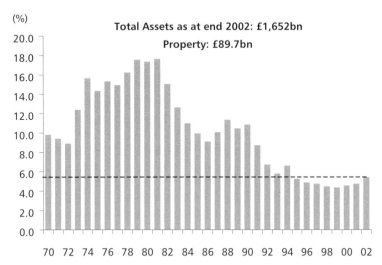

Figure 2.4.13   Share of investment by financial institutions in UK land and property
Note: Financial Institutions comprise pension funds, insurance companies and trusts.
Source: ONS

In the early 1980s, institutions had about 18 per cent of their holdings in land and property and this had fallen to just less than 6 per cent by 2002. A number of explanations have been put forward:

- Poor liquidity, that is, transacting in property is a long process. As a result, investors cannot switch between asset classes or even within property quickly to exploit profitable opportunities.

- Higher property transaction costs.

- Property investment is hampered by the large lot size, and property portfolios more costly to maintain.

- The Minimum Funding Requirement introduced in 1995 stating that the solvency of a pension fund is assessed with reference only to UK shares and UK bonds. This is under review now.

- Underperformance of property in the slumps of the early 1980s and early 1990s.

To these explanations we also need to add the fact that over time UK investors became more familiar with foreign markets and funds were shifted to both foreign equity and bond markets. Moreover, lack of investment product in the property market could have also acted as a constraint.

The question is, of course, whether investors are confident and will continue to be confident from investing in property. Our view is 'yes'. Poor liquidity, transaction costs and lot size can all be reflected in a yield premium over the more liquid assets with very low transaction costs. The underperformance of property in the previous cycles, arising from a weak demand and an over-supply, cannot wholly be attributed to misjudgements by the property sector. Lenders and investors did not foresee the slump, misjudging economic trends themselves.

The reasoning behind our expectation for investment levels to be maintained (or even increased) in real estate is in part based on the increased awareness and understanding of real estate as an investment class. The chart in Figure 2.4.14 shows the overall performance of the IPD index in 2002 and over the last 3, 5 and 10 years, clearly indicating the strong level of performance. Even over 22 years, returns are maintained with real estate only behind equities in terms of performance. On the basis of the diversification benefits of real estate, especially in times of uncertainty within the financial markets, we can expect institutional investors to maintain their portfolio weightings in property.

(% per annum)

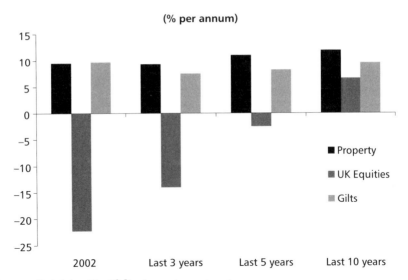

Figure 2.4.14   Portfolio investment returns
Source: IPD

Both academic work and research from property consultancy firms demonstrate the qualities of property as a true diversifier in a mixed asset portfolio. The research team of Jones Lang LaSalle has carried out such work jointly with the University of Reading. A novelty of this research work is the fact that the diversification contributions are examined in periods of financial stress. It became clear that property greatly reduces the risk (volatility of portfolio returns) but also increases overall total returns (see Tsolacos, Lee and Foxley, 2003). We also expect the private investor to maintain their representation in the investment market and offer liquidity for smaller lot sizes. Again, recent research by Jones Lang LaSalle has shown:

● Private investors now have a much better understanding of the performance of property and the importance of holding property over the longer term and not as a short-term opportunity.

● Great returns have been achieved through investing in the residential buy-to-let market, which has provided a stepping stone for commercial investments.

● Data availability has greatly improved, such as with the Jones Lang LaSalle/IPD Auction Results Analysis System, together with publications from other consultancies.

● Professional advice that explains strategy and risks is available.

● Coverage in wider business press and television.

Nevertheless, the research has also highlighted a number of factors that could impact on future investment levels or lead to a sell-off of some assets, including the following factors:

- If property enters a period of poor returns – which is not predicted.

- Should jittery banks call in loans due to tenant defaults – although the number of tenant defaults has ceased rising?

- Stamp duty, which will decrease the net return on property to the private investor.

- Renewed interest in equities.

- Interest rates rises that will erode margins from investing in property.

- Press comments that can upset the private investor.

- Lack of product following heavy sales from institutions.

Final remarks

The UK property market is a market that has offered opportunity. The fact that it is a popular destination for international investment funds is the corollary of the advanced investment environment and quality of advice that investors receive. This and the preceding chapter have demonstrated the spate of information available to an investor for decision-making. The transparency of the market and to an extent the UK lease are advantages that fund managers consider attractive. But ultimately investment decisions require taking into account several parameters relating to risk attitudes, portfolio structure and opportunities that require professional advice. Furthermore, the criticism of illiquidity, usually advanced by analysts in other investment fields, can be addressed through market monitoring and careful medium-term property performance analysis and planning. And after all how liquid are equities in a falling market?

As noted earlier, holding property maintains portfolio performance in periods of financial stress such as the currency crisis in Asia and Russian economy difficulties in the late 1990s and more recently the burst of the tech bubble.

Another advantage of the UK market is the fact that property market trends can be forecasted because the market responds to fundamentals. Although events can affect sectors in particular years, in the medium term, performance is driven by fundamentals. The empirical investigation of these relationships is of key importance to investors and has been aided by the ample availability of data. To illustrate this point, the existence of socio-economic databases at the very local level enables us to map future trends in the occupier market, which underpins value both in the development sector and the investment market. In addition, the valuation profession and the overseeing body have initiated research on valuation accuracy, aiming to address inconsistencies. Such initiatives increase investors' confidence in the profession and the property sector. Due diligence service provision is now a shared characteristic of real estate consultancy firms in the United Kingdom. It can be inferred from this discussion that the ingredients for an environment conducive to real estate investment are in place in the United Kingdom.

Further information

British Council for Offices (BCO) www.bco.org.uk
British Council for Out of Town Retail (BCOTR) www.bcotr.co.uk
British Council for Shopping Centres (BCSC) www.bcsc.org.uk
British Property Federation (BPF) www.bpf.org.uk
British Retail Consortium (BRC) www.brc.org.uk
Inland Revenue www.inlandrevenue.gov.uk
Investment Property Forum (IPF) www.ipf.org.uk
Royal Institute of British Architects (RIBA) www.architechture.com
Royal Institution of Chartered Surveyors (RICS) www.rics.org
Royal Town Planning Institute (RTPI) www.rtpi.org.uk
Valuation Office www.voa.gov.uk

References

IPD (2003) *UK Property Investors Digest 2003*
Tsolacos, S, Lee, S and Foxley, S (2003) Avoiding bull market euphoria and bear market sorrows: Real estate in the right place, at the right time, Jones Lang LaSalle/Reading University Research Paper

2.5

Agricultural and Residential Property

Richard Binning and Richard Donnell, FPD Savills

Agricultural property

UK property has traditionally been considered as a stable investment, and within the property market rural and agricultural property has often been considered the most stable sector. For this reason, it has been a popular part of most large portfolios of both individual and corporate funds. Farmland can be a spectacularly good investment and for many, this has been the case over the last 25 years. For others, the story has been more mundane. What makes the difference?

Timing

As with all investments, timing of the trading makes a huge difference to short- and medium-term performance. As shown in Figure 2.5.1, a seller of land in December 2002 would, on average, have seen annual capital growth of 4.3 per cent on farmland held for 10 years but an annual reduction in value of 4.1 per cent on land held for 5 years. The large swings in farmland value during the 1990s followed farm profitability as it surged upwards on the back of weak currency and consequentially high support levels, coupled with high commodity prices and lower interest rates. Values have been slower to fall on the downswing and they are now on the up again, buoyed by the further downward movement of interest rates, demand for residential farms from outside agriculture and the recent upturn in farm profits. In 2003, 41 per cent of the farms handled by FPD Savills were bought by 'lifestyle buyers' from outside farming.

Once the current reform of the CAP has been clarified, we see a very

active farmland market ahead of us, limited only by the long-term reduction in the amount of land offered for sale. In these circumstances, would-be buyers looking to catch the market risk being frustrated and they may need to piece together a deal privately, buying before the farm reaches the market.

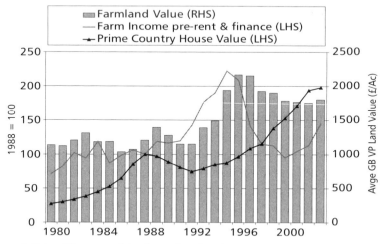

Figure 2.5.1 The trend in farm land value

Residential and amenity value

Figure 2.5.1 understates the extent to which high demand for a relatively fixed stock of farmhouses has boosted the investment performance of farms over the last 25 years. Figure 2.5.2 shows how the

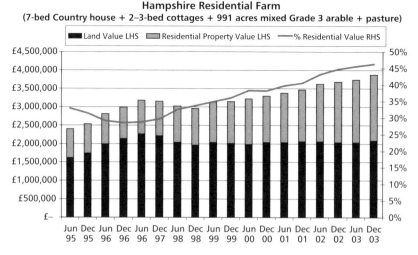

Figure 2.5.2 Change in the value of typical residential farm

value of a large residential farm in Hampshire has typically moved over just eight years – even on this large farm the residential value now makes up 46 per cent of the whole compared with 29 per cent in 1996 and 17 per cent in 1980.

Tenure

Let land portfolios generated a return of almost 20 per cent to investors in 2002 and total returns in 2003 are likely to be well into double figures. This follows a period when returns averaged around 15 per cent per annum over both 3 and 10 years. This is a niche market with generally low turnover and wide variation in the nature of the asset. Initial yields vary in a range of 1 per cent to 7 per cent. Mis-pricing is a hazard for the uninformed in such a market, so buyers and sellers should trade with care.

Those pension and life funds that bought farmland heavily in the late 1970s in a rising market (only to be part of a rush out of agriculture in the mid-1980s in a falling market) tend to be disappointed with their experience of agricultural investment. On the other hand, some of those funds have retained a reserve of strategic land with development hope value, which in many cases has paid off handsomely.

Development

With agricultural land typically worth between £1,000 and £3,000 per acre and greenfield residential building land worth anything from £150,000 to £2.5 million per acre depending on location, it does not take a rocket scientist to work out that provision of land for development can be an extremely profitable pastime. It is also an increasingly complicated activity, with government steering new housing development towards 'brownfield' land (that is, previously developed land) and looking to secure a proportion of affordable housing within the development mix.

Glossy syndicated offerings of land with development potential are increasingly common. Buyers should beware; planning permission is the principal constraint and without it your new investment is highly unlikely to be one of the top performers of the next 25 years.

Tax

Taxation advantages tend to be a significant secondary reason for holding land. One hundred per cent relief from Inheritance Tax after a qualifying period of ownership, which can be two years, is a valuable means of passing wealth to the next generation. For instance, if land is held for 10 years before death then this could add more than 3 per cent a year to the effective investment return from land, although other ways of avoiding tax are possible.

The value in rolling over capital gains into farmland, thus deferring Capital Gains Tax, is less than it was before the introduction of business asset taper relief. Nevertheless, this could add around 0.7 per cent per annum to investment returns over a 25-year period.

Conclusion

Overall, there are many good reasons to own a slice of the British countryside, with lifestyle motives tending to be high among them. From an investment perspective, there has been and will continue to be great variation in the returns from land ownership, depending on its location and characteristics. As ever, stock selection is the key to good investment return.

Residential property

Winners in the great house price race

Everyone has a good war story about how much money they have made out of the UK housing market at some point in the past. It is not surprising, given that 30 years ago the average value of a house was less than £10,000. With average values today standing at closer to £160,000, many consider owning or investing in housing a one-way ticket to riches. It has certainly kept the aspiration to own a home alive and well and, more recently, it has spurred high levels of new investment in the market. On a micro level, some locations and property types have been real winners, with growth much higher than the national average. However, it has not been a one-way ticket for everyone, and there have been some losers, even in the recent past.

One of the classic examples of a winner is Notting Hill in West London. Shunned by many buyers in the 1980s as a no-go zone, widespread gentrification over the last decade has transformed it into a truly prime location. To say those who owned property in Notting Hill before the 1990s have done very well is something of an understatement. Back in 1979, a seven-bed house in one of the better streets would have sold for around £250,000, whereas today the sale price would be closer to £7 million. This is a cool 2,700 per cent increase, some four times higher than the national average. The catalysts for Notting Hill's revival were access via the Central Line to Liverpool Street/Broadgate in the City, a large supply of period housing stock ready to be upgraded, and the communal gardens, which, while not available to all of Notting Hill or indeed unique in themselves, have created huge demand that has helped 'pull up' adjacent stock.

A similar combination of factors has spurred gentrification of the existing housing market in many parts of the country in recent years, especially where there is a good supply of period family housing. Parts of London that have benefited from this trend include Putney, Wandsworth and Islington. Locations in other cities adjacent to prime areas have done very well, including Portobello to the east of the New Town in Edinburgh and the area between Smethwick and Edgbaston in Birmingham. Other winners have been the holiday or second home hotspots around the coast, in particular parts of the South West and East Anglia. Prices in these areas have taken a major leap forward over the last decade. Some prime properties in Aldeburgh, Suffolk, have leapt ahead by as much as 1,800 per cent over the last 25 years, three times the national average rate of growth.

Forecasting tomorrow's hotspots

Most buyers would love to be in the next Notting Hill before it happens, but it is a tricky business pinpointing the hotspots of tomorrow. The property press have certainly been obsessed with the next up-and-coming area or latest property hotspot. However, there is a big difference between strong house price growth in a particular location and an area really making a quantum leap. The slowdown in house price growth we expect to occur this year and next will really sort out the wheat from the chaff. Whether an area has made it or not depends upon a complex mix of factors, in particular the scale of gentrification that has taken place. The number and quality of new bars and shops is normally a good indicator and the quality of the local school is even more important in areas where houses dominate supply. Indeed, the importance of schools has jumped rapidly up the buying agenda in the last decade. The impact of schools on house prices is clear, with premiums for property in the best catchments. Schooling will remain key in driving local house prices in future. Those who want to be really clever should try to start forecasting the up-and-coming schools of tomorrow.

Comparative losers

Buyers should watch out where they buy, in so-called up-and-coming areas. Once the hype has died down and price growth slows, those who could only afford to buy on the fringes could well see the value of their property underperform. It is akin to the tide moving out and leaving some properties high and dry. There is evidence to suggest that the heady asking prices for this type of stock some 18 months ago have already declined in some parts of London and the South East. It is part of an even greater polarization of the housing market that is set to take place in the next few years as house price growth slows to levels that are more manageable.

Not everyone who has bought a house has been a winner. Much is down to timing and despite the very strong house price growth of the last seven or eight years, a few households are still in negative equity from the early 1990s' recession. These unfortunate households have been the real losers in the housing market. Their problems have been primarily a result of localized economic decline. Local housing markets are driven by their local economies and few owners stand any chance of making money from the housing market if the local economy encounters problems. While households in the South bemoan a lack of housing and high house prices, there are pockets in Northern England and Southern Wales where house prices remain lower than they were 15 years ago. Only large-scale regeneration can help them and the government has put in place ambitious long-term plans to turn these so-called 'housing market renewal areas' around.

Forward factors for profitable investment

Looking forward, there are a number of important characteristics that will identify up-and-coming areas worthy of a potential purchase. We have already talked about the importance of a good local economy and schools as the catalysts of gentrification. However, there are one or two other trends to watch out for: in particular, transport improvements and major urban regeneration projects. New rail links or tram systems that improve journey times to previously undervalued areas are obvious ones to watch. The Jubilee Line Extension and extensions to the Docklands Light Railway have both had a material impact on property prices in parts of South and East London over the last decade. The new Channel Tunnel railway has opened up new, faster access to a number of areas in the South East and this has already generated major strategic opportunities for a number of developers. On a smaller, more accessible scale, there are a number of current proposals for new tram routes and extensions to existing routes across the country and one or two areas could certainly see a major improvement as a result. Northern parts of inner city Nottingham have already benefited from the new tram system that has recently opened. Besides running off to research the proposals for new trams, it is very important before buying to get a feel for the chances of the proposals turning into reality. Anyone who bought on the back of the Crossrail announcements more than 15 years ago is still waiting today.

One of the best long-term opportunities stems from the creation of new residential markets as part of the many major regeneration initiatives currently under way across the United Kingdom. The development of new housing stock is a form of gentrification and we have seen our city centres revitalized by a growing number of new residential developments, running from hundreds to thousands of new homes. Buyers are faced with the choice of either buying into the scheme itself or, more opportunistically, buying lower-value second-hand property on the fringes of the development. What is important to stress is that these schemes take many years to develop and mature. As such, it may not be until 15 or 20 years down the track that the full value of the investment comes through.

TaylorWessing

The legal force for inward investment into the UK and Europe

For further information on inward investment please contact
David Kent
d.kent@taylorwessing.com

Daniel Rosenberg
d.rosenberg@taylorwessing.com or

Paul Webb
p.webb@taylorwessing.com

Taylor Wessing offices
Berlin Brussels Cambridge Düsseldorf
Frankfurt Hamburg London Munich Paris
Representative offices: Alicante Shanghai
Associated office: Dubai

www.taylorwessing.com

Mergers and Acquisitions and Joint Ventures

Sara Bradbury, David Kent, Daniel Rosenberg and Paul Webb, Inward Investment Group, Taylor Wessing

Introduction

This chapter deals with three areas designed to give the individual overseas investor or an overseas company investing in the United Kingdom a major start in the United Kingdom. It looks at private company acquisitions, public company acquisitions and joint ventures.

Private company acquisitions

For the overseas investor or an inward investing company, the acquisition of a key research and development facility or of an existing distribution structure in the United Kingdom or Europe can be very exciting and strategically provide immediate traction.

English law can be different

A number of jurisdictions, including the United States, have a concept of a merger in its truest form, where one company merges with and into another, leaving a single entity as the surviving entity. In the United Kingdom, there is no such merger concept. The two principal acquisition structures (in the private arena) are the following: 1) asset and business purchase; and 2) share purchase. One of the principal differences between an asset and a share purchase is that, on a share purchase, the purchaser inherits all of the liabilities of the target group, whereas on an asset purchase, there is greater scope for selecting liabilities to be specifically excluded from the purchase.

The employees of an English company cannot, however, be 'excluded' from the purchase. If the purchaser is acquiring an undertaking (which is usually the case on a purchase of a business or a business division from a company), the provisions of the Transfer of Undertakings (Protection of Employment) Regulations 1981 of the United Kingdom will apply, such that the employees have the right to automatically transfer, along with the undertaking, to the purchaser on their existing terms and conditions of employment. (See also Chapter 5.2.)

Warranties and indemnities

There is a fundamental distinction between warranties and indemnities given by a seller to a buyer in UK transactions. The warranties in a UK transaction are not backed up by a global indemnification provision in the same way as they are in transaction documentation in certain other countries, including the United States. Indemnities in a UK transaction are reserved for covering the risk of specific, identified liabilities, for example a potential litigation claim. In the United Kingdom, the purpose of the indemnity is to provide complete cover (on a pound (sterling) for pound basis) for any losses suffered in relation to the specific matter identified, including reasonable costs and expenses. It is felt that this may result in more than what was actually owing being reclaimed. In contrast, a breach of warranty claim, if successful, results in a different measure of damages – effectively damages for breach of contract where the purchaser is also required to prove that the loss was foreseeable and the purchaser will be required to show that it has attempted to mitigate its loss.

Typically, the period of warranty cover in a UK acquisition is longer than in certain other countries, including the United States. In relation to UK taxation, it would be usual for a seller of the shares of a company or the seller of a business to provide warranty cover to the purchaser for a period of six years in relation to tax warranties (as this is the period in respect of which the Inland Revenue can examine the tax affairs of a company), for between six and 15 years for environmental/land contamination warranties and anywhere between one year and three years for all other warranties, depending on the relative negotiating power of the parties to the agreement. Typically, on a share purchase, the tax warranties are supported by various tax covenants, contained in a tax deed to which the sellers of the shares and the purchaser will be party.

In addition to the time limits for bringing warranty claims, the cap on the maximum liability of the seller(s) under the warranties also tends to be higher for UK transactions than for transactions in certain other countries. Traditionally, the seller's liability is capped at the total amount of the consideration received by the seller(s), whereas in certain other jurisdictions, for example the United States, the liability is often limited to a percentage of purchase price, for example, 10 per cent or 15 per cent, with such amount being held back in some form of escrow or retention account for the period of the warranties. As a rule, holdbacks or retentions are less common in UK acquisitions.

Disclosure

In the United Kingdom, on an asset or a share purchase, the seller(s) will invariably deliver a disclosure letter and accompanying bundles of supporting documents to the purchaser, containing the seller(s) disclosures against their warranties. These are the exceptions or qualifications to the warranties and provide the seller(s) with the requisite protection against a breach of warranty claim by the purchaser. In certain other countries, for example, the United States, the disclosures are made by way of a disclosure schedule (being a schedule to the actual purchase agreement) rather than a disclosure letter.

There are a number of public registers in the United Kingdom, including the register of companies held by the Registrar of Companies at Companies House, the Trade Marks Registry and the Central Registry of Winding Up Petitions in England and Wales, and the seller(s) will usually attempt to make various general disclosures to the effect that all matters disclosed by an inspection of the public registers are deemed to be disclosures against the warranties, in addition to the specific disclosures.

Restrictive covenants

In addition to the warranties and indemnities in the purchase agreement, another key set of provisions for any purchaser of the business and assets or the shares of a company are the restrictive covenants or 'non-competes'. The purchaser will want to obtain a covenant from the seller(s) that they will not compete with the business that they are selling to the purchaser and that they will not solicit the employees of that business employed in the business at the time of the sale, for a specified period of time after completion of the sale and purchase. Under English law, in order for such restrictive covenants to be enforceable, they need to be carefully drafted to ensure that they do not extend beyond the protection of the legitimate business interest of the purchaser. Consideration also needs to be given to the scope of the geographical area to which the restrictive covenants will apply, again, in order to provide a greater chance of enforceability by the English courts.

Stamp duty and stamp duty land tax (SDLT)

Stamp duty (effectively a transfer tax) applies on the transfer of the shares. Stamp duty is chargeable at a rate of 0.5 per cent (rounded up to the nearest £5) on the total value of the consideration for the shares and is payable on the transfer document, known as a stock transfer form, unless the transfer of the shares qualifies for a stamp duty exemption, for example, because the transfer of the shares is intra-group (although the legislation governing these types of exemption contain a number of requirements that must be met to qualify for the exemption).

SDLT is payable on land transactions relating to UK land (whether or not an instrument is executed) and will apply to the purchase of land on an asset and business acquisition. For commercial property purchases, the maximum rate is 4 per cent above the consideration payable in excess of £500,000.

Competition/anti-trust

In the United Kingdom, the national merger control rules are contained in the Fair Trading Act 1973. The EC merger regulations also need to be considered when structuring an acquisition where there is a 'community dimension'. A detailed examination of the various turnover thresholds that trigger UK or EC merger control regulations is outside the scope of the chapter, although it is important to consider the issue at the outset of a transaction as non-compliance with relevant merger regulations may result in sanctions, including the requirement to dispose of part or all of the entity that is acquired.

Financial assistance

(This is very technical and can be confusing). Section 151(1) of the Companies Act 1985 prohibits a target company in the United Kingdom or any of its subsidiaries from giving financial assistance directly or indirectly for the purpose of the acquisition of the target company's shares. Financial assistance is defined as including (under section 152(1)(a)):

- 'gifts';
- financial assistance by way of guarantee, security or indemnity (for example, if the company were to grant a charge or mortgage over any of its assets as security for a loan taken by the proposed purchaser of the shares of the target company);
- financial assistance given by way of loan or other agreement under which any of the obligations of the person giving the assistance are

to be fulfilled at a time when in accordance with the agreement any obligation of another party to the agreement remains unfulfilled; or

- any other financial assistance given by a company the net assets of which are thereby reduced to a material extent or which has no net assets.

Contravention of section 151 of the Companies Act 1985 by the giving of financial assistance constitutes a criminal offence and the company is liable to a fine and every officer of it is liable to imprisonment or a fine, or both. Lenders may also be unable to recover monies lent on a transaction that contravenes section 151.

There are a number of exemptions contained in section 153 of the Companies Act 1985, although careful consideration is needed as to whether the company actually falls within one of the exemptions before seeking to rely on it. In addition, there is a form of 'relaxation' of section 151 of the Companies Act for private companies (contained in sections 155 to 158 of the Companies Act) known as the 'whitewash' procedure.

In order to qualify for the whitewash procedure, the financial assistance may only be given if the company in question has net assets that are not reduced because of the financial assistance or, to the extent that they are reduced, if the assistance is provided out of distributable profits. The giving of the assistance must be approved by a special resolution of the company in a general meeting (that is, a vote in favour of the resolution by the shareholders of at least 75 per cent by number of the shares) unless the company proposing to give the financial assistance is a wholly-owned subsidiary. In addition, the directors of the company proposing to give the assistance are required to swear a statutory declaration in the form prescribed by section 156 of the Companies Act 1985 before the assistance is given, to confirm that they have formed the opinion that the company will be able to pay its debts as they fall due for 12 months after the assistance is given. The statutory declaration is also required to have annexed to it a report of the company's auditors. The 'whitewash' procedure therefore has timing implications when considering a proposed share purchase. The most important of the timing issues is the report of the auditors, who may wish to undertake a detailed re-examination of their last audit and bring it up to date.

Public company acquisitions

This section of the chapter deals with the purchase of UK public companies, including those quoted on the London Stock Exchange. It provides a summary only and is not intended to be comprehensive or to contain legal advice, which should always be sought at an early stage.

Certain of the areas covered in the section entitled 'Private company acquisitions' also apply to the acquisition of shares in a public company, for example, stamp duty on the transfer of shares (although please see below under 'Schemes of arrangement'), competition/anti-trust and the prohibition on companies (and their subsidiaries) giving financial assistance for the purpose of the acquisition of shares in the company. The 'whitewash' procedure in relation to financial assistance referred to above is not available to UK public companies.

The structures

A purchaser or offeror (the 'Offeror') (which is the terminology of the City Code on Takeovers and Mergers (the 'Code')) may purchase a public company in the United Kingdom, listed on the London Stock Exchange or AIM ('the Target') using one of two different procedures: 1) the Offeror can either make a general offer to the Target's shareholders (an 'Offer'); or 2) the Offeror can carry out a scheme of arrangement ('Scheme of Arrangement') in circumstances where the transaction is approved by the Target's directors.

As mentioned in 'Private company acquisitions', there is no UK equivalent to the US merger (the Scheme of Arrangement for a public company is the nearest equivalent). The Offer is the more common means of acquiring a public company in the United Kingdom.

Set out below is a summary of some of the key points in relation to cash offers. There are additional requirements for share-for-share offers, although these are outside the scope of this chapter.

The Code

The Code contains various rules as to the conduct of the Offeror and the Target during the course of an Offer, including rules on restrictions on acquiring shares, rules as to when the Offeror must make an Offer and the timetable requirements for an Offer.

The Code is in effect a self-regulatory regime and is not contained in English statutes. The Code is issued by the Panel on Takeovers and Mergers (the 'Panel'), which comprises representatives of the leading London institutions. The regime set out in the Code is also overseen by the Panel. While it does not have the force of law, the general level of compliance with the Code is very high, not least because the Panel's ultimate sanction is to order the City's advisers to refrain from acting for a company that does not comply with the provisions of the Code.

The directors of both the Offeror (and any ultimate parent company) and the Target are required, under the provisions of the Code, to take responsibility for the conduct of their respective companies during an

Offer as well as their respective documents.

Timetable

The Code sets out a strict timetable within which an Offer must be made:

- The Offer is first made by way of an announcement to the press.

- The Code prescribes a specified period after the issue of an announcement (28 days), in which to post the offer document itself to shareholders of Target, although in practice the Offeror usually seeks to post the offer document as soon as possible after the announcement. The offer document will be sent out to Target shareholders by the financial advisers to the Offeror.

- One of the key conditions of the Offer is the acceptance condition (dealing with the level of acceptances of the Offer). If the Offeror does not own or control at least 50 per cent of the Target's issued voting equity shares (whether by prior ownership, purchase or acceptances of the Offer) by the 60th day after the date of the posting of the offer document, the Offer will lapse. In these circumstances, the Offeror is usually precluded from launching a further Offer for 12 months.

Confidentiality

Maintenance of secrecy in relation to a potential Offer, prior to the making of any announcement of it is a key consideration from the Offeror's and the Target's perspective and this area is quite strictly regulated. If the fact that an Offeror is preparing to launch an Offer for the Target enters the public domain, this could significantly increase the risk of a rival offer being made for the same Target. On this basis, the initial due diligence carried out by the Offeror in relation to the Target will normally be carried on with an even higher degree of secrecy than for many private company acquisitions. Usually all correspondence relating to the due diligence and the Offeror's investigations generally will be marked with a project code name to maintain confidentiality. The Code also deals with the area of the provision of confidential information to an Offeror during an Offer and there are sanctions generally for the disclosure of inside information under English law.

The Offeror's approach to Target

Rule 1 of the Code requires that the Offer be put forward in the first instance to the board of the Target. In any case, the Offeror will be seeking to obtain the Target board's recommendation for the Offer as such recommendation is more likely to persuade the shareholders to accept the Offer on the advice of the Target's directors.

Rule 3.1 of the Code requires the Target board to obtain independent advice in relation to any Offer for the Target shares (the advice will normally be taken from a financial adviser such as a bank or broker). This should assist the directors in making a decision as to whether to recommend the Offer. The substance of such advice must be made known to Target shareholders.

If the Target board does not recommend the Offer, there are two alternatives: 1) the Offeror may decide to continue with the Offer on a hostile basis, which may have a lesser chance of succeeding due to the lack of recommendation of the Target board. Pursuing a hostile bid also has the effect of extending the Offer timetable. (Further examination of the timetable for a hostile bid and the process are outside the scope of this chapter) 2) the Offeror may decide not to continue.

Irrevocable undertakings

Normally, an Offeror would not make approaches to the Target shareholders before the announcement of an Offer in order to maintain secrecy in the run-up to the Offer being made. However, subject to specific rules, the Offeror may approach (on a confidential basis) certain major shareholders of the Target immediately before an announcement in order to obtain from them irrevocable undertakings to accept the Offer. The main purpose of seeking such irrevocable undertakings or 'irrevocables' as they are commonly known is to seek to ensure that the Offeror will achieve the minimum acceptance level for the Offer under the Code of 50 per cent of the shares.

Unless and until the Offeror's 1) acceptance condition (see below); and 2) the other conditions are satisfied or otherwise waived, the Offeror will not be obliged to complete the acquisition of any Target shares that are the subject of acceptances, including those that are the subject of irrevocable undertakings to accept the Offer.

Making the Offer

An announcement of the Offer should not be made until the Offeror is certain that it has all its funding in place in an amount sufficient to satisfy full acceptance of the Offer by all Target shareholders. The financial advisers to the Offeror will be particularly concerned to ensure that this is the case as they are required (under rule 24.7 of the Code) to make a 'cash confirmation' statement in the actual offer document to the effect that sufficient resources are available to the Offeror to satisfy full acceptance of the Offer.

Acceptance condition

As mentioned above, the minimum level of acceptances is 50 per cent of the issued voting shares. However, it is more typical for the acceptance condition to be set at 90 per cent of the shares by the Offeror in order to take advantage of the compulsory acquisition ('squeeze out') procedure (please see below for further details).

Buying Target shares in the market

The Code contains strict rules governing the purchase of Target shares (both before and after the announcement of an Offer). The Offeror may decide, from a tactical perspective, to try to build a stake in the Target from which to launch an Offer and therefore to acquire shares in the market. Various English law provisions governing use and disclosure of inside information and disclosure of interests in shares will be relevant to such market purchases; however, an exploration of these provisions is beyond the scope of this chapter.

Squeeze-out procedure

If the Offeror acquires at least 90 per cent of the shares to which the Offer relates, the Offeror can use the compulsory acquisition procedure contained in the Companies Act 1985 in the United Kingdom to acquire the remainder of the Target shares at the Offer price. As the squeeze-out procedure only applies to shares to which the Offer relates, shares purchased in the market will not count towards the 90 per cent threshold.

De-listing

Once the Offer has becomes unconditional in all respects and the Offeror is in a position to utilize the squeeze-out procedure, it is usually a formality to obtain a de-listing of the Target's shares from the London Stock Exchange. As long as the Offeror has previously stated (in the Offer document) that it intends, if the Offer is successful, to seek to cancel the listing for Target's shares, it can effect the de-listing at this time.

Schemes of Arrangement

The Scheme of Arrangement is not used as frequently as a general Offer in order to acquire a public company in the United Kingdom. A Scheme of Arrangement is a specific procedure permitted under the Companies Act 1985.

Procedure for a Scheme of Arrangement

In summary, the procedure to effect a Scheme of Arrangement involves the following main steps:

- A special meeting of the Target's shareholders is convened at which the Scheme must be approved by a majority in number representing three-quarters in value of shareholders who vote (in person or by proxy) at the meeting. Shareholders who do not vote are therefore disregarded.

- Once the special meeting has taken place, the Scheme must then be sanctioned by the court, following which it is binding on all shareholders.

- The normal structure of a Scheme of Arrangement involves the cancellation of all existing shares in the Target and the issue of new shares in the Target to the Offeror.

Advantages of a Scheme of Arrangement

Essentially, the threshold at which the Offeror can obtain complete control (that is, 100 per cent ownership), is lower for a Scheme of Arrangement than the 90 per cent threshold required for the squeeze-out procedure (please see above) on an Offer. So long as shareholders constituting a majority in number and representing at least three-quarters in value of those voting, vote in favour of the Scheme of Arrangement, once the requisite shareholder approval has been obtained, this binds all shareholders. In addition, shares in the Target already owned or controlled by the Offeror do not count towards the 90 per cent threshold in relation to a squeeze-out on an Offer. The squeeze-out procedure extends the timetable on an Offer and, if used, can mean a longer timetable than is required for a Scheme of Arrangement.

It is possible to structure a Scheme of Arrangement to avoid stamp duty on the transfer of shares in the Target. Please see above under 'Private company acquisitions' for further details in relation to stamp duty on the transfer of shares.

An SEC-regulated Offeror does not have to file an S4 containing accounts of the purchaser and Target within one month of the close. This can be a very troublesome non-requirement!

Disadvantages of a Scheme of Arrangement

As the period for the Offeror to acquire more than 50 per cent control of the Target is longer than is usually the case with an Offer, if a competing Offeror comes on the scene, such competitor will have more time to act. If a competing Offeror comes to the fore on an Offer, it is possible for the original Offeror to alter certain of the terms of its Offer and to increase its Offer. However, on a Scheme of Arrangement it is more difficult for the original Offeror subsequently to alter the terms of the Scheme. The timing and implementation of the Scheme are within the control of the Target and its directors, who may decide to withdraw the Scheme.

Shares held by shareholders who, for example, receive different consideration from other shareholders under the Scheme, will be treated by the court as a separate class of shareholder and therefore a separate vote for each class of shareholder will be required. This may make it harder to achieve the requisite shareholder majority vote(s) in favour of the Scheme referred to above.

The court, when considering whether to sanction the Scheme, has the power to require certain modifications to be made prior to giving its sanction if it is not satisfied, for instance because a minority share-holder has raised a justifiable objection to the Scheme at the court hearing. Overseas companies have used both methods, the Offer and the Scheme of Arrangement, for these purchases.

Joint ventures

A joint venture in the United Kingdom is usually structured through shareholdings in a limited company, although a limited or unlimited partnership involving two or more companies may also refer to itself as a joint venture. Here is a brief guide for the inward investor thinking of setting up a joint venture with its English counterpart.

The documentation for a UK joint venture includes: 1) the articles of association of the joint venture company, setting out the constitution of the company and 2) the joint venture agreement or shareholders' agreement between the parties to the joint venture, which contains the provisions for the management of the business of the company between the different shareholders.

Because English law is under a common law system, the joint venture agreement needs to reflect English law and lay down what happens in most situations the joint venture will face. Set out below are some of the key areas for consideration when entering into and drawing up the documentation for a joint venture in the United Kingdom.

Contributions of the parties

The parties will invariably take shares in the joint venture company. The parties may all take ordinary shares or a funder may take a different class of shares, for example, preference shares where the funder would rank in preference to the ordinary shareholders for dividend purposes and on a distribution of the assets on a winding up. Certain parties, again, usually the funder, may make loans available to the joint venture company, while other parties may contribute their expertise, personnel, business assets, technology, know-how, IP or real property in consideration for shares in the company. All these are possible under English law. Care needs to be taken to cover situations where one party is unable to provide further funds needed.

Management

A key question is always how will the joint venture company be managed. Decisions will need to be taken as to how many directors in total there should be, how many directors (if any) each shareholder has the right to appoint to the board of the company, the quorum for board meetings and the frequency and location of meetings. There will also be considerations as to whether a chairperson of the board is appointed and, if so, whether or not he or she has a casting vote. Where there are only two joint venture parties and it is a 50/50 joint venture, the quorum and the issue of whether or not a chairperson has a casting vote will be particularly important as, often, neither party will wish to concede this.

Decision-making

It is usual to have a particular class of decisions that cannot be made unless all of the shareholders in the company agree or a certain percentage holding of the shares held by shareholders vote in favour of the decision. These would usually be particular types of internal decisions of the company, that is, changing the articles of association, issuing new shares, acquiring a new business or selling a significant part of the current business or assets of the joint venture company, or granting a charge over any assets of the joint venture company.

As a matter of English company law, the holders of more than 25 per cent of the issued shares can block a special resolution. In a joint venture, however, it is typical for the majority shareholder to be required to obtain the minority shareholder's consent even for some matters where normally an ordinary resolution or a special resolution would be sufficient. Such matters are some of those mentioned above, for example, amending the company's articles of association. Just how much blocking power a minority shareholder has is often the subject of much negotiation and specialist advice on English law and minority protection may be needed.

Succession

There is often an initial period of commitment to the company required from the shareholders under the shareholders' agreement. Once any such period has expired, the agreement usually makes specific provision for how a shareholder can transfer his or her shares and thereby exit the joint venture. It is usual that, before a new person can become a shareholder, he or she will need to enter into a deed of adherence, agreeing to be bound by the same terms as the existing shareholders.

Commonly encountered restrictions on the transfer of shares include pre-emption rights. A shareholder wishing to transfer his or her shares is first required to offer the shares to the other parties to the joint venture pro rata to their existing holdings. In this event, issues are raised as to how the price of the shares is calculated. Examples of common pricing mechanisms in UK joint ventures include:

- the price that would be offered by a third party, provided that it is bona fide and at arm's length;

- a price agreed between a particular transferor and the directors of the joint venture company; or

- a price to be determined by a specific valuation procedure laid down in the documentation (usually the articles of association), for example, using an independent chartered accountant.

Other typical share transfer provisions include founder shareholders or employees of the joint venture who have shares being entitled to make permitted transfers to family members or, if the shareholder is a company, to affiliates of that company. Often, founders or employees may be required to relinquish their shareholdings in particular circumstances, for example, following their dismissal or redundancy. Sometimes the joint venture company will want to make a distinction between 'good leavers', that is, employees who leave the company through retirement, ill health or redundancy, and 'bad leavers' (employees who leave due to misconduct or resignation during the time in which the venture is still being developed). Where shares are held subject to restrictions, this can raise various tax issues, which are outside the scope of this chapter. Care should also be taken on minority holdings and their valuation, because otherwise the valuation of the minority will be substantially discounted under the normal English rules of discounts for minorities. Advice should therefore always be sought at an early stage in relation to structuring the shareholdings and the transfer provisions.

Confidentiality and non-compete provisions

There is invariably a confidentiality clause in the shareholders' agreement whereby the parties agree to keep confidential their knowledge about the joint venture company and the knowledge they learn about each other in the course of the joint venture. The shareholders' agreement should also include non-compete provisions, often known as restrictive covenants, under which the parties agree that they will not compete in any way with the joint venture company and that any new business they acquire or obtain outside of the joint venture company has to be carried out by the joint venture company.

Dispute resolution

Dispute resolution is particularly important in the context of a 50/50 joint venture. If there is a deadlock, this will affect the whole decision-making process in the joint venture if certain decisions require a particular percentage in order to obtain consent. One way around this is for each of the shareholders to appoint a certain (equal) number of directors and then a chairperson of the board will be appointed and that chairperson will be selected by both shareholders. The chairperson will then have a casting vote.

Alternative forms of dispute resolution include the following:

- Arbitration or independent expert provision, whereby an independent expert, often a chartered accountant, will come in and look at the proposed decision with an objective view as to whether it is in the best interests of the company.

- 'Russian Roulette', where either party can serve notice offering either to sell its shares or buy out the other shareholder (if the shareholders cannot agree on a decision and there is deadlock) at a given price/terms and the recipient of the notice then has the right to accept (or elect to do the opposite) on the same price/terms (this would usually only be applicable in a 50/50 joint venture).

- 'Texas Shootout', where the parties have the right to offer on the highest sealed bid basis for the business of the joint venture company on liquidation or for the other's shares.

- The right to require liquidation of the joint venture company where there is a deadlock. There is sometimes a combination of provisions, for example, first, a provision of a period of time for negotiation between the parties to see if they can reach agreement, followed by liquidation of the joint venture company if no decision is reached at the end of the specified period.

Duration of joint venture and termination

The joint venture company may have been set up for one particular project only and once that objective is attained, the joint venture company will then be wound up. Alternatively, there may be particular provisions in the joint venture agreement regarding termination, for example where a shareholder in the joint venture company becomes insolvent or commits a material breach of any of the provisions of the agreement. If a particular licence or regulatory control or permit is required in order to carry on the business of the joint venture company and such licence is lost, then this may constitute a termination event. Also, if there is a change of control of one of the parties to the joint venture, this may be included as a termination provision.

All activities of a joint venture company are governed by English law. The negotiation of an agreement is long and can be tedious because it is required to centre around the potential falling out of the parties and what happens when one party wants to terminate the arrangement or is breaching the agreement. Other conflicts occur where one party is happy with the business of the joint venture while the other or another party wishes to expand its activities substantially. Sometimes the negotiation of a licensing, distribution, or marketing agreement will provide a practical low-cost alternative to a joint venture for an inward investor. Most joint ventures end up with one party acquiring the other's shareholding. On the other hand, a joint venture provides access to the UK market place at what is potentially 50 per cent of the cost of going it alone.

2.7

Private Equity and Venture Capital

Professor Colin Mason, University of Strathclyde

Introduction

Private equity can be defined as the equity financing of unquoted companies at various stages in the life cycle of a company, from start-up to expansion, as well as management buyouts (MBOs) and buy-ins (MBIs) of parts of established companies or even entire companies. The key features of private equity are as follows:

- investments in unquoted companies;
- providing equity capital;
- medium- to long-term investment horizon;
- targeted at companies with growth potential;
- returns mostly realized through a trade sale or flotation on the public market;
- generally a hands-on investment style, with investors seeking to add value to their investee companies.

In the past, the term 'venture capital' was used to describe this form of investing. However, the term venture capital is now confined to the seed to expansion stages of investment, while 'private equity' is used for investments in established companies that are undergoing various forms of restructuring, notably the MBO or MBI of divisions or subsidiaries of larger companies, businesses in receivership, family businesses with succession problems, and privatisations.[1]

Increasingly, private equity firms are now often involved in leading such investment opportunities rather than waiting to be approached by management teams (institutional buyouts). Private equity firms are also doing public to private deals, which involve buying out the shareholders of smaller publicly listed companies where a public listing is no longer useful, to take them into private ownership for subsequent re-sale.

Venture capitalists and private equity investors therefore have very different skill sets. Venture capitalists invest in young businesses with the potential to become significant companies in their markets. The skills of venture capitalists are therefore in opportunity evaluation, the assessment of management teams and the provision of 'hands on' support to their investee companies. Private equity investors, on the other hand, are investing in established companies in situations where there is the potential to achieve growth and unlock value. Their skill sets are financial engineering and deal crafting. However, in both cases the objective is to achieve returns through capital gains.

Given this focus on investing in companies with growth potential it is not surprising to find that venture capital and private equity (VC/PE)-backed companies make a significant contribution to the economy. Research published by the British Venture Capital Association[2] reveals the performance of VC/PE-backed companies in the five years to 2002/03:

- Their sales rose 21 per cent per annum, more than three times that of FTSE100 companies.

- Their exports rose by 11 per cent per annum compared with a national growth of 3.3 per cent per annum.

- Their investment rose 21 per cent per annum compared with a national increase of 5.4 per cent.

- Their employment increased by an average of 19 per cent per annum (83 per cent of which was organic rather than due to acquisition) compared with 0.5 per cent per annum in the private sector.

Private equity-backed companies in the United Kingdom employ 2.7 million people – 18 per cent of the private sector workforce. In view of this, it is not surprising that government is supportive of the industry, with the Chancellor of the Exchequer recently noting that 'a flourishing British venture capital and private equity industry is vital to growth'.

Structure

The United Kingdom's VC/PE industry is both the longest established and the largest outside of the United States. The industry was established with the creation of the British Venture Capital Association (BVCA) in 1983 with 34 founding members. However, some venture capital firms existed before the creation of the BVCA, notably Charterhouse Industrial Development Company, which was formed in the 1930s, and ICFC, the precursor of today's 3i plc, which was created in 1945. Currently, there are approximately 165 full members of the BVCA.

There are two main types of VC/PE firm. The larger category is independent firms that are structured as limited partnerships and raise their funds from the financial institutions and other investors (for example, companies, wealthy families, government). The other main category is 'captives', which are the in-house private equity subsidiaries of financial institutions (for example, banks).

However, private individuals can invest in private equity through any of the 22 publicly quoted 'Venture and Development Capital Investment Trusts' and approximately 70 Venture Capital Trusts (VCTs) (discussed later) that are quoted on the London Stock Exchange. Many of the larger fund managers are hybrids, operating both captive and limited partnership funds (and sometimes quoted Venture and Development Capital Investment Trusts and VCTs as well).

Private equity firms are characterized by a great range in size in terms of their funds under management, from under £1 million to over £5 billion. The smaller funds tend to focus on venture capital and have an investment focus that is restricted to a specific geographical area, whereas the larger funds focus on MBOs/MBIs and related investments and operate on a pan-European basis. Over time, private equity has come to dominate in terms of the volume of funds invested.

Size

In terms of its size, The PricewaterhouseCoopers/3i *Global Private Equity 2003* report identifies the United Kingdom as being the second largest market for VC/PE in the world in 2002 (see Table 2.7.1), based on both investment value ($9.58 billion) and funds raised ($13.42 billion). This report also identifies the United Kingdom as being the second largest private equity market in terms of high-tech investment ($2.4 billion), expansion investment ($1.8 billion) and buy-out investment ($6.9 billion) (see Table 2.7.2). To further emphasize the relative size of the United Kingdom's private equity market, it accounted for 36.8 per cent of private equity invested in Western Europe in 2002 and 52 per cent of the amount raised.[3]

Table 2.7.1 The 20 largest countries for private equity based on investments and funds raised in 2002

	Country Ranking for Investment	Investment Value US$ billion	Funds Raised US$ billion
1	USA	62.68	54.89
2	UK	9.58	13.42
3	France	5.53	4.54
4	Italy	2.48	1.89
5	Japan	2.38	0.72
6	Germany	2.37	1.55
7	South Korea	1.95	0.36
8	Netherlands	1.63	1.13
9	Canada	1.57	2.07
10	Sweden	1.39	0.61
11	Australia	1.21	0.21
12	India	1.05	0.16
13	Israel	0.98	1.14
14	Spain	0.92	0.60
15	Hong Kong	0.75	0.55
16	Indonesia	0.56	n/a
17	Finland	0.43	0.68
18	South Africa	0.37	0.08
19	China	0.35	0.32
20	Belgium	0.34	0.12

Source: PricewaterhouseCoopers: *Global Private Equity 2003*

Table 2.7.2 High-tech, expansion and buyout investment in 2002

High-tech Investment US$ billion		Expansion Investment US$ billion		Buy-out Investment US$ billion	
1 USA	25.7	1 USA	13.3	1 USA	41.5
2 UK	2.4	2 UK	1.8	2 UK	6.9
3 France	1.5	3 Canada	0.8	3 France	4.2
4 Canada	1.4	4 Italy	0.8	4 Italy	1.5
5 Japan	1.0	5 Germany	0.7	5 Japan	1.3
6 Israel	0.9	6 France	0.7	6 Germany	1.1
7 Sweden	0.8	7 Netherlands	0.6	7 Korea	1.0
8 Korea	0.8	8 Spain	0.6	8 Sweden	0.8
9 Germany	0.8	9 Japan	0.5	9 Netherlands	0.7
10 Australia	0.5	10 Israel	0.5	10 Australia	0.6

Source: PricewaterhouseCoopers: *Global Private Equity* 2003

Furthermore, the United Kingdom accounted for 32.9 per cent of Western Europe's technology investments by value and 43 per cent of its buy-out investments by value.[4] Private equity investments in the United Kingdom in 2002 were equivalent to 0.62 per cent of its GDP, compared with just 0.29 per cent for Western Europe as a whole, and much higher than for France (0.39 per cent), the Netherlands (0.39 per cent), Italy (0.21 per cent) and Germany (0.12 per cent).[5] However, the United Kingdom is rather less dominant in terms of the number of investments, than their value. Because of the much larger average size of investments in the United Kingdom (which reflects the dominance of MBO investments), the number of UK investments accounted for only one-quarter (24.5 per cent) of the total number of investments in Western Europe in 2002.[6]

Investment trends

The UK VC/PE industry, like its counterparts in other parts of the world, expanded at a massive rate during the 1990s. Institutional investors were attracted by the high returns that VC/PE funds were generating from the mid-1990s, while demand for VC/PE was fuelled

Table 2.7.0   MBO and MBI investments above £100 million in 2003

Buy-out Name	Value £m	Buy-out Source
Spirit Amber/S&N Retail	2,510	Scottish and Newcastle plc
Debenhams (Baroness Retail)	1,720	Public private
Gala Clubs	1,240	Secondary buy-out
Linpac/Picnal	860	Private sale by family owners
Travelodge and Little Chef	712	Compass group
Waste Recycling Group	531	Public private
Pizza Express	278	Public private
Aviagen	255	Secondary buy-out
Warner Village Cinemas	225	Warner Brothers
Accantia	225	Secondary buy-out
Holmes Place	210	Public private
Fitness First (Moray)	204	Public private
Isle of Man Steam Packet Co	160	Sea Containers Limited
MacDonald Hotels	157	Public private
First Assist	147	Royal & Sun Alliance
IG Group (IGGHL)	143	Public private
Insinger de Beaufort	142	Anglo Dutch Bank
Xyratex	*110	Secondary buy-out
Fosroc International	*100	BP Burmah Castrol

Note: * Estimated value.
Source: Centre for Management Buyout Research, Nottingham Business School

by the growing numbers of technology companies and financial pressures on the corporate sector that created opportunities for MBOs and MBIs. Indeed, since the mid-1990s the bigger funds have begun to take an active, rather than passive, role in seeking investment opportunities by pioneering institutional buy-outs, in which they lead the transaction rather than backing a management team, and public to private deals, taking publicly listed companies private. Secondary buy-out funds[7] have also emerged. Table 2.7.3 demonstrates that, although accounting for only a small proportion of investments, because of their huge size these types of investment account for a disproportionate share of the amount invested.

The amounts raised by independent VC/PE funds, shown in Table 2.7.4, rose enormously during the 1990s, up from £749 million in 1995 to a peak of £13.6 billion in 2001, before falling back to £7.8 billion in 2002. Pension funds have been the biggest single source of investment in VC/PE funds, followed by banks and insurance companies. However, the main feature has been the increasing inflow of funds from overseas – especially US investors. From accounting for under half of the funds raised by independent VC/PE funds in the United Kingdom in the mid-1990s, overseas investors' share rose to around 70 per cent by 2001. The fall in equity markets, which has reduced the commitment by pension funds in particular to equity-based investments, has created difficult fundraising conditions for VC/PE firms in the past couple of years, although most fund managers anticipate an improvement in fundraising conditions in 2004.[8]

Table 2.7.4   Investors in UK independent private equity firms

	1995	1996	1997	1998	1999	2000	2001	2002
				Amount raised £m				
UK Pension Funds	170	734	622	553	437	817	1,640	796
Overseas Pension Funds	191	519	1,397	1,875	1,610	2,759	3,853	1,043
UK Insurance Companies	131	221	1,160	152	533	457	451	739
Overseas Insurance Companies	12	104	505	193	383	931	1,022	454
UK Corporate Investors	32	29	376	83	138	299	195	236
Overseas Corporate Investors	18	51	428	432	447	414	100	410
UK Banks	7	68	238	383	350	332	661	1,051
Overseas Banks	42	153	467	640	786	575	1,376	495
UK Funds-of-funds*	n/a	n/a	n/a	n/a	58	799	474	282

continued overleaf

	1995	1996	1997	1998	1999	2000	2001	2002
Overseas								
Funds-of-funds*	n/a	n/a	n/a	n/a	352	427	1,705	778
UK Government								
Agencies*	n/a	n/a	n/a	n/a	n/a	6	13	128
Overseas Government								
Agencies	n/a	n/a	n/a	n/a	n/a	241	561	827
UK Academic								
Institutions	4	56	10	5	29	13	86	55
Overseas Academic								
Institutions	63	82	234	434	122	47	394	103
UK Private Individuals	43	68	164	157	175	363	214	108
Overseas Private								
Individuals	4	108	142	152	100	211	429	119
UK Other Sources	25	207	228	182	56	125	173	90
Overseas Other								
Sources	7	45	525	329	237	179	287	113
UK Total	412	1,383	2,798	1,515	1,776	3,211	3,907	3,485
Overseas Total	337	1,062	3,698	4,055	4,037	5,784	9,727	4,342
Grand Total	749	2,445	6,496	5,570	5,813	8,995	13,634	7,827

Note: * Earlier years were included as part of 'Other Sources'.
Source: BVCA Report on *Investment Activity 2002*, Appendix 6O

The scale of investment activity by UK VC/PE funds has reflected this massive increase in fundraising and is exhibited in Table 2.7.5. Total funds invested (including non-UK) rose from £1.4 million in 1992 to £4.9 million in 1998, and then – driven by rising valuations – almost doubled to a peak of £8.3million in 2000, before falling back to £5.5 million in 2002 in the aftermath of the stock market crash. Paralleling the rise in investment activity during the 1990s has been the increasing share of funds that have been invested outside the United Kingdom, rising from around 14 per cent in the early 1990s to over 20 per cent by the turn of the century. Investment in the United Kingdom has followed the same trend as for overall investment, rising from £1.3 million in 1992 to peak at £6.4 million in 2000, falling back to £4.5 million in 2002 as both valuations and investment activity dropped. However, the industry raised more funds in the late 1990s than it was able to invest before the stock market crash. Furthermore, the decline in investing preceded the drop in fundraising. The consequence is that the industry still had a substantial overhang of funds available for investment. The decline in exit possibilities following the crash – arising from the loss of interest in IPOs and the drop in the number of companies making acquisitions – has meant that VC/PE funds have used this money to support their existing portfolios of companies rather than to make new investments.

Table 2.7.5 Investment trends 1992–2002

Year	No of Companies Financed in the UK	Amount Invested in the UK (£m)	Amount Invested Overseas (£m)	Total Amount Invested (£m)
1992	1,147	1,251	183	1,434
1993	1,066	1,231	191	1,422
1994	1,101	1,668	406	2,074
1995	1,030	2,140	395	2,535
1996	1,060	2,806	433	3,239
1997	1,116	3,066	1,118	4,184
1998	1,122	3,775	1,144	4,919
1999	1,109	6,169	1,678	7,847
2000	1,182	6,371	1,885	8,256
2001	1,307	4,752	1,412	6,164
2002	1,196	4,480	986	5,466

Source: BVCA (2002) *Report on Investment Activity 2002*, Appendix 6A

Stage of Investment

The dichotomous nature of the VC/PE industry is evident from recent investment trends. Table 2.7.6 shows that early stage investments account for around one-third of all investments but less than 10 per cent of the amount invested. In contrast, MBOs/MBIs and related types of investment represented 15 per cent of investments but because many of these investments are large they accounted for 63 per cent of the total amount invested. Indeed, as Table 2.7.7 demonstrates, large MBOs (over £50 million) accounted for just 10 per cent of all MBOs but over half of the amount invested in MBOs, and one-third of the total amount invested.

However, early stage investments have increased in significance in recent years, rising from 16 per cent of investments in 1995 to around one-third since 2000. In terms of value, early stage investments have risen from under 5 per cent in 1995 to peak at 11 per cent in 2000, falling back to 7 per cent in 2002. At the same time, MBO/MBI investments have become slightly less dominant. Their share of investment activity has declined from 33 per cent in 1995 to 15 per cent in 2002, while in terms of value they have fallen from just under 75 per cent in 1995 to below 60 per cent in 2000 and 2001 but recovering in 2002 to 63 per cent.

Thus, although the relatively small number of big MBO investments dominate in terms of the amount invested, the 'typical' VC/PE-backed company is an SME (a business with less than 250 employees), which raises less than £5 million (88 per cent; 61 per cent less than £1 million).[9]

Table 2.7.6   UK investment by stage

(a) Amount invested (£m)

	Early Stage	Expansion	MBO/MBI	Total
	£m			
1992	82	362	807	1,251
1993	69	393	769	1,231
1994	76	480	1,112	1,668
1995	85	495	1,560	2,140
1996	131	592	2083	2,806
1997	159	907	2,000	3,066
1998	288	822	2,665	3,775
1999	347	1,156	4,666	6,169
2000	703	2,122	3,546	6,371
2001	390	1,636	2,726	4,752
2002	295	1,374	2,811	4,480

(b) Number of UK companies

	Early Stage	Expansion	MBO/MBI	Total
1995	167	528	335	1,030
1996	184	520	356	1,060
1997	219	548	349	1,116
1998	241	561	320	1,122
1999	260	539	310	1,109
2000	409	548	225	1,182
2001	408	653	246	1,307
2002	398	619	179	1,196

Note: Before 1995 data were calculated on the basis on number of 'financings'. This is not comparable because companies can have more than one financing in a year.
Source: BVCA (2002) *Report on Investment Activity 2002*, Appendix 6Ci and Cii

Table 2.7.7   MBO investments in 2002 by size

Size of Investment	Number		Amount Invested	
	No	%	£m	%
Under £2m	54	36	80	3
£2m–£10m	45	30	240	9
£10m–£50m	36	24	846	32
Over £50m	15	10	1,493	56
Total	150	100	2,659	100

Source: BVCA (2002) *Report on Investment Activity 2002*, Table 5a

Sectoral investment patterns

Investments occur across virtually all sectors of the economy. However, the sectors containing the most VC/PE-backed companies are software and computer services, pharmaceuticals and support services. The most significant sectors in terms of the amount invested are leisure and hotels, health and retail. Technology sectors have withstood the worst of the post-2000 downturn in VC/PE investing. Thus, even in 2002, just over half of all investments were in technology sectors, virtually all of these investments being either early stage (49 per cent) or expansion financing (48 per cent). Computer software was the technology category that attracted most investments. But whereas the number of technology investments fell 17 per cent between 2000 and 2002, Table 2.7.8 reveals that the amounts invested in technology sectors dropped by two-thirds over the same period. However, the effect of this drop is simply to bring technology investing back to the level of the 1990s before the boom.[10]

Table 2.7.8   Trends in technology investments 2000–02

	2000	2001	2002
No of Companies	772	690	641
% of all UK Companies	65	53	54
Amount Invested (£m)	1,615	1,658	546
% of amount invested in all UK Companies	25	35	12

Source: BVCA (2002) *Report on Investment Activity 2002, Table 5a*

Geographical characteristics

VC/PE displays distinctive geographical characteristics. The majority of private equity firms are based in London and investment activity has tended to favour London and the South East. During the 1990s, however, there was significant growth in investment activity in some of the English regions – notably the East and West Midlands and the North West – although London and the South East continued to attract a disproportionate share of investments. The growth of VC/PE outside of the South East is clearly linked to the emergence of small clusters of VC/PE firms in such cities as Birmingham and Manchester. However, the growth of private equity investments in the regions has been largely driven by MBO and MBI investments: early stage investing has continued to be disproportionately concentrated in London and the South East, and also Scotland. The investment downturn since 2000 has had less of an impact on London, the South East and the East of England.[11]

Investment performance

The latest BVCA *Performance Measurement Survey* (conducted in conjunction with PricewaterhouseCoopers and Westport Private Equity) notes that UK independent private equity funds have outperformed the Total UK Pensions Assets over 1, 3, 5 and 10 years.[12] Looking at returns from fund inception, the best performers, for which data are given in Table 2.7.9, have been the large MBO funds and non-technology funds, whereas early stage funds and technology funds have performed poorly. This differential investment performance clearly helps to explain the dominance of private equity funds over venture capital funds.

Table 2.7.9   Overall performance of independent UK private equity firms by investment stage: returns since inception

	No. of Funds	To December 2002	To December 2001	To December 2000	To December 1999	To December 1998
Early Stage	31	11.5	14.1	15.0	9.8	8.3
Development	45	10.1	9.7	10.0	12.2	9.1
Mid MBO	50	11.0	14.2	16.3	16.7	16.5
Large MBO	40	16.8	18.8	18.7	17.1	19.2
Generalist	45	15.4	16.2	16.4	16.8	13.5
Total	211	14.6	16.2	16.4	15.9	14.9
UK	175	14.5	15.4	16.2	16.5	15.5
Non-UK	36	15.1	18.7	17.5	12.4	9.8
Technology	49	10.7	12.1	12.8	9.5	8.4
Non-technology	162	15.3	17.0	17.3	16.5	15.6
Very Large MBOs	19	18.3	20.5	19.6	17.7	17.7

Source: PricewaterhouseCoopers / BVCA (2002) *Performance Measurement Survey 2002*, www.bvca.co.uk/publications/performmeasusurv/pm2002summary.html

Government support for the early stage venture capital market

The United Kingdom is well served for larger private equity deals. However, there has been periodic concern that there is a lack of early stage funding available, especially for technology-based firms, and for amounts of under £250,000. Over the years these concerns have prompted government intervention. The present government has been particularly active in establishing various funding initiatives to ensure the supply of early stage finance.[13]

University Challenge Funds

First, it has established University Challenge Funds (UCFs). They are seed funds that help the commercialization of university research and were established in response to a perceived funding gap for bringing university research discoveries to a point where their commercial usefulness can be demonstrated to a sufficient extent that successful approaches can be made to investors for finance or to companies to take out a licence. They were funded by two charities (The Wellcome Trust, which contributed £18 million, and the Gatsby Charitable Foundation, which contributed £2 million) and HM government (£25 million). In June 1998, universities were invited to bid on their own or in consortia for a share of the money. Each recipient had to match 25 per cent of the amount awarded from its own resources. A total of 15 seed funds were established (involving 31 universities and 6 institutes). In 2000, the government contributed a further £15 million, which was awarded to 5 funds involving 38 institutions. The funds are all professionally managed. UCFs have invested £36 million in 186 university spin-outs over the past three years which has led to the development of 102 patents and 15 licences.[14] However, because of the investment downturn a number of the fund managers have reported difficulties in attracting follow-on funding for the investments that they have already made.

Regional Venture Capital Funds

Second, the government has established Regional Venture Capital Funds in each of the nine English regions to focus on sub-£500,000 investments. They are profiled in Table 2.7.10. The devolved nations of Scotland, Wales and Northern Ireland have their own separate publicly supported institutional arrangements for early stage venture capital. The funds have commercial objectives and are professionally managed. Their aims are threefold:

- to increase the amount of equity-based finance for growing SMEs;
- to ensure all regions have access to viable regionally based venture capital funds;
- to demonstrate to potential investors that commercial returns can be made by funds that invest in the SME 'equity gap'.

Table 2.7.10   The Regional Venture Capital Funds

Region	Fund Manager	Size of Fund (£m)	No of Investments	Total Invested (£m)
				At May 2003
North West	North West Fund Manager	35.5	7	1.834
North East	Northern Enterprise Ltd	15	12	1.775
Yorkshire and the Humber	Yorkshire Enterprise	25	1	0.250
East of England	Create Partners Ltd	20	–	–
West Midlands	Midven Ltd	20	3	0.450
East Midlands	Catapult Venture Managers Ltd	30	11	1.433
South West	South West Ventures	25	1	0.250
South East	South East Growth Fund	30	12	2.900
London	London Fund Managers	50	1	0.250

Source: PricewaterhouseCoopers (2003) *Early Evaluation of the Regional Venture Capital Funds: Report to the Small Business Service*

The funds have raised a total of £250 million, ranging from £15 million to £50 million. In each fund approximately 50 per cent of the finance has been contributed by the European Investment Bank (EIB) and the UK government, with the remainder raised by the fund managers from private sources (mainly banks and local authority pension funds). To help the fund managers attract private capital, the government has subordinated its investment position by putting a 'cap' on its investment return, thereby boosting the anticipated returns to the private sector and EIB, and agreed to act as 'first loss'. In other words, in the event of the erosion of the fund's capital base the government's investment will suffer the first loss. The funds, which have to be the first external investor in a business, are limited to a maximum investment of £250,000, with up to a further £250,000 in a follow-up investment. If the investment is syndicated the total deal size cannot exceed £250,000. Eight of the nine funds were established during the 2002–03 financial year. By May 2003 these funds had made 48 investments in total, averaging £195,000, which suggests that the majority of investments have been close to the £250,000 limit.[15]

The Early Growth programme and the UK High Technology Fund

Two further initiatives complement the Regional Venture Capital Funds. The Early Growth programme provides smaller amounts of risk capital (average of £50,000) for start-ups and early stage businesses. The UK High Technology Fund, a fund-of-funds, supports early stage high technology businesses by investing in technology-oriented funds. Using £20 million of government funding it has leveraged £100 million of private sector money. To date it has committed £123 million to nine specialist venture capital funds, which have made over 110 investments throughout the United Kingdom.[16]

Venture Capital Trusts

Third, the government has continued with Venture Capital Trusts (VCTs), which were established in 1995 by the previous Conservative government. The aim is to help individuals invest in small higher-risk trading companies whose shares are not listed on a recognized stock market. VCTs, which are listed on the London Stock Exchange, are similar to investment trusts. They are run by fund managers. Investors subscribe for shares in VCTs, which use the money that is raised to invest in unquoted companies and companies listed on the Alternative Investment Market (AIM) and over-the-counter markets, providing them with the finance to start up and grow. UK-based companies (with certain restrictions) can raise up to £1 million a year from VCTs. Investors gain both income tax and capital gains tax relief. This comprises 20 per cent (the basic rate) relief on amounts invested in *new* VCT shares up to a maximum of £100,000 per year. However, the average investment is £25,000. Shares must be retained for a minimum of three years. Investors also receive relief on any dividends paid by VCTs. In addition, any capital gains arising on the disposal of VCT shares are free of tax. Capital gains can also be deferred if reinvested in VCTs.

VCTs have raised over £1 billion in the five years to April 2003. An economic assessment of the scheme concluded that the large majority of this money would not have been invested by those same investors in the absence of the scheme.[17]

One of the main attractions of VCTs for investors has been the ability to defer capital gains. However, with declining equity markets in recent years, fewer people have had capital gains and consequently the amount of money flowing into VCTs has fallen sharply, from £450 million in 2000–01 to £115 million in 2001–02, and to £65 million in 2002–03. In response to this volatility, the government is proposing to make some structural changes to VCTs. Capital gains tax relief will be withdrawn and replaced with an enhancement of equal value to the incentive to invest through income tax relief. In order to make the scheme less cyclically sensitive, the government is proposing a temporary increase in the income tax relief from 20 per cent to 40 per cent, but with the value of the additional 20 per cent paid to the VCT rather than the investor. In other words, investors will be able to buy £1.20 of assets (or £1.15 if costs are included) for £0.80. In addition, the annual investment limit for investors will be raised to £200,000. Further details were to be announced in the March 2004 Budget.[18]

The Corporate Venturing Scheme

Fourth, government has sought to encourage corporate venturing – that is, investments by large companies in smaller, usually technology-based, firms for mutual strategic advantage. The Corporate Venturing Scheme gives companies 20 per cent relief on Corporation Tax on amounts invested in new ordinary shares held for at least three years, allows them to defer tax on any gain on corporate venturing invest-ments that are reinvested in another shareholding under the scheme, and they can claim against income for capital losses (net of corporation tax relief) on disposals of shares. Government has also established Corporate Venturing UK[19] in order to create a market mechanism that enables potential partners to identify one another, promote the wider acceptance of the principals and practices of corporate venturing and offer guidance on the corporate venture capital process.

Bridges Community Ventures

Fifth, government was instrumental in the establishment of Bridges Community Ventures,[20] a venture capital fund that invests in busi-nesses with high growth potential in the most under-invested parts of England. The idea was one of the recommendations of the Social Investment Task Force, chaired by Sir Ronald Cohen of Apax, which reported to the Chancellor of the Exchequer in October 2000. Inspired by the community development venture capital industry in the United States, the idea is to use the tools of venture capital – equity investment and hands-on support to companies – to grow businesses that create jobs, entrepreneurial capacity and wealth to stimulate the economies of disadvantaged communities and enhance the livelihoods of low-income people in such areas. Government accepted the recom-mendation and agreed to match on a pound-for-pound basis the amounts raised from the private sector. Bridges Community Ventures was established to manage the fund. Its aim is to demonstrate the investment potential in socially excluded communities.

The fund has raised £20 million from a range of private sector investors (companies and individuals), which the government matched. It seeks to invest in companies with fewer than 250 employees and less than £25 million turnover. Investee businesses have to be linked to their local community, for example, through their employees, markets or supply chain. Its investment range is from £150,000 to a maximum of £2 million. Its target rate of return is 10 per cent per annum (based on similar US funds). As of March 2004, Bridges Community Ventures had made nine investments, listed in Table 2.7.11.

Enterprise Capital Funds

The government's next step is a plan to launch a competitive bidding process for a 'pathfinder' round of Enterprise Capital Funds (ECFs), subject to EU state approval rules. ECFs will be private sector, commercially managed entities that adopt the US Small Business Investment Company model for the United Kingdom by investing a mix of public and private sector capital in businesses with growth potential affected by the equity gap. ECFs will be allowed to invest in SMEs in funding rounds of up to £2 million, and will put the private sector on the same basis as public sector capital.[21]

Table 2.7.11   Investments made by the Bridges Community Ventures Fund

Company	Location	Business	Stage	BCVF Investment (£'000)	Total Deal Size (£'000s)
EB2	London	Online booking engines for airlines	Early	500	1,000
Elixer Studios	North London	Video games developer	Development capital	650	2,100
Eyebright	Hull	Dedicated eye surgeries for cataracts	Start-up	500	2,220
Harlands Labels	Hull	Specialist label designer and printer	MBO	730	4,000
HS Atec	Yorkshire	Distribution of lorry parts	MBO	1,000	2,450
Simply Energy	South London	Telephone-based energy price comparison service	Start-up	125	300
The Office	London	Flexible office space in under-invested areas	Start-up	610	1,320
Trust the DJ	West London	DJ management and Web hosting	–	800	–
Touch and Glow	Coventry	Dimmer switch and security device	–	500	–

Source: Bridges Community Ventures and Financial Times (2003) Bridges over deprivation, 19 September, p 15

Business angels

Despite these government interventions, in reality the demand for smaller amounts of early stage funding is largely met by business angels – high net worth individuals (often cashed out entrepreneurs) who invest a small part of their wealth directly in unquoted companies. Most angel investors are anonymous and their investments are not reported. Thus, it is impossible to accurately assess the size of the market or its characteristics. However, one study has estimated that there are 20,000–40,000 active business angels in the United Kingdom investing £0.5 billion–£1 billion per annum in around 3,000–6,000 companies.[22] Most of these investments are in the £10,000–£250,000 range and focused on companies at their start-up and early growth stages. A further characteristic of business angels is that most of their investments are 'local' – typically within about an hour's travel time. This reflects the 'hands on' investment style of most business angels who support their investee businesses with a range of value-added contributions, such as strategic advice, networking, functional expertise and social support. As a consequence, the market for business angel finance comprises an overlapping series of local and regional markets upon which is superimposed a market comprising those business angels who invest nationally (and even internationally). These tend to be larger and more specialist investors.

The *Investor Pulse UK Angel Attitudes Survey* undertaken by C2 Ventures Ltd provides the most up-to-date profile of business angels in the United Kingdom, their recent investment record and investment intentions.[23] A study of the investment returns of a sample of UK business angels revealed a fairly satisfactory performance when compared with early stage venture capital funds: 34 per cent were a total loss, 13 per cent were a partial loss or broke even, while 23 per cent achieved a return (IRR) of over 50 per cent or above.[24]

There is evidence that business angels and early stage venture capital funds operate in a complementary, rather than competitive fashion, for example, in terms of amounts invested and stage of business development. In some cases, business angels and venture capital funds will co-invest. In other cases, the business angel will do the first round and then 'pass the baton' to the venture capital fund to finance subsequent rounds.[25]

As venture capital funds have increasingly vacated the market for smaller investments (under £2 million) so this space is being filled by angel syndicates – structured groups of up to 50 or more angels (many of whom are passive investors) fronted by an investment manager or core of active angels, which are doing deals in the £250,000 to £1 million-plus range that in the not too distant past was venture capital fund territory. One example is Archangels, an Edinburgh-based angel syndicate, which has been operating for 12 years, during which time it has invested around £35 million. In 2003 it invested £5.8 million in 19 early stage Scottish companies, comprising 24 separate deals. This is a similar amount invested as in 2002 but in more companies.[26] Braveheart, another Scottish angel group, has been operating since 1997. It has 50 members. It has made 27 investments in 19 companies (March 2004).[27] Both syndicates prefer to invest close to home and so restrict their investing to Scotland.

Tax incentives

Business angels enjoy two important tax incentives. First, the Enterprise Investment Scheme (EIS) provides various tax reliefs for investors who invest in new ordinary shares in unquoted companies: 1) income tax relief at the lower rate of 20 per cent on shares up to £150,000 per annum; 2) deferral of gains realized on different assets; 3) gains on disposal of the shares after three years are exempt from capital gains tax; and 4) if EIS shares are disposed of at a loss, such a loss can be set against the investor's capital gains or income in the year of disposal.[28] Investors are not allowed to be 'closely connected' to their investee companies prior to the investment but are permitted to become paid directors after the investment is made. There are certain restrictions in the companies that qualify for EIS.

Some £350 billion has been invested through the EIS since it was launched in 1993–94. Investment peaked in 2000–01 when £1 billion was invested. This has fallen to £480 million in 2002–03. It has been estimated that more than half of the money invested would not have been invested by these same investors in the absence of the scheme, thus it has achieved significant additionality (although not as much as VCTs). Moreover, the performance of the investee companies was changed and positively affected as a result of the hands-on involvement of investors.[29]

Second, a capital gains tax taper was introduced in the 1998 Finance Act, which reduces the rate of capital gains tax charged on the disposal of business assets held by individuals from 40 per cent to 10 per cent after four years. This relief covers all shareholdings in unquoted trading companies.

Information

Help is also available from business angel networks (BANs) to find investments. These are essentially introduction services, which, for a fee, connect investors who are looking for investment opportunities in the unquoted company sector with entrepreneurs seeking finance. A list of BANs is produced by the National Business Angel Network. This list is published as a booklet and is available on the web.[30] Many of these BANs are either operated by Business Links – government small business support organizations – or with support from them, or by Regional Development Agencies. However, there are also several private, for-profit BANs. Typically these networks bring investors and entrepreneurs together in the following ways: publication of investment bulletins, computer and web-based matching, and investment forums at which entrepreneurs 'pitch' their businesses to an audience of prospective investors. Increasingly many BANs are also providing training for prospective angels and 'investment ready' programmes for entrepreneurs.

Conclusion

Deloitte's current *Private Equity Confidence Survey* (December 2003) suggests that VC/PE investors are becoming more optimistic about the future as the industry emerges from its latest cyclical downturn. Investors' confidence about the economic climate is increasing and valuations have stabilized. The climate for fundraising is stable, while both investments and exits are forecast to increase. Buy-out funds see opportunities arising from a combination of public companies that need to sell subsidiaries because they are unable to raise money in relatively depressed equity markets or because they are under pressure from shareholders to improve performance, and because of the lack of trade buyers. However, the ability of private equity funds to achieve exits is also constrained by the scarcity of trade buyers and the slow recovery of the IPO market. Given the pressure on funds to achieve disposals some commentators expect an increase in secondary buy-outs (where one fund sells an investment to another fund). In terms of venture capital, there is anecdotal evidence that business angels are re-emerging, while entrepreneurs report more interest from investors. Government's active intervention to tackle the 'equity gap' is contributing to increased activity in the start-up, early stage and expansion markets. In short, things seem to be returning to 'normal' after the technology boom and bust. All of this suggests that the United Kingdom continues to be the most attractive place for private equity in Europe.

Acknowledgements

I am most grateful to Elissa Brodey of the British Venture Capital Association for commenting on an earlier draft of this chapter.

Notes

1. In other accounts, the terms 'classic' and 'merchant' venture capital have been used to describe these two industry segments: Bygrave,

W D and Timmons, J (1992) *Venture Capital At The Crossroads*, Harvard Business Press, Boston.

2. BVCA's *Economic Impact of Private Equity in the UK 2003*, http://www.bvca.co.uk.
3. Source: PricewaterhouseCoopers (2003), *Global Private Equity 2003*.
4. Source: PricewaterhouseCoopers (2003) *Global Private Equity 2003*.
5. Source: PricewaterhouseCoopers (2003) *Global Private Equity 2003*.
6. EVCA (2003) *EVCA Network News: Annual Survey of Pan-European Private Equity and Venture Capital*, Newsletter Number 9, Supplement, September.
7. Funds that buy companies from their original VC/PE investors.
8. Deloitte (2003) *Private Equity Confidence Survey*, December.
9. BVCA *Report on Investment Activity 2002*. Note that some of this investment could be follow-on investment rather than initial investment. In addition, these figures include investments by Venture Capital Trusts (VCTs) – see later – which are limited to a maximum company investment limit of £1 million.
10. BVCA *Report on Investment Activity 2002*.
11. BVCA *Report on Investment Activity 2002*. For a more detailed analysis of the geography of private equity in the United Kingdom see Mason, C M and Harrison, R T (2002) The geography of venture capital investments in the UK, *Transactions of the Institute of British Geographers*, **27**, pp 427–51.
12. PricewaterhouseCoopers (2002) *BVCA Performance Measurement Survey*, www.bvca.co.uk/publications/performmeasusurv/pm2002summary.html.
13. For the latest evidence on government thinking, see HM Treasury (2003) *Bridging the Finance Gap: A Consultation on Improving Access to Growth Capital for Small Businesses*, April; and HM Treasury (2003) *Bridging the Finance Gap: Next Steps on Improving Access to Growth Capital for Small* Businesses, December.
14. HM Treasury (2003) as above.
15. KPMG (2003) *Early Evaluation of the Regional Venture Capital Funds: Summary of Findings*, report to the Small Business Service.
16. HM Treasury (2003) *Bridging the Finance Gap: Next Steps on Improving Access to Growth Capital for Small Businesses*, December.
17. PACEC (2003) *Research into the Enterprise Investment Scheme and Venture Capital Trusts*, Inland Revenue Research report.

18. HM Treasury (2003) 2003 Pre-Budget report, http://www.hm-treasury.gov.uk/pre_budget_report/prebud_pbr03/prebud_pbr03_index.cfm.

19. www.corporateventuringuk.org. Also see the Inland Revenue website for information: http://www.inlandrevenue.gov.uk/pdfs/ir2000.htm.

20. www.bridgesventures.com.

21. HM Treasury (2003) *2003 Pre-Budget Report*, p 55.

22. Mason, C M and Harrison, R T (2000) The size of the informal venture capital market in the UK, *Small Business Economics*, **15**, pp 137–48.

23. www.bestmatch.co.uk/Bulletins/InvestorPulseSurvey/2003.pdf.

24. Mason, C M and Harrison, R T (2002) Is it worth it? The rates of return from informal venture capital investments, *Journal of Business Venturing*, **17**, pp 211–36.

25. Harrison, R T and Mason, C M (2000) Venture capital market complementarities: The links between business angels and venture capital funds in the UK, *Venture Capital: An International Journal of Entrepreneurial Finance*, **2**, pp 223–42.

26. http://www.archangelsonline.com. Investment statistics from *Young Company Finance*, February 2004, p 11.

27. www.braveheart-ventures.co.uk.

28. Further details in a booklet that is available from the Inland Revenue (www.inlandrevenue.gov.uk/pdfs/ir137.htm). The Enterprise Investment Scheme Association (www.eisa.org.uk) also provides information.

29. PACEC (2003) *Research into the Enterprise Investment Scheme and Venture Capital Trusts*, Inland Revenue Research report.

30. http://www.bestmatch.co.uk/Bulletins/directory.pdf.

2.8

Technology and Innovation – the Cambridge Phenomenon

Alan Barrell and Mark Littlewood, Library House, Cambridge

Introduction

Paradoxically, the East of England is both one of the most rural regions in the country and one of the most high tech. The industrial structure of the region has changed dramatically over the centuries. Thetford in Norfolk – north of Cambridge – was the first great centre of the wool trade in England. The wool trade migrated to the North West of England in the 19th century, during the first Industrial Revolution. The fishing industry has also declined – fewer than 100 fishing people now cast their nets along the coastline of the region. Leather goods, especially footwear, moved north-west into the West Midlands region in the early part of the 20th century. Farming and agricultural industry in general – including bio-agriculture – remain in place.

Since the 1960s, however, something very profound has happened to this rural part of England, and the area surrounding Cambridge in particular. It has become the most developed cluster of technology and innovation-based companies in Europe. Thanks primarily to the accelerated development of Cambridge as a high technology location, it has become the most developed region from the perspective of its capacity to attract, and show returns for, investors in innovation-based businesses. It is in the immediate vicinity of Cambridge that this effect is most noticeable.

Cambridge is situated at the heart of the East of England, an ancient seat of learning. It is 56 miles north-east of London and is now an important geographical location between the industrial West Midlands of England and the East Coast ports.

Cambridge's contribution to technology and innovation

Cambridge's importance to the UK economy today is primarily as a hotbed of innovation and as a magnet for technology investors across the world. It is a stunning fact that companies in the Cambridgeshire area (population just 454,000, or approximately 0.75 per cent of the UK total) received around 25 per cent of the private investment into innovation-based businesses in the United Kingdom in 2002.

Ingredients of success

It is generally acknowledged that there are three separate sets of institutions: the university; corporate research laboratories; and a range of technical consultancies, which have combined to give the city of Cambridge a strong technology skills base. This has produced world-class research, plenty of commercial know-how and sufficient business management expertise to develop a track record of success.

The university
Cambridge University has played a pivotal role in the transformation of the region, the city and the surrounding area from being a medieval seat of learning to a great educational centre and wealth-creating knowledge-based business centre – a transformation that has taken more than 40 years and has been largely 'bottom up' – a result of building communities of common purpose – and matching the aspirations with achievements, rather than through 'top down' government policy, intervention or funding.

There is sense of common purpose of integration and coherence at the university. This culture change has been as important as the superb science base available in Cambridge University, the intellectual capital of academics and business people and the development of support structures in enabling the formation and sustenance of many new companies in the area.

Technology consultancies
The formation of the current commercial cluster began in 1960, when a spin-out from Cambridge University – Cambridge Consultants Ltd – gave birth to a family of technology providers and consultancies and the cluster grew from there.

The university and many of these consultancies retain strong links – both formally and informally. Graduates of the university often find themselves running projects to commercialize the work of others. The technical consultancies are a vital part in the process of bridging the gap between academic research and commercial application. They have also been instrumental in blending technology transfer expertise with business creation skills and seed funding in a number of innovative ways.

Institutional research and development

Institutional change has been at the heart of the progress seen in enabling Cambridge University to commercialize research to the benefit of cluster development and to encourage investments from major corporations such as Microsoft, Hitachi, Toshiba, GlaxoSmithKline, The Wellcome Trust, Marconi and others.

Other success factors

Cultural change

Another major factor in enabling the growth of the cluster has been culture change – culture in terms of the generation of more entrepreneurial spirit – and especially the development of a belief in the common purpose in the entire community. This has been both moral and inspirational and in terms of financial resources, for example, government financing of the Entrepreneurship Centre and the Cambridge Massachusetts Institute. These have been important factors in bringing the university closer still to the business community and in enabling the university to develop commercial programmes internally. Government attention and support – not to mention funding – have been significant stimuli in bringing necessary institutional change to the university.

The economic viability of the Cambridge sub-region is not in doubt. Growth in GDP per capita of 6.5 per cent has been confirmed and is ahead of virtually all such results in European and US sub-regions. Job creation has also been impressive.

Connectivity and infrastructure

Cambridge and the East of England are served by two international airports – Stansted (40 minutes' journey) and Luton (one-hour journey). Heathrow and Gatwick International Airports are two hours' travel time away – so reasonably accessible. Rail links with London are good and services frequent to the City (50 minutes' journey time).

The Cambridge cluster

Companies in the Cambridge cluster

Much of the work for this chapter has been drawn from the work of Library House in its seminal, *Cambridge Cluster Report, 2003*, an in-depth analysis of information covering every single innovation-based company within 45 minutes' drive of Cambridge. In completing work on the *Cambridge Cluster Report*, Library House conducted 12,500 hours of research, filtering over 2,000 companies in the area. Library House is a research organization supporting investors in making investment decisions. Library House has a restricted definition of 'innovation-based' companies that excludes sales, marketing, distribution and service companies. In 2003, Library House found, based on this strict definition, 898 innovation-based companies employing 28,209 people. The average company has 31 people.

Of the seven top-level sectors, the information technology sector is the predominant sector in the cluster, containing 536 companies, which represents 59.7per cent of the cluster, followed by life sciences containing 202 companies, which represents 22.5 per cent of the cluster. When the entire cluster is viewed at the next level down, as 40 unique sectors, a different story emerges. Table 2.8.1 illustrates the breakdown of the top-level structures in the cluster and Figure 2.8.1 shows the employment figures in the different sectors.

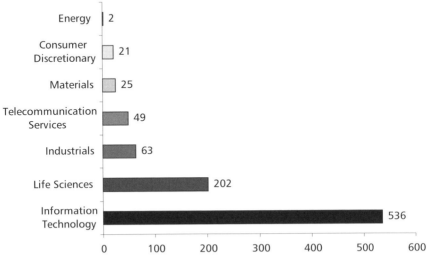

Figure 2.8.1   Employment in the Cambridge cluster

Table 2.8.1 Top-level structures in the Cambridge cluster

Sector	Company Nos.	Employment
IT	536	14,418
Life Sciences	202	6,626
Industrials	63	2,602
Telecom Services	49	2,862
Materials	25	1,238
Consumer	21	n/a
Energy	2	n/a

Note: Figures exclude employment from companies headquartered outside Cambridge.

Within the IT sector, application software is the largest single sub-sector with 160 companies, followed by electronic equipment and instruments with 106 companies. Table 2.8.2 illustrates the sub-structure of the IT sector.

Table 2.8.2 Structure of the IT sector in the Cambridge cluster

Sub-sector	Company Nos.	Employment
Application Software	160	4,208
Instruments	106	2,947
Internet	53	668
IT Services	37	659
Systems Software	34	881
Comms Hardware	29	885
Peripherals	29	1,128
Others	88	3,042

At the sub-sector level, instead of a cluster clearly dominated solely by information technology, three sub-sectors stand out: application software, biotechnology and electronic equipment and instruments, representing 160, 153 and 106 companies respectively. These three sub-sectors contain 46.6 per cent of all the companies within the cluster, which begins to show the concentration within the cluster and further, the importance of biotechnology, which is obscured at the top level.

Figure 2.8.2 illustrates the primary sub-sector classification of the cluster by number of companies and Table 2.8.3 lists the significant companies in order of rank.

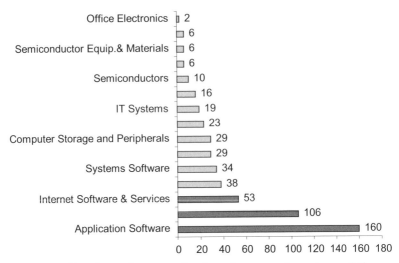

Figure 2.8.2   Number of companies in primary sub-sectors of the Cambridge cluster

Table 2.8.3   Significant companies in the Cambridge cluster

Rank	Sector	>	Sub-sector	No.	%
1	Information Technology	>	Application Software	160	17.8
2	Life Sciences	>	Biotechnology	153	17.0
3	Information Technology	>	Electronic Equipment & Instruments	106	11.8
4	Information Technology	>	Internet Software & Services	53	5.9
5	Information Technology	>	IT Management, Consulting & Services	37	4.1
6	Industrials	>	Industrial Machinery	37	4.1
7	Telecommunication	>	Wireless Telecommunication Services	35	3.9
8	Information Technology	>	Systems Software	34	3.8
9	Life Sciences	>	Health Care Equipment	32	3.6
10	Information Technology	>	Communications Hardware	29	3.2
11	Information Technology	>	Computer Storage and Peripherals	29	3.2
12	Information Technology	>	Computing Systems Hardware	23	2.6

continued overleaf

Rank	Sector	>	Sub-sector	No	%
	Information Technology	>	IT Systems	19	
	Consumer Discretionary	>	Consumer Electronics	19	
	Information Technology	>	Photonics	16	
	Industrials	>	Electrical Components and Equipment	14	
	Information Technology	>	Semiconductors	10	
	Life Sciences	>	Pharmaceuticals	9	
	Materials	>	Advanced Materials	9	
	Life Sciences	>	Health Care Supplies	8	
	Industrials	>	Aerospace and Defence	7	
	Telecommunication	>	Alternative Carriers > Broadband	7	
	Information Technology	>	Discrete Components	6	
	Information Technology	>	Semiconductor Equip. & Materials	6	
	Information Technology	>	Sub-assemblies & Components	6	
	Industrials	>	Commercial Printing, Services & Products	4	
	Materials	>	Metals, Metallurgy & Alloys	4	
	Materials	>	Speciality Chemicals	4	
	Telecommunication	>	General	4	
	Materials	>	Fertilizers & Agricultural Chemicals	3	
	Materials	>	Other	3	
	Telecommunication	>	Integrated Telecommunication Services	3	
	Information Technology	>	Office Electronics	2	
	Consumer Discretionary	>	Consumer Discretionary General	1	
	Consumer Discretionary	>	Broadcasting and Cable TV	1	
	Energy	>	Alternative Energy	1	
	Energy	>	Alternative Energy Technologies	1	
	Industrials	>	General	1	
	Materials	>	General	1	
	Materials	>	Industrial Gases	1	
Total Number of Companies				898	

These and other sub-sectors are best understood by looking at them in detail at the category and sub-category level. A selection of the largest or most interesting is described below.

Application software
The largest sub-sector within the information technology sector is application software. This sub-sector comprises 160 companies and represents 17.8 per cent of the total information technology sector. Companies producing business application software dominate the application software sub-sector. The 71 companies in this category represent 44 per cent of all companies within the application software sub-sector.

Three categories trail business application software: graphics software (11.3 per cent), communications software (8.8 per cent) and industrial applications (7.5 per cent). All other categories are smaller than 5 per cent.

Biotechnology
Seventy-six per cent of life science start-ups in the cluster are biotechnology start-ups. Biotechnology is dominated by companies either directly involved in development of health care products and services or in the creation of research tools, reagents and equipment (RTR&E). The largest sub-category within the health care category of biotechnology is in the discovery and development of therapeutics. Fifty-two companies are solely devoted to therapeutics.

Therapeutics may be examined more closely. First, most therapeutic biotechnology companies in the cluster use either small molecules or proteins/antibodies as therapeutic substances. Other technologies, such as cell or viral therapies play an insignificant role in this cluster. Second, the route for the discovery or selection of those molecules is more diversified, but there is a clear focus on 'clever' drug design, utilizing informatics (bio- and chemo-), structure-based drug design and combinatorial chemistry. Third, the therapeutic areas, in which the cluster biotechnology companies specialize, are immunology and inflammation, cancer and infectious diseases. All other areas trail those three leading sectors significantly.

The electronic equipment and instruments sub-sector
The electronic equipment and instruments sub-sector is the third largest in the cluster comprising 106 companies or 11.8 per cent of all cluster companies. In contrast to the biotechnology and application software sub-sectors, electronic equipment and instruments is not dominated by one or two large categories. Instead, the sector is more or less evenly divided into five categories: general, electronic security equipment, electronic test and measurement instruments, scientific and technical instruments and 'other'. The 'general' and 'other' cate-

gories combined account for more of 40 per cent of the companies in this sub-sector.

Wireless telecommunication services sub-sector
Although this sub-sector is only ranked seventh in terms of company numbers, some of these companies can be considered to be world leaders in wireless telecommunication technology. There are five categories with the largest being wireless applications containing 23 companies representing 65.7 per cent of the sub-sector. The 'others' category contains substantial diversity including 23 computer hardware companies, 16 in photonics, 10 in semiconductors and 6 in discrete components.

At the heart of the Cambridge cluster is IT and within that application software and to a lesser extent instruments. Cambridge has been in the instrument business since the 1890s when Cambridge Instruments and Pye were founded. Software is a more recently established business but one where Cambridge has a substantial industrial base. Within the application software category, 71 companies are in business application software, 18 in graphics reflecting early work in CAD, and 14 in communications software. The largest category within the 106 instrument companies is electronic test and measurement with 27 companies.

The life science cluster is concentrated in biotechnology, which makes up 153 of the total 202 companies. Thirty-two companies are in health care equipment. This is the most vigorous of the next generation of sectors within the cluster, particularly when it comes to capital requirements.

Investment in the Cambridge cluster

In the single month of March 2003, companies sought funding totalling £259 million. Cambridge biotech companies were seeking the lion's share of the total (£106 million) although adding up the total for IT sub-sectors at £90 million makes it only slightly smaller than the capital sought by biotech. Table 2.8.4 shows the money sought in 2003 by sector and Table 2.8.5 shows money raised in the period 2000–02.

Table 2.8.4 Money sought in 2003

Sub-sector	Amount £m	Per Deal £m
Biotech	106	3.1
Semiconductor	30	7.5
Applications Software	28	0.7
Wireless	18	1.4
Peripherals	14	6.8

Over a three-year period (not just a single month in 2003), biotech also represents the single largest invested area – larger than the total (£300 million) invested into the IT and telecoms-related areas combined.

Table 2.8.5   Money raised in 2000–02

Sub-sector	Amount £m	Per Deal £m
Biotech	362	4
Wireless	86	6
Alternative Telco Carriers	75	8
Semiconductors	70	5
Application Software	68	3

A greater number of life sciences companies as a percentage of all life sciences companies are moving through the pipeline from seed to later stage than their counterparts in information technology. But, on an absolute basis, the total number of information technology companies receiving A series funding is about the same as life sciences. Also, a greater percentage of life sciences companies is receiving subsequent rounds of funding, although that may be an artefact of life sciences funding where a greater number of rounds and a greater absolute amount of capital is typically employed across the lifetime of the company.

At the sub-sector level, instead of a cluster clearly dominated solely by information technology, three sub-sectors stand out: application software, biotechnology and electronic equipment and instruments.

Cambridge vs rest of Europe

At the top level, the funding across the cluster over the last three years appears relatively stable ranging from £245 million in 2002 to slightly over £300 million in 2001 and totalling £829 million over the three years.

In 2002, Cambridge accounted for almost 25 per cent of private investment in innovation-based companies in the United Kingdom. Within the above numbers, considerable disparity exists when comparing the relative success of different sectors in securing capital. Life sciences clearly dominates the amount of funding successfully raised. Figure 2.8.3 shows the total investment into Cambridge broken down by sectors.

Of all European provincial centres of high technology growth, Cambridge is without doubt the best served with venture capital and other financial services. It is also serviced by highly sophisticated private organizations such as Library House, which exist to facilitate activity for the investment community. Library House is an organization that effectively supports a wide range of investors and the

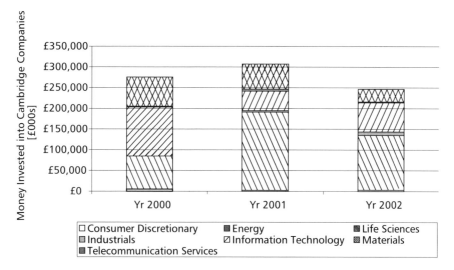

Figure 2.8.3 Total investment into Cambridge companies broken down by sectors

investment processes across the United Kingdom. Library House has collected extensive information on angel and VC investing and cluster development in the Cambridge region. This information is available on a confidential basis to Library House members. More information is included on Library House – in a specific section of the report and further details can be found at www.libraryhouse.net.

Recently, the UK public markets for technology in particular have been very depressed. IPOs effectively stopped for two years. Cambridge companies, however, appear to be among the first to begin the process of recovery. There have been issues on the Alternative Investment Market (AIM) and full listings on the London Stock Exchange (an example is Cambridge Silicon Radio – LON: CSR – which received significant venture capital and institutional rounds before floating in March 2004.

Cambridge, thanks to its well-rooted science base, and an increasing stock of seasoned entrepreneurs and executives, has been able to weather the technology investment storm of the past few years. Perhaps more than any other place in Europe, Cambridge has remained innovative, and has seen a steady stream of successful companies being funded, at every stage of development. Cambridge relies on people and money to make the cluster work. The best news is that more experienced business people are choosing to make Cambridge their home, and that investors continue to view Cambridge as one of the hottest places in Europe to find good deals. It is a place that cannot be ignored.

For information on the macroeconomics of the East of England, contact Invest East of England +44 (0) 01223 450 40, www.investeast-ofengland.com. For details about technology investment opportunities across the United Kingdom, contact Mark Littlewood, Library House, mark.littlewood@libraryhouse.net +44 (0) 1223 500 550, www.library-house.net.

2.9

Art and Collectibles

James Goodwin

Introduction

Lord Clark, the art historian, wrote that 'in a godless age and in what we call a free society, art is the only escape from materialism which is not subject to the law of diminishing returns, and one of the few which is not damaging to health'. From an economic viewpoint the art market is one of the last examples of almost unregulated laissez-faire capitalism; one where supply tends to stimulate demand and objects tend to become more highly valued as their original purpose is lost. However, it should not be forgotten that works of art are not substitutes for money. In the long run, it is therefore important to buy what you like and to develop a well-trained eye.

The market for fine and decorative art often refers to paintings, pictures, drawings, prints, sculpture, furniture, rugs and carpets, ceramics, glass, silver and vertu, clocks and watches, jewellery, Oriental, Islamic, Russian and Indian works of art, and modern and contemporary art. The smaller market for collectibles loosely refers to old cars, classic postage stamps, numismatic coins, banknotes, stock certificates, scripts, medals, vintage wines and spirits, playing cards, objets de vertu, bric-a-brac, scientific instruments, books, manuscripts, photographs, sporting memorabilia, dolls and toys, luggage, and other memorabilia.

In 2001, approximately 1.2 million art transactions took place globally and about US$23.4 billion-worth of fine and decorative art changed ownership. Worldwide, in 2002–03, 149 paintings were sold for more than £1 million, including a £45 million record for a painting by Rubens sold by Sotheby's in London.

The UK art market

The UK art and antiques market has sales of £2.29 billion or 28 per cent of the world's total, second to the United States' 42 per cent. The

UK art market is second only to the theatre in attracting high-spending foreign visitors to the United Kingdom and is larger than the UK music industry. According to a TEFAF (the world-famous antiques fair in Maastricht) survey, the UK art trade, including ancillary industries, adds at least 13 per cent directly into the UK economy. London is the greatest single global entrepôt for art and antiques, turning over £2.1 billion. In 2000, one London dealer alone generated 4 per cent of UK dealer sales.

Exports and imports

UK art exports account for 60 per cent of revenues, including supply of 56 per cent of the EU's 12 billion euro market added to the trade with non-EU countries. In 2002 exports were £2.289 billion (fine art £1.659 billion and antiques £0.63 billion) or 21.5 per cent more than 2001 and imports were £1.892 billion (fine art £1.583 billion and antiques £0.309 billion), a 16.5 per cent increase. The main export destinations were the United States (65 per cent), Switzerland (15.5 per cent), Japan (2 per cent), especially antiques, and Australia (1.9 per cent), mostly pictures. The main imports were from the United States (49 per cent), Switzerland (32 per cent), Japan (3.9 per cent) and Canada (2.5 per cent), especially pictures. Both Hong Kong and South Korea are now much stronger destinations for UK art.

Structure of the market

The UK art market comprises 10,217 businesses, including 9,463 dealers and 754 auctioneers who employ 37,063 staff (17,123 at the auctioneers). In the late 1990s Christie's and Sotheby's accounted for 25 per cent of the world's art and antique market sales and 45 per cent of the auction market. Half of all British Antique Dealers Association members, two-thirds of whom are sole traders, have a turnover of more than £1 million.

In the United Kingdom, wages and productivity are above the EU average, there is an even split of males to females, a quarter of the staff work part-time and most are degree educated.

Buying and selling art – auctioneers, dealers, trade associations and press

The trade in works of art remains a highly fragmented market today relying to an extraordinary degree on specialist knowledge, often transmitted over multiple generations. There are two routes to buying and selling: auctioneers and dealers. Evidence suggests that art experts provide an extremely accurate prediction of art prices.

Traditional auctions

The auction market in the United Kingdom is represented by the big three of Sotheby's, Christie's, Bonhams, and a number of provincial auctioneers and international internet auctioneers, such as eBay. Both Sotheby's, www.sothebys.com, and Christie's, www.christies.com, were founded in the 18th century, and are the world's oldest and most prestigious fine art auction houses. They have salerooms throughout the globe and hold over 700 auctions every year. Bonhams, www.bonhams.com, from its base in Knightsbridge, London, has 600 international sales annually in most continents, having recently bought Butterfields auctioneers, on the West Coast of the United States, and Goodmans, an Australian auctioneer.

In the United Kingdom, according to the *Antiques Trade Gazette* (*ATG*), the growth of the internet and the reluctance of the biggest auctioneers to deal with low-value goods has helped provide provincial auctioneers win more business. According to the *ATG* the three biggest provincial auctioneers in 2003 were Gorringes, www.gorringes.co.uk, Woolley and Wallis, www.w-w.co.uk, and Lyon and Turnbull, www.lyonandturnbull.com. The auctioneer Tennants, www.tennants. co.uk, which is based in Yorkshire, recorded the biggest sale outside London in 2003.

Traditionally, selling at auctions was a long, drawn-out affair and more specialist sales were as infrequent as once or twice a year. Now, with the buoyancy of the art and collectibles market and with greater numbers of collectors chasing fewer objects, not only are prices being driven up, but also the turnround is much quicker. At auction, prices often rise above 'true value' when two or more people are determined to bid.

Buyers and sellers at auction will often pay more in the major venues of New York and London as commission rates often depend on the location or prestige attached to the saleroom. At Sotheby's, the maximum commission for selling an item in the United Kingdom is 15 per cent with insurance of 1.5 per cent, and Bonhams charges vendors 15 per cent for the first £1,000, 10 per cent between £1,000–£70,000 and no commission over £70,000. Charges at other UK provincial auctioneers are less though the standard of objects on offer is generally lower.

Buyer's fees at Sotheby's are 20 per cent and Christie's 19.5 per cent up to a £70,000 hammer price and from 10–12 per cent thereafter. At Christie's' South Kensington branch, 17.5 per cent up to £70,000 is charged and 10 per cent above, while Bonhams charges between 7.5 per cent and 19.5 per cent up to £70,000 and 10 per cent thereafter.

Online auctions

The advent of online auctions since August 1999 has made sought-after items even more accessible. However, the internet is generally considered less suitable for the sale and auction of more costly art because specialist assistance is not at hand and quality and authenticity cannot be easily verified.

The online auctioneer www.ebay.co.uk advertises over 1,000 pieces of furniture for less than £1,000, with most offered under £100. It costs £2 to list on ebay and £20 once a £1,000 item has been sold. Despite this, a survey showed that the prices of comparable goods sold by an internet auctioneer showed a 25–39 per cent fall in one year.

Dealers

Although dealers have lost market share to the auction houses since the late 1960s, thanks to their concerted marketing, their collective turnover is still greater than the UK sales of the two main auction houses. There is an interdependence between both parties, with sales to dealers at the big auction houses ranging from a third to a half of their total, as well as dealers mostly buying from each other. Moreover, major sales and promotions in London and New York are often coordinated between all parties. In fact, buying and selling through a dealer can represent a more straightforward transaction though prices can be twice those paid at auction. In the United Kingdom, antique shops and collectors' fairs are the most commonly visited, with many collectors preferring this distribution channel because of dealers' increased specialization.

According to antique dealer surveys, 70 per cent of their turnover is from their shops or galleries and another 24 per cent at fairs, with only 4 per cent of sales over the internet for values mostly under £5,000. Among London picture dealers participation at trade fairs has grown, the most popular being the 20/21 British Art Fair and Art 2002 Islington. Overall, 71 per cent of their customers are private collectors, 11 per cent museums and 10 per cent other dealers.

The most reputable dealers are typically those belonging to the British Antique Dealers' Association (BADA), www.bada.org, the Association of Art and Antique Dealers (LAPADA), www.lapada.co.uk, and the Society of London Art Dealers (SLAD), www.slad.org.uk.

BADA, with 400 members in a market of 9,000 UK antique dealers, organizes fairs in March and June. The most prestigious is the 70-year-old Grosvenor House Art and Antiques Fair, which exhibits the works of 90 dealers.

LAPADA, with 700 members, stages its Antiques and Fine Art Fairs at Birmingham every January and the Royal College of Art in London in October. LAPADA promotes regional antique associations in the

Cotswolds, Bath and Bradford on Avon, Petworth, Thames Valley and the world's largest antiques market at Portobello in London.

SLAD is a founder member of the British Art Market Federation (BAMF) set up in 1996 to represent the interests of the art trade with the government and other bodies. Its members must have been in business for at least three years and have expert knowledge.

Sources of information on the international art markets, published in the United Kingdom, is available from the *Antiques Trade Gazette*, www.antiquestradegazette.com, and the *Art Newspaper*, www.theart-newspaper.com. On the *ATG*'s website, worldwide information in four languages on auctioneers and dealers can be found, including sale calendars, and catalogues with photos and lots sold. For furniture, there is an historical search facility by item type and description, provenance, sale date, estimate, realized price, buyer's premium and auctioneer's address.

Company performances

Recent comparative company performance for 108 (see Table 2.9.1) of the main UK auctioneers and dealers in 2002 indicated few of the largest by turnover being profitable; the exception being Mallett, www.mallettantiques.com. For 40 of these companies, only 10 had export sales exceeding half of their turnover and 15 recorded export growth during the previous year. The five auctioneers surveyed produced less sales per employee than the average number of dealers, while paying salaries higher than the average.

Table 2.9.1   Comparison of different types of investment

	Turnover £000s	Profit Margin (%)	Return on Capital Employed (%)	Gearing or Debt/Equity Ratio	Employees
Sotheby's	81,683 (78,115)	−22.8 (−3.48)	−305.92 (−11.12)	413.91 (70.10)	649 (660)
Bonhams	39,737 (18,001)	−12.39 (−23.79)	−9.55 (−12.93)	31.47 (34.39)	791 (873)
Mallett	25,336 (17,165)	20.50 (25.21)	18.33 (16.59)	0.41 (0.21)	49 (47)
Partridge	9,929 (10,247)	0.09 (2.99)	0.03 (0.99)	11.62 (17.97)	28 (32)
Richard Green OM	33,065	4.71	3.56	4.71	23

Source: FAME 2004

Return on capital employed is the best overall measure of a company's financial performance and gearing measures a firm's financial strength. Gearing should generally be no more than 50 per cent.

Since 1998, Christie's has been privately owned by Francois Pinault's Artemis Group, so figures are not readily available. It is known that Christie's sales fell from a record US$2.2 billion in 2000 to US$1.77 billion by 2002, and the company continues to be profitable. The most recent figures from Sotheby's for the year 2003 indicate general signs of recovery after the trauma of the 1999/2000 collusion scandal with Christie's, for which the company was heavily fined. In the fourth quarter of 2003, Sotheby's was again profitable with the share price rising 3.24 per cent on the day following the announcement.

In contrast, eBay, www.ebay.co.uk, generated revenues of US$2.17 billion or 78 per cent higher than 2002, which translated into an operating profit of US$441.8 million or 20 per cent margin. Collectables including antiques accounted for US$1.5 billion of revenues.

As well as total turnover, auctions' success or failure is often measured by the number of transactions and the auction sale rate. In 200, Christie's, www.christies.com, and Sotheby's, www.sothebys.com, both turned over more lots than in the previous year, 8,608 and 7,509 respectively, even though Sotheby's turnover was marginally higher. Bonhams, www.bonhams.com, improved its financial turnover despite handling fewer lots, 5,909 compared with 6,140 in the previous year.

External factors influencing the art market

Supply

Art now operates for rich individuals and corporations as it did in previous centuries for the courts of Europe. The major auction houses helped re-define the art market in the 1980s and have made it a global phenomenon. In the United Kingdom, antique collecting is now part of a rewarding shopping experience stimulated by an enthusiastic media, following the success of the BBC's *Antiques Roadshow* since the 1970s.

It is said that supply to the art market benefits from debt, divorce and death, while overall demand benefits from new money, which tends to buy new art. Today, sales to meet tax bills provide auction houses with the greatest flow of works. However, the supply of works of art in many of the mainstream collecting areas has contracted. As a result, the major auction houses have turned their attention to collectables of a smaller volume of top-quality works, releasing their hold on large volumes of business to others, increasingly via the internet.

Demand

On the demand side, art seems to flow towards surplus money, as it did in 19th-century United States and in Japan in the 1980s. As a country's economy improves and it becomes cash rich, the quality and subsequently the value of its art improve. Wolfgang Wilke of Dresdner Bank, www.dresdner-bank.com, demonstrated that globalization has been the driving force behind art prices, noting setbacks coinciding with war and protectionism from 1915–45. Reflecting this, currency flows are claimed to have an effect on the sale of art. In the last few years, the US dollar decline has boosted the US art market, with collectors inclined to buy at the big New York auctions. In 2003, as the dollar fell by 17 per cent and 8.6 per cent against the euro and sterling respectively, New York auction prices rose 20 per cent. Since 1996, there has been a stronger demand for Chinese artefacts thanks to a large and wealthy Chinese population. There is similar enthusiasm for Indian and Russian art.

In Western economies, it is said that people buy contemporary art when they are confident about their society and the future, and reminders of the past when they are not. Contemporary art is mostly in demand among newly affluent collectors in their thirties and forties.

Today there are over 1,000 corporate art collections intended to boost staff morale and improve company image. Some purchases are justified as benefits by investors paying high rates of tax. Ownership tends to concentrate around those of high net worth who already have a full range of safer and more liquid investments. Art collectors can be advised as much by business people as academics.

Impact of taxation

The international art market has always been strongly affected by the legal, fiscal and commercial policies of the countries in which it operates. London's European pre-eminence as an art market, especially in the decorative arts, has been built on a VAT regime that encourages international dealing in art, reasonable levels of capital gains tax, a freely competitive art market, easy export rules and modest government support for domestic buying of art.

European Union legislation introducing new VAT of 5 per cent in 1999 on the imports of works of art and the threat of introducing rules on artists' resale rights of 2–6 per cent of sales, known as *droit de suite*, have begun to undermine the UK's pre-eminent position. As well as this, an EU licence is now necessary to export a cultural object out of the Union, if its value exceeds a stated threshold – for watercolour paintings this is £18,200.

Artwork imports outside the EU, which are 40 per cent of London dealers' sales, fell by 40 per cent after the 2.5 per cent imposition. A DTI survey estimated that *droit de suite* alone could rob the United Kingdom of an annual £68 million in art sales and 5,000 jobs in the art trade. Determined campaigning against *droit de suite* resulted in its postponement until 1 January 2006 for living artists, and six years later for works by artists who have died in the last 70 years.

Investment value

Though it is difficult to make a clear distinction between the collector and the investor, the number of people who buy art solely as investment is limited. Unlike most other investments, art is based only on the capital gain when the investment is realized, since there is no interest or dividend on the capital invested. The profit on sale must be greater than the capital gain on conventional stock plus the total dividends that would have accrued, less inflation.

The theory is that as the number of buyers in the market goes up supply stays static or declines, so promising a long-term upward movement in prices. The capital appreciation also has to be substantial to make up for the initial cost of acquisition and disposal, valuation and provenance research fees as well as insurance, conservation and storage. A study by Zurich Financial Services demonstrated that a painting bought at auction for £1,000 net in 1997 should fetch a sum of £2,159 in 2007 to produce an 8 per cent compound annual return including an inflation rate of 3 per cent.

Like the stock market, everything depends on when you buy and when you sell, particularly as the art market is heavily affected by bottlenecks in supply and demand. The key to getting good value is to catch the trend early on, bearing in mind that the art market, like any other, will in the long term rebalance itself.

According to a TEFAF global survey, during 1991–2000 fine art prices increased by 63 per cent or 6 per cent per annum, declining by 9 per cent in the years 1992–94. From 1998 to 2001 the average price of a painting sold in the United Kingdom advanced 54 per cent, while in the EU they declined by 39 per cent. After the United Kingdom, the highest average EU prices were found in Italy, France and the Netherlands. In the United States they advanced by 75 per cent.

Advocates of art investment recommend clients with money to spare to allocate up to 10 per cent of their capital. Pension funds are generally free from tax on their gains in art and antiques. And today it is believed that the improvement of information facilities and impartial market intelligence might eventually help to make such alternative investments attractive for close funds. Given that investors have experienced slim returns on cash and deposits, and continuing uncertainty in the stock markets, art might become a safe haven. Conversely, those who fear political, economic, social or tax repression in their own countries tend to regard alternative investment as a means of safeguarding their wealth. Equally, it can be said that when assets fall, people feel less rich and eventually stop buying artefacts.

Current research by Professors Mei and Moses, www.meimosesfineartindex.org, demonstrates that the art market never really crashes. They calculated that from 1954 to 2003, art returned an annualized 12.6 per cent, which was slightly ahead of the SandP500's 11.7 per cent and well above Treasury Bonds. Art prices have experienced only moderate declines during the 27 recessions since 1875. Moreover, in the last four major wars, art outperformed the SandP500, growing by 108 per cent during the Korean War compared with 67 per cent for shares. Art is most closely correlated with real estate values.

Mei/Moses concluded that art gives up little return but achieves substantial reduction in risk when the holding period is increased. Others have observed that at the beginning of a recession the art business is almost always very good and that financially it is a lagging indicator, which responds slowly and comes back more slowly with a cycle lasting about eight or nine years. After declining by 5 per cent in 2002 US art prices rose by 20 per cent last year, but lagged behind the SandP rise of 28 per cent. Their advice is that the more you pay the lower the return. The outcome being that a masterpiece subsequently underperforms the market. They have calculated the long-run average holding period for art being 28 years, though demonstrated that the same works by Picasso and Rodin resold in 2002–03 appreciated in value.

Mei/Moses have further demonstrated that art shows a low correlation with the SandP and with most asset classes, supporting dealers' contentions that as an investment art provides good diversification. Moreover, a recent study using the Sharpe ratio, suggests that adding fine art to a diversified portfolio produces a slightly greater return for each unit of risk, and a significantly better return with less volatility than most other asset classes on their own.

Since the late 1980s several attempts have been made to set up different forms of art funds but so far none have been successful. The most recent attempt is being made by Lord Gowrie's Fine Art Fund. Advised by a 'Who's Who' of the art and financial world and over two years in the making, the Fine Art Fund hopes to return 10–15 per cent compound annual growth after 10–13 years. The minimum investment is US$250,000 and the fund has been structured to provide investors in some countries with a particularly attractive tax treatment. It is seeking to raise US$100 million.

Art and antique indexes

The *ACC* (Antique Collectors' Club) *Index*, www.antique-acc.com, is based on the average prices of 35 types of 1,200 typically good-quality pieces of British furniture from seven periods dated 1650–1860, as illustrated in a book from the publisher. The index has been published annually in January since 1968, and is compared to the FTSE 250,

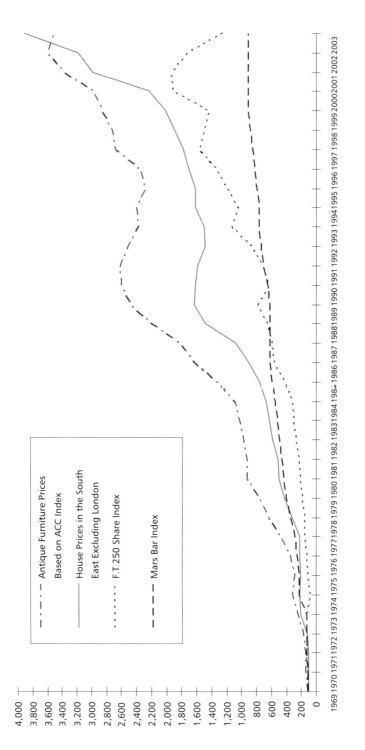

Figure 2.9.1 Comparison of different forms of investment
Source: Antique Collectors' Club, 2004

house prices in the South East excluding London, and UK inflation (see Figure 2.9.1 for a comparison). The index has risen by over 1,000 per cent over 30 years but has fallen by 2 per cent and 3 per cent in the last two; the exception being oak and country furniture and pieces with good provenance.

Also dating from 1968 but representing the fine art market is Duncan Hislop's *Art Sales Index (ASI)*, www.art-sales-index.com, which is published every August in three languages and updated continuously on the internet. Last year the index included 2.7 million pieces of data on 210,000 artists, covered by 2,400 auctions. Bought-in (unsold) items are excluded and the figures are net of auction premium and tax.

Offering the broadest range of investor prices are Robin Duthy's Art Market Research (AMR) indexes, www.artmarketresearch.com. The indexes, which are internet-based and include most fine and decorative art categories, have been compiled annually since 1976 with the help of Christie's. Data on stock markets, UK property markets and other forms of investment are also available. Its clients include the US and UK revenue services, banks, insurers, galleries and newspapers.

Located abroad but written in the English language are a number of fine art websites used by the art auction market, journalists and academics. From France, www.artprice.com provides recent data including bought-in works. Its website provides analysis of artworks, artists and their works, market segments and market overviews. Similarly, www.artnet.com from the United States links works sold by each artist in order of ascending value. Its website and magazine provide general market information including dealer locations and events. Its use is favoured by a large number of SLAD members and Sotheby's in London.

From Italy, Gabrius, www.gabrius.com, has since 1997 set itself the mission 'to become the leading partner of financial institutions and art professionals'. It provides 470,000 colour images sub-divided into Old Master paintings, 19th-century, modern and contemporary art. It also publishes a confidence index adjusted for inflation. Its clients include a number of banks and private equity groups.

Conclusion

It is often said that buying a good antique is not spending money – it is transferring your assets. And that by investing in art or antiques just to make money you are likely to lose it. The keys to success are knowledge, good advice, timing, a concentration on quality and condition and, above all, a genuine appreciation of art.

In recent years, it has been the private buyer with a sound knowledge of the determinants of quality and provenance, that is, a trained eye, who has sustained the market in art and antiques. In future, a French art expert predicts that the art market will become a kind of avant garde of museums, a selection process of what may subsequently become part of our collective memory. It also seems possible that art management specialists who take on responsibility for high-value portfolios are likely to increase in number.

For now, the traditional investor with an interest in the art market but lacking the buying knowledge may attain the best returns via traditional investment in the industry itself.

Part 3

Industry Sectors of Opportunity

UKTRADEINFO CAN HELP!

We can help to develop your business in the UK.

- Importers' Details database to find new customers

- Trade statistics to understand UK markets

- Because we are web based you can access us whenever and wherever

We are part of HM Customs and Excise which means our UK trade information is the most accurate available anywhere.

www.uktradeinfo.com

uk**tradeinfo**
trading with knowledge

HM Customs and Excise

The Automotive Industry

Mark Norcliffe, Society of Motor Manufacturers and Traders

A global business

The 20th century was once dubbed 'the age of the motor car', but, during its closing years, the automotive industry experienced a severe bout of rationalization and consolidation. Driven by the demands of economies of scale, lean manufacturing and downward price pressure, many famous names amalgamated, were taken over by erstwhile competitors, or simply faded away.

Today there are a dozen global car manufacturers – each building more than 1 million units per annum – which produce and sell vehicles around the world. Below them is a tier of regional manufacturers, which principally serve their domestic market from a single manufacturing plant. And then there are niche manufacturers, building specialist vehicles (for example, sports cars) in volumes ranging from hundreds to tens of thousands.

A similar process of consolidation has taken place in the automotive component industry, particularly at the Tier 1 level (that is, those companies that supply product direct to the vehicle manufacturer). By a process of acquisition, major Tier 1 players have positioned themselves to supply whole vehicle systems to the car makers, in whatever region of the world their customer chooses to assemble vehicles. These leading component suppliers are also taking an increasingly prominent role in the design and development of new products.

The evolution of elite groups of global vehicle and component manufacturers has major implications for states and/or regions seeking to attract inward automotive investment. The number of companies willing, and able, to contemplate major overseas investments has been reduced significantly, while their expectations of potential investment sites has increased. At the same time as there are fewer automotive investment projects for which to compete, there are more countries actively campaigning to attract motor industry investors.

It is no longer sufficient to offer competitive manufacturing and labour costs, plus access to a good local market. Investors now seek a full range of support services and skills to underpin the long-term validity of their projects.

A brief history of automotive investment in the United Kingdom

Inward investment from automotive companies is not a new feature of the United Kingdom's industrial history. Ford Motor Co started building cars in the United Kingdom as long ago as 1911, and General Motors, naming the Vauxhall brand after its first site in South London, was not far behind. Component suppliers from Europe and America arrived to support both the foreign vehicle manufacturers (VMs) and the fragmented domestic manufacturers.

The pace quickened in the 1980s with the arrival of the Japanese. Nissan, Toyota and Honda all chose the United Kingdom as their manufacturing base within the European Community. In each case Nissan in Sunderland, Toyota in Burnaston, Derby, and Honda in Swindon – they elected to construct new, modern plants in areas with a strong tradition of engineering skills, but high levels of unemployment. Key Japanese component manufacturers came to support their major customers. Some established brand new facilities, some combined with existing UK companies, and some – like Calsonic, who took over Llanelli Radiators and opened a greenfield site in Washington (County Durham, North East England) – did both.

Throughout this period of expansion, the UK government and industry pursued an 'open door' policy to inward investment, in marked contrast to some EU countries, where there were dark mutterings about 'a Japanese aircraft carrier, moored off the European coast'. Their reward was a rejuvenation of the UK motor industry. Productivity and quality standards soared. In 1982, the United Kingdom produced only 888,000 vehicles – by 2002, the figure had doubled.

In the 1990s further inward investors arrived from Europe and the United States. Ford took control of Jaguar, PSA bought the Rootes/Chrysler plant at Ryton, near Coventry, and BMW gained control of the Rover Group. All invested substantial sums in modernizing facilities, introducing new models and raising production levels. Even when BMW subsequently parted company with Rover, selling the passenger car business back to the UK management and the Land Rover brand to Ford, it maintained a substantial footprint in the United Kingdom by continuing to manufacture the best-selling Mini and a large proportion of its global engine production. And, in the luxury car sector, it concluded a complicated deal with VW, which resulted in the two German manufacturers taking ownership of the Rolls Royce and Bentley brands respectively.

Alongside their manufacturing investments, the global automakers identified another area where the United Kingdom offered attractive investment opportunities – product design and development. Vehicle manufacturers learnt – sometimes by bitter experience – that, although they are in a global business, they must offer products that have local market appeal. Again, Ford was one of the first on the scene. Its R&D Centre at Dunton, Essex, opened in the 1960s and grew to become the company's world centre for design and development work on small and medium-sized passenger models. Another key investor in this sector was Nissan, which, in 1991, created a new European R&D centre at Cranfield, Bedfordshire. The staff at Cranfield have subsequently been responsible for re-engineering the Primera, Micra and Terrano models for the European market. And Daewoo invested substantially in a technical centre at Worthing, before the Korean parent company's financial troubles led to its demise.

The UK motor industry today

The combination of native engineering and production skills with the capital and best practice injected by foreign investors – all supported by the 'open door' policy of successive governments – has created a strong, modern industry that contributes substantially to the United Kingdom's overall economic performance.

Nine major international car makers have found that the United Kingdom is a good place to build, and sell, cars, and they are complemented by more than 40 niche manufacturers to create the most diverse automotive mix in Europe. Additionally, 17 of the world's top 20 component suppliers have UK operations. The United Kingdom also boasts Europe's most productive car plant (Nissan at Sunderland) and commercial vehicle plant (Leyland).

Today, total automotive turnover is estimated at US$72 billion, with the sector providing direct employment for around a quarter of a million workers. The UK car market has reached record totals for each of the last three years, and is now comfortably the second largest in Europe. Almost 70 per cent of the vehicles produced in the United Kingdom go for export. Annual turnover in the R&D sector is calculated at US$2.4 billion, of which 50 per cent comes from foreign investors. UK companies account for around 20 per cent of the global market in independent design and development engineering services.

The changing pattern of automotive investment in Europe

In March 2004, the Korean car maker Hyundai announced that its new European car plant will be built in Slovakia. This decision reflects the growing trend in the motor industry to locate new investments in Central and Eastern Europe, where they can take advantage of low labour rates in countries that have recently become full members of the European Union. But the arrival of Hyundai perhaps also marks the last major automotive production plant investment to be made in Europe. All the major global players now have manufacturing facilities within the EU, and, while there may be future rationalization and transfer of models between plants, it is questionable whether there will be another large-scale greenfield investment.

Consequently, there will be a number of key changes in the battle to attract inward investment. First, the emphasis will switch from winning new projects to retaining the loyalty of existing investors. Second, component suppliers will become more important in the investment equation, and, third, research and development projects will take on a new significance.

In the 1980s and 1990s, the United Kingdom was a pioneer of attracting automotive inward investment into Europe. Although other competitors have subsequently emerged – some of whom can offer significant cost benefits – the early reputation the United Kingdom established as an easy and welcoming place to do business is likely to be a key factor in preserving investor loyalty. Industry and government are working together to ensure that this reputation is maintained.

The component sector is increasingly at the cutting-edge of new technology developments in the automotive industry, and component suppliers are taking more and more responsibility for the conception, design and development of vehicle systems. They therefore require a production base that is not only economically competitive but can also offer them a reservoir of research skills sufficiently large and sophisticated to meet their new development role. Again, UK industry and government are working together to ensure that the United Kingdom's engineering heritage is preserved and expanded.

The United Kingdom is home to a considerable number of independent companies, and academic institutions that perform R&D work for global vehicle manufacturers. As already noted, some of those manufacturers have also chosen to set up their own research centres in the United Kingdom. Design and development considerations are now both a crucial part of initial investment decisions, and a powerful factor in determining which plant in a manufacturer's global network will win the work to upgrade existing models and build new ones. Against this background, the government is paying increased attention to industry's call for enhanced incentives for R&D work.

What can the United Kingdom offer?

Positive economic indicators

Automotive investors have been attracted by, and have benefited from, the same macroeconomic factors that have sustained growth across many industrial sectors. These include:

- a stable, low-inflation economy, which has generally outperformed the other major European players;

- a strong domestic market, driven by consumer demand;

- good labour relations and flexible working practices, which allow UK plants to achieve high levels of productivity.

An open business environment

The welcoming approach to inward investors, categorized by successive governments' 'open door' policy, is carried over into industry and regional contacts. The Society of Motor Manufacturers and Traders (SMMT) – the trade association that represents all sectors of the automotive industry in the United Kingdom – has a multinational membership, embracing all the leading international and domestic companies that are active in the United Kingdom. Those regions that host motor industry investments have created automotive 'clusters' and other mechanisms for linking together companies within the supply chain. At the same time, the DTI's specialist Automotive Unit has designated Business Relationship Managers to maintain a business dialogue with major overseas investors. The networks offered to investors by all these organizations extend into Brussels and the heart of European Union policy-making.

A skilled and professional workforce

The United Kingdom has a strong tradition of engineering and production skills, which has long attracted inward investors. The decline in industries like ship-building and railways has given automotive investors the opportunity to establish greenfield operations close to existing pools of engineering talent. Industrial relations have improved out of all recognition in the last 30 years, and the total of stoppage time is low.

A number of British universities offer specialist automotive engineering courses at both undergraduate and postgraduate level, ensuring that there is a continuing supply of qualified engineers and technicians entering the job market. Because many of these academic institutions also conduct research on behalf of major vehicle and component manufacturers, their students have an early opportunity to gain first-hand experience of vehicle development programmes.

Government and industry are committed to maintaining, and growing, this pool of automotive talent. The Automotive Academy (see below) has recently been established with the principal objective of enhancing job skills and training at all levels of the industry.

A network of research and development centres

A multi-skilled research and development network – embracing world-class testing facilities, independent design engineering companies and academic institutions – has grown up within the United Kingdom to support development projects for major international customers. Prominent in this network are the 50 universities and colleges that have been designated 'automotive centres of excellence'. These run specialist courses and research programmes specially tailored to the needs of UK-based automotive manufacturers, as well as providing a steady stream of well-qualified graduates to fill positions within the industry.

A recent example of this collaborative approach to research and development work is the International Automotive Research Centre established at the University of Warwick in 2003. Partners in the project include the university's Warwick Manufacturing Group, component supplier Corus Automotive, Ford Motor Co, and Advantage West Midlands. Initial funding of £70 million came from the regional development agency and the industrial partners.

A unique partnership between industry and government

Both government and industry understand the importance of maintaining world-class, competitive standards if the UK automotive industry is to remain attractive to inward investors. They have, therefore, worked together to develop a range of programmes to ensure that – throughout the industry – standards are constantly improved.

SMMT Industry Forum

In 1996, SMMT Industry Forum was established to support companies in achieving manufacturing process improvement. Master engineers were engaged from leading global players to provide practical training and tuition. By a process of cascade learning, more than 450 companies have benefited from the Industry Forum programmes, and the example has been taken up by other industry sectors.

Foresight Vehicle

In the field of R&D, another joint programme – Foresight Vehicle – was instigated to stimulate the development of technologies for future motor vehicles. This programme encourages collaborative research by industry and academia under five thematic headings – engine power-train, alternative fuel vehicles, electronics and telematics, advanced structures and materials and design and manufacturing process. Although working on future automotive developments, the Foresight Vehicle programme, under industry management, has a clear focus on achieving practical and marketable solutions.

The Automotive Academy

The most recent example of government/industry cooperation is the creation of the Automotive Academy. The objective of the academy is to ensure that, at all levels, the United Kingdom's automotive workforce is continually trained to the highest standards, and to encourage talented young people to make their career within the industry. Among the first courses to be rolled out were 'The Automotive Leaders Programme', designed to hone the strategic business skills of the industry's future leaders, and 'The Team Leader Programme', which equips factory-floor workers to identify and achieve improvements in quality, costs and delivery performance. Future courses will focus on giving new graduates practical 'hands on' experience, and will target the recruitment of younger students into engineering and automotive disciplines.

Research and development incentives

The government offers a package of fiscal incentives to companies conducting R&D work in the United Kingdom. Since 1 April 2002, both large and small companies have been able to claim tax relief on both capital, consumable and salary expenditure on research and development projects. Detailed information is available at:
www.inlandrevenue.gov.uk/randd/index and
www.dti.gov.uk/support/draft- guidelines.

A further enhancement was announced in the 2003 Pre-Budget Report, to the effect that fuel used for testing purposes will, in future, qualify for tax credits.

Key areas of expertise

The United Kingdom has acquired a global reputation for excellence in some of the motor industry's most dynamic, competitive and technically innovative sectors. These include engine design and build, vehicle styling and motorsport.

Engine design and production

Companies that have been behind some of the world's most famous engines – names like Cosworth, Lotus and Ricardo – continue to offer their design and engineering skills to international customers. As electronic systems take an increasingly prominent role in engine development, new names, like QinetiQ, are coming to prominence.

Recognizing the advantages offered by the combination of these development skills and a sophisticated component supply base, many volume manufacturers have selected the United Kingdom as a key location for engine manufacture. BMW, Ford, General Motors, Honda, Nissan, Toyota and MG Rover all build substantial numbers of power units within the United Kingdom. Currently, 2.3 million car engines are produced annually – a figure that is predicted to rise to 3.5 million by 2005.

Vehicle styling

UK-born and trained stylists are behind some of the most eye-catching, and best-selling, models appearing in world markets. Peter Horbury is currently Ford's Chief of North American Design, after previous spells with Volvo and Premier Auto Group. The Callum brothers – Moray and Ian – lead the design teams respectively at Mazda and Jaguar. And Martin Smith has been top designer at both Audi and GM Opel.

British academic institutions and design houses, such as the Royal College for Arts, have a reputation for schooling top-class designers, which attracts international talent and investment from around the globe.

Motorsport

In the demanding realm of motorsport, the United Kingdom is clearly a world leader, with an estimated 70 per cent of the global market. More than half the cars on the Formula 1 grid are built and tuned in the United Kingdom. Leading teams in Indy Car racing and NASCAR also turn to UK expertise to prepare their cars for competition. And volume manufacturers like Subaru and Hyundai, who wish to burnish their brand image with world rally success, have invested heavily in UK-based operations to develop their products to the optimum performance level. This concentration of motorsport activity again testifies to the high level of engineering skills and rapid development capability available within the United Kingdom.

Investing in the future

The 21st century sees a motor industry that is more global, more complex, and more competitive than at any time in its long history. Manufacturers' prosperity and survival depend on designing and building the best vehicles speedily and economically. They need to operate in an economic and business environment that offers them the best prospects of success.

The United Kingdom has won an international reputation for offering automotive companies a world-class development and production base. Government and industry are committed to working together to maintain that status as the motor industry continues to evolve.

Key websites

www.autoindustry.co.uk
www.uktradeinvest.gov.uk
www.smmt.co.uk
www.industryforum.co.uk
www.foresightvehicle.org.uk
www.automotiveacademy.co.uk

3.2

Biotechnology

Jeanette Walker, ERBI

Introduction

While scientists worldwide celebrated the 50th anniversary of the deciphering of the structure of DNA, Cambridge had special cause to celebrate, for Crick and Watson made this ground-breaking discovery at the Cavendish Laboratory in Cambridge. Moreover, Sir John Sulston, winner of the Nobel Prize in 2001, is also a Cambridge scientist. In fact, Cambridge is home to more Nobel Laureates in medicine and chemistry than any other part of the world (see the list at the end of this chapter).

The East of England is home to over 200 biotech companies, including a quarter of Europe's top 50 publicly quoted biotech companies and over half of the United Kingdom's public biotechs. Cambridge is arguably the most successful bio-pharma cluster in Europe, and Norwich (just over 50 miles from Cambridge) is home to the largest concentration of scientists in plant, food and microbial research in Europe.

Companies are attracted to this part of the United Kingdom because they are able to access all the resources they need to research, develop, test and market products and services whether in red or green biotech. Cambridge is a highly networked bio cluster. Newcomers and start-up companies are able to integrate quickly and easily into the local scientific and business communities.

Dozens of internationally mobile companies have established operations in the East of England including Amgen and Genzyme, two of the world's most successful biotech companies. Despite the tough economic climate, the science community in the East of England is growing. The number of start-ups from universities is rising, new science parks are under construction, mature biotech companies are pursuing complex mergers and acquisitions and more and more business and scientific professionals are moving to the area.

Advantages of locating in the East of England

- access to a large research base of over 20 research institutes;
- the opportunity to collaborate with seven universities including the top-ranked University of Cambridge;
- the support of a broad network of technical service providers;
- close proximity to the global research centres of the multinationals GSK, Merck and Bayer;
- close proximity to Addenbrooke's and Papworth Hospitals, research hospitals of international acclaim, plus the recently opened Norwich and Norfolk University Hospital;
- networking in a cluster of 200 biotechnology companies;
- easy access to other significant UK biotech clusters in London, Oxford, Manchester and Scotland;
- fast, low-cost access to continental Europe;
- a large labour pool in all disciplines including research, clinical development, business development, marketing/technical sales and consulting;
- a wide choice of affordable labs and offices on world-class science, research and business parks;
- a mature network of professional advisers (lawyers, bankers, accountants, recruiters) all of whom understand the unique needs of biotechnology companies;
- the support of ERBI, Europe's most successful regional biotech industry group;
- unrivalled international partnering opportunities;
- superb quality of life for employees.

Research institutes in biosciences

There are over 20 research institutes in the East of England including the world-class Laboratory of Molecular Biology in Cambridge, dubbed 'The Nobel Factory'. The Wellcome Trust's Genome Campus at Hinxton is the largest campus of its type in Europe, housing the Sanger Centre, European Bioinformatics Institute and the Rosalind Franklin Centre for Genomics Research. The Norwich Research Park is home to the John Innes Centre, Sainsbury Laboratory, Institute of Food Research,

University of East Anglia and the Norfolk and Norwich University Hospital (see Table 3.2.1).

Table 3.2.1   Biotechnology research institutes in the Cambridge/East of England cluster

Institute	Website
Babraham Institute	http://www.babraham.ac.uk/
European Bioinformatics Institute	http://www.ebi.ac.uk/
The Rosalind Franklin Centre for Genomics Research (previously the Human Genome Mapping Project Research Centre)	http://www.hgmp.mrc.ac.uk/
Institute of Arable Crops Research	http://www.rothamsted.bbsrc. ac.uk/iacr/tiacrhome.html
Institute of Food Research	http://www.rothamsted.bbsrc. ac.uk/iacr/tiacrhome.html
John Innes Centre	http://www.jic.bbsrc.ac.uk/
Laboratory of Molecular Biology	http://www2.mrc-lmb.cam. ac.uk/
MRC Biostatistics Unit	http://www.mrc-bsu.cam.ac.uk
MRC Cancer Cell Unit	http://www.hutchison-mrc.cam. ac.uk/ccu_organo.html
MRC Centre for Protein Engineering	http://www.mrc-cpe.cam.ac.uk/
MRC Cognition and Brain Sciences Unit	http://www.mrc-cbu.cam.ac.uk/
MRC Dunn Human Nutrition Unit	http://www.mrc-dunn.cam. ac.uk/
MRC Resource Centre for Human Nutrition Research	http://www.mrc-dunn.cam. ac.uk/
National Institute of Agricultural Botany	http://www.niab.com/
Sanger Institute	http://www.sanger.ac.uk/
Silsoe Research Institute	http://www.sri.bbsrc.ac.uk/

Local universities

There are seven universities in the East of England with life science departments. The University of Cambridge is arguably the top-ranked university in the UK for science and technology as 14 of its science and related departments achieved the highest rating in the government's recent audit. Cambridge has an active technology transfer and corporate liaison office with an 'open for business' policy. Cranfield University, a post-graduate university, has an outstanding track record in providing research to industry particularly in the field of bio-sensors (see Table 3.2.2).

Table 3.2.2   East of England universities with life science departments

University	Website
Anglia Polytechnic University	http://www.anglia.ac.uk/
Cranfield University	http://www.cranfield.ac.uk/
University of Cambridge	http://www.cam.ac.uk/
University of East Anglia	http://www.uea.ac.uk/
University of Essex	http://www.essex.ac.uk/
University of Hertfordshire	http://www.herts.ac.uk/
University of Luton	http://www.luton.ac.uk/

Research hospitals

Three of the region's hospitals work in close collaboration with universities. Addenbrooke's Hospital in Cambridge is a leading international centre for biomedical research, medical education and clinical trials. The hospital shares its site with the Wolfson Brain Imaging Centre, the MRC Laboratory of Molecular Biology, the Cambridge Institute for Medical Research (CIMR), the MRC Dunn Human Nutrition, and the MRC Centre for Protein Engineering. Other institutions include the Regional Blood Transfusion Centre, the Addenbrooke's Centre for Clinical Investigation, Addenbrooke's Clinical Research Centre (ACRC) incorporating the Wellcome Trust Clinical Research Facility and Clinical Investigation Ward, the Centre for Genetic Epidemiology, the Institute of Public Health, which accommodates the MRC Biostatistics Unit and the University Department of Public Health and Primary Care. The Hutchison/MRC Research Centre houses the new MRC Cancer Cell Unit and staff of the Cancer Research Campaign Department of Oncology.

Papworth Hospital is a global leader specializing in cardiothoracic research. Research programmes include coronary heart disease, heart failure, sudden cardiac death and arrhythmia, pulmonary vascular disease, inflammatory lung disease and respiratory failure. Activity includes the assessment of new technologies and methods of service delivery, often in multi-centre trials that involve multidisciplinary collaborations.

The Norfolk & Norwich University Hospital is a recently opened teaching and research hospital, in partnership with the nearby University of East Anglia (UEA). The medical school built on the UEA campus – the first in the UK for 31 years – will train up to 110 medical undergraduates each year. When the school is fully operational, some 500 medical students will be training in Norwich.

Biotech companies

There are over 200 biotech companies in the East of England region. Eighty per cent of the commercial activity in biotechnology is focused on drug discovery, enabling technologies and technical services. These include a mix of:

- **overseas companies** that have established subsidiaries in the East of England (Amgen, Genzyme, PPD, Gilead, TKT, Ambion, Lion Biosciences, Cellzome, Medivir, Accelrys, Lark, GATC, Li-Cor, Advanced Technologies, Biogemma, Mundipharma International, Organon Labs, Prometic, Scynexis, Argenta, Dakocytomation);

- **successful locally established companies** (Cambridge Antibody Technology, Alizyme, Vernalis, KuDOS, Arakis, Amedis, Astex, Domantis, Cytomyx, Acambis, Ionix, Solexa, Biofocus, Lorantis, Abcam, HFL, Inpharmatica, Isogenica, Paradigm, MMI, NCE Discovery, Pharmagene, Xenova, Biosynergy, Cambridge Biotechnology, de Novo, Xention);

- **spin-outs** from universities, research institutes and other companies (Akubio, Pharmorphix, Sareum, Smart Holograms, Novacta, Novexin, Lumora, Purely Proteins).

As Figure 3.2.1 indicates, there is increasing focus on clinical development work as companies progress products into the clinic. Figure

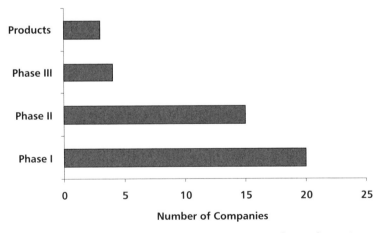

Figure 3.2.1 Number of Cambridge companies with products in the clinic and on the market

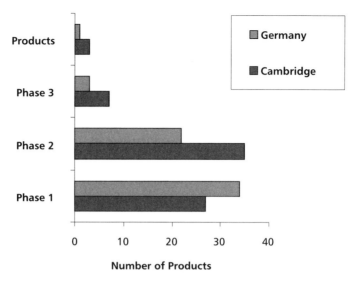

Figure 3.2.2   Comparison of companies in the Cambridge region with the whole of Germany by products in the clinic and on the market

3.3.2 shows that companies in the Cambridge area have more products in the clinic than the whole of Germany.

Science and research parks

With over 14 science parks located in the East of England (see Figure 3.2.3 and Table 3.2.3), biotech companies have a wide choice of laboratories and offices.

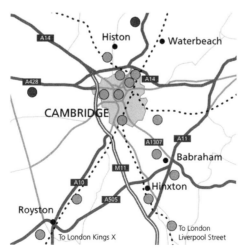

Figure 3.2.3   Science parks in the East of England

Table 3.2.3   Science parks in the East of England region

Park	History
Cambridge Science Park	The Cambridge Science Park is the most successful development of its type in Europe. Established in 1970 by Trinity College (University of Cambridge), the Park currently houses 24 life sciences companies.
Babraham Research Campus	The Babraham Incubator is arguably the most successful bio-incubator in the United Kingdom, currently providing labs and offices for 24 biotech companies on flexible terms. Larger laboratories are currently under construction at the campus to provide grow-on space for existing and new tenants. Companies also have access to Babraham Technix – a range of technical and administrative services ranging from meeting rooms, library, accounting and photographic services to production of monoclonal antibodies, microchemistry and imaging.
Granta Park	Granta Park is a purpose-built biotech research park located close to the Genome Campus and the Babraham Institute. The park has attracted some of the region's top pharma and biotech companies including Alizyme, UCB, Cambridge Antibody Technology, Vernalis (British Biotech), PPD, Gilead and Pharmion.
Great Chesterford Park	Located close to Granta Park and the Genome Campus, Great Chesterford Park is undergoing a major expansion to include biology and chemistry laboratories and a state-of-the-art amenity centre in a parkland environment. In addition to the Wellcome Trust, the Park currently houses six biotech companies.
Fyfield Park	A landscaped science park with low-cost refurbished labs located between London and Cambridge.
Cambourne Research Quarter	Design and build options are available on this park situated to the west side of Cambridge.
Norwich Bio-incubator	Offers top quality labs and offices on the Norwich Research Park available on flexible terms with access to services and equipment at the research institutes on the park (for example, John Innes Centre stores).

Proximity to other significant UK biotech clusters

There are excellent connections to other significant biotech hubs in the United Kingdom from a base in the East of England, whether travelling by road, rail or air. The region is served by four main roads: M11, M1, A1 and A14 giving easy access both north to south and east to west. Typical drive times to Oxford are 1.5–2 hours and 3.5 hours to Manchester subject to traffic. All major towns in the region have direct rail services to London. Cambridge is only 45 minutes by train to the centre of London. There are three international airports in the region. Daily scheduled flights to Scotland (Glasgow and Edinburgh) are available from Stansted and Luton airports with average flights times of less than an hour.

Fast, low-cost access to continental Europe

Stansted and Luton airports also offer daily, scheduled flights to all main European cities including Frankfurt, Paris, Milan, Stockholm, Rome, Amsterdam, Brussels and Madrid. Access to Stansted is just off the M11 motorway with short-term parking available directly in front of the terminal building. Luton is adjacent to the M1 motorway. Companies interested in reducing costs choose to fly with low-cost airlines such as Ryanair and easyJet with average return tickets to European cities of approximately £50.

Mature business infrastructure

First-class advice is on offer from experienced professional firms of lawyers, bankers, recruiters, accountants, management consultancies. Many of the companies employ dually qualified staff. Biotech companies can be confident that they are receiving advice from professionals who fully understand the unique needs of biotech companies. The 'Big 4' (PWC, E&Y, Deloittes and KPMG) all have life science offices in the region.

Access to venture capital

Having access to finance at all investment stages has also been critical to the growth of biotechnology in the East of England. The business angel network in Cambridge is one of the most active in Europe. It is estimated that there is over US$1 billion available from locally active

VCs such as 3i, Merlin, Avlar, Apax, NW Brown, Abingworth and Schroeder.

Advice and support from ERBI

ERBI is the bioscience industry group for the East of England. As Europe's leading regional science-based industry group, ERBI has an international reputation for delivering support to its member companies which makes a real difference to their top and bottom lines. ERBI is recognized for providing solutions and programmes that help its members to save costs through purchasing schemes, increase productivity, find research partners, enhance marketing and sales and improve human resources.

For companies setting up in the East of England, ERBI offers a bespoke service, free of charge, that includes help with recruitment, finding offices and labs, access to scientific and business networks, PR and general information about the East of England.

International partnering opportunities

Cambridge's reputation as Europe's leading biotech cluster means that Cambridge attracts visitors from all over the world. On these occasions, ERBI hosts formal partnering days providing a platform for local companies to meet visiting delegates to explore unrivalled opportunities for collaboration.

Access to ERBI's free confidential service is available from: ERBI, St John's Innovation Centre, Cowley Road, Cambridge, CB4 0WS. Telephone: +44 (0) 1223 421974, jeanettewalker@erbi.co.uk, www.erbi.co.uk.

Cambridge Nobel Laureates

Chemistry 1962
PERUTZ, MAX FERDINAND
KENDREW, Sir JOHN COWDERY
'for their studies of the structures of globular proteins'

Chemistry 1967
EIGEN, MANFRED
NORRISH, RONALD GEORGE WREYFORD
PORTER, Lord (GEORGE)
'for their studies of extremely fast chemical reactions, effected by disturbing the equilibrium by means of very short pulses of energy'

Chemistry 1980
BERG, PAUL
'for his fundamental studies of the biochemistry of nucleic acids, with particular regard to recombinant-DNA'
GILBERT, WALTER
SANGER, FREDERICK
'for their contributions concerning the determination of base sequences in nucleic acids'

Chemistry 1982
KLUG, Sir AARON
'for his development of crystallographic electron microscopy and his structural elucidation of biologically important nuclei acid-protein complexes'

Chemistry 1997
BOYER, PAUL D.
WALKER, JOHN E.
'for their elucidation of the enzymatic mechanism underlying the synthesis of adenosine triphosphate (ATP)'
SKOU, JENS C.
'for the first discovery of an ion-transporting enzyme, Na+, K+-ATPase'

Physiology or Medicine 1962
CRICK, FRANCIS HARRY COMPTON
WATSON, JAMES DEWEY
WILKINS, MAURICE HUGH FREDERICK
'for their discoveries concerning the molecular structure of nucleic acids and its significance for information transfer in living material'

Physiology or Medicine 1963
ECCLES, Sir JOHN CAREW
HODGKIN, Sir ALAN LLOYD
HUXLEY, Sir ANDREW FIELDING
'for their discoveries concerning the ionic mechanisms involved in excitation and inhibition in the peripheral and central portions of the nerve cell membrane'

Physiology or Medicine 1975
BALTIMORE, DAVID
DULBECCO, RENATO
TEMIN, HOWARD MARTIN
'for their discoveries concerning the interaction between tumour viruses and the genetic material of the cell'

Physiology or Medicine 1984
JERNE, NIELS K.
KÖHLER, GEORGES J.F.

MILSTEIN, CÉSAR
'for theories concerning the specificity in development and control of the immune system and the discovery of the principle for production of monoclonal antibodies'

Physiology or Medicine 1993
ROBERTS, RICHARD J.
SHARP, PHILLIP A.
'for their discoveries of split genes'

Physiology or Medicine 2002
BRENNER, SYDNEY
HORVITZ, H. ROBERT
SULSTON, JOHN E.
'for their discoveries concerning genetic regulation of organ development and programmed cell death'

3.3

Chemical Industries

Neil Harvey, International Trade and Sector Groups, Chemical Industries Association

Meeting needs and expectations

The UK chemical industry lies at the heart of the European industrial economy, serving every branch of manufacturing industry. It employs 230,000 highly skilled people nationwide, and accounts for 2 per cent of Gross Domestic Product and 10 per cent of manufacturing industry's gross value-added. It invests over £2 billion annually, representing 14 per cent of total manufacturing investment, with a further £3.5 billion being spent on R&D. It is the United Kingdom's top manufacturing export earner, with an annual trade surplus of nearly £5 billion on sales of £46 billion, of which £29 billion is accounted for by exports, with a large proportion going to other countries in the European Union.

Birthplace of the modern chemical industry, the United Kingdom's chemical sector is a powerhouse among the country's manufacturing sectors. The UK chemical industry is made up of approximately 3,800 companies. No surprise then that the United Kingdom has long been, and continues to be, one of Europe's most attractive locations for international chemical investment.

Commitment to free enterprise, low taxation, deregulated utilities, absence of restrictive labour practices and regulations, freedom to manage, English language and business practices similar to those in the United States: all these combine to make the United Kingdom a logical location for global investors. Over 200 international chemical companies with manufacturing facilities in the United Kingdom clearly agree.

Geographical dispersion within the United Kingdom

Chemical production is widespread throughout the United Kingdom in various densities. Historical, geographic, economic and social factors have led to most of the industry being concentrated in Grangemouth (Scotland), the North West of England, along the M62 motorway corridor to West Yorkshire and Humberside to the east, with another cluster extending northwards to Teesside – all of which are integrated by a national ethylene pipeline network. All four regions are within a radius of 200 miles and each has major port facilities that are interconnected by an extensive road and rail network. Another cluster is developing between Grangemouth and Teesside at Tyneside with a strong focus on pharmaceuticals, biotech and service providers.

There are smaller concentrations of chemical companies in the Midlands (Nottingham, Loughborough, Birmingham) and life science companies in Cambridge, but interaction among them is not as high as in the ribbon running from North West to North East England.

South West England (Bristol, Southampton) and South Wales have significant established chemical production centres, with Cornwall developing a new cluster of small, highly specialized research chemical producers using the very latest synthetic chemistry techniques, such as combinatorial chemistry. London and the South East of England do have chemical and big global pharmaceutical companies but many of the premises are offices, research establishments, corporate HQs or traders only.

A tabular version of geographical distribution of speciality chemical companies has been recreated below (Table 3.3.1). The North East and Teesside tend to have larger sites (more capital-intensive and less labour-intensive). The figures for London and the South East appear larger than casual observation of the environment would suggest. The reasons are that many sites, other than pharmaceutical, crop protection and catalysts, are formulators as well as offices, trading operations, storage and warehousing.

Table 3.3.1 Distribution of UK speciality chemical companies by UK region, by percentage of number of companies and by percentage of number of staff

Region	Coverage	% of Companies	% of Staff
North West	Manchester, Liverpool, Warrington, Widnes, Runcorn, Blackburn, Burnley, Nelson, Bolton, Colne, Stockport, Crewe, Nantwich, Middlewich, Northwich	23	21
Yorkshire & Humberside	Leeds, Wakefield, Halifax, Bradford, Huddersfield, Hull, York, Grimsby, Immingham, Scunthorpe, Doncaster	14	12

Region	Coverage	% of Companies	% of Staff
North/North East	Teesside including Darlington, Tyneside, Wearside including Durham, Cumbria, Carlisle, Lancaster, Preston	11	8
East Anglia	Suffolk, Cambridge, Essex	8	8
South Yorkshire & East Midlands	Sheffield, Nottingham, Loughborough, Leicester, Northampton	5	9
Birmingham & West Midlands		3	6
South West	Avon, Somerset, Devon, Cornwall, (Bristol, Taunton, Torquay)	3	4
South	Hampshire, Dorset (Bournemouth, Poole, Southampton)	3	
Scotland		4	6
Wales	Cardiff, Newport, Swansea, Bangor, Mostyn, Llangefni	6	5
London and South East	Surrey, Sussex, Herts, Berks, Bucks, Kent	20	19

Product diversity of the UK chemical sector

The United Kingdom's chemical sector is very diverse, not just geographically but in product coverage too. Petrochemicals and basic organics are produced from North Sea oil and gas reserves. Coupled with a substantial inorganic sector, the United Kingdom has also become a recognized European centre for intermediate and speciality chemical production. Further down the supply chain, the United Kingdom is a major European manufacturing and distribution point for pharmaceuticals, paints and coatings, detergents and for other manufacturing industries such as the automotive and electronics sectors. Plastics processors in the United Kingdom generate annual turnover of some £10 billion.

Table 3.3.2 provides a range of statistics explaining the size of the UK speciality chemicals industry sector versus the other industry sectors. They were derived from government surveys of the industry and reported according to Standard Industrial Classification (SIC) codes.

Table 3.3.2   UK statistics for the UK chemical commodity,
speciality, pharmaceutical and consumer products sector – 2002

Sector	Number of Companies	Employ- ment '000s	Turnover £billion	Product Sales £billion	GVA £billion	GDP % Total	Trade Balance £billion	Capital Expenditure £billion
Commodity	1,027	54	14.5	10.3	3.7	0.40	0.4	0.57
Speciality	1,541	82	13.9	9.2	4.3	0.46	1.3	0.70
	(40%)	(29%)	(27%)	(28%)	(26%)	(26%)	(27%)	(30%)
Pharmaceutical	362	71	15.6	8.2	6.4	0.69	2.6	0.87
Consumer	888	46	6.7	5.3	2.3	0.25	0.5	0.17
Total	3,818	254	50.7	33.0	16.6	1.80	4.8	2.3

UK chemical technology and the business environment

Many of the world's greatest inventions emanate from the United
Kingdom, which has some of the best university chemistry departments to be found anywhere in the world. This knowledge base serves
several multinational companies with global or European R&D centres
in the United Kingdom. They recognize that the United Kingdom
provides a business and regulatory environment to help push technological changes to meet:

- increasing demand for 'lifestyle' products;

- quality and cost improvements, especially in life science products;

- public health and environmental challenges;

- expectations for cleaner chemical processes and products with less
  environmental impact;

- requirements for protecting intellectual property and profit repatriation.

To respond to these future business drivers, the United Kingdom has
an evolving and flexible industrial, regulatory and academic infrastructure to accommodate and welcome new investments that, for
example, seek:

- the ability to perform a range of complex chemistries and formula-
  tions at scales from kilos to tonnes using flexible technology platforms;

- provision of special customer services such as research and
  screening, the supply of research and laboratory chemicals, contract

synthesis, contract and/or toll manufacture of reaction and/or formulation chemistry;

- well-supported, multi-functional assets on sites capable of operating to current good manufacturing practice (cGMP) standards, typical of the pharmaceuticals sector;

- a robust regulatory and analytical infrastructure;

- fast-track development and manufacture;

- strategic commitment to custom synthesis and formulation manufacture in order to support a complex web of alliances and joint ventures between major players, especially in pharmaceuticals;

- secure technology licensing arrangements.

Outlook for the UK chemical industry in Europe

The UK government is in the vanguard of promoting international free trade and free enterprise cultures. One aspect of this is the comparatively low level of taxation. UK corporate tax is 30 per cent (20 per cent for small companies) compared with levels of 34–40 per cent in other major chemical producing countries in Europe. Even more dramatic is the difference in social security taxation where the UK rate is 12 per cent compared with 30–50 per cent in other countries. UK personal tax rates at 10–40 per cent (basic rate is 22 per cent) are also generally lower than elsewhere in Europe.

Flexible labour laws are particularly appealing to cyclical businesses and the UK chemical industry's strike-free record in recent years is testimony to the cooperative culture that has developed between management and labour.

The United Kingdom leads other European countries in its approach to privatization. Telecommunications, electricity, water and gas are all in the private sector and domestic and industrial consumers have the freedom to purchase from competing UK and foreign companies.

While safety and environmental regulations are similar to those in many leading industrial countries, UK regulators understand that high standards can be achieved without excessive bureaucracy. Statutory consents and permits for new facilities can be obtained rapidly, usually in a matter of weeks.

Europe is the world's biggest chemicals market and the United Kingdom is an integral part of that market. This is why the United Kingdom is first choice for so much chemical investment. The East Coast ports of Humber, Teesside and Grangemouth are major chemical and container ports with large export and import flows. They also offer frequent 48-hour delivery services to Continental Europe and deep-sea access to the rest of the world. Likewise, the Port of Liverpool is the deep-sea gateway for the chemical industry hub in North West England. The United Kingdom has more transatlantic and global air connections than any other European country.

A wide variety of brown- and greenfield sites are available in the United Kingdom, many of which attract investment grants. Grangemouth and Teesside are obvious locations for the petrochemical and polymers sector. Both have the advantage of pipeline links with the North Sea oil and gas fields. Both are well-established major petrochemical locations with a wide range of utilities, services and engineering support for new investors.

BP, as owner of the major site at Grangemouth, has put together an attractive package of sites (up to 120 acres) feedstocks and utilities based on its own onsite co-generation and from a new 133 megawatt combined heat and power plant, which will be built in the area. BP's faith in its own site has been evidenced by its decision to invest some $800 million in cracker and LLdPE expansions as well as in a PP joint venture project with Elf Atochem.

Fully serviced sites of up to 20 acres, which would particular suit speciality chemical production looking to share utility costs, are also available at Grangemouth. Local companies are keen to attract new investors as part of their corporate growth and development strategies. Fully serviced sites are available, with access to combined heat and power generation. These are seen to be a selling point for incoming investment.

Some 150 miles further south on Teesside there is a similar offer, this time driven by Wilton International, which has spare land and a utilities supply infrastructure comprising one of Europe's largest chemical complexes. Sites of up to 100 acres each, utilities based on two power stations (one being the largest privately owned power station in Western Europe) are supported by a range of services including project risk management. From the large – Huntsman has recently expanded its production in Teesside – to the small – a new Pioneer Chemicals Park is planned to help the incubation of businesses developing new chemical products and processes. Teesside can also provide sites where the infrastructure exists to support investment in ammonia and methanol and their derivatives.

Further south again, the Humber also offers opportunities for methane-based investments as well as a range of intermediates and specialities and has access to the UK ethylene pipeline system. The site's location on the Humber deep-water estuary further increases the range of manufacturing options. With over 120 sailings a week to European destinations, products can be in Germany or Italy within 24 hours. Greenfield sites are available with access to 300 storage tanks alongside deep-sea port facilities.

North West England is already linked into the ethylene pipeline and has a large, well-established primary plastics sector. It is also home to the United Kingdom's flourishing speciality chemical sector, with sites available for further growth, and is the principal base in the United Kingdom for chloralkali production. Continental Europe is easily accessible via the excellent road connections to the Humber ports on the Eastern Coast.

In fact, the options are myriad. Whatever an investor needs, by way of raw materials, utilities, effluent treatment, well-located sites or partners, the solution lies somewhere in the United Kingdom – particularly in Grangemouth, Teesside, the Humber or North West England.

3.4

Creative Industries

Jonathan Reuvid

Definitions

The formal definition of the creative industries is 'those activities which have their origin in individual creativity, skill and talent and which have the potential for wealth and job creation through generation and exploitation of intellectual property'. In the United Kingdom the creative industries are within the remit of the government's Department for Culture, Media and Sport (DCMS), which works with UK Trade & Investment to aid export performance. The DCMS identifies the following main sub-sectors within the creative industries sector:

- advertising;
- architecture;
- art and antiques market;
- crafts;
- design;
- designer fashion;
- film and video;
- interactive leisure software;
- music;
- the performing arts;
- publishing;
- software and computer services;
- television and radio.

Four industry groups have been set up by DCMS to carry out the work of stimulating exports: Creative Exports, Cultural Heritage and Tourism, Design Partners and Performing Arts International Development. DCMS has also established the Creative Industries Higher Education Forum with a mandate to assess ways of improving the interface between creative industries and higher education and to address skills, knowledge transfer and entrepreneurship. The DCMS produces regular statistical bulletins, which may be found on the internet at http://www.culture.gov.uk.

In this chapter, we focus on four sub-sectors; design, designer fashion, interactive leisure software and television and radio, with less detailed comment on the others. Chapter 2.9 – Art and Collectibles – includes analysis of the markets for art and antiques. Contact references for all sub-sectors are given in Appendix II at the end of the book.

Economic contribution of creative industries

In 2001, creative industries generated revenues of US$87 billion (£54 billion), rising to US$98.5 billion (£61.1 billion) in 2002 and accounted for 1.9 million jobs (June 2002) in 122,000 companies. The gross value-added (GVA) of the creative industries (that is, GDP less taxes net of subsidies) grew by an average of 8 per cent compared with 2.6 per cent for the economy as a whole between 1997 and 2001. The fastest growing sub-sectors during this period were TV and radio at 17 per cent, advertising at 14 per cent and software at 10 per cent.

The export contribution of creative industries in 2001 to the balance of trade was US$18.1 billion (£11.4 billion), equivalent to about 4.2 per cent of all UK goods and services exported. Export growth from 1997 to 2001 was 15 per cent per annum for creative industries compared with an average 4 per cent for all goods and services.

The software and electronic publishing sub-sectors account for some 56,000 companies while music and the visual and performing arts account for 32,000 companies, together amounting to almost three-quarters of the total. Company numbers include only those above the VAT threshold.

Sub-sectors of creative industries

Advertising

The traditional main media in the United Kingdom for advertising are press and television together with cinema, radio and direct mail either by post or fax. However, in recent years the internet has developed as an alternative and, today, short messaging services in text on mobile

The Royal Opera has over 260 years of operatic tradition and The Royal Ballet celebrates its 75th Anniversary in 2005. As an organisation with such a prodigious history and an acknowledged centre of excellence with both national and international links, it is unique in supporting three performing companies, The Royal Ballet, The Royal Opera and The Royal Opera House Orchestra, along with a diversity of supporting art forms (design, visual arts, costume etc.) After a GBP214million redevelopment completed in December 1999, the Royal Opera House has become one of the most technically advanced theatres in the world, enabling us to attract the best designers, directors and artists from across the globe.

We continue to seek out new ways to reach audiences and give more people a chance to see and hear our work – the very best of opera and ballet in the world. Each year over 630,000 people from a broad range of backgrounds attend performances on the main stage. Even more diverse are the 2.6M people who view the performances broadcasted on BBC television each Season.

The Royal Opera House boasts one of the biggest memberships in the UK. Our members include many Times and Fortune 100 companies and opinion formers who regularly entertain at the House. Additionally, we run an extensive sponsorship programme that delivers qualitative brand building and hospitality opportunities to an assortment of multinational brands such as Coutts & Co, BP, Travelex, Audi and Vodafone.

Sustained artistic excellence across so many Royal Opera House performances is a tribute to extraordinary talent and dedication. Our orchestra, chorus and dancers all perform to consistently high standards and are acknowledged as among the best in the world. Creative partners are essential if we are to continue to innovate and extend our ability to reach new audiences nationally and internationally. With a great number of initiatives in the development stage we would welcome the chance to meet with you and discuss partnerships for the future. Contact the Development team **+44 207 212 9245. development@roh.org.uk**

ROYAL OPERA HOUSE
COVENT GARDEN

A ROYAL ASSOCIATION

The Royal Opera House is one of the world's great theatres. Home to The Royal Ballet, The Royal Opera and The Royal Opera House Orchestra, as well as a host of new companies and artists, it is recognised the world over as a centre of excellence and cutting-edge creativity.

Over half a million people attend the Royal Opera House each year and millions more see or hear performances on BBC television and radio. They do so because they share our passion for quality - and this makes them a perfect audience for your company.

Our Membership and Sponsorship schemes offer you a unique opportunity to communicate with that audience - and if you're launching a new product or entertaining clients, the opulent surroundings of the Royal Opera House provide the perfect backdrop.

In business and on stage, partnership is the key to a great performance.

Please call the Royal Opera House Development team on **00 44 207 212 9245/448** development@roh.org.uk
for a confidential discussion on ways to grow your business in tandem with the Royal Opera House.

phones offer new opportunities in direct marketing. Other new media include an increasing number of television channels via satellite, digital and cable, while more radio advertising alternatives are on offer via digital radio. The effectiveness of these new media remains unquantified.

The sales value of UK media advertising peaked at £14.6 billion in 2000 before dropping back to £13.1 billion in 2001 and recovering to £13.2 billion in 2002 and £13.4 billion in 2003. For 2004, increased media sales revenues of £14.0 billion are forecast. The breakdown of the media advertising spend in 2003 has been calculated as shown in Table 3.4.1.

Table 3.4.1   Media advertising spend (2003)

	£billion
Press	6,240
TV	3,478
Direct Mail	2,274
Outdoor Ads	669
Radio	536

Source: Snapshots International

At June 2002, the advertising industry employed 225,900 people in just over 10,000 registered businesses. London is the favourite location for the agencies, where they have the advantage of proximity to other creative industries. Over 80 per cent of employees in advertising are under the age of 40.

Architecture

British architects are famed for their skills in the area of master planning as well as their particular signature buildings. A prime example is the Urban Task Force initiative for urban regeneration chaired by Richard Rogers in 1998, which became the basis for a government White Paper on urban policy. As well as Lord Rogers, other noted UK-based architects include Sir Norman Foster, Zaha Hadid and Bill Dunster. Architecture contributed US$5.8 billion (£3.6 billion) to the economy in 2001 and generated exports worth US$£827.7 billion (£521.4 billion). The professional body for architects is the Royal Institute of Architects, having 4,208 registered member practices.

Crafts

The Crafts Council, part of the Arts Council, promotes UK crafts through regular trade missions as well as the Chelsea Crafts Fair in

London and a new annual event called 'Collect' at the Victoria and Albert Museum launched in February 2004. There is a long UK tradition in crafts such as ceramics, glass and metalwork, textiles and jewellery design and silversmithing.

Design

The United Kingdom has a strong reputation for good design, which plays an important role for consumers and businesses. In terms of GVA, the British Design Initiative valued the turnover of some 3,700 design consultancies at US$9.4 billion (£5.9 billion). However, these consultancies employed 66,849 people across 10 disciplines including film, video and TV, fashion and textiles, which are other areas of creative business described separately below.

La Repubblica and *Il Sole* newspapers of Milan, the design capital of the world, have acknowledged the growing UK strength in design by hailing the 'British creativity miracle'. This pre-eminence is the result of a combination of favourable factors, such as the United Kingdom's individualistic culture, first-rate art schools, the wide range of advice and support available to businesses in the industry and government recognition of the sector's significance in the knowledge economy. In the field of industrial design, the automobile manufacturers Ford and Nissan and the electronics giant Samsung are among those that have opened design studios in London.

Designer fashion

Between 1997 and 2001 the designer fashion sector's contribution to GVA grew by almost 3.5 per cent annually, reaching US$509.5 million. The sector, defined as clothing collections with a recognizable identity attributable to an individual designer or design house, has an export value in excess of $625 billion, totalling 14 per cent of all UK clothing sales.

Increasing label consciousness has been an important factor, leading to increased sales of designer fashion domestically. High street stores such as Marks & Spencer, Debenhams and Top Shop have made designer fashion more accessible by launching designer diffusion ranges, while the larger department stores have opened new stores in the larger regional cities such as Birmingham, Manchester and Leeds.

Outstanding fashion designers who have put the United Kingdom on the global fashion map include Manolo Blahnik, Stella McCartney, Alexander McQueen, Zandra Rhodes, Vivienne Westwood and Matthew Williamson, supported by top catwalk models such as Naomi Campbell, Sophie Dahl and Kate Moss. UK fashion design is showcased through two London Fashion Weeks, which are attended by approximately 4,000 and attract extensive media coverage.

Film

In 2002, the United Kingdom was the location of, or involved in, 115 movies that brought in US$907.1 million (£571.5 million) with a total spend, excluding co-production shots abroad, of US$693 million (£436 million), of which 42 were UK films on which spending was US$263.3 million (£165.9 million). Aided by favourable tax treatment, inward investment on film production in 2002 was US$426.8 million (£268.9 million).

Studios such as Disney, Warner Bothers, Amblimation and Dreamworks have all located in the United Kingdom to produce cinema-released feature films. Releases in 2003/04 to date have included the Richard Curtis production *Love Actually*, and *The Prisoner of Azkaban*, the third in the Harry Potter series.

Interactive leisure software

In leisure software the United Kingdom is the world's third largest market after the United States and Japan, producing 40 per cent of the world's computer games. Over the last five years, UK sales of PC and computer games software have grown steadily as shown in Table 3.4.2.

Table 3.4.2   Sales of UK computer and PC games software

	£million
1999	850.0
2000	934.4
2001	1,057.0
2002	1,081.0
2003	1,260.0
2004	1,403.1 (estimated)

Source: Snapshots International

In 2003, the UK sales of computer games software and hardware combined were £1,198 million against traditional toy sales of £1,788.4 million.

Divisions of multinational corporations such as Electronic Arts, Sony and Microsoft Xbox have significant leisure software development operations in the United Kingdom, reflecting the available pool of creative and technical talent. There are some 200 development houses across the United Kingdom, which places the United Kingdom in the vanguard of creativity and innovation.

Among the key players, Electronic Arts has located the headquarters of its European operations at Chertsey, employing nearly 500 people in a state-of-the-art games development studio designed by Sir

Norman Foster. More recently, it has established a second development studio in the North West at Warrington as a centre of excellence for its Formula 1 and other racing games.

In 2002, Sony launched 'The Getaway', created by an in-house development studio. This innovative game, which mapped Central London accurately, blurred the boundaries between computer games and film.

Music

The United Kingdom is renowned for consistently producing original and stimulating music as well as having one of the world's largest live music industries. The industry comprises composition, publishing, musical instruments and related equipment, classical and non-classical performance, recording, manufacturing, retailing and distribution, and education. The DCMS estimated that the music sector, including the visual and performing arts, contributed US$5 billion to the economy in 2001 with an export sales value of US$462.1 million. In the sub-sector of music publishing, the United Kingdom is the fourth largest in the world with a 9.8 per cent share of international revenues from sheet music sales, royalties and performance rights.

The performing arts

The performing arts include theatre and musical theatre, opera, ballet and contemporary dance. Investment is made in production and into developing new work. In the United Kingdom much of the funding for the latter comes from the regional arts councils.

Assigning value to the performing arts sector is difficult as it overlaps with other creative industries sectors, in particular with opera and theatre music. In evaluating GVA, the DCMS treats music and performing arts as a single sector and estimates that they contributed US$14.1 billion (£8.7 billion) to GVA in 2001.

The London West End theatres, opera and ballet are world famous and there is a strong base of regional theatres and companies. Of the many regional festivals the best known is the annual Edinburgh Festival.

Publishing

In addition to the four traditional sub-sectors of books, learned journals, newspapers and magazines, publishing now encompasses electronic publishing via the internet and other electronic media such as CD ROMs. In particular, the United Kingdom has generated some leading publishers in the specific fields of academic, business, education and scientific publishing. Excluding electronic publishing, the industry contributed US$14.1 billion (£8.7 billion) to GVA in 2001. The industry employs 292,500 people in 6,700 businesses.

Software and computer services

The software sector is treated separately in Chapter 3.12 as an industry sector in its own right.

Television and radio

As at June 2002, approximately 110,400 people were employed in TV and radio by 3,600 businesses. Their combined contribution to GVA in 2001 was US$11.6 billion (£7.2 billion), representing 1.1 per cent of total GDP and a 21 per cent increase on the previous year. The annual value of export sales was US$1,434 million (£889 million). The key growth sector in UK television and radio is digital broadcasting, in which the United Kingdom is a world leader and has introduced digital services via satellite, cable and terrestrial broadcasting.

In television, the government is encouraging its development strongly and has set itself the ambitious target of replacing 45–50 million analogue TV sets by 2010. The sector has generated the world's first multi-broadcaster, multiplexed DVB-based terrestrial broadcasting services, offering improved picture quality and numerous channels without subscription. By the end of the first quarter of 2003, 43.9 per cent of UK households, numbering 10.8 million, were accessing digital television, of which more than one and a quarter million are estimated to have digital terrestrial television.

Using the United Kingdom as a test bed for digital broadcasting technology, Japanese manufacturers such as Hitachi and Sony have consequently pioneered the introduction of idTV (integrated digital TVs) in the United Kingdom. This testing is important to the further development of the digital TV market. Analogue services will not be switched off until everybody who currently has access to them (more than 90 per cent of the population) can access free-to-view digital services. Other Japanese companies have chosen the United Kingdom as the location for their R&D centres and are establishing joint ventures with UK companies and universities.

In radio, there are more than 100 different brands broadcasting digitally in the United Kingdom and Northern Ireland. Listeners in the United Kingdom can generally receive between 30 and 50 stations on a digital radio, about double the availability on analogue. Multiplexes have on average eight or nine slots. The total number of digital radios sold by the end of 2003 was estimated to have been close to 500,000. The United Kingdom is said to be about 18 months to two years ahead of the rest of the world.

More information on digital broadcasting is available on the internet at the Digital Radio Development Bureau: http://www.drdb. org and The World Forum for DAB: http://www.worlddab.org.

2004/05 at the Royal Opera House

At the core of the 2004/05 season are two big names: Ashton and Wagner. To mark the centenary of the birth of Sir Frederick Ashton – Founder Choreographer of the Royal Ballet – the Royal Ballet is planning an exciting celebration, bringing to the main stage a wide array of Ashton's work.

2004 marks the beginning of a new *Ring*, a journey that will occupy us over the next two seasons before culminating in the full cycle in autumn 2007. Wagner's masterpiece will be conducted by Antonio Pappano, directed by Keith Warner and designed by Stefanos Lazaridis.

The season will also bring new productions of *Werther*, *Don Pasquale*, *Ballo in Maschera* and *Turco in Italia*, as well as La Scala's *Forza del destino* conducted by Riccardo Muti. For the third year the House will be staging a world premier of a new opera on the main stage – this year Lorin Maazel's *1984* conducted by the composer.

ROH_2, based around the alternative performing spaces in the House, aims to extend the range of work performed in the House and to allow artists, both those within the House and from partner organizations, to use the spaces to experiment with and develop new ideas. Both roles are crucial for any artistic institution, but especially so for one that is part funded by the public purse. For example, this year there are six chamber operas planned. They range from a world premiere of Nigel Osbourne's *The Piano Tuner* to Tippett's *The Knot Garden* and nine works written by black British composers.

Tony Hall, Chief Executive, is keen to make the Opera House a place where anyone and everyone can come, feel welcome and enjoy world-class opera and ballet. Central to this is a commitment to keep seats as affordable as possible. Next season, for the fourth year running, half the seats for every performance will be held at £50 or less. Together with the BP Big Screen relays around the country and live TV broadcasts, over 5 million people will have the opportunity to engage and experience the House this year.

3.5

Electronics Sector

Jonathan Reuvid

The UK electronics industry

With a total domestic market of US$160 billion (£100 billion), the United Kingdom's electronics industry is now the world's fifth largest producer and employed 428,600 people in 2002. Overall, the total value of the market increased by 35.7 per cent between 1997 and 2001.

The manufacturing workforce is dispersed within 7,545 companies ranging from the huge operations of multinationals to dynamic start-ups working on next generation technologies. A further 130,000 people are employed in that part of the software and services sector related to electronic applications.

The majority of electronics manufacturers are engaged in computer hardware, control and instrumentation products and communications equipment. For original equipment manufacturers (OEMs), the UK market for electronic equipment, with sales of US$13 million (£8.1 billion) from domestic production, provides a solid base for expansion into exports.

In 2002, the UK computer hardware market grew by 4.1 per cent to reach a value of US$13,425 billion (£8.4 billion) and accounted for 17.1 per cent of the European market, making it the second largest in Europe. The world demand for computer hardware is equivalent to approximately US$378 billion (£235 billion) so that the United Kingdom accounts for less than 5 per cent.

In 2001, the electronics component market was valued at approximately US$7.6 billion (£4.7 billion) and is predicted to grow to US$10.7 billion (£6.6 billion) by 2005. There are outstanding support services for the electronics industry in the United Kingdom, reflected in its long history of engineering innovation and its well-established technical support networks. Component suppliers work to the most exacting quality assurance standards with guaranteed delivery, while the United Kingdom's defence sector has generated specialist high-tech suppliers.

Regional dispersion

In Scotland the electronics industry provides up to 90,000 direct jobs and accounts for approximately 10 per cent of Scotland's economy. The Electronics Design Realisation Centre in the Scottish Borders aims to deliver 700 new and up-skilled printed circuit board designers by 2007.

Wales also has a strong electronics industry, led by overseas investment, with approximately 300 active companies. Foremost in the Welsh electronics industry is Sony, which set up its first UK plant in Bridgend in 1973 and now employs 4,500 people producing up to 10,000 television sets a day and key components for the world's leading electronics companies. The technology centre at Pencoed houses one of the most active digital research and development groups within the Sony Corporation as well as manufacturing integrated receiver decoders and colour televisions. Over 85 per cent of Sony's Welsh production is exported.

There is also a burgeoning electronics sector in Yorkshire and Humberside in the region's digital cluster. Electronics contribute US$4,800 million (£3,000 million) to the regional economy with US$2,400 million (£1,500 million) gross value-added from a workforce of approximately 24,000. The digital cluster is expected to grow 50 per cent by 2012. The overarching not-for-profit body responsible for networking activities between the region's electronic engineering companies is Electronics Yorkshire Ltd (EYL). Medium and large electronics enterprises employing more than 200 people are concentrated in Leeds, Sheffield, Bradford and York.

Nearly one-fifth of the top UK electronic engineers are based in the Yorkshire and Humberside region's universities. The University of York houses the EMC testing company and the York Electronics Centre carries out applied research and product development for industrial organizations. The Electronic Design Centre is based at the Barnsley Business Innovation Centre (BBIC) and the Bradford-based Electronics Yorkshire Centre of Excellence contains facilities that enable the region to train technicians and designers in the latest manufacturing and assembly techniques. BBIC is also home to the regional Yorkshire Electronics Design Engineers (YEDEC), a group of electronic designers and consultants.

Pre-eminent in the development of the United Kingdom's electronics industry is the cluster of high-tech companies around Cambridge University where vital links between academia and business have been forged. The Cambridge experience is described in detail in Chapter 2.8 – Technology and Innovation.

The United Kingdom's electronic strengths

The United Kingdom has the industrial design, manufacturing, planning and interpersonal skills in place to take products from the original concept through all stages of development to high-volume production. The United Kingdom's greatest strength is its leading-edge R&D, aided by close links with academia referred to above and in Chapter 2.8. The diverse experience and skills pervade the entire electronics spectrum.

UK electronics component manufacturers have a traditional strength in the design and production of bespoke components and sub-assemblies, especially for the defence and aerospace markets, which are low-volume, high-value market sectors requiring a highly skilled engineering base and well-educated workforce.

Proven world-class expertise in applications design has put the United Kingdom at the forefront of areas such as: systems integrated circuits; printed circuits (digital, analogue and mixed); higher frequency (HF) techniques; systems-on-chip (SoC) techniques; display technology and fibre optic components.

In electronics systems, including digital video, cellular communications, wireless communications, avionics systems, automotive systems and financial systems, the United Kingdom plays a leading design role.

Areas of excellence

The strength and maturity of the industry in the United Kingdom has helped develop numerous centres of excellence and innovation. There are 64 science parks offering excellent R&D facilities, including state-of-the-art telecommunications links and a range of incentives and other benefits for new entrants.

The United Kingdom leads the world in optoelectronics. Light emitting polymer displays were invented at Cambridge in the 1990s and university research-led companies around the United Kingdom have developed new products in solid-state lasers, single chip video cameras, dense wavelength division (DVD) components for telecoms networks, ophthalmic equipment and helmet mounted displays for pilots.

The United Kingdom is also a world leader in the development of new flat panel display technologies, in which indigenous companies such as CDT and inward investors such as Sharp have major operations.

In independent semiconductor design the United Kingdom holds 40 per cent of Europe's revenues with 40 per cent of the design houses. ARM Holdings is Europe's largest chipless supplier and ARM-designed chips, found in 70 per cent of the world's mobile phone handsets, are being incorporated into new generations of handheld computers.

Major investors in electronics

Leading global information technology companies have chosen the United Kingdom as their European operations hub and the continuous investment by overseas manufacturers has supported the United Kingdom's competitive position. Major electronics companies with UK manufacturing plants include: Compaq, Ericsson, Fujitsu, Samsung, Sharp, Sony and Toshiba. Other manufacturing companies that have flocked to the United Kingdom are: Agilent, Alcatel, Atmel, Bookham, Celestica, Filtronic, IQE, International Rectifier, Motorola, National Semiconductor, Nortel, Phillips, Raytheon, Solectron and Zetex.

Many of these companies including Atmel Microelectronics, Hitachi, Motorola, Phillips and ST Microelectronics have been active in setting up R&D bases in the country. Others such as Cisco, Cypress Semiconductor, Marconi, Mittel, NEC and Newbridge Networks have established design and development centres in the United Kingdom.

Government support

The Electronics Industries Directorate of the Department of Trade and Industry (DTI) supports the UK electronics and broadcasting industries (website: www.dti.gov.uk/industries/electronics). Financial support is available from the following programmes, which are described in Chapter 4.3 Development and Business Support Agencies:

- Foresight;

- LINK;

- EUREKA;

- EU's Sixth Framework Programme (FP6).

In addition, the DTI, together with other government departments and the research councils, support innovative R&D through mechanisms such as the Teaching Company Scheme (TCS), which encourages transfer of knowledge between the UK research community and industry by placing high-quality graduates (TCS Associates) in a partner company on specified technology transfer projects, normally for a period of two years.

Trade and professional associations

Intellect
Tel: +44 (0) 20 7331 2000
Fax: +44 (0) 20 7331 2040
Website: www.intellectuk.org

National Microelectronics Institute (NMI)
Tel: +44 (0) 1506 472 220
Fax: +44 (0) 1596 463 270
E-mail: nmi.info@nmi.org.uk
Website: www.nmi.org.uk

Joint Equipment and Materials Initiative (JEMI UK)
Tel: +44 (0) 131 650 7815
Fax: +44 (0) 131 650 7475
Website: www.jemiuk.com

Institute of Electrical Engineers (IEE)
Tel: +44 (0) 20 7240 1871
Fax: +44 (0) 20 7240 8830
Website: www.iee.org

3.6

Electronic Commerce

BT eLocations

The times are e-changing

So much has been written about electronic business and commerce and its impact on businesses worldwide. From online banking and shopping through to business-to-business transactions crossing continents, virtually all business today is e-business, with very few companies not trading in some form over the internet. Electronic commerce, however, continues to remain a relatively new phenomenon. It is only through a legal framework, which will encourage technology developments, technology innovators, an understanding of the barriers that remain and an agreement that all investment parties must embrace the new changes, that electronic commerce can continue to grow as part of today's business fabric. Today, the United Kingdom is making electronic commerce a central and practical means of doing business.

Support from the top

For electronic commerce to work, it is clear that there needs to be support from the top – a government committed to a deregulated telecommunications infrastructure and with the vision of a knowledge-driven economy delivered by electronic communications and electronic business. This is clearly the case in the United Kingdom today. From the office of the e-Envoy, based in the Cabinet Office with the mandate of ensuring that all government services are available electronically, through to the continued push for nationwide coverage for broadband services, there are few governments in the world so ambitious in their electronic vision. Furthermore, despite there being potential barriers in conducting electronic business throughout Europe – for example, different national legal provisions for electronic invoicing, or a different legal treatment of online and offline business – the European Commission is aware and addressing these issues. Enterprise Commissioner for the EU, Erkki Liikanen, offered words of encouragement recently: 'The EU legal framework for e-business is well and widely established. It's now time to take stock of remaining barriers and decide how to remove them.'

The United Kingdom's online annual report

The results of the fourth UK online annual report, released in December 2003, speak for themselves. Ninety-six per cent of the UK population are aware of a place where they can readily access the internet; UK electronic commerce transactions across the internet exceeded £23 billion in 2002; and broadband take-up continues to increase, with more than 3 million people having subscribed by November 2003 and 80 per cent of the population now having access to broadband enabled exchanges. A report by Booz Allen Hamilton (BAH) also found in November 2002 that the United Kingdom's environment for e-commerce was second only to the United States.

Whether it be UK companies investing domestically or international companies deciding on expanding overseas, the United Kingdom and its proficiency in electronic commerce has become a critical selling point.

The right infrastructure – telecommunications

The cornerstone of any successful electronic commerce strategy has to be its telecommunications. With 18,000 overseas companies currently operating in the United Kingdom and many of them linked to the internet economy, can the country's infrastructure cope with the huge demand in multimedia communications and transactions? In all these cases, the answer is most definitely 'yes'.

As a result of the early privatization of telecommunications, the United Kingdom today has the most advanced telecommunications network in Europe with widespread roll-out of broadband and 3G technologies, among others. Today, 8 out of 10 of the world's top telecommunications companies operate in the United Kingdom. And it is the technical innovators that will ensure that such progress continues. BT's world-renowned research and development site at Adastral Park near Ipswich is committed to consolidating the United Kingdom's position as a leader in telecommunications. Current research projects include further development of broadband technology and systems, a wealth of electronic business research including e-business payment and security systems, and a futuristic view of how communications will shape our business and personal lives in years to come.

The right infrastructure – business property

Not only is the telecommunications infrastructure already widely available but it is now starting to be pre-incorporated into business premises nationwide. The development of a state-of-the-art telecommunications infrastructure is seen as much a requirement for property landlords and business park owners today as electricity, water or air-conditioning. Take BT's specialist BT eLocations' portfolio of 60 pre-equipped business parks throughout the United Kingdom. The ability to conduct high-speed multimedia communications and e-business has become a central benefit of the sites.

From some of the world's leading science parks to city centre locations and edge of town business parks, all sites have an exceptional state-of-the-art optical fibre network infrastructure, including broadband communications; Internet Protocol (IP) technology hosting and applications; mobility solutions; next generation switching; and enhanced exchange capacity sufficient to cope with a company's ongoing communications demands. The result is a cost-effective resilient, high-speed and high bandwidth communications infrastructure, customized to the company's specific business requirements.

A sector approach

The growth of electronic commerce is also changing how certain sectors operate in the United Kingdom and it is innovators in the telecommunications industry that are meeting the new challenges.

Take the gaming industry, for example. New legislation, due before the UK parliament in 2004, is expected to transform the sector. The bill will enable companies to open high technology Las Vegas-style casinos throughout the country, to install large numbers of slot and electronic gaming machines, and enable online gaming operators to set up online sites in the United Kingdom provided they are licensed.

BT's Adastral Park has developed sophisticated ICT solutions to meet these particular needs, from electronic customer relationship management (eCRM) solutions; biometric and internet protocol security products; mobility solutions to allow customer remote access to casinos and online gaming; and secure online payment services.

In other sectors as diverse as financial services, creative media services, biotechnology, health care, pharmaceuticals and automotive, the telecommunications industry has developed specific technology solutions, products and services to meet proposed sector changes – all initiated through electronic commerce.

The UK case for outsourcing

The United Kingdom continues to provide a natural home to outsourcing in the electronic commerce sector, whether it is through either inbound or outbound call centres or a complete outsourcing of telecommunications and ICT services. In this way, overheads can be reduced, staff freed up and business productivity increased. According to a recent survey by UK magazine *Computer Weekly*, well-managed outsourcing can boost a company's share price by over 5 per cent. And, despite the continued publicity of companies looking to outsource to countries such as India and the Philippines, the United Kingdom continues to offer a compelling case for outsourcing investment. For example, there is the United Kingdom's multi-lingual resource with over 400,000 economically active foreign nationals in the Greater London area alone speaking over 200 languages.

EU labour legislation also allows for easy cross-border recruitment, enabling pan-European operators to advertise and recruit direct from mainland Europe. There is the resilient and secure telecommunications infrastructure, essential for high-value, outsourcing operations. And finally, there is the fact that the United Kingdom is a mature market with a proven track record in outsourcing and the destination of choice for investment into the European Union.

Creating a 'secure' environment

The potential dangers to electronic commerce have never been better illustrated by the growing wave of electronic attacks – viruses, hacking, denial of service attacks or electronic fraud. Furthermore, one must not forget the physical threats – terrorism, fire, flood, theft and power cuts. To address business continuity and allow electronic commerce to grow uninterrupted, the United Kingdom has brought security and business continuity to the top of the agenda. Furthermore, the United Kingdom government is continuing to urge UK-based businesses to adopt the new internationally agreed Organisation for Economic Co-operation and Development (OECD) guidelines on information security as well as setting up its own Security and Authentication Unit. Current initiatives include supporting Cabinet Office proposals to introduce the information security standard BS7799, sponsoring security technology research (CESG) and providing security guidance to UK businesses. The result is increased trust in electronic business.

The 'electronic business capital' of Europe

Digital business is changing the way we work and communicate. It is not only about improving existing business methods, but creating and establishing new channels and approaches that were not possible before electronic commerce.

The outstanding business locations and communications infrastructure the UK offers, the support from central government, the increased focus on security, the strong business case for outsourcing, and technology innovators that customize their products and services for different sectors, are all reasons why the United Kingdom will remain the 'electronic business capital of Europe' for many years to come. For further information on BT and the BT eLocations programme, visit the website at www.bt.com/btelocations or contact elocations@bt.com.

Case Study: Appian Graphics in the e-commerce capital of Europe

Appian Graphics is headquartered in Redmond, Washington, in the United States. Appian Graphics is the market leader for Xtended Desktop Solutions™, designing, manufacturing and marketing hardware, software and technology to improve productivity of the professional user by extending the desktop area and offering the attachment of multi-display devices.

Since its foundation in 1994 Appian Graphics has grown to dominate the multiple monitor industry. The company sells its multiple monitor solutions in over 35 countries worldwide through distributors, dealers, value-added resellers (VARs) and original equipment manufacturers (OEMs).

While having a strong foothold in the United States and a growing customer base abroad, Appian Graphics was keen to get closer to its customers in Europe, the Middle East and Africa. The company chose London. Kenneth Collingbourne-Smith, Managing Director of Appian Graphics Europe, explains the reasons:

> London is the electronic commerce capital of Europe. Its excellence in higher education; its well-trained workforce of 9 million; and its transportation network made London the ideal location.

> We needed a flexible office base; the latest communications infrastructure, which could potentially offer future web hosting facilities; and a location which could draw on the very best in IT skills. It was at this stage that we started to draw on the skills and expertise of BT.

Once office space had been sourced, BT's eLocations team went into action, developing a suitable communications infrastructure to meet the needs of this growing and innovative company. Today, the Appian Graphics Europe office in London is providing sales, marketing, operational and technical support for distributors, resellers and its OEM customers throughout Europe, the Middle East, and Africa.

Case Study: The International Financial Services District in Glasgow – e-enabled for the future

There are few more competitive and crowded markets in the United Kingdom today than the finance sector. Increased competition; the need for mission-critical telecommunications solutions and lower cost delivery systems; the customer always looking for a better deal; the demand for ever more innovative products; and the importance of being first to market, pose huge challenges to any finance company investing in the United Kingdom.

The Glasgow-based International Financial Services District (IFSD) is a finance-specific, pre-equipped business area designed for global finance firms. Partners include BT eLocations, Scottish Development International, Scottish Finance Enterprise and Scottish Enterprise Glasgow. Customers that have already invested in the district include global financial services firms Morgan Stanley and JP Morgan Chase.

Key highlights of the IFSD, and of particular benefit to e-commerce-focused companies, include:

- an exceptional state-of-the-art network infrastructure, including high-speed internet access; web-enabled customer contact centres; internet data centre applications; next generation switching technology; and resilient fibre ducts and exchange capacity, sufficient to cope with finance company demands;
- a resilient telecommunications infrastructure with enhanced dual optical fibre capacity; and
- web hosting solutions, with BT operating an Internet Data Centre in Glasgow, offering a complete range of web hosting facilities to investors in a 24/7, secure environment.

3.7

Financial Services

Kevin Smith, AWS Structured Finance

A brief overview

The financial services sector in the United Kingdom is, very rightly, seen to be one of the most important and most advanced financial markets anywhere in the world. Not only is it one of the world's oldest financial services markets but it also has a worldwide reputation for impartiality and integrity. Given its size and global importance it is not surprising that it is also of great significance to the UK economy as a whole. Indeed, the financial services sector in the City of London contributes around £17 billion to the United Kingdom's balance of payments, which is a respectable part of the total GDP each year.

Not only does the United Kingdom as a whole have an enviable reputation for the size and quality of the financial services companies that operate here, but the very words 'City' or 'City of London' are synonymous with the world's leading location for the financial services sector.

The statistics are impressive and the reach and depth of the markets can start to be understood when it is appreciated that there are more US banks in the City than there are in New York, or that each of the world's top 20 insurance companies operate in London or, indeed, that 375 of the top 500 global companies have offices in London. All these firms understand the importance of the UK market as a whole and the pre-eminence of the financial markets in the City of London.

In this age of sophisticated communication it is often argued that a local presence is not required, but the banks, traders, investment funds, insurers, shipping brokers, accountants, lawyers and all the other parts of the financial services sector that congregate in the United Kingdom and primarily in the City of London, create a critical mass that is not seen anywhere else in the world.

It is a dynamic place, ever-changing and evolving in order to ensure its place at the forefront of new developments, but at the same time its solidity and permanence is one of the many attractions for companies establishing a presence or investing in the United Kingdom.

The United Kingdom in general, but London more specifically, also has extremely good international flight connections. With over 170 flights each day going to countries that generate more than 80 per cent of the world's GDP and over 230 international destinations in total, more than 90 million people use London's airports each year. Yet another reason for investing in the United Kingdom.

Banks

The exact number of banks in the City varies, declining as banks merge and rationalize operations and increasing as other banks grow and expand their international presence, but at the last count there were some 450 banks operating in London, of which more than 300 were foreign owned. Indeed, almost 100 of the banks with offices in London are from other EU countries.

Foreign banks in the City manage more than US$3,000 billion on behalf of foreign clients and the volume of international lending is more than twice as high as in the United States or Germany. Consequently, more syndicated loans are completed in London than anywhere else in the world. As such, companies from around the world looking to raise large debt facilities approach the markets in London rather than the less developed markets in their home country.

The fact that the United Kingdom is not part of the Eurozone has had no impact on the markets despite predictions from some that the United Kingdom needed to convert to the euro in order to ensure the continued success of the City. Indeed, statistics show that if anything the City has prospered even more since the Eurozone was established. Eurobonds now account for the majority of bond issues, about 60 per cent of them originate in London and about 70 per cent of the secondary market in bonds is in London. Despite the euro's rise, most foreign exchange deals worldwide are still in US dollars but London still dominates the foreign exchange markets. Daily transactions total some US$637 billion and represent about one in three of all foreign exchange transactions worldwide, making the London market nearly twice the size of the nearest rival, the United States.

Mergers and acquisitions and other investment bank activities are centred on London, with many European and US banks having large operations reflecting the level of business. Often, regional head offices are based in London and cover areas as wide as Europe (Western, Central and Eastern), Africa and the Middle East. Investment bankers providing advice on matters such as privatization in the emerging markets of Central Europe, and other countries worldwide are often based in London even if they are working for large US investment banks.

It is a similar story with trade and project finance, with many foreign banks centring their trade and project finance departments in London rather than in their home countries. Not only is there more expertise and activity in London than any other centre but also the high level of deal origination leads to more opportunities for all. The secondary markets (where banks buy and sell existing debt and trade finance paper among themselves) are also centred on London. The ever-growing presence around the world of public private partnership structures to utilize private sector capital to finance public sector services is another area that is driven by the concentration of experience in the United Kingdom and the financial services expertise in the City of London.

Capital markets

The London Stock Exchange is also pre-eminent among the world's stock exchanges, with more foreign equities listed in London than on any other of the world's exchanges, with turnover in these companies accounting for 58 per cent of the world's trading in foreign companies, which is almost twice as much as the nearest rival.

London is the leading fund management centre in the world with more than £2,550 billion of assets under management. Not only is London way ahead of New York in this respect but also more funds are invested in the City than in the next 10 European centres combined. Another leading centre of fund management expertise (and life insurance companies) in the United Kingdom is Edinburgh.

There are private equity investors and venture capital funds based around the United Kingdom. Many of these are specialist funds catering for specific sectors and are based near the centres of expertise in the respective sectors, for example, a number of locations such as Oxford and Cambridge boast a cluster of funds and these tend to specialize in sectors such as high technology, biotechnology and the like, but the majority of investment funds are based in London. Tax breaks exist in the United Kingdom to encourage private investors to put money into equity funds and other capital market instruments but even more generous tax breaks exist to encourage private investors to invest in Venture Capital Trusts, which are funds that specialize in investing private equity into start-up and early stage opportunities (see Chapter 2.7).

Insurance

The world's first insurance market was Lloyd's of London and it is still the best-known name in the industry, especially for any unusual or bespoke insurance requirements. For example, space rockets and satellites are often insured here and many famous musicians and film stars use Lloyd's to insure their fingers, face, legs and many other parts of the body. Lloyd's specializes in aviation and marine insurance and it is the global market leader in these sectors. Again, the sheer number and diversity of insurance companies and brokers, both UK and foreign, clustered together in the area adjacent to Lloyd's makes the insurance market in the United Kingdom unique.

The United Kingdom insurance industry is not only the largest in Europe but it is the third largest in the world. In 1998 the value of insurance sold in London was £123 billion and this generated gross premiums of £14 billion and by 2003 Lloyd's of London alone accepted insurance premiums of £14.4 billion, demonstrating the continued rise of these markets.

The UK life and pensions market is twice the size of that of the nearest European rivals and each day pays out over £140 million of benefits, which is more than the UK government.

Other markets

The United Kingdom is also home to a range of other leading financial service markets such as metal trading, derivatives, ship chartering and the professional services such as accountants, consultants and lawyers that are an integral part of a fully functioning market.

The London Metal Exchange transacts over 90 per cent of the world's traditional metal trading and, separately, some 36 per cent of the world turnover of derivative products is handled in London. The 2,000 members of the Baltic Exchange in London transact about 50 per cent of the worldwide tanker chartering business, about 40 per cent of worldwide dry-bulk business and more than 50 per cent of new and second-hand tonnage is sold through brokers in London.

All the large accountancy firms have offices in London, employing thousands of people and, as with the banking sector, many regional head offices or sector specialist teams are based in the United Kingdom, drawing on the high degree of local expertise and attracting other experts from markets worldwide. The accountancy firms based in the United Kingdom are leaders in providing not just accounting and auditing services but also consultancy and advisory services around the world.

Five of the 15 largest law firms worldwide are City firms and more than 60 US law firms have London offices. Given the importance of the UK market and the international expertise in London, law firms from around the world have offices here. In more recent years London has become a centre for arbitration (reducing the time and costs involved in settling international contractual disputes), drawing on the expertise of the large number of law firms with operations in the United Kingdom and the worldwide reputation of English law and the impartiality of the whole of the judicial system. Indeed English law is normally the law of choice in transactions between international parties operating under different jurisdictions.

The Financial Services Authority (FSA) is the regulator of all the financial services in the United Kingdom (see Chapter 5.5) and has a worldwide reputation for striking a good balance between being sufficiently strong to ensure the integrity of the markets while being sufficiently flexible so as to ensure that competition and growth in the markets is not hindered. There is a constant demand from other regulators around the world to visit the FSA in order to learn from their expertise.

Summary

One of the strengths of the financial services sector in the United Kingdom is that it draws on expertise from around the world and its size and reputation acts as a magnet for individuals and companies wanting to take part in and benefit from its dynamism. In London alone there are resident communities (of more than 10,000 people) from 33 different countries and over 300 different languages are spoken.

The level of expertise, together with the strength and depth of the market, are a compelling reason for many companies to invest in the United Kingdom but even if this is not the primary reason for the investment decision, the quality of the financial services sector can only increase opportunities for inward investors and enhance a decision to invest based on other reasons.

3.8

Food and Drink

Jonathan Reuvid

Introduction

The quiet revolution

As in other highly developed consumer markets, the food and drink sector has undergone a quiet revolution through a steady progression in consumer attitudes and tastes over the past two or three decades. In food, there has been a slow but steady move away from traditional British foods such as fish and chips to more exotic cuisines and foods derived from continental Europe and further afield, such as Asia in particular. Many of these foods have been marketed on the basis of their health and convenience benefits.

While the provenance of quality foods has become highly prized, partly as a result of health considerations and requirements of weight loss through dieting, convenience foods that cater for a time-strapped society have gained an ever-growing share of the market. At the same time, the demand for convenience foods has been fuelled by the advent of microwave cookers, which substitute for conventional cooking methods, and an extensive range of chilled and frozen packaged meals.

Regional branding of food and drink

The United Kingdom has an abundance of regions producing premium quality foods and drinks and has maintained most of its traditional branding. Famous names include Cheddar cheese, Cornish mackerel, Cromer crabs, Devon clotted cream, Gordon's gin, Melton Mowbray pork pies, Newcastle Brown Ale, Scotch whisky, Stilton cheese and Whitstable oysters. More recently, the Prince of Wales, under his title of Duke of Cornwall, has garnered significant revenue for his charities through the introduction of 'Duchy Original' branded produce from his estates.

The restaurant scene

The United Kingdom now rejoices in a thriving restaurant industry that includes almost every exotic international cuisine imaginable. The United Kingdom is also at the forefront of movements towards organic products and fusion foods, which 'fuse' elements of several world cuisines.

Serious culinary talents, which have led the way in the continuing evolution of the United Kingdom's gastronomic culture, include the well-established Raymond Blanc, Jamie Oliver, Gordon Ramsey and Rick Stein, together with a host of rising stars.

Market overview

The food and drink industry accounted for 15 per cent of the entire UK manufacturing sector in 2003. More than 500,000 people were employed in 7,535 food and drink enterprises throughout the country. The total turnover of the food and drink manufacturing sector in 2003 was £67.6 billion. The industry bought two-thirds of all the United Kingdom's agricultural products.

In 2002, the total spent on retail food and non-alcoholic drinks in the United Kingdom was valued at US$97.9 billion (£61.2 billion) by the Office of National Statistics, while catering sales totalled US$61.7 billion (£38.6 billion). Alcoholic drink sold in the take-home or off-trade added US$17.6 billion (£11 billion) to retail sales and alcoholic drinks sold through pubs and clubs amounted to US$43.9 billion (£27.4 billion), bringing the total sales of alcoholic drinks up to US$61.5 billion (£38.4 billion). In 2003, total consumer spending on food and drink was £145.2 billion, representing 21 per cent of all consumer expenditure.

Table 3.8.1 UK retail sales of food and drink 1998–2003

	Food	Non-alcoholic Drink	Total
	(£m)	(£m)	(£m)
1998	80,089	7,877	89,966
1999	82,234	7,660	89,894
2000	85,094	8,114	93,208
2001	90,100	8,486	98,586
2002	94,560	8,866	103,426
2003 (est.)	99,042	9,247	108,289

Source: Snapshots International

Retail sales

The growth in retail food and non-alcoholic drink sales from 1998 to 2003, as calculated by Snapshots International, is logged in Table 3.8.1 showing that sales at current prices from 2000 to the end of 2003 rose 16.3 per cent (20.5 per cent over the full six-year period).

The breakdown of 2002 retail sales by type of outlet is summarized in Table 3.8.2.

Table 3.8.2   Composition of 2002 UK retail sales by outlet type

	£m
Food & Predominantly Food Retailers	104,700
of which: Non-alcoholic Drinks & Vending Machines	10,140
Supermarkets	65,852
Other Grocery Outlets	28,708

Source: Snapshots International

Household expenditure

UK household expenditure on food and drink in the United Kingdom is analysed in Table 3.8.3, showing that the two categories accounting for the largest percentages of consumers' spending are meat and alcoholic beverages, followed by bread and cereals, vegetables and dairy products. Together, these products attracted 67.5 per cent of consumer expenditure on food and drink.

Table 3.8.3   UK household food and drink expenditure 2002

Sector	Value £m	% of Retail Expenditure
Meat	12,463	17.3
Alcoholic Beverages	10,995	15.2
Bread and Cereals	9,285	12.9
Vegetables	8,368	11.6
Milk, Cheese & Eggs	7,582	10.5
Sugar & Sweet Products	6,524	9.0
Water & Soft Drinks	6,023	8.3
Fruit	4,274	5.9
Fish	2,248	3.3
Coffee, Tea and Cocoa	1,773	2.5
Other Food Products	1,411	2.0
Oils & Fats	1,134	1.6

Source: Office for National Statistics (Consumer Trends)

Value-added food and drink

With 14,500 food and drink wholesalers, just over 68,000 active food and drink retailing businesses and 104,000 catering enterprises having 367,000 licensed catering premises, the United Kingdom has a highly competitive food chain. Against this distribution background, the United Kingdom is a world leader in value-added food and drink production and marketing and responds to the constant change in consumers' health and lifestyle needs and the demand for new products. The demand for some of the biggest new sellers in 2002 by product group is illustrated in Table 3.8.4.

Table 3.8.4 Key growth sectors for new sellers (2002)

	Value £m	% Growth
Flavoured Alcoholic Beverages	1,517	33.0
Frozen Snacks	66	24.1
Cereal Bars	139	22.8
Chilled Ready Meals	1,120	17.6
Frozen Meat Alternatives	81	17.1
Chilled Pasta	105	15.2
Dried Fruit & Fruit Snacks	114	15.0
Bottled Water	991	13.6
Canned Fish	362	13.4
Honey	41	11.9
Chilled Salads	734	11.3
Chilled Sauces	87	10.0

Source: Food and Drink Federation (FDF), Leatherhead Food International

Exports

In 2002, the United Kingdom food and drink industry exported US$14.2 billion (£8.9 billion) and in 2003 exports rose 10 per cent to US$15.7 billion (£9.8 billion). More than 60 per cent of the product sales were to fellow EU members. Table 3.8.5 provides an analysis of export sales by product group and main export region.

Table 3.8.5 UK food and drinks exports by product group and export zone 2001/02

	2001(£US$m)	2002 (US$m)	% Change
UK food and drink exports by product			
Meat/Dairy/Fish	2,835	2,998	6
Cereals	1,731	1,799	4
Fruit and Veg	634	687	8
Sugar/Tea/Coffee/Cocoa	1,516	1,491	(2)
All Other Groceries	1,663	1,888	14
Total Foods	8,379	8,863	6
Drinks	5,181	5,302	2
Total Foods & Drinks	13,560	14,165	4
UK food and drinks exports by zone			
EU	8,222	8,869	8
North America	1,563	1,678	7
Rest of the World	3,791	3,617	(4)
Total	13,576	14,164	4

Note: Bracketed figures denote losses.
Source: Food from Britain marketing consultancy

The drinks category alone accounts for more than two-thirds of total exports with meat/fish/dairy products and cereals being the two largest groups within food sales.

Major players

The United Kingdom is home to a wide range of food and drink companies, of which the largest are listed in Table 3.8.6. However, there are all sizes of enterprise in the 7,535 manufacturing businesses registered.

Cadbury Schweppes – the world's largest confectionery manufacturer, Diageo – the world's largest spirits manufacturer, and Compass – the world's largest catering contractor, are all headquartered in the United Kingdom. Other large international companies with manufacturing bases in the United Kingdom include:

- Nestlé;
- Kraft;
- Kellogg's;
- McCain;
- Heinz.

Table 3.8.6   Major UK food and drink manufacturers in 2002

	Companies	Turnover (US$m)
1	Unilever (Food)	25,759
2	Diageo	17,897
3	Cadbury Schweppes	8,405
4	Associated British Foods	7,245
5	Scottish & Newcastle	6,661
6	Tate & Lyle	6,257
7	Allied Domecq	5,289
8	Nestlé Holdings (UK)	3,217
9	Mars UK	3,047
10	RHM Group One	2,752
11	Northern Foods	2,314
12	United Biscuits (Invest)	2,037
13	Coca-Cola Enterprises	1,996
14	Grampian Country Food Group	1,900
15	Dairy Crest	1,880

Sources: The Grocer/OC&C Index, annual company reports

Market trends and outlook

The following are the main trends at play in the UK consumption of food and drink and the forward development of the industry:

- In 1950, the average UK household spent one-third of its income on food and non-alcoholic drink. By 2000, the proportion had fallen to one-sixth. Increased choice at reduced real prices has been a significant factor in improving UK living standards and the ability of the food industry to deliver this benefit has fed through to export markets.

- In the catering sector, Chinese takeaway and delivery, and pre-packaged sandwiches have supplanted fish and chip shops. Food pubs, Indian and Italian restaurants all show strong growth at the expense of burger houses.

- Home entertaining has moved towards less formal dining with premium ready-made meals becoming socially acceptable for dinner party hosting.

- The organic sector is the fastest growing in the UK retail food industry although the consumer remains reluctant to accept GM foods.

- Pressure on leisure time and improved premium product offerings have increased the appeal of ready-made food for shoppers.

- The pub-restaurant movement has enjoyed a revival. The UK government restriction of the early 1990s on the number of pubs that large breweries could own has made it possible for enterprising young chefs to buy rural pubs and convert them into restaurants.

- Mid-market value in the sector previously dominated by pizza chains has improved. UK consumers now have more choice in relatively cheap quality meals at sit-down restaurants with quick and friendly service.

- The growing UK taste for wines and coffees over the more traditional beers and teas is being satisfied by New World wines and own-brand supermarket products, which are displacing premium French wines with heavy discounting. However, the British are becoming more selective as a result of the wide range on offer.

- In the retail segment there is a move from frozen to chilled value-added products, particularly in ready meals. However, the same inroads on frozen products are not expected in the food service market.

- Thanks to increased food safety concerns, consumers are demanding full traceability from suppliers for all fresh groceries in the form of origin and content labelling on retailers shelves.

- UK health lobby groups are calling for tighter curbs on the marketing of sugary or fatty foods to children and of fast foods to adults for health and dietary reasons.

- The penetration of UK supermarkets' own-brand or private label products is significantly higher than anywhere else in the world, accounting for about 45 per cent of supermarket sales in the United Kingdom.

Overall, retail volumes of food and drink sold do not tend to vary widely from year to year, but their value continues to show strong growth. This growth is mainly due to the increased demand for premium and speciality foods rather than price increases in the United Kingdom's low inflation environment. Consumers are increasingly willing to spend extra for greater convenience or for foods that also offer additional health benefits.

Contacts in government and trade agencies for advice and support and in food research and development institutes are listed in Appendices II and III at the end of the book.

Gaming

David Kent, Inward Investment Group,
Taylor Wessing

Introduction

Las Vegas-style casino resorts in the United Kingdom? A few years ago this would have seemed impossible, but the UK government has spent a considerable amount of time reviewing and researching the concept in the United States and has undertaken its own review in the United Kingdom and gone out to consultation. This chapter examines the current proposals for new laws together with the opportunities that they will create.

The gaming divide between the United States and the United Kingdom

In the United States, there are now over 400 casinos. Casino revenue alone is said to be at least US$40 billion each year. Those casinos employ well over 400,000 people bringing job security to those involved. In the United Kingdom, because of the regulation, there are around 100 small casinos and they together with bingo clubs and small betting offices employ a fraction of the number of people employed in the United States. The concepts in the United States and the United Kingdom are currently very different due to the UK regulatory environment brought in during the 1960s, designed to protect the UK public.

Reports show that most British people gamble, indeed some 73 per cent of households gamble each year. However, overall spending in gambling equates to a mere £3.90 per household per year, the vast majority of which is spent on the National Lottery! The UK restrictions on club membership, the restrictions on alcohol and live performances, together with restrictions on numbers of slot machines and the prizes available have held back the UK gambling market dramatically when compared with the United States.

The Budd Report and subsequently

Her Majesty's government asked Sir Alan Budd to produce a report on the state of gambling in the UK in 1999. The review covered all aspects of UK gambling, which at that stage comprised mainly fixed odd betting, which was centred mainly on horses and greyhound racing, although in recent years it has moved to other sporting events, bingo, arcades, lotteries and competitions. The report also included a review of online betting and looked at the potential supply and support services to the gaming industry such as the supply of gaming machines.

After the Budd Report, the government produced a White Paper 'A Safe Bet for Success' in March 2002 based on the Budd recommendations and later that year a policy position paper on 'The Future Regulation of Remote Gambling'. These papers were followed in November 2003 with a draft Gambling Bill, although further clauses and draft legislation is expected after Easter 2004. The Gambling Bill covers all gaming apart from the National Lottery. The Gambling Bill, once enacted, will repeal all of the 1960s' legislation, in particular The Betting, Gaming and Lotteries Act 1963, The Gaming Act 1968 and The Lotteries and Amusements Act 1976.

Having worked through the figures, the government estimates that it can produce an additional £500 million each year for the next five years once its reforms in the Gambling Bill have taken effect.

What is proposed in the Gambling Bill

The set up of a Gambling Commission

There will be a new regulator called The Gambling Commission, which will regulate commercial gambling and will replace the existing regulator, The Gaming Board. The Secretary of State will appoint the commissioners of The Gambling Commission, but their functions will be independent. The Commission's objectives will be to control gambling by means of its powers of licensing in accordance with written objectives. The objectives will be the prevention of gambling from being a source of crime, from being associated with crime, or being used to support crime. The objectives will also ensure that gambling is conducted in a fair and open way and to protect children and other vulnerable persons from being harmed or exploited by gambling.

Gambling licences

The Commission's power will be the issuing of operating licences for commercial gambling and the issuing of personal licences to the individuals who are involved in the business of gambling. The licensing will cover casinos, betting, bingo and adult gaming centre operators. Licensing will also cover gaming machine manufacturers and suppliers of those machines, certain lottery operators and managers, Pools promoters and others offering gaming products through remote technologies including the Internet. This means that licences will be needed for all parts of the chain and in that way the government believes that the Commission will be able to regulate the whole gaming industry.

The Commission's powers will be to assess the integrity, financial standing and competence of applicants before granting an operating licence, they will assess criminal records and relevant information held by other bodies and where appropriate they will be able to attach conditions to licences and issue codes of practice. They will also monitor compliance with the licensing conditions and have powers to review, amend and revoke licences and to impose unlimited financial penalties.

Licensing premises for gambling

Obtaining a licence for premises for gambling will be achieved through the local licensing authority, which is currently and will remain the Magistrates Court. The Commission will issue guidance on the exercise of its powers under the Act to the Magistrates Court and the Secretary of State will set out licence fees, which will then be paid to The Gambling Commission. Under the existing law, a potential licence operator needs to prove 'unmet demand' in their chosen location and to ensure that it is within 'a permitted area' designated by local legislation before a licence can be granted. All of those constraints will be abandoned and regional planning bodies will, once the Act has been passed, work on plans for leisure developments of regional significance, that is, including plans for large casino resorts. Regional planning bodies will look to identify suitable locations that will maximize contribution to tourism and the economic development of their regions. In this regard, there has been substantial press coverage about the potential for a number of casinos in Blackpool, Manchester, Coventry and various London sites such as the Dome, Olympia, Battersea Power Station, King's Cross and Piccadilly, which have already been highlighted as potential areas for development.

Casinos

Casinos will no longer be required to be private clubs operating a 24-hour rule between membership and the ability to play. In addition, they will be able to offer any kind of legal gambling including betting, bingo and unlimited prize gaming machines linked within the individual premises to allow for a larger pooled prize. There will be a prohibition on casinos only providing gaming machines. No casino will be licensed unless it has a table area larger than 5,000 square feet and there will be a limit of no more than three gaming machines for each table game. There will be no limit for the number of gaming machines permitted in larger casinos (defined as over 10,000 square feet) as long as more than 40 table games are available.

Gaming machines

There will be a new licensing framework for gaming machines, which will be for adults only. Children will only be permitted to use amusements machines with the lowest stakes and prizes. Betting offices, bingo premises and betting tracks are going to be permitted to have a limited number of machines with prizes up to £500.

Betting

Betting tracks will be permitted to offer betting to adults over the age of 18 on non-race days and other rules will be relaxed.

Internet gambling

There are currently no rules providing for internet gambling in the United Kingdom. This is because the internet had not been devised at the time that the old legislation was drafted. The government would like to see internet gaming companies come to the United Kingdom, but it is acutely aware of the need for them to be competitive with those based offshore. Therefore, all internet gaming will be licensed in the United Kingdom.

Bingo

Bingo premises will no longer need to be members' clubs and subject to the 24-hour rule. There will be no limits on prizes for linked or multiple bingo subject to a licensing regime.

Lotteries

The laws on lotteries will be updated but the National Lottery Commission will continue to license the National Lottery under separate legislation.

General

A gambling debt will become a binding obligation and enforceable as such.

Timetable for the Bill

The timetable for the introduction of the Bill into the Houses of Parliament is not clear. Lord McIntosh of Haringey is said to have support from both main political parties, and it is said to be a priority of the Prime Minister. We shall therefore have to see if the Bill is introduced in the next session of parliament commencing September 2004, as is widely hoped.

The moral and religious view – helping the addict

The Methodist Church is said to have always been against gaming of all sorts. Its opposition in the United States to gaming is well documented. Its opposition to the Bill in the United Kingdom is expected although, no doubt, consultations with the Church and other pressure groups will continue throughout.

The American Gaming Association came to London in January 2004 to lecture and advise on the issues as it saw them. This Association was set up by the US casino operators to lobby in Washington, and to carry out independent research to address the issues and to document the benefits of casino gaming. Not surprisingly, in the Association's view, the economic benefits of casino gaming far exceed the social costs. More details about the Association can be found on its website: www.americangaming.org.

In recognition of these issues and with prompting from government, The Gambling Industry Charitable Trust was set up in 2003 by the UK gaming industry to research into the problems of gambling and to support treatment that would not otherwise be available through the National Health Service. The trust currently runs a 24-hour helpline and counselling. The government is considering whether to charge an annual levy on gambling operators as an additional charge to provide support for those in need of help, education and/or treatment.

The gaming opportunity in the United Kingdom

Gaming in the United Kingdom is now subject to unparalleled interest from gaming machine manufacturers and casino operators from all over the United States and Europe as well as the United Kingdom's homegrown industry. The United Kingdom provides a relatively untapped area where casino revenues could potentially provide enormous growth. This will probably take two forms. The first will be the acquisition of existing hotel and casino accommodation by larger groups, and its refurbishment and operation under the licences and guidelines of The Gambling Commission. The second but more delayed activity is potentially even more exciting. This involves the identification of key existing sites, and some brownfield sites away from main areas, for the licensing, planning, construction and operation of casino resorts combining shows, hotels and shopping malls, with very large casino premises and car parking.

It is said that in the United States, revenues from casino resorts are split 50/50 between the gambling and the non-gambling activities. The additional investment and employment that these new UK resorts bring will provide greater long-term prospects for the people involved.

It would appear that very little guidance is going to be given as to an overall number of casino resorts, in that in the end it will be the market itself that determines those that will survive and those that will fail. As and when the large casino operators come into the United Kingdom there will be an overall increase in the support companies and services companies involved in the sector. These will range from machine operators to software companies. The US operators have become excellent at tracking and keeping the punter in its resorts not only by means of the entertainment available but also by means of tracking software linked to personnel on the floor. Some casino owners are considering using tokens that track the punter throughout the complex; this is a very new industry indeed!

It will be interesting to see whether the UK public has really matured in its interest in gambling so that it immediately fills the casinos and other licensed gambling premises in accordance with the predicted growth curve. Maybe it will take a generation or half a generation for this to happen. After all, the failure of some of the online gambling companies set up in the Channel Islands, and the initial failures of Euro Disney, may give food for thought. What is certain, however, is that whether it is the year after the legislation comes through, or in subsequent years, so long as it is coupled with the promised but so far unidentified tax reforms, the gaming industry in the United Kingdom will become part of the overall entertainment and leisure scene in a big way.

3.10

Pharmaceuticals

Lilly

Nearly a quarter of the world's top 100 medicines were discovered and developed in the United Kingdom and almost 50 per cent of the top 25 medicines prescribed by GPs on the NHS are UK in origin. As well as helping to improve the nation's health, the pharmaceutical industry in the United Kingdom also makes a major contribution to its wealth through exports and as an employer. The industry is consistently in the top three for trade surplus – in 2003 it brought in a trading surplus of £3.6 billion.

Nearly £10 million per day is spent by the pharmaceutical industry on discovering and developing much-needed new medicines, making it the single largest investor in research and development in the United Kingdom. This contribution has not gone unnoticed. The government has now not only increased spending on science to its highest level for over a decade, but plans to introduce a long-term strategy to support UK science, the funding for which was announced in the July 2004 Comprehensive Spending Review (CSR).

As the Chancellor of the Exchequer, Gordon Brown, said in his March 2004 Budget Statement: '…we cannot be a strong economy if we are weak in education and science. So first on science and innovation, we will work with the scientific community and our science-based companies so that in this spending period we can raise the level of science funding as a share of national income, with one purpose: to make Britain the best and the most attractive location for science and innovation in the world.'

The announcement was timely, coming shortly after the Association of the British Pharmaceutical Industry (ABPI) published the results of an opinion poll that showed overwhelming support for the government to support medicines research and encourage pharmaceutical companies to invest in the United Kingdom. The survey, aimed at testing public perception of the industry, showed that around 90 per cent of people felt that the government should do more to help research into new medicines and to encourage investment in the country by pharmaceutical companies. 'Both the survey and the government's announcement are very encouraging because they show that there is a great deal of understanding about the importance of research and development into modern medicines,' says Andrew Hotchkiss, Managing Director of Lilly UK.

As a global and UK top 10 research-based pharmaceutical company, Eli Lilly and Company is a leader in providing innovative medicines and health information in many of the major disease areas, including cancer, mental health, diabetes, osteoporosis and heart disease. 'Last year we launched a treatment for erectile dysfunction and a ground-breaking treatment for osteoporosis that stimulates the formation of new bone,' Andrew reveals. 'During the next few years we plan to introduce new treatments for stress urinary incontinence, depression, attention deficit hyperactivity disorder, asbestos-related lung cancer and diabetic complications. Our company is in an unprecedented period of growth and the United Kingdom has, and we hope will continue to have, a major role to play in our global success story. This is why we took the decision last year to invest a further £220 million in our UK operations and, in turn, increase our workforce over the next two years.'

This investment further cements a relationship that goes back to 1934 when Lilly opened its first UK office. Lilly was founded in 1876 in Indianapolis in the United States, where the headquarters is still based. Now the company employs more than 43,000 people around the world, 2,500 of whom are in the United Kingdom, spanning research, manufacturing, sales and marketing.

The first Lilly manufacturing facility outside the United States was opened in Basingstoke, Hampshire, in 1939. It now produces over 50 million packs of medicines a year and exports to more than 100 countries. 'Lilly exports from the United Kingdom are worth over £1 billion annually, making us one of the top exporters,' says Andrew. 'In fact, Basingstoke has received the Queen's Award for International Trade on three occasions.'

There is a second Lilly manufacturing facility at Speke on Merseyside, the largest bulk biotechnology manufacturing site in the United Kingdom. Lilly Speke manufactures a human growth hormone and the antibiotic capreomycin. It is playing a major role as part of Lilly's global $70 million programme with the World Health Organization and other partners to combat multi-drug resistant tuberculosis (MDR-TB).

One of the world's leading antipsychotics for the treatment of schizophrenia and bipolar disorder was discovered at the Lilly Research Centre in Windlesham, Surrey. When it opened in 1967, it was Lilly's first R&D site outside the United States. Since then it has expanded steadily to become the company's European Centre of Excellence for neuroscience research. The first phase of a projected

£100 million expansion project that will create laboratory space for up to 120 additional scientists is underway. Both UK Trade & Investment and the South East England Development Agency (SEEDA) were instrumental in helping make this happen.

Lilly's decision to increase its investment in the United Kingdom is significant. Plans to launch several new drugs are a major factor but, as Andrew, points out, there are many reasons why it makes sense for pharmaceutical companies to invest in the United Kingdom: 'Lilly's business is based around people and the skills and capabilities of the people that we employ,' he says. 'We are fortunate enough to employ some of the world's top scientists and a good supply of high-quality science graduates is a major factor for Lilly. The supply of graduate scientists in the United Kingdom has been growing since the mid-1990s and the proportion of graduate scientists in the young adult labour force is higher here than in most other countries, with the exception of France.'

Similarly, Lilly's investment in Speke is being made because of the skills and capabilities of the workforce. Emphasizing this, Andrew reveals: 'Through good working practices – minimizing down time and eliminating errors – our staff at Speke increased production to 500 per cent of the human growth hormone plant's original capacity. It was their expertise that drove Lilly to invest £45 million in expanding the site.'

Of course, a favourable investment climate is still important. The government's monetary and fiscal framework, including making the Bank of England independent and imposing inflation targets, has put the United Kingdom in a better position to cope with the ups and downs of the economic cycle. As a result, the UK has avoided recession and continued to grow in the six years since 1997. In addition, the corporate tax rate of 30 per cent is the third lowest among comparator countries and the 25 per cent R&D tax credit is a significant incentive.

However, the general feeling is that the United Kingdom could do more to reward and encourage investment and that the government should continue working with businesses to improve the tax regime and so provide incentives for investment in wealth creation and greater rewards for success. The industry particularly welcomes plans for a simpler 'purpose test', which will further expand the scope of the definition of eligible expenditure to include expenditure, not capital, incurred for R&D. 'Pharmaceutical R&D in the United Kingdom is equivalent to 30 per cent of sales,' says Andrew. 'No other British industry returns even 10 per cent to R&D. Lilly currently re-invests nearly 20 per cent of sales revenue in R&D, which is why we are regularly acknowledged as having one of the best, if not the best, new product pipelines in the pharmaceutical industry.'

The political stability of the United Kingdom and the close

partnership with the government is another important factor in the success of pharmaceutical companies in the United Kingdom. As the ABPI states, 'the ability of this country to retain world-class pharmaceutical company investment is critically dependent on the willingness of the government to understand the complex issues involved and to support an environment in which the industry can conduct its research, manufacturing and marketing activities as effectively as in all the other countries that are competing for investment'.

In recent years, the government and industry has worked together to set up the Pharmaceutical Industry Competitiveness Task Force (PICTF). This group looked at what needs to be done to retain and strengthen the United Kingdom as an attractive business environment for an innovative pharmaceutical industry. From more than 50 recommendations the task force has addressed a very broad range of issues relevant to the industry and its relationship with the government, regulators and the NHS. Areas covered include clinical research, licensing, intellectual property rights, the science base and the domestic market framework.

Under the terms of the five-year Pharmaceutical Price Regulation Scheme (PPRS), companies continue to have freedom to set launch prices, with a cap on profits. This makes the United Kingdom more attractive than some other countries, where launch prices are more regulated.

The industry also believes there is scope to work even more closely with the NHS to help improve the nation's health. Says Andrew: 'A partnership framework has been developed between the pharmaceutical industry and the NHS in Scotland, which is providing a useful template for how we can work together ethically on areas of mutual interest for the benefit of patients across the United Kingdom.'

But despite the success of companies like Lilly and a sound fiscal and political environment, there are two important issues dogging the pharmaceutical industry – manufacturing and spending on new medicines. With the exception of Lilly, the share of manufacturing investment by major pharmaceutical companies in the United Kingdom has fallen significantly since 1997, in sharp contrast to the growth in R&D investment. Jobs in the UK manufacturing sector are forecast to fall by 16 per cent between 2002 and 2005.

As Andrew says, 'In terms of being a global business therefore, we need incentives to build new manufacturing capabilities in the United Kingdom. At present these are likely to go elsewhere. In fact, Lilly are currently building two new insulin plants – in the United States and Puerto Rico.'

Turning to medicine spending, Andrew says that the growth in spending on branded medicines in the United Kingdom has averaged 7.9 per cent over the past five years and was just 5 per cent in 2003.

'This means that the medicines bill has grown at less than the overall rate of increase in NHS spending over the past five years and accounts for just 12 per cent of total NHS costs,' he adds. 'Disappointingly, medicines consistently make up a smaller share of the market in the United Kingdom than in many other countries.'

Historically, the NHS has been slow to take on board new medicines. This is still the case, even though the National Institute of Clinical Excellence (NICE) has been established. While NICE has generally issued guidance recommending the use of newer treatments, there has been a tendency by the NHS to wait for NICE – so-called 'NICE blight' – and once the guidance is made, implementation can still be slow. 'While we welcome NICE's aim to provide faster access to modern medicines, clearly there is still more to be done to ensure that patients have the opportunity to be prescribed newer treatments,' says Andrew. 'This is particularly important at a time when the government is actively encouraging scientific innovation.'

3.11

Renewable Energy

Allan Taylor, Renewables UK

UK government policy framework

The UK government is strongly committed to increasing renewable energy usage in order to help reduce greenhouse gas emissions and thereby contribute to national and international targets for emissions reductions. Increasing usage of the various renewables technologies will also contribute to greater diversity in the UK energy supply. The growing importance attached to this form of energy production was reinforced in 2003, with the launch of the government's energy White Paper, which set the United Kingdom four clear goals in energy policy:

- to put the United Kingdom on a path to cut the United Kingdom's CO_2 emissions by some 60 per cent by about 2050, with real progress by 2020;

- to maintain the reliability of energy supplies;

- to promote competitive markets in the United Kingdom and beyond, helping to raise the rate of sustainable economic growth band improve our productivity; and

- to ensure that every home is adequately and affordably heated.

The government's target is that by 2010, 10 per cent of the United Kingdom's electricity sales will come from sources eligible for the Renewables Obligation. This target was increased to 15 per cent of the United Kingdom's electricity supply from renewables sources by 2015 with the energy White Paper aspiring to a figure of 20 per cent by 2020.

What is the Renewables Obligation?

The Renewables Obligation is the key policy mechanism by which the government is encouraging the growth necessary to reach the United

Kingdom's renewable energy targets. Introduced in April 2002, the Renewables Obligation calls on all licensed electricity suppliers in England and Wales to supply a specified and growing proportion of their electricity sales from a choice of eligible renewable sources. The Renewables Obligation Scotland is the equivalent instrument in Scotland. Suppliers are offered a number of means to comply with the terms of the Obligation:

• Each supplier will have to sell a target proportion of their sales from renewables, or prove that someone else has done so on their behalf.

• Compliance will be demonstrated to Ofgem (Office of Gas and Electricity Markets) through a system of Renewables Obligation Certificates (ROCs).

• ROCs are issued to accredited generators, and can be sold separately from the electricity to which they relate. This allows for open trading of certificates, and thus allows those who have surpassed their Obligation requirements to sell on to those suppliers who have been unable to purchase enough renewables-generated electricity.

• Individual suppliers can also choose to 'buy-out' their Obligation commitment. The buy-out price is currently set at £30.51 per megawatt/hour.

• All payments will be recycled to those suppliers who have chosen to demonstrate compliance by presenting ROCs to Ofgem.

Table 3.11.1   Technologies under the Renewables Obligation

Source	Eligibility
Landfill Gas	✓
Sewage Gas	✓
Hydro Exceeding 20MW Declared Net Capacity (dnc)	Only stations commissioned after 1 April 2002
Hydro 20 MW or Less dnc	✓
Onshore Wind	✓
Offshore Wind	✓
Co-firing of Biomass	Eligible until 31 March 2011 for up to 25% of a supplier's obligation At least 75% of biomass fuel must be energy crops from 1 April 2006
Other Biomass	✓
Geothermal Power	✓
Tidal & Tidal Stream Power	✓
Wave Power	✓
Photovoltaics	✓
Energy Crops	✓

In order to provide a stable and long-term market for renewable energy, the Renewables Obligation will remain in place until 2027. Yearly targets have been set up to 2015/2016.

Eligible renewables

Table 3.11.1 shows the eligibility of the various renewables technologies under the Obligation.

Other support mechanisms

The Obligation itself is underpinned by a capital grants programme, which provides grants for the deployment of near-commercial technologies, for example, offshore wind. The UK government has committed nearly £360 million over four years to support these technologies.

The New and Renewable Energy R&D Programme provides support for research into renewable technologies and particularly helps emerging technologies, for example, wave and tidal and fuel cells. This programme supports up to £19 million worth of projects each year.

The Department of Trade and Industry's (DTI) Renewable Energy Industry Directorate manages the capital grant and R&D programmes.

Renewables UK

In April 2002, the DTI created Renewables UK (RUK), part of the Renewable Energy Industry Directorate, whose role is to promote the UK renewable energy industry to help secure maximum benefits for UK industry from the rapidly growing worldwide renewables market. RUK works and contributes towards achieving the government target of 10 per cent of the United Kingdom's electricity from renewable sources by 2010. RUK works to assist in overcoming barriers to renewables projects in the United Kingdom through the Renewables Advisory Board and to optimize the benefits to the United Kingdom of renewable energy in order to maximize opportunities in manufacturing, services, exporting and jobs. Contacts and information on the work of Renewables UK can be found at www.dti.gov.uk/energy/renewables.

Renewable technologies

Wind power

Wind power equipment has been developed to provide a range of power outputs, from less than 100 watts up to over 3 megawatts from a single turbine. Multiple wind turbines can be arranged in wind farms that have capacities of hundreds of megawatts. The new offshore wind farms planned in the United Kingdom will have capacities of up to 1 gigawatt. The overall reliability of wind turbines is high – 97–99 per cent availability is standard for modern turbines, and they are designed to have a useful life of about 25 years. Turbines can have fixed or variable speed rotors, can be pitch or stall regulated, or in the case of small turbines can have furling rotor blades. When used for electricity generation, turbines can generate either direct or alternating current. The flexibility of design of individual turbine components means that machines can be matched to areas with high, medium or low average wind speeds, from the Arctic to the Sahara, and from mountain tops to locations out at sea.

Wind power offers differing applications:

- Large-scale, grid connected generation – a large number of turbines grouped together on one site, either on or offshore.

- Small-scale, grid connected generation – individual or small clusters of turbines, sometimes in areas where electricity grids are unable to accommodate large amounts of generation.

- Stand-alone applications – these are more varied and could be as small as a charger used to charge batteries or megawatt size used for powering a desalination plant on an arid coastline.

- Hybrid systems – wind power is very suitable for hybrid systems. These offer flexibility and wind/diesel combinations are common, but most recent developments include wind/PV.

Many UK wind companies draw their expertise from practical experience of the expanding domestic market, while others have been active in different parts of the world for many years. Onshore wind is one of the fastest growing renewable energy technologies in the United Kingdom and more recently, UK companies have been at the forefront of new initiatives to develop large offshore wind farms. The first of these was completed in 2003 and many more are expected to follow in the next few years, capitalizing on the United Kingdom's expertise in both wind power and offshore engineering. Contacts and information are available from:

British Wind Energy Association
Renewable Energy House
1 Aztec Row, Berners Road
London
N1 0PW
General enquiries: +44 (0) 20 7689 1960
General fax: +44 (0) 20 7689 1969
General e-mail: www.offshorewindfarms.co.uk

Biomass

Biomass fuels are derived from plant material and animal wastes and are used worldwide as an important source of energy, mainly for heating and cooking. The renewable nature of the resource means that it is creating great interest; new technologies mean that it is also being used increasingly to fuel power generation.

Traditional methods of disposal of biomass wastes can lead to environmental problems. For example, slurries have traditionally been spread on land, which can lead to pollution of rivers and aquifers in areas of intensive animal husbandry. Using the biomass wastes as an energy resource not only provides an environmentally acceptable method of waste disposal, but also gives economic benefits through provision of heat and power and the creation of employment.

Biomass fuels are increasingly being used with advanced conversion technologies, such as gasification systems, which may offer superior efficiencies compared with conventional power generation. Gasification is a thermo-chemical process in which biomass is heated with little or no oxygen present to produce a low-energy gas. The composition of the gas will depend on the nature of the gasification process used. The gas can then be used to fuel a gas turbine or a combustion engine to generate electricity. A very wide range of biomass resources can be used as a fuel. The nature of the fuel will determine the way that energy is recovered from it.

Dry biomass fuels

The most straightforward way to recover energy from dry biomass fuels is by combustion to provide heating or hot water. These types of applications range in size from simple log fires and stoves, to sophisticated wood or straw fuelled boiler systems, usually with automatic fuel handling and control systems. Electricity can be generated from dry biomass by using the heat from combustion to raise steam, which is then used to drive a steam turbine. This application applies many of the proven technologies used in power plants fuelled by coal. However, the nature and composition of the fuel often means that specialist features not needed in fossil fuel plant have to be incorporated into the biomass plant if it is to work efficiently. For example, certain materials have a tendency to 'slag' and block the grate if they are fed into it incorrectly.

Combined heat and power (CHP)

CHP is becoming an increasingly attractive option for biomass plant, offering a reliable low-cost heat source for industrial or commercial uses (such as a district heating system for a small community), together with electricity that can be sold to the local grid. Forest residues, industrial wood wastes and a range of agricultural wastes are often readily available as fuel for CHP plant. However, energy crops, such as wood coppice (willow or poplar in cooler climates, wattle and eucalyptus in warmer climates), or perennial grasses such as miscanthus, are becoming increasingly important. These may be grown specifically for use as a fuel, and can provide long-term secure resources.

Wet wastes

Cattle, pigs and poultry all produce slurries that can be used to produce biogas. The slurries (and sewage) are fermented in an anaerobic digester to produce a gas that is mainly methane and carbon dioxide. The gas can be used in gas engines to generate electricity or in boilers to provide process heat or space heating. Some 40–60 per cent of the organic matter present in the slurry is converted into biogas. After maturation, the remainder provides a stabilized residue that can be used as a soil conditioner.

A very wide range of municipal or industrial wastes may be used as fuel. The nature of the waste and the waste disposal method will determine the way that energy can be recovered. Dry household, commercial or industrial wastes can either be burned (combusted) as raw waste, or they may first undergo some sorting or processing to remove waste components that can be recycled separately.

Combustion with energy recovery

Waste combustion with energy recovery is an established way to dispose of wastes. It decreases the volume of the waste and allows for recovery of metals and other potentially recyclable fractions. After further basic treatment, most of the remaining residue can be combined with other materials and used as an aggregate material. Any residue that is landfilled is biologically inactive and does not generate potentially harmful emissions.

The heat recovered from these plants can be used to generate electricity or can be used for industrial heat applications. The size of energy from waste plant is designed to meet the waste disposal needs of the community taking into account the potential for waste minimization and recycling. Plants that generate electricity can typically process between 20,000 and 600,000 tonnes per year, and from this they can generate from 1 to 40 megawatts of electricity. Power is produced from these wastes by using the steam raised in the combustion process to drive a steam turbine to generate electricity, in a similar manner to a conventional coal-fired power station.

Advanced thermal technologies

Where the waste stream is of a uniform nature, for example, if it has been processed into a homogeneous fuel, it is better suited to the more 'advanced technologies' such as gasification or pyrolysis. Wastes that are not uniform in composition, for example, municipal wastes, are less suited to treatment by advanced technology, although the technology is rapidly developing to handle more challenging wastes.

Gasification

Gasification is one of the newer technologies that are increasingly being used for waste disposal. It is a thermo-chemical process in which biomass is heated in an oxygen-deficient atmosphere to produce a low-energy gas containing hydrogen, carbon monoxide and methane. The gas can then be used as a fuel in a turbine or combustion engine to generate electricity. Gasifiers fuelled by fossil sources such as coal have been operating successfully for many years, but they are now increasingly being developed to accept more mixed fuels, including wastes. New gas clean-up technology ensures that the resulting gas is suitable for burning in a variety of gas engines, with a very favourable emissions profile. Gasifiers operate at a smaller scale than incineration plant, and can also be provided in modular form to suit a range of different scales of operation. A number of UK companies are leading in this emerging technology.

Pyrolysis

Pyrolysis is another emerging technology, sharing many of the characteristics of gasification. With gasification, partial oxidation of the waste occurs, while with pyrolysis the objective is to heat the waste in the complete absence of oxygen. Gas, liquid and char are produced in various quantities. The gas and oil can be processed, stored and transported, if necessary, and combusted in an engine, gas turbine or boiler. Char can be recovered from the residue passed to a gasifier and the char gasified.

Strict environmental standards now apply in all European countries governing the emissions from energy from waste plant, particularly of heavy metals, furans and dioxins. All energy from waste plant must now meet these standards, which can be achieved through the installation of extensive state-of-the-art gas cleaning systems.

Landfill gas

Energy can also be recovered from waste that has already been landfilled, in the form of landfill gas (also known as biogas). This is a mixture comprising mainly methane and carbon dioxide, formed when biodegradable wastes break down within the landfill as a result of anaerobic microbiological action. The biogas can be collected by drilling wells into the waste and extracting it as it is formed. After cleaning it can be used in an engine or turbine for power generation, or used to provide heat for industrial processes situated near the landfill site, such as in a brickworks. Landfill sites can generate commercial quantities of landfill gas.

The UK biomass industry has experience across a range of applications and has high-quality products and services. This experience includes agriculture and silviculture, R&D, project development, manufacturing, construction and operation, engineering and financial and legal services.

British Biogen
16 Belgrave Square
London
SW1X 8PQ
United Kingdom
Tel: +44 (0) 207 235 8474
info@britishbiogen.co.uk

Renewable Power Association
2nd Floor
17 Waterloo Place
London
SW1Y 4AR.
Tel: +44 (0) 207 747 1831
www.r-p-a.org.uk

Environmental Services Association
154 Buckingham Palace Road
London
SW1W 9TR
Tel: +44 (0) 207 824 8882
ddorkin@esauk.org
www.esauk.org

Hydropower

Conventionally, hydropower is produced when the kinetic energy of flowing water from a reservoir, in a river or in a tidal current, is converted into electricity by a turbine connected to an electricity generator. For conventional hydropower, the amount of power generated depends on the rate of flow and the volume of water available to drive the turbine. Hydropower schemes are designed to offer power generation with high levels of availability over a long operating life. Civil engineering works (weirs, channels) can last for many years with suitable maintenance and the mechanical and electrical lifetime of a hydro power plant can be up to 50 years.

Large-scale hydro
Large-scale is typically taken to mean more than 20 megawatts of grid-connected generating capacity and is usually associated with a dam and a storage reservoir. The largest schemes are well over 1,000 megawatts in size and can take years to construct. However, most

large-scale schemes were developed prior to 1990 and the potential for identifying new large-scale schemes is now more limited, not only because there are fewer commercially attractive sites still available, but also because of environmental constraints.

Pumped storage

Pumped storage schemes are large hydro schemes that are designed with a storage reservoir that is larger than justified by the natural flow of water into it. At times, when electricity demand is high, water is released from the reservoir to drive the generators in order to send power to the grid. Conversely, when electricity demand is low, the generators draw electricity from the grid and become motors, which are then used to drive the turbines in reverse. They then pump water back into the reservoir. Pumped storage schemes play a major role in many countries in smoothing out imbalances between supply and demand, and providing rapid response capabilities that help stabilize the grid.

Small-scale hydro

Schemes of less than 20 megawatts now offer a greater opportunity for providing a reliable, flexible and cost-competitive power source with minimal environmental impacts. Although these small-scale schemes currently contribute only about 3 per cent (21 gigawatts) to the total hydropower capacity, they are making an increasing contribution towards new renewable energy installations in many regions of the world, especially in rural or remote regions where other conventional sources of power are less readily available. Small-scale schemes can be associated with a dam and storage reservoir or can be located in a moving stream ('run of river').

Small-scale hydropower generation is a well-established technology. It is characterized by relatively high initial capital outlay but these high initial costs are offset by the long lifetime of the scheme, its high reliability and availability, low running costs and the absence of fuel costs. Capital costs can often be reduced by making use of existing engineering structures or by refurbishing existing plant and equipment. The cost of generating power from small-scale hydro schemes depends on the characteristics of the site and in particular the height of the hydraulic head (the vertical distance from the reservoir or river to the turbine). Economic viability decreases as the head decreases. Where the grid supplied by a scheme is isolated from the main national or regional grid, hydro plant can be run in conjunction with another form of generation, typically diesel. See the text on hybrid systems below.

Micro hydro

In certain locations, even very small hydro schemes can be developed to provide an economic source of power. Micro hydro plant are typically a few hundred watts up to a few hundred kilowatts. They are generally 'run of river' schemes, frequently utilizing water wheels that were previously used to drive water mills. Micro hydro has a particular role to play, from recovery of energy from water pipelines to providing electricity in remote locations that are not connected to the national grid. It is increasingly used in less developed parts of the world, where the provision of electricity is seen as a major factor in improving living standards.

Hybrid systems

Micro and small-scale hydropower are very suitable for incorporation into hybrid systems. They offer flexibility, because they can provide power even when there is little water in the river or reservoir during dry periods. Hydro diesel combinations are common, but more recent developments include hydro photovoltaic units, a hybrid option that offers power generation from 100 per cent renewable sources.

Tidal power

Tidal power can use either conventional or new technology to extract energy from a tidal stream. It is usually deployed in areas where there is a high tidal range. Typically a barrage with turbines is built across an estuary or a bay. As the tide ebbs and rises, it creates a height differential between the inner and outer walls of the barrage. Water can then flow through turbines and drive generators. Some tidal barrages operate on both the rising and falling tide, but others, particularly estuarine barrages, are designed to operate purely on the falling tide.

It is also possible to make use of the tidal flow that occurs between headlands and islands or in and out of estuaries. This is known as tidal stream. It is this application that is the focus of much research and development and new products for this purpose are now being commercialized. These 'in-flow' tidal turbines can be arranged singly or in arrays, allowing a range of power outputs to be produced.

Wave power

Wave energy depends on the height, length, frequency and speed of the waves. The power of the waves is readily visible on nearly every ocean shore in the world. There has been much research to harness the power of these waves and various machines have now been developed. These fall broadly into three categories:

• Machines that channel waves into constricted chambers. As the waves flow in and out of the chamber, they force air in and out. These airflows are in turn channelled through a specialized turbine, which is used to drive a generator. This type of machine is principally designed for use on or near the shore, or for incorporation into break-waters. Commercially, this mechanism is the most advanced and is particularly advantageous when incorporated into coastal protection.

- Fixed or semi-fixed machines that utilize the pressure differential in the water that occurs at a submerged point as the wave passes over that point. The pressure differential is used by a variety of means to cause a fluid to flow in a circuit, which is then used to drive a turbine and generator.

- Machines that utilize their buoyancy to cause movement in a part of the device as it moves up and down in the wave. The movement is used either directly or indirectly to drive a generator.

The UK waterpower industry offers high-quality products and services for a range of applications. It is based on a tradition of excellence, from design and engineering through to insurance, and backed by proven expertise in developing innovative hydropower projects. From micro hydro run of river systems to multi-megawatt installations with large storage reservoirs, UK companies are ideally placed to provide a comprehensive range of services and solutions in all aspects of the use of water as an energy resource.

Many UK companies draw their expertise from practical experience of the expanding domestic market, which at the small and micro scale is now growing rapidly, while others have been active in different parts of the world for many years. UK-manufactured hydro-turbines of many sizes from micro to large are operating in many locations around the world, providing electricity at low cost, with high efficiency and high overall productivity. UK companies are also expert at the restoration and refurbishment of existing hydropower schemes and can, in addition, offer expertise in providing appropriate hydro technology to support the development of indigenous industries.

More recently, UK companies have been at the forefront of new initiatives to develop tidal and wave power systems, the first of which are now being installed off our coasts and the coasts of North America. These technologies are aided by the United Kingdom's enviable expertise in offshore engineering in some of the most difficult marine conditions in the world. For contacts and information:

British Hydropower Association
Unit 12
Riverside Park
Station Road
Wimborne

Dorset
BH21 1QU
Tel: +44 (0) 1202 886622
infor@hydroplan.co.uk
www.british-hydro.org

Solar power

Solar power is produced by the conversion of sunlight into DC (direct current) electrical power using PV cells. PV cells, modular and light, have no moving parts, have no direct impact on the environment, and require only minimal maintenance. They therefore offer many potential advantages compared with more conventional power generation systems, including ease of installation, long life and durability and low operating costs.

When PV cells were originally developed in the 1970s, they were expensive and inefficient. Since then, PV technology has been developed to improve efficiency and reduce costs. Today, three main types of PV cell are available:

- Onocrystalline silicon PV cells are made from a single, continuous crystal lattice structure.

- Multicrystalline silicon PV cells are cast from molten silicon obtained many different lattices of monocrystalline silicon.

- Amorphous silicon PV cells use a homogeneous layer of silicon atoms rather than a crystal structure.

Photovoltaic technology continues to develop rapidly, and several alternatives to silicon are already being used in PV cells. These include gallium arsenide (GaAs), cadmium telluride (CdTe) and copper indium diselenide (CIS). PV cells made from these new materials can be manufactured more cheaply than crystalline silicon cells, and are more efficient than amorphous cells.

Each crystalline silicon PV cell generates around 0.6 volts, and cells are combined in series and in parallel to make modules. A typical module may produce 50 watts of power at 24 volts (DC), and modules may then be combined into arrays to meet the higher power and voltage demands of typical applications.

The output from a PV module varies depending on the amount of incident light and other factors such as temperature and the cleanliness of the cell surface. Modules are rated in terms of their peak output (peak watts or Wp), which is the maximum power that they will produce given optimum solar input and operating conditions. It follows that the average amount of power produced will be closer to the rated (peak) output in locations where there is a high level of incident radiation – in tropical countries with low cloud cover for example. However, PV cells do produce useful quantities of power in less than ideal conditions, such as those that prevail in the United Kingdom. Today, PV cells are used in a wider range of applications, including stand-alone systems, grid-linked systems and building integrated systems.

UK companies play a prominent role in the PV industry and several of these are now world leaders in the PV market, and the number of UK companies active in the field is increasing steadily. Many of these companies are already exporting into countries where the PV market is growing more rapidly. UK companies operate at all stages in the supply chain, that is, supply of equipment and systems, design and specification, installation and commissioning, project management, testing services, training and consultancy. For further information contact:

The British Photovoltaic Association
National Energy Centre
Davy Avenue
Knowlhill
Milton Keynes
MK5 8NG
Tel: +44 (0) 1908 442291
Fax: 0870 0529193
E-mail: enquiries@pv-uk.org.uk
Website: www.pv-uk.org.uk

Export and technology programmes

The DTI has two programmes to help UK companies export their knowledge and capabilities into export markets, and to facilitate international technology partnering. They are the Trade Promotion Service and International Technology Partnership respectively.

Trade Promotion Service

The Trade Promotion Service has been running since 1994, with specialist trade promotion advice since 1995. In that time it has earned a well-respected reputation and is widely considered to be delivering a useful and valued service. Typically, the Service has worked by promoting the UK renewable energy industry at home and overseas, raising the profile of UK companies and increasing their involvement in these markets.

The programme has been managed by Renewables UK since April 2002, and although it continues to promote and raise the profile of the

UK industry, it also focuses on industry sponsorship activities and targeted company support for existing UK exporters and providing support activities for UK companies to develop their export potential and activities.

The Trade Promotion Service is delivered by two dedicated trade promoters and information on the service can be obtained from:

Barry Holmes
Trade Promoter
Oak House
Oakwood Road
Burgess Hill
Sussex
RH15 0HZ
Barry.holmes@pera.com

John Buckley
Trade Promoter
PO Box 33
Huntington
Cambridgeshire
PE28 9HN
john.buckley@pera.com

International Technology Partnership

DTI Global Watch Technology Partnering connects UK companies with 16 International Technology Promoters (ITPs), which provide a practical route to leading-edge technological developments from the world's major investors in research and development in the sectors of electronics and ICT, life sciences, performance engineering and energy and the environment.

ITPs offer flexible and free support to UK companies whose strategic plans could be advanced through partnerships with organizations abroad, to develop and transfer products, technologies, processes or management practices, set up business alliances, overcome language barriers or enable effective entry into new industrial and geographical markets.

By capitalizing on commercial and scientific synergies through alliances of all kinds, from research collaborations to co-development projects, licensing agreements to joint ventures, companies can ensure that they maintain a frontline position in the exploitation of emerging technologies and new markets. By bringing in partnering professionals, key cultural and linguistic barriers to successful partnering can also be overcome.

To find out more about the DTI Global Watch Technology Partnering, visit www.globalwatchonline.com/itp or call the ITP helpdesk at Pera on +44 (0) 1664 501551.

Opportunities for investors

Renewables UK has recently analysed the opportunities for investors in the energy renewables industry by carrying out a detailed GAP analysis. The final report, titled *Renewable Supply Chain GAP Analysis*, will be published shortly on the Renewables UK section of DTI website: www.uktradeinvest.gov.uk.

3.12

Software

Charles Ward, Intellect UK

The UK vs Europe

With a value of 64 billion euros in 2003 the United Kingdom accounts for 22.2 per cent of the European IT market, and is by a narrow margin the largest market ahead of both France and Germany. In terms of internet adoption, the United Kingdom's penetration was 57.6 per cent of the population in 2003, significantly higher than the European average of 48.9 per cent. Only the Nordic group of countries exceeds the United Kingdom's adoption, which is projected to reach 75.4 per cent by 2007, equivalent to 47 million users. E-commerce in the United Kingdom is predicted to grow dramatically from 85 billion euros in 2003 to 429 billion euros in 2007 with the B2B share increasing from 80 per cent to 85 per cent of the total. The United Kingdom is only exceeded by Germany in e-commerce (*source: EITO*).

UK IT market – general picture

Along with most other Western IT markets the United Kingdom has suffered from the post-Y2K and DotCom effect. The UK market shrunk by 0.3 per cent in 2003, though is predicted to achieve modest growth of 2.4 per cent in 2004 and 4.3 per cent in 2005. Indeed, a number of commentators point out that the underlying decline of the traditional IT market is masked by the positive impact of infrastructure and business processing outsourcing (BPO) and to some extent public sector spending. The main victims of this decline are project services (8 per cent) and software (1 per cent). Verticals' shares of IT spending are shown in Table 3.12.1.

While there are a multitude of forces at play leading the comparatively depressed state of the market, the UK economy is a key influencing factor. The general mood in the market has been one of caution

Table 3.12.1   Verticals' shares of IT spending

	2003 Share (%)	2006 Share (%)	2004/2006 AAGR (%)
Manufacturing	17.3	16.6	1.9
Finance	18.9	17.0	−0.5
Public Sector	23.5	29.0	9.6
Telecoms/Utilities	8.8	7.2	−0.6
Retail, Services & Transport	31.5	30.3	1.9

Note: AAGR = compound average growth rate.
Source: Ovum Holway

it is important to understand customers' general attitudes and behaviours:

- emphasis on leveraging existing IT investments;

- emphasis on cost reduction and operational efficiency – *a key driver for outsourcing*;

- excessive focus on ROI for new investments with longer sales cycles and rigorous internal approval process;

- large projects broken down into smaller bite-sized pieces to reduce risk and increased use of pilot implementations and proof of concept projects;

- Compliance is now starting to become a driver for IT investment in certain sectors.

The impact of these conditions on the supply side has been companies experiencing reduced turnovers and shrinking workforces though there have been signs in early 2004 of improved conditions leading to a more positive outlook in the sector.

Looking forward there are optimistic signs, not least the impact of the massive waves of public sector spending on IT. That said, as with any huge market there are sectors/sub-sectors in expansion that present opportunities for existing and new players. Increasingly it is the ability to spot these exciting 'micro-markets' that can lead to business growth way beyond the headline average.

The UK software market – product perspective

Growth rate in the UK software market peaked at 10.1 per cent in 1998 and has fallen since. Sized at £4.92 billion, the UK software market is forecasted to shrink by 0.6 per cent in 2004, remain static in 2005 before growing 1 per cent in 2006. Growth in packaged applications, systems infrastructure software (SIS) and tools will be offset by decline in enterprise software. Middleware is the reason that the SIS product category continues to grow, albeit modestly, as it is a tool to leverage extra value/performance out of existing systems and deal with complexity. In the applications segment, CRM will remain a focus in many organizations with the emphasis moving to back office integration. Similarly, supply chain management will continue to be a source of productivity improvement with a focus on purchasing, inventory management and workforce management.

Absence of a 'killer' application to boost the market combined with the 'excess IT inventory' problem has impacted new licence sales of established software vendors. Such suppliers have been able to compensate by developing services and consultancy revenue streams, with the larger well-financed players even developing BPO offerings. In addition, the established players are attempting to adapt their products, pricing and distribution in order to address the mid-market level opportunity. In the longer term, developments in packaging and delivery will allow vendors to offer their software as a service. Web services, hosted applications and managed IT services will shape the new business models.

Tension between 'best of breed' and 'generalist' suppliers is expected to mount as the established players who have enjoyed a long period of prosperity serving the corporate market seek to outperform the market growth by developing their product portfolios and addressing the mid-market opportunity. Many existing small and medium-sized specialists will inevitably become acquisition targets or victims as the bigger players reposition themselves. Nonetheless, the United Kingdom has been and will continue to be a fertile ground for small, innovative, agile software companies operating either in niche markets or on the periphery of the established players.

Business process outsourcing (BPO) is the fastest-growing segment within outsourcing and is relevant to the software community because niche software providers are successfully developing BPO offerings in response to customers wanting to cut costs, improve productivity, disengage from non-core activities, as well as transferring technology and operational risks. While this would normally be seen as the market of the traditional outsourcers, a key customer requirement is domain intimacy, which is often more important than generic service capability.

Over the medium term the penetration of broadband and improved broadband service will act as a stimulant for growth in the digital content and interactive services. It is expected that the 'new media' type companies that largely disappeared after the DotCom crash? will return and fuel growth in this sector which is a hybrid between software, creative arts and communications.

The UK software market – vertical perspective

The immediate market horizon is inevitably dominated by developments in the public sector driven by the UK government's ambitious modernization targets. As expected, the massive investment plans have triggered something of a 'feeding frenzy' in the market. It should be noted that developments in the United Kingdom are being closely observed by other European countries that could well adopt a 'follow the leader' strategy to modernization of their own public services.

Public sector market overview

The Prime Minister has stated that 100 per cent of public services should be available electronically by 2005. Therefore, spending on public sector IT has risen significantly over the last five years. It is expected that the public sector's total IT budget will exceed £10 billion during 2002/03, while the market for IT services alone in the Public Sector is expected to be worth £4.75 billion by 2004. The Comprehensive Spending Review included a number of IT-related measures in the departmental Public Services Agreements and £3 billion of ring-fenced spending for electronic service delivery.

The statistics illustrate the scale of the challenge confronting both government and industry in achieving the 2005 objectives over 200 agencies and 400 local authorities; more than 750 services provided by local government and over 520 provided by central government; nearly 5 billion transactions undertaken annually, of which 80 per cent are conducted at the local level; and, of course, close to 60 million citizens.

For new entrants into the Public Sector marketplace, the current environment presents a number of exciting opportunities but also a number of daunting challenges. The level of public investment into electronic service delivery together with the relative slowdown in the private sector market has led to an increasing number of ICT companies attempting to enter the public sector making competition increasingly fierce. Nonetheless opportunities exist for those companies who are willing to be patient and develop and understanding of the markets they find attractive.

In central government, the majority of contracts have already been issued and given the size of many of these multi-million pound tenders contracts are traditionally awarded to one of a select number of larger, multi-national companies with existing relationships. Nevertheless, it is important to note that opportunities do exist for smaller companies within the Framework Agreements these larger players have in place. Understanding the nature and timing of these opportunities is not easy.

The criminal justice market (covering the police, courts, probation and prison services) will shortly become the next 'big' area of procurement. Again it is likely that Government will award the majority of their contracts to larger players, with smaller companies or new entrants only able to benefit via the Framework Agreements or through the development of niche products. Both approaches require a significant level of commitment, both in terms of time and resources.

It is the local government market place that probably presents the most accessible opportunities for new entrants. Within the United Kingdom, there are over 400 local authorities, each demographically different, resulting in a disparity in the manner in which e-government strategies have been implemented. Many urban authorities have taken a notable lead in implementing strategies, which have been considered, in some cases, to be superior to the work that has been undertaken by central government. In contrast, smaller rural authorities, lacking the necessary resources and expertise to attract suppliers to their tenders have found it increasingly difficult to implement their strategy effectively. This does not mean that smaller local authorities are any less attractive than larger authorities, it merely presents smaller suppliers or new entrants with an opportunity to enter the public sector market at a level that would allow for genuine partnership to develop and flourish.

Health
In terms of both scale and degree of change IT developments in the United Kingdom's National Health Service are unparalleled. For almost a decade the Health Trust model has existed whereby individual large hospitals or groups of smaller hospitals have managed themselves autonomously. The same applied to GP practices. There was no central IT purchasing by the NHS. This decentralized fragmented model has favoured specialist SMEs, as many large IT players were forced to abandon their direct presence in the sector altogether due to unsustainable selling costs. In March 2002, the UK government announced the National Programme for IT (NPfIT), designed to radically modernize the NHS.

The modernization programmes themselves cover:

- Integrated Care Records Service;

- E-Prescriptions;

- E-Bookings.

Eight major contracts have now been awarded. The six largest of these form the core of the modernizing agenda of NPfIT and include five regional Local Service Provider (LSP) contracts, covering England, for a Care Records Service, and a further contract as a National Application Service Provider (NASP) to deliver the data spine where all the care records will be held. Two additional contracts have also been awarded to deliver an e-bookings service and broadband infrastructure known as N3:

- LSP London region – BT (Capital Care Alliance);

- LSP North East – Accenture;

- LSP North West & West Midlands – CSC;

- LSP Eastern region – Accenture;

- LSP South – Fujitsu;

- NASP – BT;

- e-bookings – Atos Origin (Formerly SchlumbergerSema);

- N3 – BT.

Each LSP has put together a consortium of companies to deliver its solution. Most SMEs have found it hard to win business with the LSPs, and coupled with a stall in local IT spending as IT buyers interpret and digest the plans, are looking carefully at their future. Many companies are waiting until the LSPs work is underway until approaching them, hoping to fill any gaps that may appear in the consortium solution. Others are marketing their skills and domain knowledge, rather than their product, to address the growing need for skilled personnel in LSPs delivery teams. NPfIT has caused confusion and instability in the UK health market both on the buy and supply sides. This uncertainty means that companies with no NPfIT contracts are unable to plan for the future. Many key questions remain unanswered such as: How will LSPs treat installed legacy systems? Will LSPs need to add to their consortia in the future? What, if anything, can still be procured locally by the NHS? Clearly, in this climate new suppliers will find it particularly difficult to become established. Only once further clarity exists on what is inside and outside the scope of NPfIT, and whether or not LSP consortia are a closed door, will companies be able to plan strategically with any degree of confidence. In other words it's a confused market place at the moment and fraught with danger unless a new entrant has a very clear and certain picture of their opportunity

Key private sector verticals

Retail
Consumer spending is a key factor behind the relative strength of the UK economy compared with continental Europe. IT spending in retail

remains healthy, the main areas of focus being supply chain management, improving productivity and efficiency as well as technology developments to reduce fraud. Chip and Pin is now being rolled out in the UK and the banking community is becoming more coordinated. One question is whether the retailers themselves can keep pace with its introduction.

RFID tagging is seen as having the potential to deliver improved supply chain information, tighter security and reduced losses through fraud and theft. Adoption of these new technologies will create substantial opportunities in integration and associated software products. Currently the driving force for RFID appears to be major retailers such as Wal-Mart and Tesco undertaking major projects with their supply chains. However opportunities are emerging in other sectors such as pharmaceuticals and it is apparent that as the technology becomes more widely understood new applications will be found. For example there is excitement within the direct marketing and postal communities that use of RFID and related technologies could enable a single item of promotional mail to be tracked through to delivery to the recipient allowing for coordinated follow up through other communications channels.

Nonetheless there are going to be standards and interoperability issues as is often the case with new technologies not to mention the potential issues with consumer rights and privacy laws.

Financial services
The key drivers in banking and finance, a sector that has consistently invested heavily in IT, are largely regulatory. The impact of the post-Enron world and the recent Basel II Accord will keep the sector buoyant. Other drivers are e-money and possibly euro adoption in the longer term. The major objective is improved capital risk management. This drives demand for CRM, data warehousing, data management and integration with legacy systems though the requirement from this community of experienced buyers is for integrated solutions as opposed to point products and services.

The UK's regulatory body FSA (Financial Services Authority) is widening its scope to cover other areas of the industry such as mortgage companies and insurance providers. This therefore increases the size of the opportunity driven by compliance, particularly integration, as companies' reporting requirements become more detailed.

The insurance and pensions sector has had to adapt to the '1 per cent world' created by the 1 per cent cap on charges stipulated by the government on stakeholder pensions introduced in 2000 though increased to 1.5 per cent in 2004. While the 1 per cent only applies to this single product type the 'low charges' precedent has been set. This has led to consolidation in the sector with a focus on end to end supply chain efficiency and process streamlining. Simultaneously, the marketing of financial services has become more adventurous with new brands entering the market, that is, supermarkets and affinity schemes.

3.13

Telecommunications

BT eLocations

Why the United Kingdom?

There are many reasons why international companies decide to invest in the United Kingdom. Some opt for the fast, easy access to the European Union single market of over 450 million; others the skilled, multilingual workforce; and many executives cite the business-friendly environment in the United Kingdom, with low corporation tax and a host of other financial incentives. For many international businesses, however, the single main attraction to investing in the United Kingdom is its state-of-the-art telecommunications infrastructure – an infrastructure that is currently undergoing dramatic transformations. From the advent of broadband communications through to Internet Protocol (IP) technologies and the very best in mobility solutions, there is little doubt of the positive impact that the UK telecommunications infrastructure is having on inward investors.

A strong market environment

Since privatization in the 1980s, the United Kingdom has always been known to have a strong market environment for its telecommunications services. Today, the United Kingdom is one of the leading locations within Europe for telecommunications and related industries.

In 2003, UK telecommunications revenues were £54.1 billion, and UK telecommunications revenue as a proportion of GDP grew from 2.4 per cent in 1985 to 4.1 per cent in 2003. According to the most recent data (1999–2003) from the industry regulator, OFCOM, net capital expenditure by the UK telecommunications industry was on average £8.8 billion per year – rising faster than the UK economy as a whole over the same period.

There are knock-on effects as well. The government's recent UK online annual report, released in December 2003, found that the United Kingdom remains one of the best environments in the world for e-commerce, with transactions exceeding £23 billion in 2002. And a recent report by the World Economic Forum found the United Kingdom to be third placed in the world in relation to its strong market environment for IT and telecommunication services.

Today, in the United Kingdom, there are 170 public fixed telecommunications providers, 5 mobile providers, 59 mobile service providers and 700 internet service providers. Eight out of 10 of the world's top telecommunications companies operate in the United Kingdom and the country has one of the fastest growing telecommunications markets in the world. Yet how has the United Kingdom managed to secure this position and what are the telecommunications innovations that inward investors can look forward to today?

The great broadband roll-out

Over the last few years, the United Kingdom has been characterized by the deployment of ever more sophisticated and faster technologies, one such example being broadband. Broadband is essentially a way of providing high-speed 'always on' data and voice links, and significantly increases the amount and the speed of data that can be carried between users. For any large organization with regular communications with its customers, suppliers or employees and requiring flexibility in the development of its multimedia communications, broadband is fast becoming a business necessity.

Meeting these demands has led to a nationwide roll-out of the technology. According to recent research from OFCOM, broadband services in the United Kingdom are being taken up at a greater rate today than in France or Germany, with 29,000 new connections per week. More than 4.5 million people had subscribed to broadband by June 2004, and 90 per cent of the population now have access to a mass-market broadband service.

And, through a series of regional partnerships with regional development agencies and other public sector partners as well as the development of alternative access technologies such as radio broadband, BT is confident that there will be broadband coverage for 99.6 per cent of the United Kingdom's population by 2005.

Broadband in practice

Yet how does broadband operate in practice and how is the technology going to help investing companies? Call centres are a good example of the importance of broadband applications. With many call centres incorporating ever more sophisticated technologies, such as Voice-over-Internet Protocol (VOIP), video conferencing and web collaboration, the development of a resilient infrastructure with high-speed and increased bandwidth is essential.

Fast broadband connections will allow call centres to deploy real-time data analysis and intelligent decision-making technologies, to build individual customer profiles and to identify cross- and up-sell opportunities. Furthermore, whether it is through e-mail, video conferencing or multimedia communications, all communications channels with customers can be developed – principally as a result of broadband.

Another great innovation – the wire-free office

Another technology that is having an impact on today's UK business environment is the wire-free office. In the future, the supply of wireless technology is likely to be as integral a part of the office as electricity, water or air-conditioning. Facilitating these developments are technologies such as Bluetooth and 3G.

Bluetooth is a short-range radio technology that allows portable devices, such as mobile computers, mobile phones and other portable handheld devices to communicate at up to 1,500 feet, without the need for wires. This, together with the growing market acceptance of third generation (3G) mobile wireless technology, is making the wire-free office of the future a distinct reality.

The benefits of a mobile workplace, totally unconstrained by cables, are 'mouth watering' – a flexible workplace, where everyone has their own, individual mobile communications package, combined with leading-edge wireless technology. The flexible workspace and the concept of every person having their own mobile communications solution will also allow employees to either work individually or in teams, depending on what is required of them.

Furthermore, there will also be tangible cost savings to the tenant, with the reduction in cabling allowing a greater concentration of employees to be based in the same location or offering up the opportunity for companies to move to higher-rent offices. The days of large servers taking up valuable office space will be a thing of the past.

Telecomms in the office

Although the wire-free office may be a few years off in achieving mass-market acceptance, a high bandwidth communications infrastructure has become very much part of today's property portfolio for investing companies. Gone are the days when an investing company just expects 'bricks and mortar' in the offices it locates to. Today's companies want a total support package combining workspace with a sophisticated telecommunications infrastructure and turning the traditional relationship between a property owner and a tenant into that between a service provider and a customer.

UK property owners are having to be proactive in developing and marketing services such as broadband, as more and more of their tenants are demanding their telecommunications to be pre-installed. For example, BT's inward investment division is addressing this need through a series of pre-equipped business parks across the United Kingdom – all equipped with the latest fibre optic technology (see case study on BT eLocations) – and many other property management companies are following suit.

The result is that companies can look forward to fast set-up times and a cost-effective and resilient broadband communications infrastructure that provides all the necessary tools to compete in a rapidly changing business environment. Commercial property owners understand that it is only through enhancing the desirability of their properties that they can attract the new, high-value tenants of tomorrow. Certainly, in terms of a telecommunications infrastructure, they are prepared.

And telecomms outside the office

The United Kingdom's telecommunications infrastructure is not just thriving in the office. It is thriving outside as well. The last few years has seen a significant increase in mobile working with innovative technologies, such as Bluetooth and 3G enabling this development. Leading IT consultancies Meta Group and Gartner both estimate that, within five years, 75 per cent of sales and service professionals in developed nations will use mobile technologies in their day-to-day operations.

According to OFCOM, the number of UK mobile subscribers has recently exceeded 50 million and 75 per cent of UK adults now own or use a mobile phone. Average monthly retail revenue per subscriber has also increased to almost £18, the highest level in three years, the result of GPRS increasing average call and SMS usage – some of this for business use.

There are other mobile technologies growing in the United Kingdom as well – Wireless Local Area Networks (WLAN) and Wireless Fidelity (WiFi), for example. WLAN/WiFi are local area networks that transmit over the air, typically on an unlicensed frequency such as the 2.4GHz band. Already, companies are queuing up to make the most of the new opportunities WiFi provides, with the utilization of public spaces for wireless internet access such as airport lounges, coffee shops, hotels and railway stations. For a fee, anybody equipped with a notebook or handheld PC can fill time while waiting for a flight or for their coffee to arrive by catching up on e-mails, surfing the web or sending reports through high-speed internet, without the need for a physical connection.

The continuing outsourcing push

Despite the news stories about telecommunications outsourcing going to countries such as India and the Philippines, the United Kingdom and Europe continue to remain a key market for such outsourcing. Recent research from outsourcing specialist, TPI, found that the value of European outsourcing contracts signed during 2003 increased 66 per cent over 2002 to reach 26.4 billion euros. The United Kingdom intends to remain at the very centre of the outsourcing market, with its resilient and secure telecommunications infrastructure – essential for high-value, outsourcing operations – skilled and multilingual work-force, and flexible business environment proving to be key selling points for investors.

A sector approach

Advanced telecommunications can also have a significant impact on specific UK sectors, especially when legislation changes are pending. Take the automotive market, for instance. Since 1985, supply, distri-bution and servicing arrangements within the car industry have bene-fited from a block exemption from European Union competition rules. This regulation, however, expired on 30 September 2002, and the new regime is likely to lead to increased competition within the automotive market with new means of selling cars, easier cross-border purchases of new vehicles and better access to after-sales servicing.

Car manufacturers will also have to choose between 'exclusive distribution' arrangements (where each dealer is allocated a sales territory) and 'selective distribution' where dealers are selected on the basis of qualitative and quantitative criteria. Dealers will also be allowed to sell cars of more than one brand and will no longer need to have facilities to carry out repairs, being able to sub-contract after-sales servicing.

With increased competition comes increased demand on the United Kingdom's telecommunications infrastructure. Customer relationship management will be vital, with car dealers realizing that their oppor-tunities for repeat business may lie in fully understanding the consumer's behaviour. There will also be a continued focus on call centre technology to manage customer requirements, and a greater need to link the communications infrastructure between repair and sales outlets.

Companies such as BT are already using their telecommunications experience to address these sector needs, and as other sectors evolve, the United Kingdom will make sure that its telecommunications infrastructure evolves with it.

The security question

Sadly, recent months have demonstrated more than ever the need for companies to have disaster recovery or business continuity processes in place to protect their telecommunications infrastructure, with international terrorism joining the more traditional threats to companies such as fire, flood, theft and power cuts. Security and business continuity is at the top of the agenda in the United Kingdom and companies are increasingly ensuring that their properties have the very best in resilient communications.

Conclusion

The state of the United Kingdom's telecommunications infrastructure has never been in better shape. Today's companies need secure, fast, integrated and seamless communication services, and the ability to access data and communicate it with customers, suppliers and employees, whenever and wherever they need it. The United Kingdom is committed to achieving this, and to ensuring that communications remains a unique selling point to inward investors for many years to come.

Case Study: Telecomms in practice – the BT eLocations portfolio

BT's inward investment division – BT eLocations – and UK property developers are taking on the challenges of fast, sophisticated and secure telecommunications within a business environment through a portfolio of 60 business, technology and science parks across the United Kingdom, already housing leading blue-chip businesses such as Capital Bank, Coca-Cola, HSBC, IBM, Oracle and JP Morgan.

From some of the world's leading science parks, such as in Cambridge and York, through to city centre locations in Cardiff, Manchester, Edinburgh and Glasgow; edge of town business parks in Birmingham, Liverpool and London; rural locations in Wales, Scotland and the North of England; and finance-specific parks such as the Financial Services Districts in Glasgow and Cardiff, the United Kingdom and BT are building a telecommunications infrastructure for future international investment.

BT eLocations has pre-equipped all these sites with an exceptional state-of-the-art optical fibre high bandwidth network infrastructure, including Internet Protocol (IP) technology hosting and applications; mobility solutions; next generation switching; and enhanced exchange capacity, sufficient to cope with a company's ongoing communications demands.

To address business continuity, each site also has pre-installed dual optical fibre network infrastructure from the customer back to both a primary and secondary exchange. The result is an ideal setting for inward investors, with fast set-up times and fast, integrated and seamless communication services.

For further information on BT's inward investment programme, visit the website at www.bt.com/btelocations or contact elocations@bt.com.

3.14

Utilities

Neil Gould, Powergen

A great time to invest

For small business enterprises (SMEs) looking to invest in the United Kingdom from overseas, a key consideration will be the availability and cost of vital infrastructure and support services. Of these, energy will be one of the foremost concerns as, increasingly, SME bosses are using large amounts of electricity to run their businesses and a company's energy bill will form a major slice of its total overheads. However, the good news is that there has never been a better time to be buying energy in the United Kingdom. The advent of privatization in the early 1990s has brought with it a new era of lower prices for the energy consumer. And these days, energy companies don't simply sell energy as a commodity. At Powergen, for example, we can now offer a range of services alongside the energy we sell to the small business sector to help ensure our customers are getting maximum value out of every megawatt of electricity or therm of gas they buy from us.

How the industry has changed

It hasn't always been like that in the energy sector, however. Before privatization, small businesses – like other customers – had no choice in the supplier of their energy needs. Electricity was bought from the local regional Electricity Board and gas from the Gas Board, later British Gas. At privatization in 1990, the electricity industry was split into separate areas of operation. Generation was in the hands of three major companies – Powergen, National Power and the nuclear generator British Energy. The distribution of electricity was the remit of 12 regional companies (RECs) – effectively the regional Boards – which were also responsible for retailing electricity directly to homes and businesses in their franchise areas. The gas industry had been privatized a few years earlier with the establishment of British Gas, responsible for both supply and transmission. Both the electricity and gas industries were overseen by regulatory bodies that looked after customers' interests by setting price controls.

However, many key figures both inside and outside of the industry believed that the future lay in vertical integration. Powergen believed that the market would evolve into a structure where a small number of major players would be involved at every aspect of the supply chain – effectively making, selling and then delivering the product. We believed that such companies would be able to make major cost savings, which could in turn be passed on to the customer.

Today's retail markets

The vision we had for the industry's future has largely come to pass. The energy sector has continued to evolve, such that there are now a number of large integrated companies in the United Kingdom that sell gas and electricity products and competition has helped bring real price savings for customers and many other benefits besides.

Today, the energy retail sector is split into three distinct markets. The first to be liberalized in the early 1990s was the industrial and commercial market, which includes the nation's largest businesses and those that consume the most energy. This was followed in the mid-1990s by the SME market for smaller businesses, or companies with multiple sites – a supermarket chain, for example. Finally, in 1998, full competition was achieved when the nation's 26 million households became free to buy their electricity and gas from whichever company – or companies – they chose.

Tailor-made service

Companies quickly learned that the best way to win and retain business customers is by not just supplying them with the electricity they need – but by offering them a complete product that is tailored to their specific needs. Research showed that, while price is an important factor, particularly for SMEs wanting to keep overheads to a minimum, even more important is the level of service and support a company can offer. So, by listening to our business customers and finding out about the things that are important to them, Powergen has developed a range of electricity products that have helped establish us as the market leader in this area.

For example, Powergen is able to offer Business Electricity Plans that provide fixed price guarantees over a one-, two- or three-year period, with the savings increasing with the length of contract. It is innovations such as this that have helped establish Powergen as the country's leading supplier in this sector. Around 400,000 – one in every four – SMEs buy either gas or electricity or, in many cases, both from the company.

Energy over the internet

For most companies, doing business over the internet has become a way of life, and the power sector has been among the leaders in embracing the advantages the e-commerce explosion has brought. Most energy companies can now offer a full range of online services for SME customers. For example, prospective customers can visit www.powergen.co.uk and fill in some key details to receive a quote. Once a business has chosen Powergen as its supplier, the option exists for the company to manage its account entirely online. This includes viewing the account details on a 24-hour basis, registering meter readings and making direct payments. Many companies appreciate the flexibility of being able to manage key services like energy supply outside of normal office hours. Many companies also have dedicated 24-hour call centres where staff are on hand to answer account queries, offer advice or point the caller in the direction of more specialised help.

Putting energy efficiency into practice

The most effective way of using energy is to use less of it. Businesses are increasingly under pressure to reduce their overheads and the energy industry is able to offer small business customers access to a range of energy efficiency advice and services to help reduce energy costs in their business. It is only by giving businesses a better under-standing of how they use their energy that they are able to see where potential savings could be made.

Powergen has a team of experienced energy efficiency specialists who work to provide individually tailored information and advice. Their skills cover all aspects of energy use, including heating, lighting, air-conditioning, refrigeration and manufacturing processes. If more detailed help is required, or financial support is considered appropriate for energy investments, companies will often be directed to government-backed schemes, which can provide financial support and advice. A good example of this is the 'Action Energy' programme that can fund services such as:

● detailed on-site energy assessments for a business;

- premises in-depth feasibility studies for energy improvements;

- interest-free loans for energy efficiency investments.

Advice to customers comes in many forms. Much of it is common sense, but, in the hustle and bustle of today's busy business world, many companies simply do not have the time – or money – to appoint someone to manage this vital area. That is where energy efficiency experts in the power industry can make a real difference.

For example, Powergen has produced a free energy- and money-saving guide that they believe can help drastically reduce energy bills – in some cases by up to a fifth. The guide was produced after they carried out research into more than 400 SMEs in the United Kingdom. That research showed that, while 93 per cent rated their energy efficiency as 'fair' or better, more than half (54 per cent) admitted to never having taken steps to improve it. The majority (78 per cent) admitted they did not have anyone dedicated to managing their energy efficiency. Alongside the booklet, Powergen has also established an energy efficiency helpline, staffed by energy experts with knowledge of a wide range of energy efficiency practices and equipment.

A waste of time and energy

Powergen is constantly looking for new ways to help its customers reduce waste around their business and so we also carried out an in-depth study into patterns of energy consumption to check if businesses were getting the best value for money. The results were startling. They showed that wasted time and energy is costing the United Kingdom's SMEs a staggering £29.6 billion a year, with many businesses massively underestimating the cost of time and energy wasted in their businesses. The survey revealed that, while most businesses believed they were not wasting energy, many were failing to take simple steps that could reduce their energy wastage and also save them money. On the basis of its customer base, Powergen believes that average UK SME energy consumption is £1,000 for electricity and £500 for gas. Yet they estimate that SMEs could save up to 20 per cent – around £300 – a year by taking simple energy-saving steps.

While some of these factors were beyond their control, small business bosses appeared to underestimate the amount of energy being wasted by staff. When asked how energy efficient their business was, 93 per cent said 'fair' or better. Yet 37 per cent said they left lights on in empty rooms, 28 per cent left heating on, and 26 per cent left PCs, mobile phone chargers and other equipment switched on or on standby overnight. It is through carrying out this kind of research and passing on their findings, together with relevant advice, to their customers that energy suppliers can add real value to the relationship with their customers.

Conclusion

The privatization of the energy sector, and the move to full market competition over the past decade, has brought with it major benefits for customers. As with any commodity market, energy suppliers now operate in an environment that is wholly customer-driven, which has led to lower prices and better levels of service.

But that's not all. In its energy White Paper the Government outlined its future strategy for the energy industry. A key factor is a greater promotion of energy efficiency as a way of achieving drastic cuts in the United Kingdom's greenhouse gas emissions. This means that, increasingly, energy companies will be working with their customers to look at reducing the amounts of energy they consume.

All of which spells good news for small businesses looking to invest in the United Kingdom. Such companies are usually limited in the resources they have available, in terms of both budget and people, to manage the basic services that are critical to the success of their business. As far as buying energy is concerned, that need no longer be a problem.

Part 4

Investment and Start-up Considerations

Legal Overview for Inward Investors

David Kent, Inward Investment Group, Taylor Wessing

Introduction

This book is designed for the individual inward investor and for an overseas company investing in the United Kingdom. This chapter focuses principally on private limited companies and registered branches as these are the most typical forms of entity for investors doing business in the United Kingdom, although the section headed 'Choice of entity' below outlines a number of different types of entity or means of doing business in the United Kingdom. Further details of these entities can also be found elsewhere in this book (see Chapter 4.5). In each case, advice should always be sought at an early stage in respect of the most appropriate form of entity and the choice will often be tax driven.

This chapter also looks at the other legal issues faced by investors, many of which are also referred to elsewhere in this book and many of which are linked. It therefore acts as an introduction to the details that follow in this chapter and Part 5.

There are three principal UK entities

There are three principal ways for an investor or for an overseas company to carry on business in the United Kingdom. The company can either:

- set up a subsidiary company (a private limited company) in the United Kingdom;
- register a branch of the overseas company in the United Kingdom; or

- establish a more limited presence in the United Kingdom pursuant to the place of business registration scheme (this entity is sometimes also called a representative office as it is not regarded as a permanent establishment for tax purposes (see Chapter 4.10) and is sometimes better referred to as a non-taxable branch).

In addition, business activities may also be conducted through a sole proprietorship, a partnership, a limited partnership, the relatively new limited liability partnership (LLP) (see Chapter 4.5) or a joint venture (see Chapter 2.6). Goods and services may be supplied through contractual arrangements such as distributorship agreements and agency arrangements without actually setting up business in the United Kingdom (see Chapter 5.1 and Chapters 4.9 and 4.10 covering taxation).

The Companies Act 1985 (as amended by the Companies Act 1989) (the 'Companies Act') is the principal legislation that regulates each of a subsidiary company, a branch and a place of business in the United Kingdom. A company incorporated in the United Kingdom can be either a private company or a public company (see Chapter 4.5).

In practice, public companies are not formed by overseas companies to be wholly owned subsidiaries in the United Kingdom. A public company is an inappropriate vehicle as it is a vehicle used normally where there are to be many shareholders. Its use would therefore look wrong to potential UK customers. In the case of a subsidiary there is normally only one shareholder, which is either the overseas company or a purpose-built holding company overseas, which itself is wholly owned by the overseas company.

Legal personality

Neither a place of business nor a branch of an overseas parent has a separate legal existence in the United Kingdom. They will simply be a part of the overseas parent company. (See later.)

A subsidiary company of an overseas parent in the United Kingdom will be a separate legal entity with its own liability. This means that if the overseas parent elects to set up a UK subsidiary, the parent will not be liable for the debts and other liabilities of its subsidiary beyond the amount of the subsidiary's share capital unless the overseas parent has provided an express guarantee in relation to its subsidiary's liabilities.

Filing requirements

There is a key difference between a UK branch of an overseas company and a UK subsidiary of an overseas parent from the perspective of filings required to be made with the Registrar of Companies. On registering a taxable branch and annually thereafter, the overseas company is required to file its accounts (in a form acceptable to the UK Registrar of Companies, although this is rarely enforced) with the Registrar of Companies.

A UK subsidiary of an overseas parent is required to file its own accounts annually in accordance with various provisions of the Companies Act, although it is not also required to file any separate financial information in respect of its overseas parent (see Chapters 4.5 and 4.9). The UK subsidiary will, however, be required to identify the overseas parent as its shareholder in an annual filing, which it makes known as the annual return (please see below under the heading 'Annual return' for further details).

The issues leading to the choice of entity

Here are some factors:

- The fact that the overseas company's accounts become a matter of public record in the United Kingdom when a branch is set up may not be acceptable to many overseas private companies, thereby steering them to set up a subsidiary in the United Kingdom to avoid this filing requirement. An alternative is for the overseas company to set up a new international subsidiary overseas to own the UK branch.

- A subsidiary may offer an advantage when doing business in the United Kingdom as it is more readily understood by those who do business with it than the structure of a branch. A subsidiary may also provide a greater sense of security to those who do business with it as both types of branches can be dissolved in one day.

- An overseas company that is looking at the United Kingdom may consider setting up a place of business (a non-taxable branch) where its activity is preparatory or auxiliary before setting up a full trading operation.

- The initial business activity should be examined carefully together with the likely further needs of the business in the coming months and years to see whether the choice of entity really works for the overseas company. For instance, there is no point in setting up a place of business (a non-taxable branch) if the entity should have been a (taxable) branch because the inevitable result will be that the Inland Revenue will seek to tax the entity as if it were a taxable branch. The result is that the overseas company will waste valuable time defending the position. It would have been more cost-efficient to set up a taxable entity with a sensible method of trading for tax purposes in the first place.

- The regulatory cost of running a subsidiary is higher than that of a branch because of the requirement that the books of account should be kept in the United Kingdom and because a subsidiary needs an audit where the overseas groups turnover exceeds £5.6 million (see Chapter 4.9). The cost difference between a branch and a subsidiary can be estimated at between £7,000 and £20,000 depending upon the auditors who have been chosen.

What is the most often-used entity in the United Kingdom?

In the end, there is little difference between the two taxable entities of a subsidiary and a taxable branch. The entity chosen by most inward investors in the period up to 2002 was a subsidiary. Since then, and even at the time of writing in 2004, branches are what the inward investment companies are choosing. This is because of the reduced ongoing regulatory expense mentioned above, and because a branch can be closed in a day. The liabilities of the branch remain with the overseas company that was its owner.

Subsidiary company

A private limited company may not be incorporated with the same name as a company already registered on the UK company register. Other details in relation to the formation of a private limited company are set out in Chapter 4.5.

Where the private limited company is to be used as a wholly owned subsidiary the articles of association should be tailored specifically to allow the shareholder control over the subsidiary at the stroke of a pen in relation to the holding of meetings of the directors (and of the shareholders) and in relation to the appointment and removal of the directors of the company.

The use of a third party's trademark, whether registered or unregistered in the name of a UK company or a branch, should be avoided. Chapter 5.1 under the heading 'Passing off' sets out the reasons for this in more detail. Detailed searches should be carried out before the entity is set up.

The process of changing the name of a UK company usually takes five to seven working days (at a filing cost of £10) following receipt by the Registrar of the necessary documentation. If a name change is required more quickly, there is also a same day name change procedure (at a filing cost of £80). The use of certain words in a company name is prohibited, for example, 'International', 'British', without the prior approval of the Registrar of Companies.

Funding

An investor should normally seek tax advice when considering the proportion of debt to equity capital when financing a company (which is governed by the 'thin capitalization' rules, see Chapter 4.9). If the overseas parent is considering some form of interest-bearing loan to its UK subsidiary, it needs to take into account the detailed rules prescribed by the Inland Revenue in the United Kingdom in relation to the payment of interest by a UK company to its overseas parent. If the UK subsidiary has a very small proportion of equity compared to debt capital, the Inland Revenue may deem the interest paid on the inter-company loan to be a distribution and the distribution would be taxed as a dividend. Tax advice should therefore always be sought on the implications of this.

When determining the amount of equity capital, although there are no rules set in stone, it is often advisable to consider an initial equity capital of at least £1,000. It is relatively simple and quick to increase the authorized share capital of a UK company. This can be done by a member's written resolution, requiring over 50 per cent of the shareholder vote in favour by number of shares held (known as an ordinary resolution). When issuing and allotting shares to shareholders, the company must also ensure that the requisite authority of the directors to allot the shares is in place (again this authority can be given by the shareholders passing an ordinary resolution) and it is also likely that the company will need to disapply pre-emption rights (both statutory and any such rights contained in the company's articles of association). The shareholders can disapply the pre-emption rights by passing a special resolution (requiring over 75 per cent of the shareholder vote by number of shares held).

Auditors

Under section 384 of the Companies Act, every company is required to appoint an auditor or auditors. The only exceptions are for dormant companies that are exempt from the audit requirements and certain small companies (in the case of private companies, different rules will apply in relation to the appointment of auditors depending on whether or not the company has elected to dispense with the laying of its accounts before the annual general meeting). This election is one of a number of elections (known as the elective regime or elective resolutions) that a private company may pass in order to simplify its administrative burden. In the same way, a private company may elect to dispense with the annual re-appointment of its auditors in general meeting. Whether or not the various elective resolutions are appropriate for each private company is likely to depend on the number of shareholders in the company.

Statutory registers

Every company is required to keep a register of its shareholders (known as 'members'). This register must include the names and addresses of shareholders, the number and class of shares held and the date when each person became (and subsequently ceased to be, where appropriate) a member of the company. This register of members must be kept at the company's registered office unless the company specifically elects to keep the register at a different location (which must be in England and Wales for a company registered in England and Wales or, in the case of a company registered in Scotland, at a place in Scotland), in which case, the company must lodge a notice in the prescribed form with the Registrar of Companies.

In the same way, a company must keep a register of charges (mortgages or security interests) granted by it over all or specified parts of its property or undertaking. A company should register the details of any such charges, in the prescribed form with the Registrar of Companies in the United Kingdom, failing which they will be unenforceable. It is usually the company secretary who takes responsibility for maintaining these and the other statutory registers.

Annual return

Every company is obliged to deliver to the Registrar (on Companies House form 363a), a return made up in every year to a date not later than the company's 'return date'. The details, which must be included in the annual return, include the address of the company's registered office, the company's principal business activities, the names and addresses of each director and the company secretary and the date of birth, nationality, business occupation and any other directorships of every director and the number of issued shares in the company and details of the shareholders.

Failure to file annual returns and accounts of a company punctually may lead to the Registrar of Companies taking steps to fine the directors and even to have the company struck off the register. If a company is struck off the register, all of the company's assets will vest automatically in the Crown. It can be an expensive and time-consuming process to apply to the court to have a company restored to the register once it has been struck off, therefore it is always advisable to keep up to date with Companies House filings.

Directors

It is unusual and unnecessary for an overseas company to appoint a non-executive director to its UK subsidiary (see Chapter 4.5). This looks rather strange to customers when searching the company's details at Companies House. It also adds to the overall cost of running the subsidiary. In most cases, the Chief Executive Officer and the Chief Financial Officer of the overseas company will be appointed as the directors of the UK subsidiary. In fact, there needs to be only one director as long as the secretary is a different person.

It is unusual for the leading UK employee to be appointed as a director of the subsidiary at the time of start-up unless he or she is very senior indeed. If he or she is appointed then it would be usual for there to be two overseas directors.

The duties of directors of a UK subsidiary are set out in Chapter 4.5. While they look daunting, the most important issue is that the UK subsidiary is a separate legal person and needs to be managed as such. The danger time for the directors of a wholly owned subsidiary is when the overseas company is facing financial difficulties. At this stage, specialist advice can be obtained in discussing how a reasonable person would manage the subsidiary in those circumstances with a view to the subsidiary continuing to be able to pay its debts as they fall due and with a positive balance sheet. Those discussions need to form the basis of board meetings at which detailed minutes should be recorded and kept in order to protect the directors from potential personal liability.

Branches of overseas corporations

Introduction

The Companies Act contains two regimes that regulate the registration of an overseas company in the United Kingdom: the branch registration regime (for the setting up of what can be referred to as a taxable branch) and the place of business registration regime (for what can be referred to as a non-taxable branch). Under English law, a branch is regarded as part of the overseas company and will be organized to conduct business on behalf of the overseas company. The term 'branch' is used in a sense close to the concept of a subsidiary, although the main distinction is that it will not be a separate corporate body in the United Kingdom. In general, a place of business (a non-taxable branch) will not amount to a branch if the business carried on at that place is only ancillary or incidental to the company's business as a whole. Examples of such operations include warehouse facilities, administrative offices and some offices seeking sales but where no sale has yet resulted from the activity. The choice of entity is an area where detailed specialist advice is paramount (see above).

Procedure for branch registration

Every limited company incorporated outside the United Kingdom and Gibraltar that opens a branch in the United Kingdom is required under the Companies Act to register under the 'branch registration' regime. Within one month of opening a branch, the overseas company must deliver to the Registrar of Companies various particulars of the overseas company on form BR1, including the corporate name of the overseas company, details of the overseas company's registration, if registered, a list of the directors and secretaries (officers) and the extent of the authority of the directors to represent the company in dealings with third parties and in legal proceedings. A certified copy of the instrument defining the constitution of the overseas company must also be submitted to the Registrar with the form BR1 and, where this is not written in English, a certified translation of the constitution must be submitted.

In respect of the branch itself, the following particulars must be given: address, the date on which it was opened, the business carried on by the branch, the name in which that business is carried on if different from the name of the overseas company, the names and addresses of all persons resident in the United Kingdom authorized to accept service on behalf of the overseas company in respect of the branch, and the names and addresses of all persons authorized to represent the company as permanent representatives of the business of the branch and the extent of such persons' powers.

Letterhead

An overseas company that has registered a branch must:

- display the company's registered name and its country of incorporation at every place where it carries on business in the United Kingdom;

- state the company's name and country of incorporation on all stationery, notices and other official publications of the company;

- if the liability of the company's members is limited this must be stated on all stationery, notices and other official publications and be displayed outside every place of business; and

- state on all letterhead and order forms the place of registration and registration number of the relevant branch.

In addition, if the company is not incorporated within the EU and is required to be registered by the law of the country in which it is incorporated, it must state on its letterhead and order forms used in the business of the branch, the place of registration of the parent company and its registration number, together with the legal form of the company, the location of its head office and, if applicable, the fact that the company is being wound up.

A branch letterhead for a non-EU overseas company, for example, the United States, should include the following information:

Xco, Inc.
[UK address]
Registered in England under branch No ZZZ
Head Office address: [   ]
A US corporation registered [with limited liability] in California under No YYY

Disclosure of annual reports and accounts

Where disclosure of annual reports and accounts is required in the state of incorporation of the overseas company that has registered a branch, it must deliver for registration, along with the other documents required to be submitted with the form BR1 on registration of a branch, copies of its latest accounts prepared and disclosed in accordance with that law.

Where the company is not required to publicly disclose its accounts, it is required to prepare and deliver its accounts in a less detailed form without the requirement for the accounts to be audited. Thereafter, accounts must be delivered to the Registrar within 13 months of the accounting reference date.

Method of trading (transfer pricing)

This section only applies to wholly owned subsidiaries and (taxable) branches. The UK Inland Revenue too will expect to receive its cut from a business entity trading in the United Kingdom. Transfer pricing is looked at in Chapter 4.10. Transfer pricing describes the relationship between the overseas company and its UK entity and in particular describes the trading relationship.

The trading relationship can vary from a subsidiary completely trading in its own right at one end of the scale, being various arrangements of buy/sell, distribution, so-called stripped distributors and commissionaire structures through to simple arrangements whereby the United Kingdom acts as a marketing representative being rewarded on a third party arrangement of cost plus or commission. This choice is part of the overall choice of entity and is linked to the other topics covered in this chapter and in this book in that each aspect should reflect and endorse the chosen method of trading and each other topic.

A mistake made by many overseas companies with their UK entities is that they allow their UK employees freedom to sign up contracts without having first decided on the correct method of trading. This can create many accounting issues and be bad for morale within the UK entity. It is best to deal with method of trading first and have an open discussion with the UK employees as to what their duties are in line with the chosen method of trading.

UK regulatory permissions and licences required to undertake business

Most investors and overseas companies wishing to do business in the United Kingdom will not need to obtain a permit or licence to undertake their business activity in the United Kingdom. However, the proposed trading activity needs to be legally reviewed to see what, if any, regulatory framework governs that industry. Examples would be the regulation required under the Financial Services Act for banks and advisors in financial and investment transactions (see also Chapter 5.5), licences from the telecoms regulator for the provision of telecom systems and services in the United Kingdom, broadcasting licences and restrictions, the laws on pyramid selling for multi-level marketing companies, and licences for gaming (see Chapter 3.9).

European holding companies

These are appropriate for large successful multinationals of overseas companies whose European sales have gained substantial traction in Europe and large profits are being made or predicted.

Many overseas companies are approached by advisors selling them European structures based in either Switzerland, the Netherlands or Ireland before sales traction has started in Europe. While there is no harm in making plans, some overseas companies suffer delayed European sales because they are waiting for the European holding structure to be set up. In addition, they suffer unnecessary infrastructure costs in recruiting and training the headquarters team based in a country that is not one of the main sales areas in Europe. Further issues will be encountered in setting up complicated methods of trading and should the Netherlands be chosen, the overseas company will then discover the unwarranted straightjacket and prescriptive nature of Dutch employment law.

European structures are essential for major multinationals. For a young or emerging growth overseas company, a European holding structure can become an unwanted and costly structure that does nothing to promote sales.

Place of business registration regime

If an overseas company has established a place of business (a non-taxable branch) in the United Kingdom it must deliver to the Registrar of Companies within one month of establishing that place of business, a form 691, which includes details of the company's directors and secretaries, details of the names and addresses of persons authorized to accept delivery of documents on the company's behalf, a statutory declaration stating the date on which the place of business was established and a certified copy of the charter, statute or memorandum and articles or other instrument that defines the overseas company's constitution.

The company is required to deliver in respect of each financial year copies of its reports and accounts prepared in accordance with the Overseas Companies (Accounts) (Modifications and Exemptions) Order 1990, which means that the accounts do not need to be as detailed as those required for a company incorporated in the United Kingdom, nor do they need to be audited.

Real estate

The process of acquiring real estate under English law is lengthier than in other countries. A typical lease in the United Kingdom sought by most property owners is for 15, 20 or 25 years. These are unacceptably long leases for an overseas company starting up in the United Kingdom.

By examining the market, the overseas company will discover that one-year sub-leases are possible. Five-year sub-leases are more normal. It is possible to negotiate break clauses after two of three years. Care needs to be taken that the service charge and 'extras' to be charged are fair. The form of lease or licence should be legally reviewed.

Where a wholly owned subsidiary has been formed, the property owner may require that the overseas company guarantee the lease obligation. This should be resisted for many reasons. The solution is to offer a three- or six-month rental deposit at the beginning of negotiations instead of a guarantee.

Transfer between UK entities

An existing place of business or branch may need to be upgraded to a branch or a subsidiary respectively. Transfers between UK entities are dealt with in Chapter 4.10. A transfer agreement is necessary for account, VAT and employment purposes. Stamp duty tax exemption or relief is available for inter-group transfers. TUPE (see Chapter 5.2) applies and reasonable notice must be given to all the employees (and unions if any) before the transfer.

Why should a UK entity be set up at all?

There are five reasons for this as follows:

- Registration under the UK Companies Act. It is a requirement under the Companies Act that an overseas company with an address in the United Kingdom registers a branch or a place of business. This applies only if the overseas company has not already set up a UK subsidiary.

- Corporation tax. Failure to register an entity will mean that the UK Inland Revenue (once it discovers that the overseas entity has an address in the United Kingdom) will deem the business as a branch that will be taxable to corporation tax. There will be no agreed method of trading and therefore no inter-company services agreement setting out the terms of the transfer pricing arrangements (see also Chapter 4.10). The Inland Revenue will fine entities that have failed to put an inter-company services agreement in place. Worse still, the Inland Revenue will deem the total sales revenue to be that of the UK entity resulting in substantial administrative costs and accounting fees to rectify the position.

- Stock options. Stock option grants to UK employees where no entity has been set up cannot be subject to Inland Revenue election agreements (see also Chapter 5.2) because the UK registered entity is required to be a party to the election agreement before it is sent to the Inland Revenue for approval.

- Immigration. Only a UK subsidiary (or taxable branch) is able to make an inter-group work permit application.

- Limitation of liability. As mentioned previously the operation of an unregistered (taxable) branch in the United Kingdom is the operation of the overseas company in the United Kingdom without any barrier of limitation of liability between the branch and the overseas company. This is undesirable and the suggestion that a new overseas international company should be set up to hold the branch appears earlier in this chapter.

Why is the appointment of consultants in the United Kingdom not a sensible action?

Many overseas corporations are unsure of the potential size of both the UK and European market for their product. As a result, they will appoint an individual as a 'contract worker' or 'an independent contractor' whose responsibility is to obtain the first sales. Using consultants in this way is full of hidden obstacles and will cause the overseas company unexpected additional expenditure to correct the taxation position.

The UK Inland Revenue will deem an individual consultant working full time in the United Kingdom as an employee. An exception to this rule is where the consultant is employed by his or her own limited company or by a partnership and is recognized by the Inland Revenue as an intermediary.

The consequences for the overseas company of appointing an individual as a consultant who will be deemed as an employee by the Inland Revenue are as follows:

* failure to pay the income tax (under the PAYE systems) and the employee's National Insurance contribution (see Chapter 5.2);

* failure to pay the employer's National Insurance contribution of 12.8 per cent (see Chapter 5.2);

* a fine of up to 100 per cent of the above taxes not paid and other fines (these can be reduced down in negotiation);

* the five other issues set out above under the heading 'Why should a UK entity be set up at all?'

Summary of key legal aspects for an overseas company setting up in the United Kingdom

English law is easier to understand and (with the exception of employment law) most overseas companies feel more at ease with it than European civil law countries. The choice of entity is in practice a choice between:

* a subsidiary (taxable);

* a branch (taxable), or

* a place of business (a non-taxable branch).

The method of trading with the parent overseas company, the employment contracts, proprietary information and confidentiality agreements, stock option plans, if any, and the form and content of its contract with customers are all linked to each other.

The United Kingdom has the fairest employment law of any of the European countries and the overseas investor will have opportunities by means of appraisals and reviews, of reducing its potential substantial liabilities when dismissing employees by reviewing new employees' conduct and dismissing where appropriate, before the one-year cut off (see Chapter 5.2).

There are regulatory licences required for certain industries and all overseas companies should ensure their UK entity notifies the commissioner for data protection and enters into an appropriate inter-company agreement. Local law reviews of all customer contracts are necessary because the local law will override the overseas company's choice of governing law. Use advisors who can show a substantial track record in advising overseas companies with start-ups and ask to speak to their clients direct.

4.2

Grants and Incentives within EU Parameters

Siegfried Doetjes, PNO-j4b

Thousands of grants worth well over £5 billion each year are dangled in front of companies in the United Kingdom in an attempt to encourage economic development, and any company looking to invest in the United Kingdom is potentially eligible to apply for most of them. While not being as important as the available skills or infrastructure, these financial incentives can be quite considerable and are certainly worth exploring further before deciding where to locate an investment. Companies may already have an idea of which funding sources are relevant to their circumstances, and it is not too difficult to find further details, but a great deal of advance consideration should be given to how easy it will be to make a successful application.

The cost of 'free money'

Although the majority of grant schemes provide financial assistance that does not have to be repaid, there will be a cost in terms of the amount of time and effort you will need to put into the application. Individual funding schemes are usually designed to achieve specific objectives and the awarding bodies will require plenty of evidence to reassure them that the project is not only viable, but will benefit the United Kingdom or one of its regions by creating or safeguarding jobs, increasing exports or encouraging economic development. The information they require is rarely straightforward, with the general rule being that the more money you are applying for, the more complex the requirements will be.

Other factors to be considered

There is no guarantee that an application will succeed, regardless of its merits, because UK grants are discretionary, meaning that they are awarded on a competitive basis. It is therefore of vital importance to ensure that the application is of the highest quality so that it stands out against the competition. It is also prudent to maximize the chances of success by considering all possible grants rather than pinning everything on just one application.

One golden rule that is easily overlooked is that applications need to be made in advance of making an investment, as applicants need to demonstrate that the project cannot go ahead without this financial assistance. The amount of assistance rarely equates to more than 50 per cent of the project costs, and will be determined largely by negotiation, during which all companies are treated equally, irrespective of nationality.

An awareness of current political issues and pet government projects is very important as they are subject to change and therefore the timing of an application is often crucial. Applications can also take several months; so you will need to factor this into your plans and provide for possible contingencies. Those sectors that currently attract the most funding include agriculture, food services, manufacturing, chemicals, waste management, bioscience, aerospace and ICT, while pet projects the government bodies are currently seeking to encourage are those involving energy, transport, the environment, education, research and development activities and training.

Not 'playing the game' in the right way may mean an application is either denied or perhaps delayed, which could cause significant difficulties. Political lobbying can dramatically increase the chances of a successful bid, so knowing whom to contact, when, and with what kind of information can be vital.

Assistance with applications

Very few companies possess the specialist knowledge or experience required to successfully handle complicated grant applications. The wiser operations choose to maximize the opportunities while minimizing the hassle, especially in applying for the larger schemes, by calling on external expertise.

Support and advice can be found through the Business Link network, which is managed by the UK government's Department of Trade and Industry. There is also a sprinkling of grant consultants of varying sizes, but their reputation has been tarnished in the past by the actions of a handful of cowboys who have charged large upfront fees and ended up delivering little if anything in return.

In continental Europe, where grants appear to be taken far more seriously than in the United Kingdom, many large organizations, including Henkel, Akzo, Polaroid, Numico and Corus Steel, look to

Europe's leading grants firm, PNO Consultants, to maximize the available grant opportunities. These clients are serviced by over 160 PNO staff in nine offices across Holland, Belgium and Germany.

These high-level services are now available in the United Kingdom for the first time following the launch in 2003 of PNO-j4b (www.pno-j4b.com), a joint venture between PNO and funding information specialist j4b plc, which has already assisted several companies with their external funding strategies, including Procter & Gamble, Caterpillar and Cargill. The services provided cover three main areas: the identification and building of fundable projects; proposal writing and submission; and support in project management and administration.

PNO had long recognized the United Kingdom as the largest potential market for grant consulting services due to its relatively poor record in accessing the larger EU grants. j4b had continually received requests for help with grant applications since 2001, when it began to re-energize grants in the United Kingdom with its range of pioneering online funding information services. These include the award-winning grant search website, www.j4b.co.uk, and various bespoke online funding solutions that have been developed for the websites of over 130 public sector bodies in the United Kingdom, including Regional Development Agencies, councils, Business Links and government departments.

Finding out what funding is available

Officially launched in September 2004, www.grant-guide.com not only allows companies to look for schemes within their own countries, but to compare the inward investment support across Europe, so they can assess which areas offer the most support. The site will encourage companies to invest into Europe as well as move within the Continent. Initially providing information on the public and private sector grants and loans available in the United Kingdom, Holland, Belgium, Spain and Austria, the intention is to roll out a commercially viable service across all the EU member and affiliate nations by 2006. Companies can log on to www.grant-guide.com to participate in testing and provide feedback.

To find out what support is available in specific regions, companies can contact the United Kingdom's network of Regional Development Agencies (see www.rdauk.org), some of which help to fund specific inward investment websites such as www.surprising-sy.com, which was developed for Renaissance South Yorkshire by j4b.

Identifying the grant 'hot spots'

While government funding schemes are often purpose- and sector-specific depending on the areas that the government is particularly interested in supporting, location is the most important factor for companies looking to invest into the United Kingdom, as locating in certain areas will make them potentially eligible for the most lucrative and the greatest number of grants.

In addition to the EU's designated 'Objective' areas referred to below, the UK government provides support through the discretionary Regional Selective Assistance (RSA) grant schemes to the Assisted Areas of England, Scotland and Wales (see also Chapter 4.3). These areas, defined in the map in Figure 4.2.1, see http://www.dti.gov.uk/assistedareas/annex_a.htm#top, are designed for companies in the services and manufacturing sectors that are planning expansions, modernizations or rationalizations, or investing in the United Kingdom for the first time. In England, RSA has recently been substituted by the Selective Finance for Investment (SFi) Scheme; in Scotland and Wales the name RSA is maintained. This scheme is delivered by the Regional Development Agencies. The scheme is designed for projects that provide employment opportunities and increase regional competitiveness and prosperity, with the amount offered depending on the needs of the project, the number of jobs safeguarded or created, and the impact the project will have on the economy. The amount provided and the terms of this assistance is generally negotiated as the minimum amount that would ensure the project can go ahead.

If overseas companies investing into the United Kingdom qualify for SFi or RSA, the amount of funding that they can receive ranges from tens of thousands to many millions of pounds, although it is unusual to amount to more than £1 million.

Companies locating in Northern Ireland are eligible to apply for grants and incentives that are not available to companies in other parts of the United Kingdom. These schemes, including Selective Financial Assistance to cover the cost of new buildings, plant or machinery, are provided by Invest Northern Ireland. Another source of funding is the (Smart) Grant for R&D scheme for SMEs that provides funds of up to £200,000 (£500,000 for exceptional projects) for new products and process development projects, and interest-free loans for environmental initiatives and projects that help reduce operating costs.

Certain local authorities in England, Scotland and Wales also offer financial assistance through grants or special loans, and all local authorities can be important sources of general support.

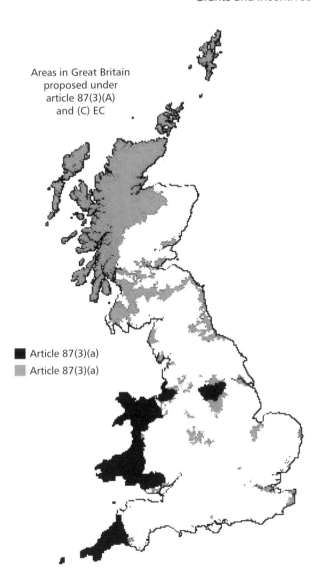

Areas in Great Britain
proposed under
article 87(3)(A)
and (C) EC

■ Article 87(3)(a)

▨ Article 87(3)(a)

Figure 4.2.1   Assisted areas

Availability of funds from the European Union

The EU's structural funds are available at varying levels in the United Kingdom depending on location (as defined in the map in Figure 4.2.2). They are generally intended for public sector bodies to bid for in partnerships with other public sector bodies or specific private sector organizations, with successful partnerships then setting up schemes to benefit end users. This means that businesses often benefit from

EU-funded schemes without realizing, as the EU only subsidizes a proportion of the project costs, with the rest 'match funded' from other sources. These schemes may involve cash but can also be workshops, seminars, subsidized consultancy or exhibitions, etc.

EU funding is available to companies investing in an area that benefits from 'Community Initiatives', including certain designated rural areas, urban areas, border regions and projects involving transnational cooperation, which are designed to promote equal opportunities in the labour market.

The European Union also provides assistance in the form of low-interest rate loans from the European Investment Bank (EIB) that can cover up to 50 per cent of the cost of eligible projects.

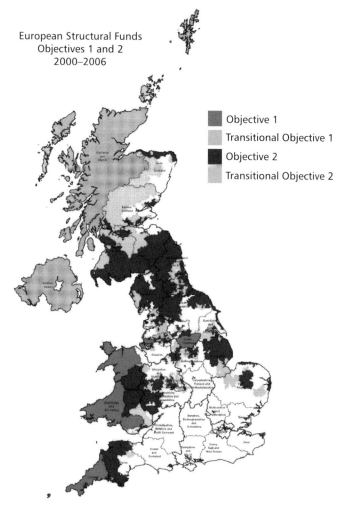

Figure 4.2.2   Objective areas

Direct applications to the EU

Many EU schemes do not encourage direct applications but some do, including research and development and technology projects. Measures have been put in place to give businesses better access to EU funds, and although applications can be complex and time-consuming, they can also be very rewarding.

The GUIDE project itself is a good example of what can be achieved by applying direct to Europe for grant funding. The pilot to develop this trans-European online grants information service (www.grant-guide. com) was part-funded by an 800,000 euro EU grant through the eContent programme, following a successful partnership application by j4b plc, PNO Consultants, and Econet of Madrid. The partnership members were introduced to each other by an EU representative, whom j4b had met at a UKIS (Information Society) Help event.

The EU's main way of providing funding for collaborative research and innovation is through the Framework Programme, which aims to strengthen European research and technological capability and encourage Europe's international competitiveness. It is open to all types of organizations in the EU, as well as a number of non-EU countries. The current Framework Programme, called FP6, has an overall budget of 17.5 billion euros and will run until the end of 2006.

The government, recognizing the vital importance of this research to the UK economy, has long provided a wide range of expert help and support to UK organizations seeking funding under the many areas of Framework Programmes through its network of National Contact Points. Last November, the Office of Science and Technology launched a single, centralized information and promotion service to make it easier for UK organizations to find out how to access this funding. This service includes a website developed by j4b: http://fp6uk.ost.gov.uk, and a central telephone support number +44(0) 870 600 6080.

Conclusion

Grants can help companies to achieve their aims, and although they can potentially involve a lot of work, with the correct approach and some thorough planning, companies can minimize the hassles and maximize the possible returns. There are some very lucrative schemes around, but they generally require more complex applications, which is where many companies decide to employ the services of grant consultants.

Development and Business Support Agencies

Jonathan Reuvid and the Small Business Service (SBS)

UK Trade & Investment – the first source of advice

UK Trade & Investment combines two agencies under the UK Department of Trade and Industry, known formerly as Trade Partners UK and Invest UK. It has two primary functions: to support companies in the United Kingdom, trading internationally, and overseas businesses seeking to set up or expand in the United Kingdom. The merger of these two agencies reflects the UK government's commitment to providing through a global network a fully integrated service that can deliver both inward and outward business opportunities.

For inward investors, UK Trade & Investment offers a one-stop advisory service that assembles and channels available information from government and public agencies. This free and confidential service can deliver a complete information package combining advice on locations, financial incentives, employment and product sectors that addresses a company's specific needs.

The UK Trade & Investment service comprises:

- thorough regional analysis and informed advice to assist selection of the right location;

- relevant information, as required, on key commercial considerations such as company registration, immigration, financial incentives, labour, real estate, transport, utilities and regulatory issues;

- introductions to industry leaders, chambers of commerce, universities and other centres of excellence and R&D;
- contact channels into central government that help to safeguard investors' interests;
- assistance, through their Global Partnerships programme, in building collaborative relationships between businesses championing cutting-edge technology;
- support for overseas entrepreneurs and management talent in developing innovative UK business opportunities.

The last two elements of the service emphasize the UK government's particular interest in securing projects that introduce new technologies or management techniques, or generate long-term jobs, and that improve the competitiveness of UK business.

In order to provide this comprehensive service, UK Trade & Investment works in close partnership with the English regional development agencies and the national development agencies in Scotland, Wales and Northern Ireland. The 12 regions that these agencies represent are featured in Part 6 – UK Regional Options.

Delivery of the service

UK Trade & Investment increased its overseas personnel by 12 per cent in 2003 and now deploys more than 130 staff at overseas locations with appropriate staffing increases in London to support the bigger international network. Although the United States remains the largest source of inward investment projects, the teams in new markets in Asia and in Europe have also been reinforced. With 25 years' experience working with inward investors, UK Trade & Investment has built up considerable expertise and knowledge to match the UK's position as the leading country in Europe for attracting inward investment. UK Trade & Investment continually strives to improve its service to clients, paying particular attention to the need to provide its clients with intelligence, advice and information that is tailored to their precise individual needs.

UK Trade & Investment continues to benefit from staff on secondment from its UK partners in business and industry, such as British Telecom and PricewaterhouseCoopers. A more recent extension of that programme has been short-term secondments between UK Trade & Investment and its UK regional partners.

Regional Selective Assistance

Regional Selective Assistance (RSA) (see Chapter 4.2) is available from the UK government in the designated Assisted Areas of Great Britain and Northern Ireland, in which just over 30 per cent of the UK population live. RSA is available to overseas-owned, as well as domestic, companies opening a new plant, or expanding or modernizing an existing plant. Most manufacturing and some service sectors are eligible for RSA, the government's main form of direct financial assistance to companies.

Of course, the UK government's aims are to:

- attract and retain inward investment that would otherwise not go to the United Kingdom;
- increase prosperity through the enhanced productivity and competitiveness of the national and relevant regional economies;
- create or safeguard skilled and other jobs in the RSA.

Forms of RSA

The most normal form of assistance is a grant, which is subject to tax. In some circumstances, loans may also be offered. RSA is classified as state aid and the approval of the European Commission (EC) may be required. Like RSA, the benefits of the government's Enterprise Zones provisions are also monitored by the EC and are described below.

There is no automatic formula for allocating RSA or entitlement to assistance. Government makes offers at its discretion and each case is determined on its own merits, judged against common criteria. The main elements against which the quality of a project is judged are:

- the extent to which a project is expected to increase Gross Domestic Product (GDP) over 10 years;
- age and salary levels;
- the amount of R&D;
- whether the jobs are new or safeguarded;
- the extent to which indirect jobs are created or safeguarded;
- impact on the regional economy;
- innovatory products and/or processes; general impact on the sector;
- relationship with the UK supply chain;
- the extent to which employee skills are transferable.

From the applicant's point of view, RSA is negotiated on the basis of the minimum required to enable the project to go ahead in the form proposed.

Levels of assistance

As an indication of possible levels of assistance, amounts offered range from less than £5,000 per job created for needed employment in areas of particular deprivation and low skill levels, to over £17,000 per job for projects of exceptional quality that can be justified on grounds of need. As a percentage of capital expenditure, offers tend to be in the range of 5 per cent to 15 per cent.

Normally, a grant is paid in instalments, linked to the creation of jobs, capital expenditure and to the project's progress. The investment and jobs have to be maintained for a minimum period; either five years after the first instalment has been paid or at least 18 months after the last instalment, whichever is the longer.

Regional variations

In England, the fixed capital expenditure must exceed £500,000 and the minimum threshold for a grant application is £75,000. There is no upper limit. In Northern Ireland, there are special arrangements for financial assistance, of which the details are available from Invest Northern Ireland. In Scotland, there is no minimum level for a grant and no upper limit. In Wales, grants of more than £50,000 are available without an upper limit.

Applications

Within England, potential investors can contact the relevant Regional Development Agency (RDA) in the region of interest. For Scotland and Wales contact is with the Scottish Executive or the Welsh Assembly government. In each case, they will be able to advise whether the project is in an Assisted Area. From outline project details, they will identify all forms of public assistance, including RSA, which could be available.

Offers of RSA are normally made within 30 days of receiving a complete application for all but the largest and most complex projects. In England, the largest cases, where assistance exceeds £2 million, are appraised by the DTI's Industrial Development Unit (IDU); a timetable for appraisal will be agreed with the applicant at the outset.

If work on a project has already begun, investors will find it difficult to establish whether they need RSA support. Applicants are strongly advised not to commit themselves to projects until they have applied for assistance and have received a firm offer.

Enterprise Zones

The UK government designates Enterprise Zones (EZs) for a period of 10 years. EZs usually comprise a number of sites with individual

planning regimes to be developed as business parks, devoted to manufacturing or for more varied uses. They are intended to encourage
vigorous private sector activity by removing certain tax burdens or
speeding up the application of some statutory or administrative
controls. Although the sites can continue to benefit from whatever aid
may be available under other policies, EZs are not connected directly
with other existing policies such as those for inner cities or derelict land.

EU restrictions

As indicated above, certain businesses may be subject to EC state aid
rules, which restrict their entitlement to state subsidies and may affect
their ability to locate with advantage into an EZ. These rules are
intended to ensure that aids to industry (like the EZ scheme) do not
inhibit free and fair competition throughout the EC. Currently, the
restricted sectors include:

● agriculture;

● coal and steel;

● fisheries;

● food processing;

● metalworking;

● motor vehicles;

● shipbuilding;

● synthetic fibres.

Advice on which businesses may be protected can be taken from the
Zone Authority or promoter in the first instance.

Summary of benefits

The following benefits are available to both new and existing industrial and commercial enterprises in an EZ for the duration of its desig-
nation as a Zone:

● Allowances of 100 per cent for corporation and income tax purposes
  for capital expenditure on industrial and commercial buildings
  whether owner-occupied or let (any balance of the allowance not
  taken initially at the owner's option will be given in straight-line
  annual allowances of 25 per cent).

● Exemption from the National Domestic Rate (Uniform Business
  Rate) on industrial and commercial property.

- A simplified planning regime; developments that conform to the published scheme for each Zone do not require individual planning permission.

- Streamlined administration of statutory controls remaining in force (for example, planning).

- Employers' exemption from industrial training levies and from the requirement to supply information to Industrial Training Boards (ITBs).

- Relaxation of certain criteria and priority processing of applications from firms in EZs for certain customs facilities (for example, inward processing relief and customs warehouses).

Current EZs

There are a total of 30 current designated EZs, of which seven are in the East Midlands (expiring between 21 September and 15 November 2005), six each in the Dearne Valley, Yorkshire and in East Durham (expiring 28 November 2005) and 11 in Tyne Riverside (expiring between 18 February and 20 October 2006).

R&D assistance

The United Kingdom has a number of existing schemes that offer assistance to companies within the area of research and development (R&D), aimed at the exploitation of innovative ideas. Foreign companies planning to establish a business in the United Kingdom can apply for R&D assistance under the following schemes:

- R&D tax credits and allowances;
- EUREKA;
- LINK;
- Foresight;
- EU Sixth Framework Programme (FP6) for research, technological development and demonstration (RTD);
- Grant for Research and Development;
- Grant for Investigating and Innovative Idea.

R&D tax credits

An R&D tax credit for small and medium-sized enterprises (SMEs) came into effect on 1 April 2000. Spending on qualifying R&D attracts relief for 150 per cent of the expenditure. For a company already bene-fiting from the small company rate of corporation tax (19 per cent), the relief will reduce the cash cost by 28.5 per cent. Companies not yet making a profit may take the relief upfront and reduce their cash cost by 24 per cent.

The Government introduced a further new tax relief in its 2002 Budget to encourage R&D and innovation by large companies that applies to all qualifying R&D expenditure from 1 April 2002. In addition to the normal 100 per cent deduction from their taxable income, large companies are entitled to an additional deduction of 25 per cent of their current qualified R&D spending. For example, a company that pays the main rate of corporation tax of 30 per cent and spends £100,000 on qualifying R&D will be able to deduct an addi-tional £25,000 under the R&D tax credit, giving a reduction in tax of £7,500. Information on tax credits may be found on the internet at: http://www.dti.gov.uk/support/taxcreditb.htm.

EUREKA

EUREKA is an EU programme designed to create trans-border, market-oriented, high-tech European R&D projects, thereby supporting the competitiveness of European companies through inter-national collaboration. The criteria for a project to qualify for EUREKA support are that it:

- is a high-tech, market-oriented R&D project;

- involves partners from at least two of the 34 EUREKA member countries;

- aims to develop a cutting-edge, civilian product, process or service;

- is funded by the partners themselves, who may receive public financing from their national governments.

The UK Department of Trade and Industry (DTI) may be able to assist with costs for UK-based companies. With priority given to SMEs, up to 50 per cent of eligible costs may be met by the DTI. At the last count, around 1,000 projects had been successfully completed under the EUREKA programme.

In the United Kingdom, participants' national contact to EUREKA is National Project Coordinators (NPC). The NPC assists companies or research centres in proposing or launching a project that will qualify for the EUREKA label and in finding international partners for project proposals. The NPC website address is: www.eureka.be/ifs/files/isp-bin/eureka/ifs/isps/publicHome.isp.

LINK

LINK is the UK government's principal mechanism for promoting partnerships in pre-competitive research between industry and the R&D sector. It provides financial support to individual programmes of research. All new programmes address priorities under the government's Foresight programme described below.

Various government departments and research councils currently sponsor LINK programmes covering a wide range of technology. Each programme supports a number of collaborative research projects, each lasting around two to three years. Government funding provides up to 50 per cent of eligible costs, which is at least matched by industrial support. Levels of funding for each partner are determined by the allocation of work within a project.

All UK companies are eligible in collaboration with the UK R&D sector. Although priority is given to SMEs, multinationals with significant manufacturing and research operations in the United Kingdom can also participate, provided that the benefits of research are exploited in the United Kingdom or elsewhere within the European Economic Area.

LINK programmes fall into five industry sectors:

- electronics/communications/IT;

- food/agriculture;

- biosciences/medical;

- materials/chemicals;

- energy/engineering.

The scope of the LINK scheme has been broadened by franchising to the following organizations that run other government schemes:

- Biotechnology and Biological Sciences Research Council (BBSRC);

- Medical Research Council;

- Innovative Manufacturing Initiative (IMI), of the Engineering and Physical Sciences Research Council (ESR).

These organizations now have the flexibility to fund LINK projects across their own selected research areas.

The two research councils listed above are among the seven UK research councils that support Research Councils UK (RCUK), a strategic partnership set up to promote science, engineering and technology. Through RCUK, they work together to create a common framework for research, training and knowledge transfer. RCUK also works alongside the Office of Science and Technology (OST) to support the United Kingdom's best academic researchers and deliver the best investment for society. For further details of the LINK scheme, visit website: www.dti.gov.u/ost/links.html.

Foresight

The UK Foresight programme is managed by the OST and is tasked to identify and help realize potential opportunities from new science and technologies. Projects in the current five-year programme, launched in April 2002, include cognitive systems; flood and coastal defence; cyber trust and crime prevention; and exploiting the electromagnetic spectrum.

The starting point for a project area is either a key issue where science has potential solutions or an area of cutting-edge science where the potential applications and technologies have yet to be considered and articulated. Further information can be obtained by visiting the Foresight website at: www.foresight.gov.uk.

The EU Sixth Framework Programme (2002–06)

The Framework Programme (FP) is the EU's main instrument for research funding in Europe. Each FP covers a period of five years with the last year of one FP overlapping with the first year of the following FP. FP6 became fully operational from 1 January 2003 and aims to contribute to the creation of the European Research Area (ERA), reflecting a vision for the future of research in Europe, an internal market for science and technology.

The overall budget for FP6 covering the four-year period 2003–06 is 17.5 billion euros, representing an increase of 17 per cent on FP5 and accounting for 6 per cent of the EU's public (civilian) research budget. The seven key areas on which the largest part of the FP6 budget will be spent and the total budget division is identified in Table 4.3.1.

There are no national quotas for FP funds. The key principles for project allocation are:

- The EU will only fund projects that involve several partners from several countries.

- FP funds are allocated following competitive 'calls for proposals' published by the Commission on a regular basis.

- Projects will only be eligible for FP funding if their objectives reflect priorities outlined in the 'calls for proposals'.

- Quality and technological relevance of projects are assessed by external independent experts.

- FP funds are not subsidies to research organizations or companies.

Table 4.3.1   FP6's thematic priorities and budget division

Thematic Priority	Budget (million euros)
Life Sciences, Genomics & for Health	2,255
Information Society Technologies	3,625
Nanotechnologies, Multifunctional Materials and New Production Processes	1,300
Aeronautics & Space	1,075
Food Quality & Safety	685
Sustainable Development, Global Change & Ecosystems (Including Energy and Transport Research)	2,120
Citizens and Governance in a Knowledge-based Society	225
TOTAL	11,285

Source: European Commission, Research Directorate-General, 2002

More information about FP6 and current 'calls for proposals' may be found by visiting the following internet websites: http://europa.eu.int/comm/research/fp6/index en.html and www.dti.gov.uk/ostinternational/.

Grant for Research and Development

Grant for Research and Development is the Department of Trade and Industry's (DTI) initiative that provides grants to help individuals and SMEs to research and develop technologically innovative products and processes. The new initiative is available in England where it replaces the previous SMART scheme. Scotland, Wales and Northern Ireland each has its own initiative, of which the details may be found on the following websites:

Scotland: www.scotland.gov.uk/wh/elld/rndSMART1.asap
Wales: www.wales.gov.uk
Northern Ireland: www.investni.com/invest/

The Grant for Research and Development offers the following range of assistance:

- Micro projects. Simple low-cost development projects lasting no longer than 12 months with a novel or innovative product or process prototype as the output. Up to £20,000 is available to businesses with fewer than 10 employees.

- Research projects involving planned research or critical investigation of 6 to 18 months' duration. A grant of up to £75,000 is available to businesses with fewer than 50 employees.

- Development projects involving the shaping of industrial research into a pre-production prototype of technologically innovative product or industrial process. For businesses with fewer than 250 employees, grants of up to £200,000 are available.

- Exceptional projects involving higher cost technology development with wider potential economic benefits that must be recognized as of 'strategic importance' for technology or industrial sector. For qualifying projects undertaken by businesses with fewer than 250 employees, a grant of up to £500,000 is available.

Grant for Investigating an Innovative Idea

The previous Technology Reviews and Technology Studies scheme has been superseded since 31 May 2003 by a new initiative called 'Investigating an Innovative Idea'. The product is intended to help businesses that have an idea to develop an innovative product, process or service but are unsure about taking it forward successfully. The grant will reimburse some of the costs of consultants chosen to provide expert advice and to develop an action plan.

Further information on the Grant for Research and Development or the Grant for Investigating an Innovative Idea is available from the local Business Link at the national helpline on +44 (0) 845 600 9 006 or at either of the following websites: http://www.businesslink.org/r-d or www.businesslink.org/innovative-idea.

The Small Business Service

According to the Small Business Service (SBS) Report and Accounts 2002–03, small businesses account for 99 per cent of all UK firms and employ over half of all the UK private workforce. Many of the businesses that inward investors start up will be classified as small businesses and, once registered, will therefore qualify for the support of the SBS.

The SBS was established as an Executive Agency of the DTI in April 2000. Its stated ambition is that the United Kingdom should be the best location in the world to start and grow a business. SBS expertise is used by the whole government in developing policies that affect small businesses. The SBS activities described below are relevant to inward investors whose UK-based businesses fall within the SBS scope.

Encouraging a more dynamic start-up market

SBS leads the government's relationship with UK Business Incubation (UKBI), and with the UK Science Park Association (UKSPA), which reflects the role of science parks in supporting innovation-led, high-growth, knowledge-based businesses.

Building the capability for small business growth

SBS delivers its support to small businesses in England through its national network of 45 Business Link offices that was restructured radically in 2002–03. In that period, Business Link Operators (BLOs) working with their local Learning and Skills Councils (LSCs) made more than 3,500 significant workforce development interventions with small businesses to support skills development. SBS also provided business improvement solutions to 37,000 businesses with estimated benefits totalling £149 million achieved as a result of SBS management best practice interventions.

Small Business Research Initiative

The Small Business Research Initiative, which is coordinated by the SBS, is designed to help smaller businesses in obtaining contracts from government bodies to conduct R&D. The existing R&D programmes of government departments and the research councils, worth up to £1 billion in total, have been opened up to small firms. The government departments involved aim to buy at least 2.5 per cent of their R&D requirements from smaller businesses with a target of £50 million worth of government research. Details of SBRI are provided on pilot information and inquiry website www.sbri.org.uk.

Improving access to finance for small businesses

The SBS works with the private sector and the government to address gaps and weaknesses in the finance market for SMEs, and to help SMEs to access the finance appropriate to their needs in the following ways:

- Access to the Small Firms Loan Guarantee (SFLG) programme has been widened since April 2003. Previously excluded business sectors, including retail catering and motor vehicle repairs, are now eligible.

- Working with eight Regional Venture Capital Funds, £230 million of venture capital was made available in 2002–03 for investment in SMEs with growth potential.

- Three Early Growth Funds were established in the same period to assist up to 1,000 small businesses seeking to raise capital. The three funds have a mandate to invest up to £50 million over three years.

- The 'Bridges Fund', a £40 million Venture Capital Fund, was launched in 2002–03 to increase the flow of venture capital to businesses with growth potential in the most disadvantaged areas in England. The fund combines private sector finance with government funding on a £ for £ basis. The SBS invests on behalf of the government using resources from the EU Phoenix Fund.

- In England, the Phoenix Fund provided £35 million in 2002–03 and £30 million for 2003–04. The life of the fund has been extended to 31 March 2006 and a further £25 million has been provided for each of the two remaining years. The Phoenix Fund also supports City Growth Strategies to put enterprise and business at the heart of regeneration plans.

Global Partnerships and Global Entrepreneurs' Programme

UK Trade & Investment operates a Global Partnerships service, which was rolled out to address the growing demand from companies looking for partners in the UK market. The service plays an important part in facilitating partnerships between international clients and UK businesses focused on the innovative technologies and skills available in the United Kingdom.

Allied to the Global Partnerships service, UK Trade & Investment launched a pilot scheme in 2003 to attract to the UK international entrepreneurs, including expatriates, with 'ideas of exceptional potential'. The pilot was initially focused on the United States and targeted at the global entrepreneur, based on the credibility, experiences and networks of successful UK entrepreneurs who acted as dealmakers within their areas of expertise, namely the sciences and technology. UK government agencies and the British consulates in the United States, as well as the Home Office, also played key roles in gaining early successes. After six months, the initiative generated 18 client entrepreneurs who are considering exploiting their talents or ideas in the United Kingdom.

4.4

Business Risk

Norman Cowan, Wilder Coe

Introduction

An entrepreneur is constantly balancing the elements of risk and reward; since managing risk will not only help protect the business but also help it grow. However, there is a distinction between a carefully considered risk and one taken without any thought as to the possible downside.

Identifying risk

The first and most important step is to identify a particular risk or a number of risks. These need to be monitored on a regular basis, with an early warning system to recognize changes in primary factors underpinning the business.

To manage a particular risk there must be an agreed benchmark to measure whether the problem area is under control, and also to strengthen it so it no longer becomes a threat to the well-being of the business. The risk must not only be graded into categories of high, medium or low, but also be assessed as to its dependence on other factors in the business. However, any one particular risk should not be looked at in isolation since there could be an imbalance within the following internal and external constituent parts of a business:

- economic factors;
- environmental;
- financial;
- human resources;
- operational;

- political;
- regulatory and legal requirements;
- technological.

Ranking the risks

Risks must be evaluated in terms of their likelihood of occurrence and impact, particularly where it is not possible to eliminate or reduce them to an acceptable level, by considering the following benchmarks:

- The threat of the risk materializing.
- Capability in reducing the impact of the occurrence of the risk.
- By ranking the risks, management will be better placed to establish the priorities and have a greater appreciation of the effect each will have on the other.

Awareness of areas to be changed

To survive the changes in business cycles, product trends and the results of world events, a business must be prepared to change the way it operates. Change must be considered and actioned with speed in order to minimize the impact on the well-being of the business. It is therefore essential to be aware of the present overall health of the business and control its shortcomings, since, if not controlled, they could quickly become a risk that threatens continuance of trade.

For example, is the rate that cash resources are utilized in inverse proportion to the level of profitability? Is there increasing creditor pressure; are stock levels at an acceptable level; is turnover at the budgeted level and are key employees leaving? The one certainty is that should a risk occur, the chance of overcoming it will be made that much more difficult where the business has other underlying problems.

Monitoring continuous risks

Once the outcome of the risks have been evaluated it is necessary to put in place a reporting and monitoring system. This should show clearly how these risks have been properly considered and whether the business objectives are now on track. To measure this, *key performance indicators* should be set up. These are independent and objective ways to measure the goals set by management. For example, the stock turnover ratio, which indicates how often stocks flow through the business in the course of a year.

In some industries certain non-financial indicators can be instituted to monitor product quality. For example, if a tyre business encounters an unusually high number of faults reported by the consumer, this may indicate a rise in injury compensation claims sustained as a result of accidents caused by these faulty tyres.

Outsourcing the impact of risk

Third parties can sometimes protect the financial consequences of a risk materializing through unforeseen circumstances. Insurance can be taken for product liability, loss of profits due to fire and an anticipated loss attributed to a key member of staff suddenly dying.

There are those risks associated with business legislation. Obtaining the assistance of support services, which provide help and indemnity against breaches in employment law, that is, a claim for unfair dismissal. Likewise, insuring against the professional costs of an in-depth tax investigation by the Inland Revenue. Indeed the risk of bad debts can also be insured, which could also cover the legal costs of pursuing recovery through the courts.

When a risk turns into a crisis

When a risk materializes or if an unplanned adverse factor emerges that materially affects the underpinning of a business, then there could very well be a 'crisis'. Careful thought and planning should be considered on how best to deal with this.

The first step could be to take immediate control of the business with strong leadership by putting in place a person who is able to cope with the stress of dealing with the crisis. This could even be achieved by obtaining temporary support from an expert interim manager, a turnaround specialist or someone with the necessary skills to recognize and deal with the crisis without any preconceived ideas.

At the outset an effective strategy must be prepared to manage the crisis and develop a clear thought process in order to address the following key issues:

- Look at the cause of the crisis and what part of the business was initially affected.

- Measure the disruption to ongoing trading and whether the damage can be limited.

- Is it possible to limit knowledge of the crisis within the organization? If it were leaked to competitors, would it damage the relationship with existing customers?

- An estimate of the time it will take for the problem to be resolved.

- What resources are needed to take full control of the crisis and what is the cost?

- A financial model must be produced that projects the anticipated outcome that the crisis is likely to have on the business together with the projected results of taking positive action to resolve the problems.

- Restoring confidence in lenders and key suppliers in order for the business to continue trading. This may entail having a full and frank dialogue with them as to how to resolve the problems created by the crisis.

Management that is not confident that it can deal with the above matters should consider seeking expert advice.

Repairing the damage may be achieved by concentrating on the short-term capabilities of the business rather than those that are long-term. The crisis is in the here and now. Preservation and generation of cash should be the one primary task. Once this is achieved then attention can be turned to viability and performance.

Lastly, it is essential that key personnel need to work as one cohesive force, with their actions prioritized as to importance. They must be aware that it is essential to deliver the targets set for the areas within their responsibility.

Conclusion

The best way to continue in business is to plan for success and the problem areas too. Keep the initiative on performance by identifying possible problem areas before they go into a downward spiral. Bearing in mind that it is human nature for proprietors and managers to ignore an approaching crisis, nevertheless there must be a strong infrastructure to monitor all aspects of the business.

For those unforeseen circumstances that will threaten the existence of a business, irrespective of the way it is run, there can only be firm and decisive action to manage the position. It is for these reasons that there can be no room for complacency. The watchwords must be *forewarned is forearmed*.

Company Formation – Methods and Legal Implications

Ian Saunders, Artaius Limited

Registration

There is no formal requirement in the United Kingdom to register with the tax authorities before commencing business. A person wishing to start a business in the United Kingdom has a choice between the registration of an incorporated vehicle (a company) or an unincorporated vehicle (a sole trader or partnership).

Unincorporated vehicles

Sole trader
A person who carries on business as a sole trader is personally liable for all the debts and obligations incurred by his or her business; accordingly all of his or her business and personal assets can be called upon to meet payment of any liabilities incurred by his or her business.

Partnership
A partnership is usually governed by a written agreement, which binds the partners and is subject to the provisions of the Partnership Act 1890. With some exceptions, partnerships are limited to 20 partners. The partnership has no separate legal entity and a trader who carries on business through this vehicle is jointly and severally liable with his or her other partners for all debts and obligations incurred by the partnership while he or she is a partner. Furthermore he or she is jointly and severally liable with the other partners for loss or damage to third parties by the wrongful acts or omissions of any partner in the ordinary course of the partnership business.

Limited partnership

These are governed by the Limited Partnerships Act 1907. As long as there is one or more partners liable for all the debts and obligations of the partnership, the Act allows a partner to limit his or her liability to the amount contributed by him or her by way of property or capital on joining the partnership. Such a partner is not entitled to take part in the management of the partnership.

Incorporated vehicles

Corporations have distinct legal personality separate from that of their members. The private company limited by shares ('limited company') and public company limited by shares ('plc') are the most important and common business corporations in the United Kingdom. There is no statutory minimum capital requirement for a limited company but the minimum capital requirement for a plc is £50,000. If contributed in cash, only one-quarter of the value of each issued share is required to be paid up in the plc (effectively £12,500) for it to obtain a certificate to commence trading.

A private company is prohibited by law from offering any of its shares to members of the public, so no offer of shares of any kind can be made. It is the vehicle used mostly for owner/managed companies and new business start-ups. A plc can, under strict procedures, issue a prospectus and offer shares to members of the public.

There are three other types of corporation that may be incorporated in accordance with the Companies Act 1985, as follows.

Private company limited by guarantee and not having a share capital

This vehicle is used chiefly by trade associations, clubs, charitable companies and management companies for apartment blocks. There is no share capital. Instead each member 'guarantees' that in the event of the company being wound up they will pay a specified sum towards the funds. The articles of association govern the terms of membership of the companies.

Unlimited companies, with or without a share capital

The members' liability is unlimited with this type of company. The chief advantage of this organization is that accounts are not required to be submitted to Companies House and are thus not available for public inspection.

Limited liability partnership (LLP)

Introduced 6 April 2001, an LLP comprises a corporate entity distinct from companies incorporated under the Companies Act, but sharing many characteristics. An LLP is a legal person quite separate from its members, with capacity to contract in its own name. Members of an LLP enjoy limited liability; they do not have to be employees of the LLP.

LLP incorporation
A minimum of two people is required when the LLP is incorporated; they subscribe their names to an incorporation document. The LLP must carry on a lawful business with a view to profit. The incorporation document, in a form approved by the Registrar of Companies (Form LLP 2), must contain the LLP's:

● name;

● registered office; and

● names and addresses of members on incorporation.

On receipt of a properly completed incorporation document the Registrar will issue a certificate that the LLP is incorporated in that name, and register the LLP accordingly.

An LLP must prepare and publish accounts similar to those regarding a company and file an annual return accordingly. An LLP may change its name and registered office. Members may change.

Unless members agree otherwise, they share profits and losses equally and may all participate in managing the LLP. Members may enter into an agreement that, among other things, deals with profit shares, involvement in management and remuneration. As with incorporating a company and settling its Memorandum and Articles of Association, those intending to incorporate an LLP and drafting a Members' Agreement should seek expert advice at an early stage. Members of an LLP are taxed as if the business was carried on by a partnership, rather than by a company.

The process of forming a company

Private company limited by shares

The great majority of companies formed in the United Kingdom are private companies limited by shares and the process of the formation of these companies will be examined first.

Company name
The proposed company name should be checked to ensure that it is not identical to an existing registered name or does not contain a word restricted or prohibited. The UK authority dealing with the registration of companies ('Companies House') maintains a list of already

registered names and restricted words. This is available at its website www.companieshouse.gov.uk/info.

Care should also be taken to avoid clashes with companies of similar names. Although this will not prevent the registration of the name, a new incorporator may find a subsequent objection to the new name has been made and in such cases Companies House have power to direct a new company to change its name.

New companies should also be advised to ensure their proposed name does not conflict with any registered trade or service marks. (See Chapter 5.1 under the heading 'Passing off'). The company name chosen must end with the word 'Limited' or 'Ltd' and these words must not appear anywhere other than as the last word in the name.

Shareholders

A private company limited by shares can have one or more share-holders. The first shareholder(s) of the new company will be the person(s) who subscribes for shares in the Memorandum of Association of the company, which is a document required to be submitted for the incorporation and which is detailed below.

Subsequent to the incorporation, the directors of the company may allot further shares that are available in the 'authorized capital' of the company as stated in the Memorandum of Association. The liability of any shareholder is limited to any amounts unpaid on the shares agreed to be taken.

Directors

The directors of a company will be those persons who consent to act as such on Form 10 submitted with the incorporation papers. The directors are required to provide their full name and residential address, date of birth, nationality, business occupation and to list any other directorships held in the United Kingdom.

There is no restriction on non-UK residents acting as directors, but there may be restrictions on what work some nationals who are not based in the European Economic Area can do in the United Kingdom. For further information please see the UK Home Office website at www.ind.homeoffice.gov.uk. (See also Chapter 4.1.) A private limited company requires a minimum of one director.

The directors will be responsible for managing the business and affairs of the company. As such, they are required to act at all times in the best interests of the company and are regarded as the equivalent of trustees of the company's monies.

Secretary

The company must have a secretary, who will be responsible with the directors for ensuring that the company meets its obligations with filing accounts and returns, etc, in good time. If there is only one director, this person may not also be the secretary. If there are two or more directors, one of these persons can also act as secretary.

Registered office

A company incorporated in England and Wales must have a registered office in either England or Wales and a company incorporated in Scotland must have a registered office in Scotland. A company is required by UK law to keep at its registered office registers of directors, shareholders, directors' interests in the shares of the company, legal charges, debentures and minutes of directors' and shareholders' meetings. Certain of the registers must be made available for inspection by any member of the public presenting himself or herself to the registered office. The registered office should therefore be a place where such inspection can take place and where any legal notice should be served on the company.

Documents required by Companies House to form the company

MEMORANDUM OF ASSOCIATION

This sets out the name of the company, whether the registered office is to be situated in England, Wales or Scotland, and its business activities (its 'Objects'). The Objects of the company may be stated as 'to carry on business as a general commercial company' and in which case the company may undertake any activity allowed under UK law. The Memorandum also states that the liability of the members is limited, the authorized share capital of the company and contains a page for the subscribers (or first shareholder or holders) to sign.

ARTICLES OF ASSOCIATION

These set out the rules for the running of the company's internal affairs, that is, the rules for meetings of directors and shareholders and the relationship between the owners (shareholders) and mangers (directors), transferring of shares, etc. There is a default set of Articles of Association, which will be implied if no Articles are submitted, but these are not always appropriate for a newly formed small company. It is therefore recommended that Articles of Association be submitted.

Company registration agents will be prepared to supply both the Memorandum and Articles of Association for a proposed company for a small fee.

COMPANIES HOUSE FORM 10

This sets out the details of the directors and secretary of the company and its registered office address. It must be signed by these officers and by the subscribers to the Memorandum and Articles of Association or an agent for the subscriber.

>84   Investment and start-up considerations

STATUTORY DECLARATION (FORM 12)

This must be signed by a director or the secretary in the presence of a commissioner for oaths, notary public or solicitor having the powers of a commissioner for oaths and is a statement that all the requirements of the Companies Act 1985 have been met.

CHEQUE FOR COMPANIES HOUSE FEES

Companies House require a cheque for the sum of £20 to complete the incorporation. If the documents submitted are in order, Companies House usually issues a Certificate of Incorporation within four to five working days.

UK company registration agents can assist with the whole process of forming a company and can arrange for the relevant declaration to be carried out very simply. In addition, it is possible for agents with the necessary software to file private limited company incorporations electronically at Companies House. This speeds up the process still further and companies can now be formed within 24 hours.

Public company limited by shares

The process for forming a public company is very similar to that of forming a private company; the differences being:

- Company name. The name must end with the words 'Public Limited Company' or 'plc'.

- Shareholders. A public limited company must have a minimum of two shareholders and must have an issued capital of £50,000 minimum.

- Directors. There must be a minimum of two directors.

Secretary

The secretary must be qualified, that is, be a barrister, solicitor or advocate admitted in the United Kingdom, or be a qualified Chartered Accountant, Certified Accountant, Certified Management Accountant or Chartered Secretary.

The documents required to be submitted to Companies House for the formation of the company are the same as for a private company, but the Memorandum and Articles of Association must be suitable for the management of a public company.

In addition, following incorporation, a public company must undertake a further declaration that it has met the minimum capital requirements and that it has paid up its capital as necessary (one-quarter of the nominal value of each share). It will then be issued with a further certificate allowing it to borrow money and trade.

Statutory requirements

Accounts

Companies are required to submit accounts prepared in accordance with the Companies Act 1985. Companies House and the UK tax authorities must receive these not later than 10 months following the company's year-end date (seven months for public limited companies).

A company's year-end will be set automatically by Companies House as the anniversary of the end of the month of incorporation, that is, a company incorporated at any time during April 2004 will have a year-end of 30 April 2005. A company's year-end can be changed by the submission of a form to Companies House and can be extended to a period of up to 18 months. However, directors of new companies should note that if this extension is made, the first set of accounts will still be due 22 months from the original incorporation date (19 months for plcs), that is, 10 months from the original year-end date (seven for plcs) (see Chapter 4.8).

Annual return

Companies are required to submit an annual return to Companies House within 28 days of the anniversary of the date of incorporation. This return sets out the current business activities, details of directors and secretary and shareholders of the company. A fee of £15 is payable to Companies House with this return.

Other documents

The Companies Act 1985 specifies that returns shall be made to Companies House in the event that the company undertakes certain actions. For example, the increase of capital, the issuing of shares, changes being made to the Memorandum or Articles of Association, the granting of a charge over the company's assets, changes to the details of any director or secretary or the resignation or new appointment of these officers. There are various time limits imposed for the submission of these returns and the officers of a company are advised to familiarize themselves with these requirements.

The management of a company's statutory affairs (such as the submission of annual returns and changes to shareholders and directors) is often carried out by specialist company formation agents, company secretarial service providers, solicitors or accountants.

Review of company law

A fundamental revision of UK company law is now under way following
an independent three-year review. This has the aim of cutting costs
and red tape for businesses of all sizes. The government published its
response to the Company Law Review's major recommendations and
set out its core proposals for reform on 16 July 2002 and in July 2003
the government announced its plans to change company law.

4.6

Commercial Banking Services

Jonathan Reuvid and HSBC

The information provided in this chapter and in Chapter 4.7 is drawn from the published material of HSBC but the services described are available from the other major banks offering commercial banking services in the United Kingdom. The commercial banking services available to international companies and UK banking practices are among the most reliable and sophisticated in the world.

Introduction

All businesses want to receive payments quickly and efficiently and to have access to a range of solutions for receiving and making payments that fit their business activities in as tailored a way as practicable. To stay in control of cashflow, the business needs to keep track of payments made, to have rapid advice of receipts and to have funds credited quickly and efficiently.

The starting point of the banking relationship for the customer is the opening of a current account and the issue of a cheque book. Cheques remain the simplest form of payment for low-volume transactions. However, there is a wide range of alternative payment methods from card payments to telephone and electronic banking services described in this chapter.

Making payments in the United Kingdom

For companies wishing to make payments, the services that will be the most appropriate vary depending on whether payments are made in the United Kingdom or overseas and upon the volumes and speed of payments required.

Making multiple normal payments in the United Kingdom

For a large number of payments each month with payment times of three days or more the following methods are suitable: 1) Faxpay – a fax- or telephone-based payment service that provides a convenient, secure and inexpensive way to make payments to regular suppliers and all wages and salaries payments. The method provides for simultaneous debiting and crediting, detailed reports confirming all payments made and password protection; 2) ACH (known in the United Kingdom as BACS) direct debits and credits software – easy to use Windows-based software packages provided by banks that allow customers to make or collect payments direct from PCs within their organizations. The software has inbuilt security, allowing full control of the payment process from creation/generation, authorization and transmission. Each action can be allocated to a specific 'user' with relevant authority. This solution caters for fully euro-denominated credit payments within the United Kingdom.

Other appropriate services for customers in this category include cheques, business cards, corporate cards, purchasing cards and payroll services, which provide a full calculation facility, the printing of payslips, management reports and payments direct into employees' accounts by wire transfer/BACS or Faxpay.

Making multiple urgent payments in the United Kingdom

For companies making multiple urgent payments with same- or next-day payment the appropriate solution is internet banking, which allows 24-hour access to bank accounts and offers the following benefits:

- real time balances on business accounts;
- transaction details on individual accounts;
- immediate transfers between customers' own accounts;
- payments of up to £100,000 per day using Bill Payments or BACS;
- forward date payments up to 45 days in advance;
- viewing and cancellation of standing orders or direct debits;
- delegated access to the service to other company users;
- download of transaction details to Quicken©, Microsoft Money© or spreadsheet packages;
- security routines including unique usernames and passwords, automatic log-off after periods of inactivity and protected

communication across the internet using data encryption and digital certification.

Most full service banks offer a priority payment facility providing a simple, cost-effective way of making payments from a PC. These enable customers to initiate same-day sterling and euro payments in the United Kingdom and urgent payments to beneficiaries outside the United Kingdom. Templates with details of regular beneficiaries may be held and payments submitted for transmission around the word at any time of the day or night.

Companies wishing to make more than 100 payments a month with same-day or next-day payment will find PC-based priority payments or their equivalent system an appropriate facility. Alternative methods are by Business Card, Corporate Card or Purchasing Card. The differing key features of these three types of card, available for both UK and overseas purchases as offered by HSBC, may be summarized as follows:

- Business Card:
  - up to 38 days interest-free credit;
  - accepted at over 600,000 suppliers in the United Kingdom, and 21 million throughout the MasterCard network worldwide;
  - separation of business from personal expenses with itemized monthly statements;
  - individual credit limits (minimum £500);
  - allows telephone and internet purchases;
  - no transaction fees on purchases.

- Corporate Card:
  - up to 56 days interest-free credit;
  - company chooses number of cards and maximum spending limit on each card;
  - itemized monthly statement for each card;
  - balances settled centrally or by cardholder.

- Purchasing Card:
  - available to corporate customers whose annual purchases exceed £1 million;
  - VAT returns supplied in line with HM Customs and Excise regulations;
  - cards issued to selected employees with maximum spending limit on each card;
  - monthly statements for each card with all balances settled by a single payment;
  - suppliers paid within three to four days.

Making payments overseas

Making fewer than five payments a month overseas

Companies making fewer than five payments a month overseas and needing same-day or next-day payment are recommended to use their bank's branch priority payments facility, which provides a fast and secure method of payment that can be sent to most countries in any tradable currency. Payments to Eurozone countries will be received within one day. Payments outside the Eurozone will normally be received within four working days.

Flexible payment methods include:

- by credit to a specified bank account;
- by payment to the beneficiary at a stated address;
- collected by the beneficiary upon production of appropriate identification.

If payment times of three days or more are required, HSBC offers its 'Worldpay' solution for the prompt and cost-effective transmission of low-value payments abroad from the customer's local HSBC bank branch. Worldpay involves one simple document only and instructions received before 2.30 pm will be acted upon the same day. The system is available for payments of £2,000 or less and may be used to pay salaries, fees and expenses to employees abroad and pay subscriptions to trade organizations and publications. The countries to which payments by this means may be made are: Australia, Austria, Belgium, Canada, Cyprus, Denmark, Finland, France, Germany, Hong Kong SAR, Ireland, Italy, the Netherlands, New Zealand, Portugal, South Africa, Spain, Sweden, Switzerland and the United States. Other high street banks offer a similar service through their local branches.

For non-urgent payments overseas or non-urgent payments in euros within the United Kingdom, International Drafts are an appropriate alternative, offering the following customer advantages:

- low cost;
- ability to attach relevant documentation and correspondence;
- no time limit within which a draft supplied by the bank has to be sent;
- drafts available in sterling and most currencies.

The alternative payment methods available are Business Card, Corporate Card and Purchasing Card.

Making multiple payments overseas

Urgent multiple payments overseas needing same-day or next-day payment may be serviced by the priority payment system described above or by Business Card, Corporate Card or Purchasing Card. Standard multiple payments overseas with payment times of three days or more may be serviced by HSBC Worldpay (or other bank equivalent described above) or by any of the three types of credit card.

Receiving payments within the United Kingdom

For companies wishing to receive payment from the United Kingdom in person, there are two alternatives: 1) banker's draft – provides a near certainty of payment upon presentation and is therefore attractive for receipt of large sums, particularly where immediate delivery of goods or the transfer of title to property is concurrent; 2) electronic card processing – an efficient and swift system for dealing with sales transactions, which accepts all major credit cards via terminals provided by the bank and software providing monthly statements showing the previous month's card transactions. Companies preferring to outsource their invoice payments and collections may consider using their bank's credit management service.

Receiving payments from abroad

Inward payment

Companies that request a wire transfer from the sender against full banking details, including SWIFT and sorting codes and account number may take advantage of their bank's inward payment service. The bank applies the appropriate exchange rate in force at the time of the transaction on receipt of a payment in currency that is to be credited to the customer's sterling account and effects the credit. An advice with all details of the receipt, including exchange rate and commission is mailed to the customer on the next working day.

Euro bulk paper clearing

For UK-based companies, the ability to pay euro cheques directly into a UK bank account has become an essential need as more and more businesses deal in euros in their foreign trade transaction. UK banks that participate in the Euro bulk paper clearing system offer clearance of most euro cheques along similar lines to the sterling clearance system. Funds can be credited to either a sterling or euro account and will be available for withdrawal three working days after paying in the cheque.

Cheque negotiations

Most banks offer a cheque negotiation scheme to clear cheques received that are payable outside the United Kingdom, foreign currency cheques payable in the United Kingdom or sterling cheques drawn abroad. The proceeds of cheques credited to a customer's sterling account are made immediately available, subject to recourse while costs are much lower than those incurred with cheque collection. A forward value date is applied when crediting a foreign currency account with funds of the same currency. The cheque negotiation scheme is also the only way in which the proceeds of travellers' cheques payable outside the United Kingdom can be paid.

Cheque collections

Businesses receiving cheques payable outside the United Kingdom, foreign currency cheques payable in the United Kingdom, or sterling cheques drawn abroad, can take advantage of their bank's cheque collection scheme. However, proceeds of cheque collections are only made available to the customer when the funds have been received by the bank, unlike a cheque negotiation where the proceeds are made available before the cheque has been cleared. As a part of the service:

- The bank will provide the exact date on which proceeds or advice of non-payment will be received for certain cheques.

- The collection process can be accelerated by requesting the bank to send cheques to the Drawee Bank by courier for an extra fee.

- The bank's international cheque processing department monitors progress of each transaction and will chase for the proceeds or an advice of non-payment.

- Since receipt of proceeds usually means that a cheque has been paid, customers can use the cheque collections mechanism to withhold the release of goods or the provision of services where advance payment is an agreed term of business.

Foreign cheques can be paid in any UK branch of most commercial banks.

US dollar and European lockboxes

If a company's goods or services are bought by customers in the United States, prompt and efficient processing of cheques receivable is paramount. For example, HSBC provides a US Dollar Lockbox service whereby funds are credited up to 10 days faster to customers' accounts by processing all cheques through the US clearing system rather than with traditional cheque negotiations. There is no need to open accounts with different banks in the United Kingdom and the United States, charges are fixed, paperwork is kept to a minimum and the documentation sent by the US customers is returned to the company.

There is an equivalent Euro Lockbox system to process all cheques from customers based in continental Europe through the relevant European clearing system. Use of this system will result in the earliest possible crediting of cheques to their accounts, up to five days earlier than with traditional cheque negotiations. The transaction information provided can be linked to new or existing electronic balance reporting and payments services.

Cash management

Physical cash management

Standard physical cash management services include the time-saving facility to place payments in self-sealing packets that can be handed over at branch counters and secure enquiry positions or deposited in automated paying-in machines to be verified later, and a range of solutions available to bank customers receiving over £10,000 in cash every week. These include cash collection services by secure carrier from the customer's own premises with delivery to the bank and cash in transit services where the collections are delivered to one of the bank's network of cash centres across the United Kingdom.

At many banks there is a parallel bulk cheque service for organizations receiving more than 100 cheques per week whereby cheques are collected by an authorized carrier from the customer's outlets/premises and delivered to a cheque-processing centre within the UK network, which processes all branch and commercial cheque items.

Outsourcing payment collection

Finally, for companies preferring to outsource payment collection there is the option of using their bank's credit management service. Credit management is one of the three service elements of invoice finance (see Chapter 4.7 – Finance for Companies) linked to credit protection and sales-linked finance services. For companies selling upon credit terms to other businesses in the United Kingdom or overseas, full service banks offer a credit management service providing consistent, professional credit control and efficient collection, which strikes a balance between the customer's need to be paid and the maintenance of good public relations.

Finance for Companies

Jonathan Reuvid and HSBC

Fundraising requirements

Most businesses will need to raise finance at some stage in their development either to fund growth or to enhance short-term cashflow. Raising finance wisely and tax efficiently can make a major contribution to a company's profitability, whereas badly planned inappropriate finance may be burdensome. The first step in identifying appropriate financing solutions is to clarify the purpose for which a company needs to raise funds. Broadly, there are four main reasons for a company to seek external funding.

To assist cashflow

The need for external support may be driven by a requirement to convert sales invoices into cash faster than a company's customers are willing to pay, by the wish to finance a large project or by other situations that cause a credit gap in cash flow. Easily accessible solutions range from invoice financing services to an extended overdraft or the use of a bank Business Card or loan.

To finance international trade

International trade can put a strain on a company's cashflow and expose the business to a variety of risks. A number of specific solutions are available, depending on whether a company is engaged in import or export trade or both.

To acquire fixed assets

The acquisition of new premises, the expansion or improvement of existing buildings may all require funding of a longer-term nature for which there are several solutions. Equally, a number of funding options are available for company acquisitions of equipment and business vehicles.

To fund business growth

Companies needing a cash injection to facilitate growth should be sure to choose an option that supports their expansion plans constructively. The needs of a business planning to expand by organic growth may be very different from those of an enterprise expanding through franchising or a company growing through acquisition.

Alternative solutions for all these funding scenarios are discussed in the sections that follow. As in the previous chapter the range of solutions is drawn from the HSBC reference book but all full service UK banks offer a similar range.

Assisting cashflow

Companies trading within the United Kingdom have access to a variety of financing services through the commercial banks.

Overdraft

Often the most convenient way for a company to pre arrange the working capital it needs to ride out the troughs in its business cycle is to arrange an overdraft facility with its bank. The company will need to satisfy the bank as to why the money is needed, how much is required and for how long. Subject to a favourable credit assessment and agreement on the overdraft limit, the bank will confirm arrangements by a facility letter. The bank may require security.

Interest is charged at a pre-agreed rate and debited monthly or quarterly to suit the customer. Small businesses may protect their overdrafts, typically up to £15,000, against death or disability for up to four eligible employees through a Small Business Protected Overdraft.

Business card

The same Business Card facility identified in Chapter 4.6 as a payment method can be used as a means of easing cashflow by taking advantage of its 38-day interest free credit in paying for everyday expenses.

Invoice finance

Comprising three service elements – sales-linked finance, credit management and credit protection – invoice finance offers greater working capital flexibility, relief from the burden of chasing customers for payment and safeguard against bad debt to businesses selling in the United Kingdom or overseas on credit terms.

Invoice finance is suitable for most businesses with a sales turnover of £100,000 or more and is available as a stand-alone service for larger, longer-established companies. It is also available in combination with the credit management and/or card protection services that individual banks offer. Other non-bank invoice finance houses offer services up to lower limits.

Financing international trade

Loans and overdrafts

Loans and overdrafts are the first source of finance for international trade, as in the normal course of domestic UK business. For longer-term needs, fixed or variable rate loans in sterling or foreign currency are available from full service banks with the repayment terms structured to suit a company's business cashflow.

Foreign currency loans on fixed terms are an attractive option for companies involved in international business. By taking out a loan in any major currency, a company can reduce its exposure to fluctuating exchange rates and is enabled to make and receive payments in the overseas currency without the cost and effort of conversion back into sterling. It opens an appropriate foreign currency account in the United Kingdom, which is simpler and may be more cost-effective than opening an account abroad. Foreign currency loans can be medium or short term and the borrower can have the option to repay in single or multi-currencies to suit its requirements.

Where these facilities are not suitable and either the lender or the borrower requires more structure, the following services are available from those banks that specialize in the finance of international trade.

Discounting/negotiation of Export Documentary Credits

Also known as letters of credit, Export Documentary Credits are a popular method of reducing the risks in overseas trade and are in global usage. They provide a measure of security for both buyer and seller. Having given credit to an overseas customer using an Export Documentary Credit, an exporter may find that its cashflow becomes tight during the credit period. If compliant documents have been presented to the bank, in most cases the bank will be able to give the exporter immediate value for the documents under the Documentary Credit, less a discount/negotiation fee.

Import Usance Documentary Credit

By asking their bank to issue Documentary Credits on their behalf to buy goods, an importer reduces the risk of non-payment for the exporter and may enable itself to negotiate a period of credit, such as 30, 60 or 90 days, from the supplier, thereby giving itself the opportunity to sell on the goods before having to pay for them.

Import loans for traders

There are two basic types of import loans. The first addresses the situation where a company has imported goods under an Import Documentary Credit, but has not received sufficient supplier credit to allow collection of any proceeds from selling on the goods. In this instance, an import loan can be used to pay the Documentary Credit on the due date. The loan is repaid when the proceeds are received from selling on the goods.

In the second instance, import loans are taken out to cover situations where a company wishes to import goods without using trade finance instruments, but still needs structured borrowing. The bank will require some assurance that the proceeds from selling on the goods will be used specifically to repay any debt associated with the original purchase of the goods. Therefore, the bank will probably provide an import loan for each transaction, with a repayment date set to match the expected date for receipt of proceeds from any onward sale of the goods.

Export loans for manufacture

If a company is the named beneficiary under an Export Documentary Credit advised to it by its bank, but needs working capital to manufacture the goods to be sold, an Export Loan may be appropriate. The Export Documentary Credit and the Export Loan will be repaid once compliant documentation has been presented to the bank, with any surplus being credited to the exporter.

Financing export sales

International commercial banks provide a range of services that allow companies to offer attractive open account terms to overseas customers, while protecting their business from the associated risks of severely delayed payment or non-payment. The banks will provide between 80 per cent and 100 per cent of invoice values on the next working day and, in this way, help to give exporters a competitive edge over local suppliers as well as reducing pressure on cashflow.

In addition, such services iron out the risks of currency fluctuation, give professional assistance in assessing creditworthiness of potential customers and allow exporters to focus on negotiating the most appropriate terms.

Advances against export collection

Documentary Collections are an alternative to the relative complexity and cost of Documentary Credits and provide a cost-effective, more secure alternative to trade on open account. Basically, the method relies on using the overseas customer's bank as an intermediary. The exporting company sends the shipping documents to its own bank, which forwards them to the customer's bank, with instructions to only release them in return for payment or a promise to pay at a later specified date. The exporter's bank can advance funds against the subsequent collection of payment.

Acquiring fixed assets

Property purchases

The commercial mortgage is the most commonly used financial package to purchase existing or new business premises or to extend premises acquired previously. Mortgage finance is available from a number of financial institutions including life assurance companies and pension funds. Mortgages are also available from commercial banks, typically up to 75 per cent of the purchase price for new or existing buildings or the professional valuation – whichever is the lower. There are no set maximum amounts but typically there is a minimum amount for the sum borrowed.

Loans from HSBC are for a minimum period of five years and a maximum period of 20 years. For loans up to £100,000 rates are charged at a margin over the bank's base rate and for those of a greater value variable rates linked to the London Inter-bank Borrowing Rate (LIBOR) are also available. Fixed interest loans are agreed by negotiation. Interest is applied monthly with an optional moratorium on capital repayment of up to two years from draw-down.

Property associated purchases

The small business loan
A quick and easy way to fund the refitting of premises or the purchase of new business equipment, such as PCs, which will minimize the effect on cashflow, is through a small business loan. Small business loans available may typically be for any amount from £250 to £15,000 without arrangement or security fees. To assist budgeting, the interest rate is fixed from the start and loan repayments therefore remain the same even if bank base rates should rise. Repayment schedules can match the

expected lifespan of the items purchased and may be spread over six, nine or 12 months or at six-month intervals thereafter up to 10 years.

Banks usually offer an optional business loan protection plan under which the borrower's payments are covered for one year against sickness and disability and repayment in full is provided in the event of death. The cover can be extended to up to four people and the insurance premium can be added to the loan as principal.

The flexible business loan

A similar type of facility is the flexible business loan, which HSBC offers for amounts over £10,000 as a cost-effective way for a company to finance fixed investment in the business or, indeed, business expansion. There is no maximum to the amount for which a loan application can be made.

Like the small business loan, LIBOR-linked interest rates are available for loans over £100,000. From £10,001, variable interest rates are charged and from £25,001, fixed interest rates are negotiable. There is an option to pay interest either monthly or quarterly.

Repayments may be spread over up to 15 years, although, in the case of equipment, the length of the loan is expected to match the useful life of the asset. For loans over £25,001 a capital repayment holiday of up to two years may be taken. On certain types of loan, an option is granted to defer up to two monthly payments a year.

Vehicle and equipment acquisitions

A range of alternative financing arrangements is available for the acquisition of vehicles and equipment, which are inappropriate for other fixed asset purchases.

Business motor finance

For small companies or unincorporated businesses running up to, say, 25 business vehicles, the alternative motor finance packages offered by the vehicle finance subsidiaries of commercial banks provide the funds to source, purchase and dispose of own vehicles, through motor purchase or contract hire by simply stating which vehicles are sought and leaving the rest to the finance company.

Motor purchase allows the acquirer to negotiate their own deal and to own the vehicle at the end of the contract. Contract hire (with maintenance) removes the uncertainty surrounding the cost of running vehicles and provides for the hirer to return the vehicle at the end of the contract without regard to its residual value. In both cases the same kind of payment protection insurance as for small business loans is available to cover the contingency of key employees being unable to work through illness or disability or their death.

Vehicle finance

Tailor-made and cost-effective solutions for fleet funding and management are also available from bank finance subsidiaries to companies having fleets of more than 25 vehicles, either exclusively in the United Kingdom or across Europe and North America. Arrangements can include fuel cards, fixed cost maintenance and provisions to offer employees a cash allowance instead of a company car and to help them source their own vehicles through personal contract purchase schemes.

Equipment finance

Finance packages are similarly available from the equipment finance subsidiaries of the commercial banks for the purchase or lease of equipment. Hire purchase enables a company to select its own supplier and negotiate its own deal, acquiring ownership at the end of the agreement. Alternatively, a finance lease enables a business to have the use of an asset over a predetermined period without leading to ownership. At the end of the contract the rental can be extended or the lessee can sell the asset and retain a part of the proceeds. As previously noted, the purchase of equipment can also be funded by a small business loan or a flexible business loan.

Funding business growth

The most suitable finance product to help fund a company's growth is based on its expansion plan. For example, a company planning to expand through franchising may have need of a bank Franchise Support service. Companies operating in the field of new technology will have special needs, while professionals wishing to buy into a partnership may require a Partnership Capital Loan.

In each of these scenarios bank customers will require the attention and advice of a specialist service that leading banks are organized to provide. For example, HSBC has formed an Innovation and Technology Unit with a nationwide network of Technology Bank Managers offering guidance to organizations providing specialist financial support. The bank also has its own range of 'in-house' equity funding programmes and can provide free assessment of technological proposals together with appraisals of their commercial viability from the HSBC Chairs of Innovation at University of York or Brunel University.

At a further stage, well-managed companies with ambitious long-term plans may require to raise equity capital to support their organic business expansion, to fund management buy-outs or to provide the cash consideration for acquisitions.

Structured finance

Major commercial banks provide a range of complementary financial products giving structured solutions for complex financial needs. Funds are generally available from £1 million to £100 million to established companies with a proven record of cash generation. The structured finance may serve a variety of purposes from management buy-out to acquisition of a business or company or for a specific working capital requirement.

The three main types of finance product available are: term loan facilities, revolving credit facilities and overdraft facilities. Term loan and revolving credit facilities both provide funding for a specific purpose, which is then repaid from the future cashflow of the corporate borrower. In previous sections of this chapter, overdraft facilities and a range of commonly used asset-based solutions have already been described.

Venture capital and equity funding

The anatomy of venture capital and private equity finance in relation to specific niche market opportunities is discussed at length in Chapter 2.7. For established companies with an eye to stock market flotation and both institutional and private funds, the route to a stock exchange main market listing is explained in Chapter 2.1 while a more detailed account is given in Chapter 2.2 of the requirements for listing on the stock exchange's Alternative Investment Market (AIM), which offers a cost-effective alternative for smaller companies with proven management to raise capital.

4.8

Financial Reporting and Accounting

Michael Bordoley with Jitendra Pattani, Wilder Coe

Introduction

All business entities that are operational are required to produce, at least once a year, a financial account for the latest period or year of activity. In the case of limited companies, it is the responsibility of the directors to prepare and submit annual accounts (financial statements), which are 'true and fair'. Limited companies, which are dormant, that is, no transactions have occurred in an accounting period, are required to produce and file a dormant company balance sheet.

The main contents of the accounts are the balance sheet, showing the entity's financial state of affairs at a given date, plus a profit and loss account showing gross revenues and expenditure and the resultant net profit (or loss) for the period ending on the balance sheet date.

Companies and limited liability partnerships (LLPs – see Chapter 4.5) are required by law to file copies of their financial statements with the Registrar of Companies at Companies House. The contents of filing requirements depend on company 'size criteria'. UK financial reporting and accounting standards are governed primarily by the following:

- For limited liability companies, by Company Law in the form of the Companies Act 1985 and extended by the Companies Act 1989. The main sections governing the financial reporting regulatory framework are contained within specific schedules of the Act.

- Financial Reporting Standards (FRSs) as well as pre-existing

Statements of Standard Accounting Practice (SSAPs), unless super-seded by FRSs.

● The Consultative Committee of Accountancy Bodies (CCAB), who have been responsible since the late 1980s for the setting up and monitoring of the Financial Reporting Council under whose policy-making directives the Accounting Standards Board is responsible for the issue of Standards under its own authority, and the Financial Review Panel, who monitor and enforce compliance with those Financial Reporting Standards.

Although not statutory in the nature of their implementation and enforcement, Financial Reporting Standards have been defined as 'authoritative statements of how particular types of transactions and other events should be reflected in financial statements, and accordingly compliance with the accounting standards would normally be necessary for financial statements to give a 'true and fair view'. The concept of 'true and fair' is a statutory requirement as laid down in the Companies Act 1985.

Audit requirement

Limited companies and limited liability partnerships are required to have their financial statements audited unless they are exempted in accordance with 'size criteria' as laid down by statute. At the time of writing the Department of Trade and Industry (DTI) had announced that the audit exemption turnover ceiling would be raised to £5.6 million per annum, and the gross asset level £2.8 million, but the new Statutory Instrument had not yet been passed by parliament.

Audit exemption size criteria

A company needs to have been classified as 'small' for the prior financial year, and satisfy the criteria as shown in Table 4.8.1.

Table 4.8.1   Audit exemption size criteria

	Single Company	Group of Companies
Turnover less than		£6,720,000 gross
	£5,600,000	£5,600,000 net
Gross assets less than		£3,360,000 gross
	£2,800,000	£2,800,000 net

Gross assets consist of the total of tangible, intangible and current assets. For the group criteria, 'gross' includes inter-company transactions and balances, which would be eliminated in Consolidated Group accounts. The new thresholds for audit exemption will take effect in relation to financial years ending on or after 30 March 2004.

Non-exemption

These include, irrespective of size, ALL publicly quoted companies, banking or insurance companies, registered insurance brokers, companies registered with the Financial Services Authority, or if a company's Articles of Association require an audit. Nevertheless, there still remains the right of the shareholders, even of a statutorily exempt company, to require an audit, if at least 10 per cent of them so elect and they apply through formal application to the company for an audit to be carried out.

Basic definition of an audit

An audit includes an examination of the financial statements by a registered auditor who, on completing the audit, makes a written report to the shareholders. The examination is on a test basis of evidence relevant to the amounts and disclosures shown in the financial statements. It also includes an assessment of significant estimates and judgement utilized by the directors in their preparation of the accounts. The audit will also look at the appropriateness of the accounting policies the directors have adopted.

On completion, the auditor will provide an opinion as to whether the financial statements give a 'true and fair' view of the state of the company's affairs at the balance sheet date, and of the profit or loss for the year or period ended at that date. In giving an opinion, the auditors state that they would have performed the audit with a view to obtaining reasonable assurance that the financial statements are free from material mis-statement, whether caused by fraud, other irregularity or error. This is the core statement of an auditor's report.

Materiality is an expression of the relative significance of a particular matter in the context of the financial statements as a whole. An item would be considered material if its omission would reasonably influence the decisions of those using the accounts.

If auditors discover areas of uncertainty or deficiency in evidence, etc, or have areas of disagreement with the directors, they would qualify the audit report as appropriate to the circumstances as disclosed in the report.

True and fair concept

The Companies Act does not provide a full definition of 'true and fair' nor does the Statement of Principles for Financial Reporting, issued by the ASB. Brief comment extracted from the Statement of Principles provides a view of the true and fair concept, as follows:

- It is a concept that lies at the heart of financial reporting in the United Kingdom and the Republic of Ireland.

- It is a dynamic concept, because it evolves in response to changes, such as in accounting and business practice.

- It is inherent in the nature of the concept that financial statements will not give a true and fair view without containing sufficient quantity and quality of information to satisfy the reasonable expectations of the readers to whom they are addressed.

Sources of accounting principles

The framework of FRSs together with the tradition of applying those correctly, and in a form that has received general acceptance by the authorities and commerce within the United Kingdom, has been established as 'Generally Accepted Accounting Practice' (GAAP). However, there are fundamental accounting concepts that remain at the core of accepted proper accounting principles, and which must be applied to the financial accounts drawn up periodically, usually on a historic cost basis. These are as follows.

The going concern concept

This assumes that the business or enterprise continues in operational existence for the foreseeable future and that there is no intention to wind-up, to liquidate the business, or to cut short its activities.

The accruals concept

This means that income or revenues are to be included in the financial accounts on an earnings basis rather than when the money is received. Also, costs should be included in the accounts when they are incurred rather than when they are paid. This also preserves the principle that income and revenue dealt with in the profit and loss account of the financial statement must be matched with the associated costs in order to determine profit or loss as the case may be.

Profit and income recognition concept

Profits and income are recognized when they have been realized, either in cash or other assets such as trade debtors, where conversion into cash can be foreseen with reasonable certainty (Ref FRS 18 Para 28). A recent amendment, in November 2003, to FRS 5 (Reporting the Substance of Transactions) discusses principles and offers guidance on how to recognize revenue (income and profit) and how to measure it for inclusion in the accounts on five particular areas only. It suggests, for example, in the area of long-term contracts that revenue should be measured at the fair value of the right to the consideration, not necessarily corresponding with expenditure incurred. However, as mentioned above under the paragraph dealing with the accruals concept, the Statement of Principles also discusses the matching concept as having two aspects of recognition timing:

- matching by timing;
  - receipts and payments are recognized as gains and losses according to the periods that they are intended to cover;

- income/expenditure matching:
  - where they are associated. Expenditure is recognized as a loss at the time gains are made, instead of during the period in which the expenditure is made.

The practice in the United Kingdom is drawing closer to adoption of, and a merging with, International Accounting Standards, which do include revenue/income recognition standards for accounting purposes. For publicly quoted companies the merging of UK standards with International Accounting Standards is expected to be implemented by 2005.

Provisions

With regard to liabilities that are known and measurable, provision should be made on the basis of certainty of economic benefit passing and the best estimate that is available as to the quantum value of the liability. FRS12 directs that the prudence concept can no longer be applied to making provisions for liabilities; provisions cannot be made unless the following three criteria are satisfactorily met:

- There has to be a legal or constructive liability for a current or past event or transaction.

- The amount of the liability should be measurable and estimated with reasonable accuracy.

- There has to be reasonable certainty of economic benefit passing.

Any liability that cannot meet the three criteria would be a contingent liability and it would be necessary only to provide a disclosure note in the financial statements with no provision being allowed to reduce profits.

Accounting policies

The accounts of a limited company must disclose the accounting policies that have been applied when producing the financial statements. The rules as to the principles and format of these policies are now set out in FRS 18.

Valuation of assets

In line with the going concern concept, tangible and intangible assets of a business should be included at a fair holding value in the balance sheet. This does not mean a fair value at which they could be sold immediately, but a sustainable value, subject to wear and tear, that will produce a foreseeable revenue stream for the business. To the extent that such assets are prevented from yielding revenue or become impaired, there is a requirement to make an impairment provision against the profits of the business.

Tangible assets would include, for example, freehold and leasehold (real estate) property, plant machinery, motor vehicles and office furnishings and equipment. Intangible assets may include goodwill, patent costs, brand costs, etc. Costs incurred in acquiring goodwill can be written off out of profit over a period considered to be a reasonable life span, but cannot usually exceed 20 years. Similar consideration applies to other intangibles.

Tangible assets are depreciated (an amount written off the cost and out of profit each year) over the useful life of the asset, after allowing for any residual end value. Financial Reporting Standards allow for revaluation of certain tangible assets to replace historic cost or previous revaluations, but these must be carried out at regular intervals (every three years and then every fifth) consistently. It is difficult to change the policy once adopted.

Whether adopting or not adopting a revaluation policy, companies are required to depreciate freehold and leasehold (real estate) buildings (not land) owned and utilized in the trading operations. In all other respects historic cost is always applied in the first instance to all expenditure, whether revenue or capital.

Current assets

This is the terminology used in the United Kingdom to describe those assets utilized in a business operation, which are revolving and are the working capital of the business. These, in the main, are:

- trading stock (inventory) and work in progress;

- loans payable by instalments;

- other sundry debtors and prepaid expenses;

- trade debtors (receivables);

- cash at bank;

- cash in hand.

Valuation in general is at book cost, but trading stock (inventory) must be valued at the lower of cost or net realizable value. Where, for example, stock items are moving very slowly or there is an element of obsolescence, those items may need to be valued at lower than cost in the accounts.

Net realizable value is defined in SSAP9 as 'The actual or estimated selling price (net of trade discount but before settlement discount) after deducting: 1) all further costs to completion; and 2) all costs to be incurred in marketing, selling and distribution'.

Urgent Issues Task Force (UITF) and true and fair override

The Companies Act 1985 requires a company's financial statements (accounts) to give a 'true and fair' view of its state of affairs at the end of the financial year and of its profit or loss for that financial year. To comply with the true and fair principle, financial accounts will generally follow, and not depart from, Financial Reporting Standards. Any departure from the Standards would not be regarded as normal, therefore, disclosure and explanation would be required in the accounts if the true and fair requirement is to be met.

The Urgent Issues Task Force (UITF), which is an arm of the Accounting Standards Board, issues abstracts on topics where over-riders to FRSs can and should be adopted when necessary, to enable a 'true and fair' view to be expressed. An example of an overrider pre-UITF is found in SSAP19 with reference to depreciation of freehold and long leasehold property. The Companies Act mandates the provision of depreciation of a tangible asset over its useful economic life as part of the true and fair presentation. The ASB decided that property (buildings and land), held for investment were not to be regarded in the same way as property utilized in the operations of a trading company. Consequently, investment properties should not be subject to periodic charges for depreciation, but should be included in the balance sheet at open market value. The Standard is, therefore, a departure from the legal requirement set out in the Companies Act 1985, as well as the earlier SSAP12 now superseded by FRS15, for the overriding purpose of giving a true and fair view.

Distribution of profits

A company may only distribute profits to its members (shareholders) in accordance with the rules or conditions laid down by the Companies Act 1985. There are special additional rules to the general conditions that apply only to publicly quoted companies. Distributions can be paid out in cash or as a transfer of other assets. Not included under this heading of profit distribution, are distributions in a winding up (liquidation of a company), bonus issues of paid up shares, and certain types of share redemption or reduction of share capital.

Restriction of distributions

In respect of all companies, the distributions can only be made out of profits available for the purpose, that is, net accumulated realized profit. Public companies are prohibited from paying a dividend unless net assets exceed share capital plus undistributable reserves – the dividend must not cause a decrease in net assets to below this total amount.

Assets leased

Businesses that have not chosen to make an outright purchase of certain of their operating assets will usually lease them instead. Such a lease would be treated for accounting purposes as a simple rental or hiring arrangement, requiring the rental cost to be debited as a normal item of expenditure in the profit and loss account of the entity. The cost is spread evenly over the period of the leasing agreement and charged accordingly in the accounts.

There are, however, other classes of leasing arrangement, which are basically finance arrangements, and may or may not entail actual acquisition and ownership of the assets. Payments made under the terms of the lease will consist of capital and interest. The interest element only is, therefore, a charge against profits in the profit and loss account. The entity is, however, required, for accounting and disclosure purposes, to treat the assets as if they had been purchased, with depreciation written off against the cost. The corresponding capital finance liability is also to be shown in the accounts for amounts due at the accounting date after reduction by the capital payments element.

Accounting basis by lessors

Where the lessor is the owner of the plant and simply rents it out under an operating lease, the lessor retains ownership and is merely receiving an income for the use of it. The asset should be treated as a normal trading asset of the business and depreciated over its useful life, in terms of its rentability. Those companies offering finance leases are in effect lending money on the security of the asset, and that asset is a lease receivable in their accounts.

Partnerships and sole traders

The accounts of ordinary partnerships and sole traders are not governed by any statutory or mandatory format, as are the accounts of limited companies. However, accounting rules as applied to companies will also apply to limited liability partnerships where the format and regulations are set out in the Companies Act 1985 (as amended for Limited Liability Partnerships Act 2000).

Nevertheless, it is common practice for the accounts of partnerships and sole traders to generally follow the format of the accounts of limited companies. Traditionally, more detail is shown on the face of the balance sheet and the profit and loss account, and fewer disclosure notes are provided, in comparison with company accounts. In fact, there is no requirement for additional disclosures.

Although there is no statutory requirement to format these accounts in any specific manner, the 'true and fair concept' is still expected to apply, and fundamental accounting principles, as mentioned briefly above, should be adhered to. Under current taxation legislation and practice, the Inland Revenue authorities of the United Kingdom accept, and will expect, that the accounts of limited companies as well as those of partnerships and sole traders be drawn up in accordance with the 'true and fair concept' and in accordance with Generally Accepted Accounting Practice (GAAP). Therefore, Financial Reporting Standards and Statements of Standard Accounting Practice need also to be considered and applied appropriately when producing the accounts of partnerships and sole traders, as well as companies.

4.9

Business Taxation

Bob Tranter, Wilder Coe

Introduction

This chapter is divided into three parts:

1. general tax considerations relating to various types of business entity formed to trade in the United Kingdom;
2. information as to the types of income, the payment of tax, and the rates of tax applicable;
3. a description of how taxable business income and gains are determined, and the deductibility of certain income and capital expenditure.

General tax considerations on UK business formations

In determining the method of trading in the United Kingdom, commerciality must determine the vehicle to be used: corporation, branch, limited liability partnership (LLP) or general partnership. Each type of entity has its own merits and downsides. Below are some comments about the alternatives.

Representative office versus permanent establishment

If it is not desirable to create a taxable entity or legal presence in the United Kingdom then care has to be taken to ensure that any presence in the United Kingdom is purely representative, without the creation of a permanent establishment (PE). The comprehensive list of double tax agreements (DTAs) between the United Kingdom and other trading nations will set out what will contribute to the creation of a permanent establishment and therefore bring the foreign entity within the UK tax regime.

The basic difference between the two, and what establishes whether or not there is a permanent establishment, is whether the overseas entity is trading *with* the United Kingdom, or is trading *in* the United Kingdom. From 1 January 2003 under provisions in Finance Act 2003 (FA2003) non-resident companies are *only liable* in the United Kingdom if they carry on a trade via a PE.

Under the FA2003 provisions, a company has a PE if it has a fixed place of business in the United Kingdom and an agent acting on behalf of the company who habitually exercises authority to do business on behalf of the company. If a foreign company has a PE, it is chargeable to tax on the profits *wherever* arising, which are attributable to that PE.

The losses arising in a PE may be available for offset against the profits in the main country of residence of the foreign company. As losses frequently arise in the initial periods of trading, PEs are frequently set up for the first periods of trading, with incorporation following at a later date.

Factors influencing the decision will be complex and will include the nature of the activities, the ability to enter into contracts or commit the foreign entity to a course of action. Care and advice are necessary.

Branch versus subsidiary

The UK branch of a foreign company is taxable on the profits arising in the United Kingdom. The calculation is as for a separate entity (for example, a subsidiary) so that transactions will need to be on a proper commercial basis. Profits arising in the branch can be remitted to the head office without restriction and without any form of withholding tax.

Branches come within the normal corporation tax methods of calculation, and so if the profits are high enough the branch will be subject to the quarterly instalment regime for large companies. In assessing this, the number of associated companies on a worldwide basis has to be taken into account.

If the UK entity is a subsidiary then, subject to the appropriate DTA, withholding tax might be applicable, but only on certain specific types of income. There is no UK withholding tax on the payment of dividends. There is little or no difference in the UK taxation position arising from trading through either a UK branch or a UK subsidiary. In both cases, the rules relating to thin capitalization will need to be considered.

The subsidiary is a separate legal entity in the United Kingdom and so normally, any claims would stop at that level. A branch is part of the overseas entity and so any claim could be followed through to the overseas entity.

Direct investment versus holding company structure

Direct investment through a branch, corporation or partnership is easy to establish and will normally be the preferred method. There are usually no adverse taxation consequences and ongoing administration and compliance is at a minimum. Sometimes, however, a UK holding company route can be appropriate. This is dependent upon the functions and activities of the UK business entity, the need for financing both in the United Kingdom and elsewhere, exit strategies, and the interaction with other non-UK entities.

Residence

Taxability in the United Kingdom will come from residence here. Incorporation in the United Kingdom or elsewhere does not determine the residence status of a company. A simple, accepted, guideline is that residence is where the 'central management and control' of the company reside. This is where the strategy of the company and decisions relating to that strategy are formulated and actioned.

Value-added tax (VAT)

The harmonization of VAT within the EU means that, generally, goods can be moved around the EU without undue VAT consequences. When goods are imported from outside the EU, import VAT is payable. From that point onwards, the goods are freely moveable between EU countries.

Any business investing or trading in the United Kingdom will have to consider whether it has a 'business establishment' for UK VAT purposes. The rules for the establishment of a 'business establishment' are different from those applicable to the residence position of the company. Other general VAT rules will also apply.

Different types of income

The UK tax system works on a schedular basis of taxation, with each type of income subject to specific rules as to how it will be calculated. The main types of income are set out below with a general description of the method of calculation of the income.

Companies and branches

Trading income

The starting point for the calculation of taxable business income is the profit shown in the accounts of the entity – the accounting treatment of expenditure is often the key to how the expense will be treated for taxation purposes. The accounts profit is then adjusted to exclude certain expenditure not allowable under UK taxation rules, and then this revised profit is adjusted to grant various taxation-only allowances and reliefs, which are not part of the accounting records. The calculations relating to general expenditure incurred in the United Kingdom apply whatever the nature of the entity in the United Kingdom. The treatment of charges from the foreign entity can differ in the United Kingdom depending upon whether the UK entity is a PE or a separate legal entity such as a limited company.

Some of the adjustments are set out below. This list is not exhaustive and advice should be taken in respect of any particular item of expenditure.

NOT ALLOWED

- capital expenditure or depreciation (see comments on capital allowances below);

- certain legal and professional charges;

- entertainment;

- fines and illegal payments;

- general provisions in respect of any expenditure;

- gifts.

ALLOWED

All employee costs are generally deductible if there is a business element. However, if the employee receives a benefit – under UK tax law this can be quite complex – the employee can have an additional tax charge and the employer an additional National Insurance (NI) charge.

Accounts depreciation is replaced by capital allowances under a complex but comprehensive system – allowances run from 4 per cent up to 150 per cent depending on the nature of the expenditure. Capital expenditure disallowed in the accounts might obtain an allowance if it falls within the capital allowances regime. There are specific provisions for certain types of expenditure, for example, bad debts.

Deduction dependent upon nature of UK entity

Although interest and royalty payments by a UK company will be deductible (subject to transfer pricing rules), payments to a head office by a PE will not be deductible. Relief could be obtained if the payments were to a foreign affiliate: a separate legal entity.

Management charges can be deductible in both cases, subject to transfer pricing rules. In the case of a company, the charge could be based upon the services provided by the offshore parent. In the case of a PE the allocation could be on a 'share' basis of total costs, provided they can be shown to be used by the UK PE.

Land and property

Income from land and property is taxable under different schedules of the Taxes Acts in the United Kingdom depending upon whether the property is situated in the United Kingdom or overseas. However, the rules for calculating the profit are essentially the same.

Income and expenses from all UK sources are pooled and treated as a separate rental business, with a separate business in respect of overseas properties. The calculations of the profits generally follow the rules for general trading activities, and accounts must be prepared on an accruals basis and in accordance with generally accepted accounting principles.

Where commercial properties are involved, capital allowances may be obtained for certain capital expenditure, but no relief can be claimed for such expenditure on residential properties. Certain other allowances might possibly be available for residential lettings, but this will depend upon the type of letting. Losses from a commercial letting business can, in a company, be offset against other general income of the same or later accounting periods while the same trade is being carried on.

Interest

Interest is, as with other company income, usually taxed on an accruals basis. However, certain types of income under this heading have different treatments. Care has to be taken on the receipt of income out of the ordinary to ascertain the correct taxation treatment. The company regime differs from the position for individuals mentioned below.

Capital gains

The capital gains arising from the sale of assets is added to other profits for the year in the company and taxed at the same rates. In calculating the gain, costs of purchase and sale can be taken into account. If there have been improvements to the asset after original purchase, and the improvements are still reflected in the asset at the date of sale, the costs of the improvements can be deducted from the sale proceeds in calculating the gain.

The original cost, and any other allowable expenditure, is indexed upwards from the date the expenditure is incurred up to the date of sale. The date of sale is taken as the date of exchange of contracts binding seller and purchaser to the sale. The indexation rates are announced monthly and are broadly the retail price indices.

Dividends

With the abolition of the imputation system, no refundable tax credit is now given at the shareholder level. Individual shareholders do receive a notional tax credit, which covers their UK liability unless they are liable at the higher rates of income tax. Corporations receive no credit, but no further tax is due.

Individuals and partnerships

Income

The income from a partnership is allocated to the partners in accordance with the partnership agreement. The income so allocated from each source or type of income is then assessed on the individual partner – be it a company or an individual.

An individual's income is calculated in the same way as for a company where there is a 'trading' aspect. The calculations and points made above with reference to trading income, land and property and investment income are therefore the same for individuals. The other types of income and capital gains are dealt with differently, and the differences are set out below.

Interest

In the main, for individuals, interest and other investment income will have been received after deduction of lower rate tax. The income is assessed on the arising basis and not the accruals basis used for companies.

Capital gains

The basis of calculation of the gain arising is the same as for companies in respect of the deduction of costs from the sale proceeds. However, indexation relief is only available up to April 1998. From this date, a new relief, taper relief, applies. The effect of taper relief is to reduce the amount of gain chargeable to tax dependent upon the period of ownership of the asset. Frequently, the effect of the taper relief is shown as a tax percentage. Different rates of relief apply to the asset depending upon whether it is a business asset or a general investment asset.

For business assets, the maximum taper relief of 75 per cent is reached after only two years of ownership and has the effect of reducing the maximum tax rate from 40 per cent to 10 per cent. Investment assets achieve maximum relief of 40 per cent after 10 years. The maximum tax rate therefore reduces from 40 per cent to 24 per cent.

Land and property

As indicated above, profits are calculated in the same way for companies and individuals. However, if losses are incurred they are treated differently. The company position is as set out above. For individuals, the losses, if they arise from letting of commercial properties can be offset against the general income of the year. Alternatively, they will be carried forward and used against future income from the same trade. Where the losses arise from residential lettings, they can only be carried forward, and not offset against other income.

Dividends

Dividends from UK companies and qualifying unit trusts received by a UK resident are deemed for taxation purposes to have had notional tax of 10 per cent deducted before receipt. If the individual is not liable for tax at the highest rate, the notional credit covers any liability due. If the individual does not pay tax, no refund of the notional tax can be obtained. If tax is paid at the highest level further tax will be due.

Payment of tax

Companies

The corporation tax liabilities of companies are payable nine months and one day after the end of the accounting period. Accounting periods generally run for a period of 12 months to the same accounting date each year. If the accounting period is extended or shortened, special rules apply to the method of calculation of profits, capital allowances, etc, and adjustments will be made to the tax payment dates.

Large companies pay on a quarterly instalment method based upon an estimate of the current year's corporation tax liability. The basic definition of a large company is one with profits in excess of £1.5 million (for the 2003 period). Various rules apply to companies in the first years in which they come into the large company definition to ascertain in which accounting period they have to start the quarterly payments.

When there are associated companies the £1.5 million lower limit is divided between the companies. Associated companies include overseas companies, so in large groups it is possible that the quarterly instalment procedures will apply at much lower profit levels.

Applicable tax rates

These rates for companies in Table 4.9.1 apply to all income and gains.

Table 4.9.1 Applicable tax rates for companies

	Taxable Profits/Gains	Tax Rate (%)
Starting rate	0–£10,000	0
Small companies rate	£10,001–£300,000	19
Main rate	> £1,500,000	30

Note: The above rates apply for the Year Ended 31 March, 2004.

If profit is above the small companies profit maximum of £300,000, but below the main rate threshold of £1,500,000, marginal calculations apply to the excess over £300,000. The effect is to bring the tax at £1,500,000 back to 30 per cent. The result is that tax in the margin has an effective rate of 32.75 per cent.

The small companies rate threshold of £300,000 is divided between all associated companies. Thus, if there are four associated companies, each would be entitled to £75,000 of profit taxable at the 19 per cent rate before going into marginal calculations. Associated companies include both UK and overseas companies.

Partnerships

Tax within a partnership is based upon the profits allocated to each partner. Partners are responsible for their own tax liability. If the partner is a limited company the rates are as shown above in Table 4.9.1. If the partner is an individual, the rates are those applying to individuals as set out below in Table 4.9.2.

Table 4.9.2 Applicable tax rates for individual partners

	Taxable Income/Gains	Tax Rate (%)
Starting rate	0–£1,920	0
Next slice of income of	£27,980	22
balance	>29,900	40

The rates of tax are applied cumulatively. Each individual who is a partner will be entitled to offset against the allocated profit share, allowances and reliefs, according to their personal circumstances.

Payment of tax

In respect of trading income from a partnership the tax is payable twice yearly on 31 January within the year of assessment, and on 31 July following the year of assessment. Special rules apply on commencement of trade.

Once the trade is running the payments are based upon the profits earned in the previous year. In the January tax payment adjustments are made to correct the payments on account based on the previous year's profits to the actual tax due on the profits shown in the accounts.

The result of this is that where profits are rising the January payment will always be the greater payment. If profits are falling, so that it is expected that the tax due in total will be less than that paid for the previous year, claims to reduce the payments can be made. However, if the calculation is inaccurate, leading to an underpayment of tax, interest will be charged. In extreme cases, there can also be penalties.

Capital allowances

The UK system of capital allowances is comprehensive and covers the majority of assets from general plant and machinery (which includes fixtures, fittings, computers, etc), to allowances on certain types of buildings, to intangible assets, patents, research and development expenditure, etc.

The allowances are based upon the cost to the entity, and where connected parties are concerned (for example, acquisitions from the head office in the case of a PE, or from a parent in the case of a separate company) the cost to the UK entity will broadly be as shown in Table 4.9.3.

Table 4.9.3   Cost to UK entity for capital allowance

	Acquired from: Head Office	**Foreign Associate**
Plant & Machinery	Market value	Lowest of actual cost, book value or market value
Hotels/Industrial Buildings	Calculated written down value for tax purposes	Calculated written down value for tax purposes
Intangible Assets	Book value	Market value

Certain assets have an initial allowance, which varies from 40 per cent to 100 per cent of the cost. Thereafter, the most common annual allowance is 25 per cent of the balance brought forward after previous allowances have been deducted.

Although not necessarily a capital allowance relief, mention should be made of special allowances available to companies for expenditure on research and development. Dependent upon the size of the company, relief of up to 150 per cent of the expenditure can be obtained. This relief is normally by deduction against profits, reducing the taxable amounts. In some cases, where the company has losses and so obtains no immediate relief, cash credits can be paid to the company in place of the corporation tax deduction.

Losses

Trading losses are calculated in the same way as trading profits. Capital allowances can increase losses or change a profit into a loss. Once determined, a loss can be utilized in a variety of ways. Examples are:

- Offset against total profits, income and gains of the year in which the loss arises.

- Offset against total profits, income and gains of the year prior to the year in which the loss arises.

- Carried forward indefinitely against profits of the trade arising in later accounting periods.

- Surrendered to other UK group or consortium companies in the year in which the loss arises for offset against the income and gains of those companies in that year. The surrender to other group companies can include surrenders between PEs and subsidiaries.

Where a company is acquired that has losses arising from previous trading activities, care has to be taken to try to ensure that those losses are available to the new owners of the company. Consideration has to be given to the way in which the trade will be carried on after the change of ownership.

Rollover relief

Where a company disposes of a business asset within a list of types of qualifying assets (see below) and reinvests the proceeds into other assets within the list of qualifying assets, the capital gain arising on the sale can be deferred until the sale of the second asset. Rollover can be applied on all subsequent sales until the ultimate final sale without reinvestment. The list of the main qualifying asset types is:

Class	Asset
1A	Land and buildings
1B	Fixed plant and machinery
2	Ships, aircraft and hovercraft
3	Satellites, space stations and spacecraft
4	Goodwill

Other, less common assets, are also included.

Thin capitalization

Funding of the UK company must also be on a commercial basis or adjustments can be made under the transfer pricing rules (already mentioned) or, where the UK company is a 75 per cent or greater subsidiary of an overseas company, under the rules relating to thin capitalization. There are requirements for appropriate debt/equity ratios, and of course if the lending is intra-group, on the interest rates applied. The reason for the legislation is to stop 'over financing' of a company, allowing the profits to be extracted by way of interest charges. At the moment, parts of the legislation are under review and discussion to ensure that they are in line with EU tax harmonization rules generally.

Stamp duty land tax/stamp duty

From 1 December 2003, Stamp Duty Land Tax (SDLT) replaces the old stamp duty regime with respect to land and property transactions in the United Kingdom. As with corporation tax and income tax in the United Kingdom, SDLT is a self-assessment tax and the obligation to notify the Inland Revenue that a transfer has taken place falls on the person paying the tax – the purchaser.

Under stamp duty the tax was payable on the completion of the contract. This gave rise to various arrangements to postpone payment. As a result, although the SDLT is also payable on completion of the contract, there are provisions that charge the tax on substantial completion of the contract. Under English law this could be on the exchange of contracts. Substantial completion is not defined but is, in broad terms, receipt of most of the consideration, taking possession of the property, the entitlement to receive the rents or profits from the property.

Rates of tax

The rate of SDLT depends upon whether the property is residential or commercial. The rates of tax are not on slices of value. If a value is within one of the slices shown below in Table 4.9.4 the whole of the price is subject to tax at that rate. For example, if the residential value is £60,000 no tax is payable. If the value is £60,001 the rate on the whole is 1 per cent, or £600.01.

Table 4.9.4   Rates of stamp duty land tax

Residential Property	%	Non-residential or Mixed Property	%
Consideration	%	Consideration	%
Up to £60,000	0	Up to £150,000	0
£60,001 to £250,000	1	£150,001 to £250,000	1
£250,001 to £500,000	3	£250,001 to £500,000	3
Over £500,000	4	Over £500,000	4

Where transactions are linked the aggregate consideration determines the rate of the tax payable.

4.10

Taxation Planning

Bob Tranter, Wilder Coe

Introduction

This chapter carries on from the overview in Chapter 4.9 and sets out planning pointers, both in terms of taxation savings and in avoiding an increased charge. It describes the taxation consequences of various courses of action.

Taxation consequences of operation via a UK resident company

- Profits will be liable to corporation tax (CT).

- The gain on the eventual sale of shares of the UK company is likely to be exempt from UK tax if held offshore.

- In several jurisdictions, the sale by the resident *company* of shares in a non-resident company (for example, UK company) will be exempt. In most jurisdictions, *individuals* would have a liability.

- The timing and manner of repatriation of profits can be flexible and assist in planning in the offshore jurisdiction.

- European Union (EU) parent companies might be able to claim that the UK loss-making subsidiary should be included in local tax consolidations.

- Disclosures by UK companies are limited to the activities of the company itself. In the case of a PE, the UK Inland Revenue might require information about non-UK transactions to determine and agree liabilities to CT.

- Royalties and interest paid by a UK company to overseas associates are tax deductible if on arm's-length terms. Payments made by a PE to its parent/head office are not deductible.

- Any problems, if applicable, in setting up a PE and subsequently incorporating it are avoided. These might include a tax charge in the foreign jurisdiction on the transfer of assets from the PE to a foreign subsidiary.

- Generally, there are no UK tax consequences on the incorporation.

Key tax planning issues

Purchase of shares

The acquisition of the shares of a company means that the purchaser also acquires within the company all of the assets and liabilities – both known and unknown. The company is a continuing legal entity and a change in its ownership does not affect its obligations from the past. Because of this, indemnities are needed on any share acquisition in respect of a full statement of liabilities and indemnity for other liabilities arising after the acquisition.

It should be noted that the acquisition of the company means that there is no uplift in the value of the assets held by the company. Any gains on those assets remain in the company and will be taxable on the company on a sale of those assets. This in-built liability needs to be reflected in the price paid for the shares. However, if the owner of the shares is non-resident and remains so, no capital gains tax would be payable on the share disposal and so in-built gains would only be of concern in assessing the price to be paid for the shares.

Purchase of assets

The purchase of the assets from a company does mean that the vehicle into which they are purchased is 'clean' with no unknown liabilities. The new vehicle will have acquired the assets at current value and so there will be no inbuilt gains to take into consideration in the future. This can be of advantage where the assets might have to be sold prior to any future disposal of the company.

Tax grouping

The association of companies can have an effect in the United Kingdom on the rate of tax payable by both resident companies and branches. There are different types of tax grouping in relation to trading profits and capital gains, and the surrendering of losses between companies with economic interests such as where a company is owned by a consortium.

Association normally comes from common control of companies. Thus, if the same individual, or group of individuals, has control of companies those companies, for UK taxation purposes, will be associated (and connected). This has effect in the following ways: 1) Transfers of assets between associated companies must be at an arm's length value. Where this does not happen the Inland Revenue can deal with the calculation of tax as though it had been at arm's length by substituting the open market value for the actual transfer value. 2) The number of associated companies will affect the rate of tax where the small company rate is involved (on profits up to £300,000). The limit of £300,000 will be divided between the associated companies.

Grouping comes from direct shareholdings of one company by another. The share percentages of such holdings are followed through. If, for example, Company A held 80 per cent of the ordinary capital of Company B, which in turn held 90 per cent of the ordinary capital of Company C, then A would be held to have an interest in 72 per cent (80 per cent × 90 per cent) of C.

If the percentages held are 51 per cent or more up to 75 per cent the companies would be group companies for capital gains tax purposes. If the percentages followed through are above 75 per cent, the companies are group companies for all UK corporation tax purposes. The effect of a grouping >75 per cent is to allow: 1) transfers of assets within the group without taxation consequence and without need for open market value to be used; 2) trading losses and capital losses to be surrendered between group companies, so that the tax rates can be averaged for best effect.

Transfer of a UK permanent establishment to a UK company

As mentioned previously, it can be the best solution, if losses are expected in the initial trading periods, to start trade in a UK branch by way of a PE so that the losses can be utilized in the overseas jurisdiction (subject to the taxation laws in that jurisdiction). When the entity becomes profitable the UK trade could then be transferred to a UK company. The usual route would be for the foreign parent to incorporate a company in the United Kingdom and then transfer the trade and assets of the PE to that company.

Using the group rules mentioned above the transfer in the United Kingdom would be achieved without taxation consequences. Care would have to be taken in considering whether the transfer triggered any offshore liability to the parent making the transfer.

Frequently, any losses incurred in the UK branch can be carried over into the subsidiary for use against future profits in the new company. One of the possible benefits from this route is that the losses initially arising in the UK branch can be utilized twice.

Sale of a UK permanent establishment

Unlike the situation for the sale of the shares of a UK company, mentioned above, the situation with regard to the sale of the assets (including goodwill) of a branch or PE of an overseas company will differ. The PE is resident and trading in the United Kingdom and is thus taxable on the sale of its UK assets.

The foreign company (head office) will be taxable at 30 per cent on the gain, subject to indexation relief. Assets owned by individuals for at least two years (provided they are business assets) will suffer tax at a maximum of 10 per cent because of the taper relief provisions.

Controlled foreign companies (CFC)

When considering the best structure overseas, investors will need to take account of the use of low-tax third countries for functions such as holding, trading, financing or management. Using such countries complicates the structure and there will need to be detailed consideration of CFC rules in all countries affected by the structure. In using such low-tax jurisdictions, transfer pricing legislation will also be a factor.

Investment in UK properties

If property is acquired in the United Kingdom by a non-resident individual or a non-resident company for rental return purposes, coupled with capital gain on disposal, the taxation position differs in terms of rates applying. An individual, even though non-resident, will be taxable at the rates set out previously. Thus, the highest rate could be 40 per cent. A non-resident company, however, pays tax on such income at a flat rate of (currently) 22 per cent.

Special administrative provisions apply in both cases in that, if there is not a collection agent in the United Kingdom, tax will have to be deducted at source on the gross rental by the tenant. The individual or company would then have to claim a refund in respect of any expenses available to offset against the income.

Repatriation of profits

In general, there are few UK taxation implications in repatriation of profits to the parent company or head office:

- There are no taxes on distributions so a remittance of retained profits, in any form, does not attract a liability.

- There is no withholding tax on UK dividends paid to offshore share-holders.

- As mentioned previously, there is a notional tax on dividends and for non-resident individuals this is deemed to cover their UK liability.

- Non-resident companies receiving dividends from UK resident companies are similarly protected from additional tax.

- Under the provisions of certain tax treaties a refund of 50 per cent of the tax credit can be repaid where the shareholder is a company holding 10 per cent or more of the UK company.

- However, other provisions provide in most cases for a 5 per cent UK tax to be deducted from the grossed up dividend (the cash dividend plus the tax credit refund). The effect of this is to almost cancel out the benefit of the refund – probably leaving the refund at only 0.9 per cent of the UK company's pre-tax profits.

Transfer pricing

The UK legislation relating to transfer pricing can impact on any transaction carried out between the UK entity (whatever its nature) and any foreign associated entity. The rules are similar in most juris-dictions and any resulting double taxation can usually be resolved under the DTAs.

The broad expectation is that any transaction between a UK entity and its associated foreign entities will be on normal commercial terms and that no tax advantage will be obtained by the pricing method used. If it is not, the legislation allows adjustment to recalculate profits to what they would be under an 'arm's-length' transaction. It also allows for the charging of penalties of up to 100 per cent of the tax due. The adjustments to recalculate the profits only apply if UK profits are understated. There is no adjustment if they are overstated. Transactions, which could therefore be affected, include:

- financing;
- licensing;

- management fees;

- property leases and other transactions;

- sales of products;

- services provided.

The onus, under UK compliance rules for the submission of returns, is for the UK taxpayer to confirm that all related party transactions are carried out on an arm's-length basis. In cases where the transfer pricing determination of arm's-length transactions might be very complex it is possible to agree arrangements and methods in advance under advance pricing agreements with the Inland Revenue.

Value-added tax

All foreign businesses operating in the United Kingdom are likely to need to register for VAT. This is so even if the profits generated by their supplies are not liable to UK tax. VAT is chargeable on the supply of goods or services made in the course of business. For UK VAT to be chargeable, the place of supply must be within the United Kingdom. Different rules apply for goods and services and can be complex. Each transaction or type of transaction contemplated should be considered for VAT purposes before the first supply is made.

Supplies in the United Kingdom for VAT purposes are divided into different categories to establish if tax is payable, and if so the rate of tax. The rates and categories are:

- Zero rate: 0 per cent VAT applies on certain transactions. The supply is still a taxable supply, so there is still a requirement to register the business.

- Lower rate: 5 per cent VAT applies on a limited number of transactions. These are mainly in relation to public corporations and will not affect most trading companies.

- Standard rate: 17.5 per cent applies as the standard rate on the majority of transactions.

- Exempt supplies: certain transactions are exempt from VAT. This means that no VAT is chargeable, but also that no refund of input VAT on costs associated with the supplies can be obtained.

Compliance

Any business with activities undertaken in the United Kingdom, where the value of supplies is (currently) in excess of £56,000 per annum *must* register for VAT. It is also possible to voluntarily register even though supplies will be less than this figure. This could be the case where it was expected to incur substantial costs, for example, during the start-up of the business, to enable refund of the VAT incurred on purchases. It is possible for groups of companies to register for VAT as a single VAT entity thus requiring a single return only. Also, transactions between group members will be disregarded for VAT purposes. VAT is self-assessed and registered persons are required to submit returns on a periodic (usually quarterly) basis and account for tax due with the return.

Trade Information Services from www.uktradeinfo.com

uktradeinfo is an information service provided by the UK government department HM Customs and Excise. One of its principal aims is to make life easier for people trading with the UK. Their Web services, available from www.uktradeinfo.com cover three main areas. The publication of UK trade data, the provision of information that is useful to the trading community, and online services to facilitate dealings with the Customs and Excise department.

Trade data

The primary use of uktradeinfo data is a market intelligence – to identify new trade opportunities for your products across the world, to measure market share, to identify growth areas, to forecast trends and to analyse patterns. Their data is the most accurate, authoritative and timely information on UK import and exports available anywhere. As the data is sourced from official documentation, you can be sure it is the most accurate possible: it is taken direct from the returns and reports submitted for every export and import consignment.

Trade data tables can be created to meet your own specific needs. Once this has been done, tables can be automatically updated as subsequent data is published. Tables can be downloaded to an Excel spreadsheet for further analysis.

Key features

- UK trade figures within 24 hours of release;
- analysis by quantity, values, periods, flows and countries;
- sophisticated search engine;
- ability to 'custom build' analysis;
- data can be downloaded to Excel;
- trade tables translated into French, German and Spanish.

Importers' details

If you are interested in exporting to the UK, our Importers' Details database can be used for an effective marketing campaign. This service offers unlimited access to over 130,000 names and full postal addresses of importers. The details are updated monthly and subscribers can have unlimited use of names and addresses and create mailing labels.

The database is very flexible and is capable of searching for a variety of information. If you want to know who imports a particular type of goods, you can search by the name of the items or by their commodity code. If you are interested in research on a particular business, you can search by company name. If you want to know who imports into a particular area, you can search by postcode or county.

Regional trade statistics

These describe the trends in UK regional trade and can be used to establish new markets. They cover the nine Government Office Regions in England, plus Scotland, Wales and Northern Ireland. The data is available on a quarterly basis and can be found with the choice of the following format: Time series – 1996 to date

- value in pounds sterling;
- quantity in tonnes;
- Standard International Trade Classification (2 digit);
- region;
- trading partner country;
- flow (import and exports).

PRODCOM

Products of the European Community Inquiry (PRODCOM) is a survey of manufactured products governed by EU regulation. PRODCOM can provide invaluable statistics on UK exports allowing organizations to measure their market share and market potential. PRODCOM combines Customs and Excise information with Office for National Statistics data and covers 4,800 products assigned to 249 standard classification codes with 47 industries classified on a quarterly basis and the rest annually. The system is easy to access and use and facilitates the recording of tables for future reference manipulation.

Additional features and service of uktradeinfo

- World Links – e-mail links to statistical sites and trade authorities around the world, useful for contact information;
- exchange rate information used for statistical purposes, when comparing rates with other counties in a graph format;
- online journal *Trade Trends* with informative articles in relation to trade;
- EU country profiles – easily accessible and standardized information on all EU member states, including candidate countries.

If you have any questions regarding their services please contact them by e-mail to uktradeinfo@hmce.gsi.go.uk or by telephoning +44 (0) 1702 367 485.

4.11

Outsourcing

Alfred Levy, Artaius Ltd

General principles

In most businesses, the management team and skilled staff have specialist abilities. Those skills are usually entrepreneurial and cover the creative parts of the company such as design and production, purchasing, selling, training, manufacturing and specialist services side of the company. These relate to the core roles of the specific business.

In addition to the roles above, there are many functions common to most businesses, which require completely different skill sets. This involves the processes covering most functions normally incorporated in the back office, financial and administration departments of the company.

In the embryonic stages of a business, many teams do not have the experience or skill sets to overcome the hurdles of the administrative 'red tape' that faces management in the United Kingdom. As a company begins to grow, cashflow can become a major problem, as can budgetary control and reporting upon results. Credit control, book-keeping, issuing of invoices, payment of suppliers, payroll, VAT and Corporation Tax can all present formidable problems that can cause management to lose the focus on the important core functions that differentiate one business from the next.

The solution, of course, is to outsource the day-to-day routine processes to a service company that specializes in ensuring that the whole administration and financial accounting process operates efficiently and acts as tools for management rather than an impediment. These operations, which are under the control of an entirely separate organization, are known as business or financial outsourcing.

Who might undertake the role of outsourcing in the United Kingdom?

Over the last few years, a number of specialist firms have set themselves up in the United Kingdom to meet the demand for outsourced business and financial services. The company offering outsourced services normally comprises a team that ranges from data entry clerks to experienced bookkeepers, management accountants, financial directors and business development advisors. Most of the team will have commercial backgrounds although a number of the qualified accountants will have had a wide experience working for professional firms and in commerce. In addition to their own team, the outsourcing company may well subcontract out, but control, other processes such as insurance, HR management, recruitment or procurement of office equipment and phone systems, etc.

The benefits of outsourcing

In the United Kingdom, some of these companies will charge fixed monthly fees, no matter what work they undertake. By spreading the time of each team member among a portfolio of clients, the resulting charge to a business will, in most cases, be less than employing the staff itself. It should be borne in mind that most businesses when they set up are relatively small. However, they still need everything from a part-time bookkeeper to a payroll operator, a VAT expert, a management and cost accountant, a credit controller and a financial director. However, they could not expect to employ those people full time, and in the United Kingdom, part-time specialists are rare and expensive. So, the benefits of outsourcing are having a supply of experts processing all the paperwork and working through all the red tape efficiently at a fixed affordable monthly price.

In the United Kingdom the employment legislation is complex, and, can be quite onerous on the employer. It is quite difficult to terminate an employment contract after one year and there is a grave danger that the ex-employee could claim 'Unfair Dismissal' in the United Kingdom. The courts usually tend to be biased towards the employee and damages can often be substantial sums of money.

A further benefit relates to the automatic support given should there be illness, holidays or absence for any other reason. The outsourcing company can always provide the support required, whereas the company that performs the back office functions in-house, cannot normally afford to double up on the headcount.

What are the possible outsourced services?

On set-up of a company:

- formation of a UK limited company with an agreed name;
- dealing with all the statutory formalities including:
  - appointment of directors and secretary;
  - situation of registered office;
  - preparation of all company annual returns;
  - writing up of statutory books;
- registering a company for VAT;
- registering a company for PAYE;
- arranging for UK contracts of employment to be prepared;
- preparing a chart of accounts;
- compiling a business plan incorporating budgetary forecasts;
- setting up credit procedures;
- introduction to UK banks and assessing the formalities of opening a bank account;
- introduction to specialist solicitors to draw up terms and conditions;
- treasury control – internet banking, issuing and signing cheques on behalf of the company. Organizing cheque signatories and procedures.

Once the company is established:

- acting as back office:
  - stock and order processing;
  - pre-sales credit control;
  - preparation of sales invoices;
  - sending sales invoices to customers;
  - post-sale credit control;
- maintenance of all accounting records:
  - sales ledger;
  - bought ledger;
  - nominal ledger;
  - inventory control;
  - bank reconciliations;
  - payroll processing;
  - maintenance and submission of VAT returns;
  - agreement of suppliers' statements;

- production of management information:
  - weekly management information;
  - monthly management accounts;
  - production and interpretation of key performance indicators;
  - comparison of actual results with forecasts;

- liaison with overseas holding companies:
  - timetable;
  - reporting in depth using any format required on any accounting matters, complying with International Accounting Standard;

- liaison with government bodies:
  - dealing with all statistical returns for VAT purposes;
  - dealing with all PAYE returns;
  - dealing with corporation tax returns;
  - dealing with data as required by UK Data Protection Act;

- liaison with statutory UK auditors:
  - preparing year end file in format required by all UK firms of auditors;
  - dealing with all audit queries;
  - ensuring that all group audit timetables are adhered to.

Conclusion

Outsourcing in the United Kingdom is a growing service industry, offering skills to businesses at an economic price, which those organizations could not readily acquire or control independently without impacting a hefty financial burden upon themselves. The result is a fixed overhead that leaves the company free to concentrate upon its core activities knowing that the administration and financial side of the business will run smoothly, seamlessly and efficiently.

Re ———————➤ location to the UK?

DOWNSIZING?

Mergers?

Re- BRAND -ing

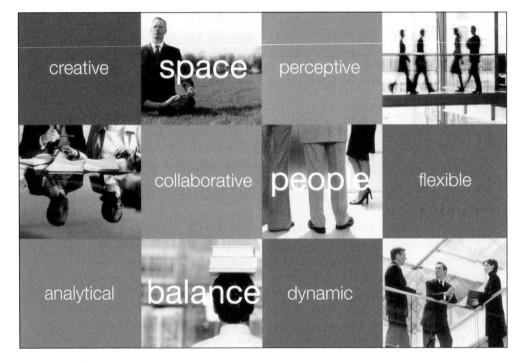

SPB³ the business relocation specialists – will provide you with a bespoke
package that will cover assistance in premises selection and evaluation,
SPACE PEOPLE BALANCE   office planning and design, compliance with statutory regulations,
furniture and equipment supply, construction procurement, project management,
cost advice and cost control, and project funding.

*Organisations we have worked with include: Dow Jones International Ltd, PricewaterhouseCoopers,
J Sainsbury plc, Telewest Communications plc, GlaxoSmithKline, NCH (National Children's Home),
The Home Office.*

SPACE PEOPLE BALANCE

For more information contact: Stephen Heath on:
T: +44 (0)20 7419 7400
SPB³, 70 Charlotte street, London W1T 4QG
Info@spb3.co.uk   www.spb3.co.uk

4.12

Relocation Issues

Stephen Heath and Johan Taft, SPB[3]

Introduction

Investors in the United Kingdom will need to address at an early stage the issue of selecting or developing premises in the specific region, town or city that they have chosen for their UK operations. Market entry as a result of merger or acquisition will most likely bring with it inherited facilities – either a factory, distribution warehouse, retail outlets or, in the case of service providers, perhaps office accommodation.

Regional Development Agencies are the first source of advice for manufacturers and distributors preferring to purchase or lease their own premises for business start-ups, and the professional services of conventional experts such as commercial estate agents, surveyors, architects and project management practices are widely available from national practices or other firms having more specialist knowledge of local facilities and markets. The UK commercial property market, its structure and its investment potential are examined in some detail in Chapters 2.3 and 2.4. However, there is an alternative source of advice and expertise.

In recent years some commercial design practitioners have broadened the range of their service offering and now operate across all business sectors as a business-to-business profession providing innovative workplace solutions. They operate either in partnership or in competition with the established professions.

Commercial interior design services

The client base for this new arm of the commercial design profession is focused on the non-manufacturing sector but covers a broad spectrum of service providers, professions and institutions ranging from leisure and retail, healthcare, science and technology, creative and media industries to accounting and financial services, law firms and communications and even charity organizations.

Most investors entering the United Kingdom will not require a bespoke new building, involving the use of traditional architectural practices experienced in working with property developers. However, when taking on an existing building, they will almost certainly require to engage in a 're-branding' of the premises, in addition to the reorganization of the accommodation and the logistics of relocation. Re-branding in this context goes beyond refurbishment to instilling the incoming occupant's corporate identity and culture into the building so that it is instantly recognizable by customers, clients and visitors and is a familiar corporate environment to management and staff. Sometimes, the corporate image may require adaptation to the UK market and this task can be included in the commercial interior designer's brief.

Clients' focus

Clients look for solutions to property or culture-related issues and will often initially require the preparation of premises evaluations and accommodation strategies. This may also lead to the further commissioning of workflow analysis, resource evaluation and relational studies, all of which a specialist commercial interior designer such as SPB[3] can provide.

Space planning, interior design or corporate re-branding, building-work procurement advice and management are the logical next steps in service requirements, followed by cost planning, programme and logistics management, with office furniture and artwork procurement the final 'bolt-on' services to be demanded, being the only non-business-to-business activity.

A complete workplace solution

Primarily, SPB[3] is in the business of selling business relocation, re-branding and restructuring expertise. Its clients benefit from SPB[3]'s specific expertise in a comprehensive evaluation of their business property, an evaluation and transformation of their business activities, their culture and corporate image. Its products and services are intended to: 1) provide all specialist advice to create and execute a comprehensive and effective business environment, which represents who the client is as an organization, and what they aspire to – a one stop service; 2) provide independent specialist advice in exploring the benefits of rationalizing and restructuring a client's property portfolio; determining the best possible match between people, activities and property; capturing and expressing through design the client's corporate vision.

SPB³'s processes focus on discovering and revealing the client's 'hallmark' and integrating it into the fabric of the design, rather than imposing its own hallmark on the client's organization.

Demand drivers for commercial interior design services

The drivers for demand in this service sector are diverse and may take the form of one or more of the following:

- the need to relocate – lease termination;

- improving the working environment – social responsibility;

- re-branding – cultural change;

- operational improvements – gaining competitive advantage;

- compliance with statutory legislation – changes in working practices;

- new ways of working – technological advances.

Service delivery

SPB³ is committed to customer service, a high level of competence and to bringing a quantifiable commercial benefit to its client's projects. To that end, its organization, for example, is more akin to that of a management consultancy than to a commercial design agency. It maintains a relatively small support office and puts its experts in its clients' workplaces. This 'project office' approach improves client relatedness and keeps running costs to a minimum. The support office provides additional programming and other back-up resources, quality assurance and administrative support.

Case Study: Improving operational efficiency

Working with a leading firm of international management consultants, SPB³ was tasked to observe the firm's working practices and provide strategic solutions to its effective use of time and space. The objective was achieved by redesigning the client's environment to meet the demands of an increasingly dynamic workplace and at the same time by a considerable reduction in overheads. The outcome was a refurbishment in occupied premises, which reduced the client's rentable space by 20 per cent.

One-stop finance solutions

Establishing a physical presence for an organization in a new market and relocating businesses brings up a whole host of obstacles and concerns. Inward investors will benefit from a complete, unique business solution to such major ventures, both financially and operationally.

Through its partnerships, SPB[3] offers a unique funding package, which gives clients simplicity in the form of a one-stop service agreement. The package can provide clients with flexible payment terms and deferred payment opportunities, which, coupled with lower rates of repayment, enables their relocation plans to be achieved fully and their working capital freed up for other business purposes.

Case Study: Financing high technology through investment

A firm of City brokers was paying £70 per square foot for poor-quality office space in the City of London. Property requiring renovation was found a short walk away. SPB[3] worked with the client to buy the building for £6,750,000, refurbish it for £5,000,000 and sell it on for £11,800,000 to a property owner from whom they then leased back a custom-designed state-of-the-art financial environment for only £28 per square foot.

Part 5

Corporate and Personal Legal Environment

5.1

Protection of Intellectual Property (Brand Protection)

Christopher Benson, Chris Jeffery, David Kent and Jason Rawkins, Inward Investment Group, Taylor Wessing

Intellectual property refers to inventions and other intangible assets and how they can be protected – through, for example, patents, registered trademarks, passing off, confidential information, copyright, registered designs and design rights. The advent of the internet and technological advances across many industries, when combined with the increase in cross-border trade, have all helped to heighten the commercial importance of intellectual property. This chapter concentrates on how the inward investor should protect its intellectual property. It looks at trademarks as well as looking at issues in the sphere of copyright and patents and in particular technology licensing and protection of confidential information about individuals (which is called data protection in the United Kingdom and is referred to as privacy in the United States).

Trademark law

Among a business's most valuable assets are its trading names, brand names, trading logos and general trading style. These assets can be protected in the United Kingdom in two main ways: either by applying to register them as registered trademarks, or under the common law action of passing off, which is similar to the law of unfair competition in other jurisdictions. Logos and distinctive scripts may also be protected by copyright.

The law on trademarks in the United Kingdom is contained in the

Trade Mark Act 1994 (the '1994 Act'), and in the common law action of passing off. The 1994 Act implements the EU Trade Mark Directive in the United Kingdom. The purpose of the directive is to harmonize the law on registered trademarks throughout the European Union (EU).

Registration of a trademark is not compulsory, although registration confers a statutory monopoly in the use of that trademark in relation to the class of goods or services for which it is registered and similar types of goods and services. An action for infringement by the owner of a registered mark is a much simpler action than seeking recourse under the common law by means of a passing off action.

Registered trademarks

There are three separate ways of obtaining a registered trademark, which covers the United Kingdom:

- by applying for a UK registered trademark ('a UK mark');

- by applying for a Community mark, which is one mark covering all the countries that are members of the European Union) ('a community mark');

- by applying for an international mark (an 'IR mark') under a treaty known as the Madrid Protocol. This is a system where one central application can result in multiple separate national trademark registrations, which are treated independently. An IR mark is a bundle of national trademark rights and can be obtained in countries that are signatories to the Madrid Protocol. The United Kingdom is a signatory.

Who may register?

Any person, partnership or company, whether resident in the United Kingdom or not, can apply to register a UK mark. Practically anyone may apply for a Community mark. The owner of a registered trademark or a pending trademark application in any country that is a party to the Madrid Protocol ('the base mark') may apply for an IR mark provided that the owner is a national of that country, or is domiciled in it, or has a real and effective commercial or industrial establishment in that country. In each case, the trademark has to be used by the applicant or with his or her consent or the applicant has to have a genuine intention to use the mark.

An application for a UK mark is made to the UK Trade Marks Registry (a division of the UK Department of Trade and Industry). The name and address of the applicant, a list of goods or services in relation to which the trademark is used or proposed to be used, a representation of the trademark and the application fee must be sent with the application. An application for a Community mark is made to the Community Trade Mark Office in Alicante, Spain, and the applicant has to give the same information. An applicant for an IR mark applies to the Trade Mark Registry in the country where the base mark upon which the IR mark is based was obtained. The Registry forwards the application to the World Intellectual Property Organization in Geneva. The application designates the countries to be covered by the IR mark.

If an applicant has filed an application in a Paris Convention country, and within six months applies for a UK, Community or IR mark for the same trademark, then by virtue of the provisions of the Paris Convention the date of filing of the second application is deemed to be the earlier date of filing of the first application, if that application is the first application filed anywhere in the world for that mark. This is a useful means of claiming priority over other applications.

What can be registered?

All applications to register a UK mark or an IR mark are examined by the UK Trade Mark Registry to verify that the trademark qualifies for registration under the 1994 Act. The Registrar can reject an application if among other things the mark in question is not distinctive, if it is descriptive, or if it is a mark that has become commonplace in the trade in question. These objections can be overcome if the mark applied for has become distinctive through use. The same principles apply to Community trademarks.

The UK Trade Marks Registry also carries out a search of its records to see if there are any earlier registrations or applications that block the path of the application. The Community Trade Mark Office carries out a search of prior Community registered trademarks and pending applications and 16 of the current 25 EU member countries carry out searches of national trademarks. Five of the current EU member countries do not carry out searches of national trademarks and four of the EU member countries have not yet decided on their position as regards national trademark searches. However, these are not used as grounds for an official objection.

A trademark has to satisfy two tests to be registrable as a trademark: 1) it must be capable of being represented graphically; and 2) it must be capable of distinguishing the applicant's goods or services from the goods or services of other businesses. It is possible to file applications for words, designs, three-dimensional shapes and colours if such marks can be represented graphically and distinguish the applicant's goods or services.

While it is possible in the United Kingdom to obtain a trademark registration for semi-descriptive marks and 3D shapes, recent case law has led to it being more difficult to obtain registered trademarks for these marks than originally envisaged when the 1994 Act came into force. Multi-class applications are permissible. One application can be filed covering several classes of the Register.

After acceptance by the UK Registry, UK and IR trademarks are advertised in the *UK Trade Marks Journal*. After acceptance by the Community Trade Marks Office, a Community mark is advertised in the *Official Journal*. In each case, third parties have a limited period to oppose the registration of the mark. Any person may submit written observations to the Trade Marks Registry or the Community Trade Mark Office (as appropriate) as to why the application in question should not be registered. This is an extremely useful way trademark owners and others can object to confusingly similar applications filed by third parties.

Duration and renewal

After initial registration, a UK, Community or IR trademark lasts for 10 years from the date of filing of the application. The registration may be renewed indefinitely thereafter for further periods of 10 years upon payment of renewal fees.

Exclusive rights

Valid registration of a trademark confers on the owner the exclusive right to the use of the trademark in relation to those goods or services for which it is registered.

Infringement

The proprietor (and in certain circumstances) both exclusive and non-exclusive licensees, can take action for registered trademark infringement. A proprietor of a trademark cannot sue for registered trademark infringement until the trademark is registered. However, his or her rights are backdated in respect of a UK or IR mark to the date of application and in respect of a Community mark to the date of advertisement so he or she can sue for acts that take place between the date of filing or advertisement (as appropriate) and the date of registration. A registered trademark is infringed if a third party uses in the course of trade:

● an identical mark on identical goods or services to those registered;

● an identical mark on similar goods or services; or

● a similar mark on identical or similar goods and services to those registered;

- and in the case of the last two scenarios there is a likelihood that the public will be confused.

A registered trademark is also infringed if a third party uses in the course of trade an identical or similar mark in relation to dissimilar goods or services to those registered, or if the mark is used without due cause and takes advantage of or is detrimental to the character or repute of the registered trademark.

The following are examples of infringing acts (these are very wide as can be seen):

- using the mark on goods or packaging;

- offering goods for sale or supplying services under the mark;

- importing or exporting goods under the mark;

- using the mark on business papers or in advertising;

- using the mark as part of a corporate or trading name;

- using the mark on a website; and

- infringing orally, for example, in a radio advertisement.

There are various defences to registered trademark infringement. These include the following:

- One of the most important defences is in relation to comparative advertising. A trader can use another person's registered trademark in an advertisement provided that its use 'is in accordance with honest practices in industrial or commercial matters' and the use would not take 'unfair advantage of or be detrimental to the distinctive character or repute of the registered trademark'. The UK courts have interpreted this wording as allowing comparative advertising provided it is not significantly misleading.

- If goods bearing a registered trademark are put onto the market within the European Economic Area (EEA) by the registered proprietor or with his or her consent then the registered trademark is not infringed if the goods later enter the United Kingdom without the proprietor's consent, unless there are legitimate reasons for him or her to oppose their entering the United Kingdom, for example, if the condition of the goods has been changed or impaired since they first appeared on the market. However, this defence does not apply to goods put on to the market outside the EEA by the registered proprietor or with his or her consent. These rules are the rules on parallel importing, the rules governing the so-called grey market.

Remedies for infringement include an injunction; damages or an account of profits; delivery up of infringing goods; obliteration of the offending sign from the goods; and destruction or forfeiture of the infringing goods. There are detailed rules governing in which country proceedings for infringement of a Community mark must be brought. It is possible to obtain an injunction covering the whole trade in the EU in respect of infringement of a Community mark.

Assignment and licensing

A UK Community or IR trademark may be assigned or licensed. The assignment of such a trademark must be in writing and the registered trademark may be assigned with or without the goodwill of the business in which it has been used. An assignment of a registered trademark can be limited to only some of the goods and services for which it is registered, or in respect of a UK or IR mark for use only in a particular area of the United Kingdom. For an IR mark, the new owner must be a person or entity qualified to hold an IR mark. It is not possible to assign rights in a Community mark only in some of the European Union countries. It has to be assigned to the same assignee in all member states. A registered trademark can also be licensed either generally or for some of the goods or services for which it is registered or only for particular areas of the United Kingdom.

If a company is a licensee of a registered trademark, although it is no longer a legal requirement, it should apply to have its licence recorded at the UK Trade Marks Registry or Community Trade Mark Office in order to ensure that if the registered trademark is assigned the assignee is bound by the licence.

Revocation

A registered trademark is vulnerable to attack and can be removed from the Register if:

- in respect of a UK or IR mark, it is not used for a continuous period of five years or more in the United Kingdom in relation to the goods and services it covers and in respect of a Community mark if it is not used for a continuous period of five years or more anywhere within the European Union in relation to the goods and services it covers – use in each individual European Union country is not necessary;

- the applicant had no genuine intention to use the mark when filing the application;

- the mark was wrongly registered in the first place;

- the mark has lost its distinctiveness or become misleading because of acts by the proprietor.

Marking® and TM

Use of the words 'Registered Trade Mark' in relation to a trademark is optional. Use of the word 'registered' or the symbol® on or in relation to goods or services are taken as a representation that the mark is registered in the United Kingdom unless it is shown that the reference is to registration elsewhere and the mark is in fact registered elsewhere. It is a criminal offence for any person to make representation with respect to a trademark not registered in the United Kingdom to the effect that it is a registered trademark in the United Kingdom. Use of the symbol™ indicates an unregistered trademark and is permissible.

For the avoidance of doubt as to the status of the trademark in the United Kingdom it might be prudent to say, for example, 'Registered in the USA' or '® USA' if the mark is registered in the United States but not the United Kingdom but is being used in the United Kingdom.

International aspects

The Community Trade Mark is an 'all or nothing' trademark. If an application is refused in any member country, the whole application fails. It is possible at that stage to convert the Community Trade Mark application into national applications in those countries where there are no objections and the original filing date is retained subject to the applicant paying national filing fees for those countries.

An IR mark is tied to the base mark for the first five years. If during that period the base mark is withdrawn, rejected or cancelled, the IR is invalid. It is possible to convert the IR into national applications in those countries where there are no objections and maintain the original priority date subject to payment of conversion fees charged by national registries.

Passing off

Trademarks (both registered and unregistered) may be protected under the English common law of passing off (as well as under the principles of unfair competition under civil law in the various European countries). Generally, English common law will prevent one trader expressly or impliedly representing that his or her goods and services are connected with or approved by another trader. Use of another's trademark is one way of making such a representation. In order to succeed in an action for passing off the claimant must establish:

- a reputation in the trademark in question so that members of the public associate the mark with his or her goods and/or services;
- actual confusion, or the likelihood of confusion by members of the

public as between the infringing goods/services and the claimant's goods/services; and

- damage.

This makes such actions more expensive than actions for infringement of registered trademarks. Accordingly, registration of marks is to be preferred.

Trademark searches should be obtained before a mark is used in the name of a company or a business to be started in the United Kingdom. In addition, using an internet search engine will highlight any unregistered use of the proposed mark elsewhere in the world. Great care needs to be taken in this aspect. A French judge under the French law of unfair competition has found that a US website infringes the unregistered rights of a French proprietor with prior use of the name just because any French person can access the US website. This area causes much heartache for overseas investors who have set up their company or branch without undertaking trademark and internet search engine checks. Specialist advice is needed here on most occasions.

Domain name disputes

Domain name disputes continue to increase as more businesses and celebrities go online. Disputes can be categorized in two ways. First, there is the person who fraudulently registers the name. This is known as 'cybersquatting'. The second is where a person registers the name innocently for a legitimate website. Cybersquatting is regarded in the United Kingdom as 'an instrument of fraud'. Innocent use of a domain name is often subject to an action for passing off although this can be difficult to prove. An alternative is to complain under the Uniform Domain Name Dispute Resolution Policy established by the Internet Corporation for Assigned Names and Numbers. A further alternative is to ask for the dispute to be settled by Nominet UK where the domain name is a '.uk' name or brand.

Patents

Patents protect new inventions. A patent gives an inventor a monopoly over his or her invention for a fixed period. This provides an incentive for people to invent. In exchange for the patent, the inventor must disclose his or her invention to the world. Patents may be granted for products and processes.

In the United Kingdom, to be patentable, an invention must be new, involve an inventive step (that is, it must not be obvious to someone who is skilled in the particular area) and be capable of industrial application. The date by which the novelty and obviousness of an invention is judged is called the priority date. The priority date of a patent will be the filing date of an application, unless the date of an earlier application in a Patent Convention Country is validly claimed. To claim the date of an earlier application as the priority date the earlier application must have been made within 12 months (for example, an overseas investor from the United States has 12 months from the date of his or her US application to file in the United Kingdom).

In the United Kingdom, patents can be obtained either nationally in the Patent Office or centrally as a European Patent in the European Patent Office. However, on grant, a European patent becomes a 'bundle' of separate national rights. In the cases of infringement of either a UK patent or a European patent, infringement has to be dealt with on a country by country basis.

For an overseas investor, obtaining UK and European protection for its patents is often paramount. The rules are complicated and specialist advice will be needed. Patent licensing, collaborations and joint research and development are similarly complex and can create much heartache where they are entered into on heads of terms rather than negotiated agreements. Overlaying these issues is a further set of issues provided by the EU competition rules with some leeway given by the block exemption. Again, specialist advice should be taken as a matter of priority.

Copyright

Copyright is the exclusive right of the authors of certain original works, including literary, dramatic, musical and artistic works, sound recordings, films, broadcasts and cable programmes to prevent persons from copying, using or exploiting their work without permission for a period of time.

Copyright arises automatically on the creation of a work in the United Kingdom and registration is not required. Copyright works include books, musical compositions, computer programs, photographs, drawings, logos and sculptures. Modern methods of storing and manipulating information have developed copyright law so that computer software is protected by UK copyright law as a literary work. Databases, similarly, but in addition there is a separate database right.

For the inward investor who has copyright protection in their home country it is likely that their copyright is also recognized in the United Kingdom under one or more of the various copyright conventions.

Employee inventions

Employee inventions, when covered by any of the UK laws of

intellectual property, belong to the employer, that is, the individual investor's company or the UK subsidiary of an overseas inward investor. However, the rules are not straightforward and it is important that clauses following the procedures set out in both the UK patents and copyright legislation are included in a proprietary information and confidentiality agreement signed with each employee. In addition, the inward investor should consider whether vesting new IP rights should occur in the UK subsidiary or in the overseas company. See Chapter 5.2 in relation to confidentiality and non-compete clauses.

Protection of technology

There are a number of legal areas relating to developing, protecting and exploiting technology in the United Kingdom, the key ones being:

- Contracting with customers, suppliers and partners.

- Regulatory issues relating to personal information: data protection and privacy.

- Specific regulatory and contractual issues relating to online sales. These include the effectiveness of online contracts, digital signatures, relevant law and dispute resolution, information to be provided to users and specific consumer rights (including cancellation of online orders).

- Liability for defective products and insurance, and equipment safety and labelling rules.

- Specific sectoral regulation, such as telecoms and broadcasting licensing regimes.

- UK and EU export controls.

- UK and EU competition rules (known as 'anti-trust' in the United States), for example, abuse of market power as alleged by the EU authorities against Microsoft, and contractual provisions that restrict competition, particularly relevant when appointing resellers and distributors.

In the following section, we will outline briefly the two areas that are likely to impact all technology companies doing business in the United Kingdom: contracting with customers, suppliers and partners and data protection/privacy.

Contracting with customers, suppliers and partners

The area of law relevant to technology contracts is vast; there is not scope to provide a comprehensive guide in this book. Instead, here are some of the key points that often arise in practice for an overseas company selling or licensing to a UK customer.

Choice of law

Consideration needs to be given as to which law should apply to the contract and how disputes should be resolved. It is important that in practice one can force the other party to comply with the contract and have practical means to sue for compensation when they do not. This may mean, for instance, that insisting on one's home law and jurisdiction of home courts is not appropriate. For the overseas company supplying a UK customer, an open mind should be kept on using English law and local courts or arbitration. As a minimum, it will be necessary to protect intellectual property and trade secrets by getting emergency court orders wherever they may be needed.

English common law

Readers from civil law countries should be ready for long agreements! UK contracts, like their US counterparts, tend to be longer than those used in continental Europe. This is because in the latter, many principles are imposed on commercial relationships by legal codes (such as the French civil code and commercial code and the German civil code). In the United Kingdom, as in the United States, nothing can be taken for granted: the guiding principle is that if it is not there in black and white, it is not part of the contract. Do not therefore assume that an overriding principle of good faith, for instance, will 'fill in the gaps' when dealing under English law.

Local law of customer overrides

Remember that where a sale is to an English customer a review by an English lawyer will always be advisable to be sure the contract can be enforced in practice. This applies even where a law other than English law is chosen to govern the relationship and a court or an arbitration body based outside the United Kingdom is to hear disputes. It is true that in some cases, paying a UK lawyer to review the contract may not be viable because of the value of a contract or project or other factors. There is a balance to be drawn between legal concerns and the realities of corporate budgets. Different companies will strike that balance in different ways, but as a general rule of thumb, where a significant level of business is expected in relation to a particular relationship or territory, then a local review should be obtained (the same applies where a sale is made to a European country and a different law is chosen than the local law of the customer. A local law review should be obtained).

Exclusion and limitation of liability clauses

Under English law there is legislation protecting both the consumer and the commercial customer against defective products or services. The United Kingdom has very strict rules on the effectiveness of exclusion clauses and various consumer protection carve outs will be needed. Typically in the United Kingdom, suppliers will look to cap their total exposure at a specific level (for example, the value of the contract or order) and to exclude liability for certain kinds of loss altogether (such as loss of profit). The issue is that, where these kinds of provisions do not comply with the relevant UK statute, they are void – that is, they are effectively deleted from the document. A UK judge will not amend the wording to make it valid.

Shrink-wrap licences

Although shrink-wrap and click-wrap licence agreements are widely used in the United Kingdom for high-volume, low to medium value software sales, they may have no legal effect. They are used principally because there is no practical alternative. As a result, the supplier takes a view on the risks of the clause being ineffective (and hopes to rely on the general principles of intellectual property to fight piracy). Alternatives should be considered where possible, although it is sometimes possible to make changes to the ordering process to increase the chances of these clauses being effective.

Method of trading of an overseas company

Ensure that the correct entity is used as the party to a technology sale or licensing contract. The tax and revenue recognition structures referred to earlier in Chapter 4.1 typically require that revenue-generating contracts are signed in the name of a specific member of the (overseas) corporate group and there is a risk of creating unnecessary tax liabilities and a management headache if this does not happen. This is one of the most frequent mistakes made by overseas companies with new businesses that have just been set up in the United Kingdom. The mistake occurs when an overzealous salesperson makes a sale in his or her first quarter and commits the UK entity to making the supply instead of the overseas company.

EU competition rules

When licensing software, all EU countries require that users can decompile the product in order to obtain the interface information (that is, a portion of the product's source code) to be able to make the licensed product inter-operable with another product. It is not possible to avoid this right through contractual wording, or by choosing a non-European law. If a licence includes restrictions that are wide enough to prevent this right being exercised, there is a significant risk that those restrictions will be void – potentially leaving the kinds of thing the user can do with the software unclear. There are ways around this issue but advice is needed as to the most appropriate method.

Sales representatives, agents and distributors

Some issues are largely relevant only to arrangements with local representatives: these could be agents (usually referred to as 'sales representatives' in the United States), resellers or distributors:

● In all EU countries agents/sales representatives who have the power to negotiate and/or sign contracts on behalf of their principals, have a number of important rights that cannot be contracted out of and that apply even if a non-European law is stated to apply to the contract. These rules are therefore mandatory. Most important of these rights is the right to compensation of a year's receivables on termination or non-renewal.

● Damages of one year's receivables can apply also to the termination of distribution arrangements in countries such as Belgium and Germany. Worse, in France, when terminating a distributor in order to set up a direct operation the employees of a distributor automatically transfer to the terminating company, under the French civil code in accordance with the EU Acquired Rights Directive.

● In the United Kingdom, distributors and resellers (those who buy from the supplier and then sell on to customers on their own account) have no such automatic rights to compensation. However, it is always important to make sure that any termination of one of these contracts is made strictly in accordance with the timing and notice requirements of the relevant contract, failing which damages will be payable for breach of contract.

● Competition or anti-trust rules apply to the appointments of resellers and distributors in Europe. This gives rise to a number of issues that need to be borne in mind, key among them being that any contractual restrictions on the price, which the distributor or reseller charges to the purchaser, is likely to be illegal (although a maximum resale price and a recommended retail price may be lawful depending on the circumstances of the case and the drafting). When considering what territory a distributor/reseller should be permitted to sell in, it should be borne in mind that there are complex rules restricting the freedom to split the European territory between the seller and its various distributors or resellers. In particular, non-exclusive distributors or resellers should be entitled to sell the product(s) throughout Europe. Exclusive appointments for particular territories within Europe, are however in principle legitimate, but need to be drawn up carefully to ensure compliance with the rules.

Data protection/privacy in the United Kingdom

The use by businesses of information about individuals is subject to a complex array of data protection laws, principally those enshrined in the UK legislation called The Data Protection Act 1998. These laws are roughly mirrored throughout the EU, being based on an EU directive. However, as always with what is loosely termed 'EU law', the rules and the way they are implemented (because they were brought in by directive and not by regulation) differ from one EU country to the next.

The Data Protection Act 1998 (DPA)

This Act:

- sets out the rules and practices that must be followed when processing information about individuals;

- grants rights to those individuals in respect of their information; and

- creates an independent supervisory body to enforce these rules, rights and practices: the Information Commissioner.

Scope of the DPA

The DPA regulates the processing of 'personal data'. Personal data are data relating to individuals (referred to in the DPA as 'data subjects') who can be identified from those data, or from those data together with other information that is in, or is likely to come into, the possession of the entity who decides what the data will be used for (the 'data controller' – see below).

The DPA applies to information that is processed automatically (that is, data held on computer); and information recorded on paper (but only if there is a significant element of structure to the paper records so that specific information about an individual can be found).

The term 'processing' has a very wide meaning under the DPA. It is intended to cover any conceivable operation on data, ranging from collecting, recording, holding of data and the carrying out of any operation on those data, through to their subsequent disclosure and eventual destruction.

'Data controllers' are the entities (companies, firms, sole traders, etc) who, either independently, or jointly with others, decide how personal data will be used and what they are to be used for. 'Data processors' are the entities who process personal data on behalf of data controllers. For example, if a business uses a payroll bureau to process its payslips and payments to staff, then that payroll bureau is acting as a data processor, and the business appointing it is a data controller.

The DPA only places obligations on data controllers, not on data processors. However, if a controller uses the services of a processor, it must have a written agreement in place with the processor in which the processor is obliged to: do only what the controller instructs it to do with the personal data; and maintain appropriate security measures in place with respect to the personal data.

The notification obligation in the United Kingdom

Generally speaking (there are some exemptions), before processing any personal data, it is necessary to first notify the United Kingdom's Information Commissioner of the intended processing activities giving specified information on the data that will be held, the purposes for which it will be used, and the entities and countries it may be sent to. Notification must be renewed annually and a fee paid. That information will then appear on a public register.

The Data Protection Principles

The DPA is based on eight Data Protection Principles. The first principle is particularly important; it requires that personal data are processed, that is, obtained and subsequently used, 'fairly and lawfully'. There are two aspects to this: making sure that the processing is legitimate by satisfying one or more specified preconditions (of which one is the consent of the data subject); and providing individuals with certain information when collecting data from them (or, if data is not collected directly from them, then before undertaking any processing of their data). Data subjects must also be provided with certain specified information including:

- the identity of the data controller(s) for the data;

- the intended uses for the data; and

- any other information that is necessary to enable the processing to be fair (for example, informing someone of their right to object to direct marketing).

Other principles relate among other things to how long personal data may be held, and security measures that need to be taken.

Rights of data subjects to copies and to object

The DPA confers a number of rights on individuals in respect of their personal data, including the right to be provided with copies of the personal data that relates to them (known as 'data subject access requests') and rights to object to direct marketing and to compensation for breaches of the DPA.

Transfers of personal data outside the European Economic Area

Under the DPA, transfers of personal data to countries outside the EEA are prohibited unless either the destination country in question ensures an 'adequate' level of data protection for individuals or one or more preconditions that allow the transfer to take place applies. This means that transfers from one country within the EEA to another are not restricted, although other provisions of the DPA may still be relevant. The EEA is composed of the 25 EU member states – Austria, Belgium, Cyprus, the Czech Republic, Denmark, Estonia, Finland, France, Germany, Greece, Hungary, Ireland, Italy, Latvia, Lithuania, Luxembourg, Malta, the Netherlands, Poland, Portugal, Slovenia, the Slovak Republic, Spain, Sweden and the United Kingdom – together with Norway, Liechtenstein and Iceland.

At the time of writing, only Canada, Hungary, Switzerland and Argentina are regarded as providing adequate protection. The United States in particular is not so regarded. If the destination country outside the EEA does not provide adequate protection, then the transfer will only be permitted where one or more specified preconditions (which are additional preconditions to the ones for general processing described above) can be met. Examples of preconditions are:

- where the data subject has consented;

- the transfer is necessary for the performance of a contract with the data subject; or

- the rights of the data subject are protected by a contract based on the European-approved terms in place between the UK entity and the overseas company (in practice the most common means of compliance); or

- in the case of transfers to the United States, the recipient has signed up to the Safe Harbor scheme.

Often, the UK entity will want to send various kinds of data back to the overseas head office for processing. That data could be HR and payroll data relating to employees, or information relating to individuals at potential or actual customers. In either case, the transfer would come within these rules where sent outside the EEA. As mentioned above the execution of a contract between the UK entity and the overseas company is the most usual way of compliance with the data protection rules. As third parties may examine the contract it needs to be carefully thought out and drafted.

Direct marketing rules

There is not scope to go into the detail in this chapter, but there are rules restricting the ability of organizations to contact prospective customers by fax, phone, post, e-mail and SMS. These rules are a combination of opt-in and opt-out and specific advice should be taken before contacting UK businesses and individuals for direct marketing.

5.2

Employment, Pensions and Stock Options

Paul Callaghan, Michael Porter, Fleur Benns and David Kent, Inward Investment Group, Taylor Wessing

Introduction

This chapter gives a brief outline of the main legislation that applies to UK employees. The aim of the chapter is to focus on the main issues of employment law from the point of view of an overseas person who has come to the United Kingdom to set up a business or from the point of view of an overseas company setting up a place of business, a branch or a subsidiary in the United Kingdom. UK employees have a number of statutory rights including the right not to be unfairly dismissed after attaining one year's service and the right not to be discriminated against on the grounds of sex, race, disability, sexual orientation, religion or belief. There are also rights relating to the family, including extensive maternity leave and pay provisions, paternity leave and pay and a further right to parental leave. There is further legislation relating to areas as diverse as sick pay, maximum working hours, minimum holiday entitlement and a National Minimum Wage.

Nothing in English employment law is intuitive, in fact the correct procedures and methods of dealing with HR issues are counter-intuitive from the point of view of the incoming investor. However, even so, English employment law is seen as the fairest and most reasonable of the employment laws of the European countries. Procedures are available for a much speedier resolution of HR issues than in France, Germany, the Netherlands, etc.

Contracts of employment

The most significant piece of legislation relating to employees rights is the Employment Rights Act 1996. Under the Employment Rights Act 1996, every employee should be given a written statement or written contract of certain terms and conditions governing his or her employment within two months of commencing employment. The statement should cover an extensive list of issues including:

- holidays;
- hours of work;
- job title;
- notice of termination;
- pension entitlement;
- salary;
- sick pay.

Whether or not a written contract of employment is given to an employee, they will be deemed to have a contract of employment under law. Quality specialist advice should always be obtained in the provision of an employment contract. The above provisions first became law in 1972 and many draft contracts that are used in the United Kingdom were prepared at that time and are out of date.

Investors should ensure that they have in addition to the standard contract (which complies with the Employment Rights Act 1996) a form of proprietary information and confidentiality agreement, which is governed by English law. This agreement will often include a non-competition clause.

Non-competition clauses (non-compete clauses)

It is possible to insert provisions in the employment arrangements with an employee to protect a company's confidential information. It is also usual to include restraint of trade provisions (non-compete clauses) to prevent key employees from either joining a competitor or, more frequently, soliciting or dealing with the company's customers or soliciting or employing other key employees once the employment relationship has come to an end. However, there are very strict rules about what is enforceable and what is not. A company will need to show that it has a legitimate business interest to protect and that the drafted restrictions are as narrow as is absolutely necessary to protect those interests. If there is no provision in a contract of employment then only trade secrets will be protected by law following the termination of an employee's employment.

Maximum working hours and holiday entitlement

Under the Working Time Regulations 1998 workers are protected by a 48-hours maximum working week averaged over a period of 17 weeks. At present, there are derogations for specific sectors such as transport and more general derogations including those for 'autonomous decision-takers' such as those who manage their own time. As currently interpreted, this derogation includes most management-type employees. Employers are required to keep certain records regarding the working time of their workforce.

The Working Time Regulations provide for a minimum of 20 days' paid holiday each year (which includes the eight public holidays in the United Kingdom). Holiday entitlement accrues from the start of the employment. Pay in respect of holiday taken is usually based on the average pay over the 12 weeks prior to the holiday.

National Minimum Wage

All workers now benefit from the National Minimum Wage ('NMW'). The genuinely self-employed and people under the age of 18 are outside of the scope of the NMW.

The basic rate for payment of the NMW is £4.50 per hour (rising to £4.85 on 1 October 2004). Young workers aged between 18 and 21 are entitled to the NMW at the lower rate of £3.80 (rising to £4.10 on 1 October 2004). Employers are required to keep full records of payments to workers.

Statutory Sick Pay

All employees (other than some specified exceptions) who are absent from work due to illness or injury are entitled to receive Statutory Sick Pay from their employer for up to 28 weeks in a rolling three-year period. The provisions operate when the employee is absent for at least four consecutive days. Shorter absences would normally, but need not, be paid as salary. The level of Statutory Sick Pay is set by statute and is regularly revised. It currently stands at £66.15 per week but many employers make up any salary shortfall at least for a specified period of illness.

Employers are required to keep records for Statutory Sick Pay purposes and an investor should put in place an internal procedure whereby there is a specified person to whom all sickness absence should be notified and who is responsible for maintaining records.

Employment protection

The Employment Rights Act 1996 provides for employee protection in general areas, the most important of which are discussed below.

Minimum notice

There is no such thing as employment 'at will' under English law. An employee is entitled to one week's minimum notice after four weeks' continuous service. After two years' service he or she becomes entitled to two weeks' notice, which then increases by one week for each year of service, up to a maximum of 12 weeks' notice after 12 years' service. These statutory notice requirements apply only where the contractual notice is less than the statutory minimum. The agreed contractual notice must be given if that is the longer period (also see Redundancy and dismissal below).

Pregnancy

All female employees are entitled to 26 weeks' ordinary maternity leave. This applies regardless of length of service. The contract of employment continues during ordinary maternity leave and during such leave the employee must continue to receive all her contractual benefits except commission, contractual bonus, wages and salary.

Female employees with 26 weeks' continuous employment are also entitled to additional maternity leave for 26 weeks. Additional maternity leave commences at the end of ordinary maternity leave and therefore some employees will be entitled to take up to a year of leave. The contract of employment continues during additional maternity leave but only certain terms and conditions apply unless there is an agreement between the employer and employee that says differently.

Those employees with at least 26 weeks' continuous service are entitled to 26 weeks' statutory maternity pay. Statutory maternity pay currently stands at 90 per cent of the employee's average earnings for the first six weeks of maternity leave, dropping to £102.80 for 20 weeks thereafter. Many employers make payments in addition to this statutory minimum.

Women returning to work within the periods set out in the relevant legislation must be reinstated in their former position or be given an equivalent job, unless the employer can bring itself within certain statutory exemptions. All pregnant women are entitled to time off to attend antenatal clinics. Parents may take up to 13 weeks' unpaid parental leave per child up to the age of five years. Dismissal on grounds of pregnancy is automatically unfair and would also amount to sex discrimination.

Adoption leave and pay

Adoption leave and pay rights are available to parents with 26 weeks' continuous service who adopt a child up to 18 years of age where the child is newly placed. Eligible employees will be entitled to 26 weeks' ordinary adoption leave during which they will receive statutory adoption pay of £102.80 per week or 90 per cent of weekly earnings if this is less. Adopting employees with 26 weeks' continuous service are also entitled to 26 weeks' additional adoption leave, which is unpaid. This means an eligible employee can take up to a year's adoption leave.

Paternity leave and pay

Eligible employees can take two weeks' paid paternity leave within eight weeks of a child's birth in blocks of a week. To be eligible an employee must have 26 weeks' continuous service, have or expect to have responsibility for the upbringing of the child and be the biological father of the child or married to or the partner of the child's mother. Paternity pay is currently £102.80 per week or 90 per cent of the employee's average weekly earnings if this is less.

Flexible working

Employees with at least 26 weeks' continuous employment who have the appropriate parental relationship with, and responsibility for the upbringing of, a child under six (18 if disabled), are able to make an application to work flexibly by altering the terms of their contract of employment with respect to:

- the number of hours worked;
- the times required to work;
- where work is carried out (that is, to work from home).

An employer must take the request seriously by following a statutory procedure in dealing with the application. An employer may refuse the application on certain specified objective business grounds.

Deduction from wages

An employer cannot deduct any amount (for example, loan repayments) from an employee's salary unless that deduction is authorized by law or by the employee in writing.

Redundancy and dismissal

An employee with two years' continuous service has a right to compensation if he or she is dismissed because of redundancy, even if there is not an unfair dismissal (see below). Redundancy payments are calculated on a sliding scale depending on age and length of service. The maximum redundancy payment is one and a half weeks' pay up to a maximum of £270 per week for each year of employment up to a maximum of 20 years (this amounts to a maximum payment of £8,100). An employee who is offered suitable alternative employment and unreasonably refuses such employment is not entitled to a redundancy payment.

Under the Employment Rights Act 1996, compensation may be payable to employees who have more than one year's continuous service at their date of dismissal if they are unfairly dismissed. The period of service is usually only continuous where it is with the same employer. However, it may also be continuous where there is some connection between the two employers, for example, they are associated or there has been a business transfer. Complaints of unfair dismissal are made to an Employment Tribunal.

The concept of unfair dismissal is well established in the United Kingdom. Statute sets out five reasons for dismissals that are potentially fair, as follows:

- capability;
- conduct;
- redundancy;
- that continued employment would contravene any restriction imposed by an enactment; and
- some other substantial reason.

For the dismissal to be fair not only must an employer dismiss for one of the above five fair reasons, but the employer must also follow a fair procedure in reaching the decision to dismiss. There are minimum procedures set out by law which must be followed. If they are not followed, a dismissal will be held to automatically be unfair. Depending upon the reason for dismissal, previous warnings or consultations with the employees may also be necessary. Many overseas investors this procedure will be regarded as unwieldy and uncommercial and they will wish to dismiss the employee immediately. A dismissal that is immediate will always be unfair.

If employees are found to have been unfairly dismissed they will be compensated by a basic award and a compensatory award. The basic award is calculated on the same basis as a redundancy payment. The current maximum compensatory award for unfair dismissal is £55,000 where the dismissal occurred on or after 1 February 2004. This may be paid in addition to any sums due in respect of an employee's period of notice. In order to settle a claim for unfair dismissal with an employee it will be necessary for a compromise agreement to be agreed between the employee and the employer. The compromise agreement will only be effective once signed by the employee and his or her solicitor. This last requirement is often overlooked by overseas investors when settling an employment dispute with an ex-employee. The failure to obtain the solicitor's signature means that the settlement is non-binding. In the case of multiple dismissals, there are various notification and consultation procedures that must be satisfied where 20 or more employees are to be dismissed within a period of 90 days or less.

Investors should ensure that all employees receive regular appraisals so that issues are addressed with them as soon as possible. In relation to new employees, appraisals should take place at least at six months and depending upon the notice period at eight or nine months from the beginning of the period of employment. In this way, the cost of an unfair dismissal claim can be negated.

Trade union activities, collective bargaining and employee representation

There are recent requirements in the United Kingdom that an employer must recognize a trade union for collective bargaining purposes where certain criteria are met. There are also general requirements to inform and consult with employees, or appropriate representatives, in the case of collective dismissals (dismissals of 20 or more employees) or in the case of a transfer of an undertaking. The detailed requirements for information and consultation are beyond the scope of this chapter, but an employer failing to comply with its obligations may be exposed to obligations to pay compensation. A failure to inform and consult may also make it more likely that there will be a finding of unfair dismissal.

Collective bargaining agreements are relatively uncommon in the United Kingdom and in any event do not have the same status and authority as in many other European countries. However, it is possible for collective bargaining arrangements to be included in individual employees' contracts of employment, whether expressly (verbally or in writing) or as a result of custom and practice. It is unlawful to refuse a person employment on the grounds of membership or non-membership of a trade union. Peaceful picketing during industrial action is generally allowed but must in general be restricted to the employees' own place of work. Neither individuals nor unions can be sued for properly constituted strike action.

The European Works Council Directive ('EWCD') applies to companies that employ more than 1,000 employees within the European Economic Area; and employ 150 of those in each of two member states. The EWCD states that employers should inform and consult their employees in relation to a wide range of business-related decisions taken by the employer. The EWCD has been implemented in other member states for some time. Consequently, many UK companies have had to take steps to comply with the EWCD as they employ significant numbers of people in member states already covered by the directive.

Discrimination

It is unlawful for an employer to discriminate against employees or applicants for employment on grounds of:

- colour, race, nationality or ethnic or national origin;

- disability;

- religion or belief.

- sex or marital status;

- sexual orientation; and

- from October 2006, age.

Colour, race, nationality or ethnic or national origin

Legislation makes it unlawful to treat a person less favourably than others on the grounds of race, colour, nationality and national or ethnic origin (racial grounds). It is also unlawful for an employer to indirectly discriminate by applying an apparently race-neutral requirement or condition that, in practice, is more difficult for members of a particular race to comply with. Finally, harassment of an employee on racial grounds is also illegal.

Disability

It is unlawful for an employer to unjustifiably treat a disabled person less favourably than another a person on the grounds of that person's disability. Additionally, employers have to take reasonable steps, including modifying premises, to accommodate the needs of disabled employees or potential employees.

An inward investor acquiring leasehold or freehold real estate in old or quaint business premises should be aware of the hidden traps in this area, for example, are the doors large enough to allow wheelchair access?

Sexual orientation and religion or belief

It is unlawful for employers to treat employees less favourably than other employees because of their religion, religious belief or similar philosophical belief, or because of their sexual orientation (homosexual, bisexual or heterosexual), with respect to all aspects of the employment relationship.

Employers can be held responsible for any harassment suffered by an employee because of their religion, belief or sexual orientation. Employees are also protected from victimization, which occurs when an employee is treated less favourably because he or she has asserted a right in relation to discrimination on the grounds of sexual orientation or religion/belief.

Sex and marital status

Discrimination on the grounds of sex or marital status is made unlawful by the Sex Discrimination Act 1975. An employer may not directly or indirectly discriminate against a person on the grounds of sex.

Under the Equal Pay Act 1970, women are required to be given equal treatment to men in respect of pay and conditions of work when working in the same or broadly similar jobs. Grievances may be brought before an Employment Tribunal, which may make an order for compensation. A typical example of discrimination may relate to the exclusion of part-time workers from occupational pension schemes. As part-time workers are more likely to be women than men, the exclusion would have a disproportionate impact on women and would therefore amount to indirect sex discrimination.

Generally, there is no limit on compensation for any of the above categories of discrimination, unlike the general limit in connection with unfair dismissal. An employer will be liable for any acts of discrimination or harassment committed by its employees in the course of employment – whether or not it was done with the employer's knowledge or consent, unless the employer can show it took such steps as were reasonably practicable to prevent the conduct. Normally, an employee will need to raise a formal grievance with an employer before they can bring a claim for discrimination. Investors should ensure that all employees receive regular equal opportunities training.

Part-time workers

The contractual terms and conditions on which an employer may engage a part-time worker are affected by legislation that aims to prevent part-time workers' terms and conditions being less favourable than those of comparable full-time workers. In some cases, an employer may be able to justify the different treatment on objective grounds (for example, if it can show that the different treatment is necessary and appropriate to achieve a legitimate business objective).

Fixed-term employees

Employees on fixed-term contracts or hired to complete a specific project or task cannot be treated less favourably than comparable permanent employees on the grounds they are fixed-term employees, unless this is objectively justified. This right applies both in terms of contractual terms (including pay and pensions), and to any other detrimental treatment by an employer.

Health and safety at work

An employer is under a general direct duty to have regard to the safety of all employees. The employer is also liable for accidents caused by acts of employees where the employees were acting in the course of their employment.

An employer is obliged to maintain insurance, under one or more approved policies with an authorized insurer, against liability for bodily injury or disease sustained by employees and arising out of and in the course of their employment. There are detailed regulations setting out specific requirements for employers to assess risks to health and safety at work.

Transfers of undertaking

Statutory regulations (known as the Transfer of Undertakings Protection of Employment Regulations – TUPE – and which became part of English law following the EU Acquired Rights Directive) provide for the rights of employees to be automatically transferred with continuity of service and on existing terms and conditions of employment in the event of the sale of a business (or part of a business) as a going concern. Therefore, the rights and liabilities of the employees against the transferring company are automatically transferred to the acquiring company on a sale of the business. The only exceptions are certain rights relating to an occupational pension scheme. While TUPE applies on a transfer of assets it does not apply where a company's shares are sold to a purchaser.

Any termination of employment that is related to the transfer will automatically be an unfair dismissal unless it can be shown to be for technical, economic or organizational reasons. Such technical, economic or organizational reasons are very narrowly defined. Any attempt to change terms and conditions of employment connected to a transfer will be void and detailed advice will be needed on a business transfer. There is also a requirement to consult with trade union or employee representatives before a transfer; failure to do so entitles the employees to damages.

Pensions

When considering employment law, the significance of pensions provision should not be overlooked. In the United Kingdom, pensions provision takes three forms: state provision, provision by individuals and provision by employers.

The state pension scheme is in two parts: the basic pension and the State Second Pension or S2P. The basic pension is a fixed weekly amount, which is uprated each year in line with price inflation. It is payable from state pension age to all employees who have paid sufficient National Insurance contributions over their working life. State pension age is 65 for a man and currently 60 for a woman, although state pension age is being 'equalized' over time so as to be 65 for both men and women. The S2P pension is an earnings-related top-up to the basic pension and is payable on earnings up to an upper limit – currently £24,600 per annum. Employees can contract out of S2P if they have a suitable alternative arrangement.

An individual may provide benefits for him- or herself under a personal pension plan or under a stakeholder pension scheme. Under both types of arrangement, the individual effects a plan with a provider, usually an insurance company or a bank or sometimes an investment management company. There are limits to the amount of contributions an employee may pay each year. The limits are determined according to the employee's age. Both types of arrangement can be used to contract out of S2P.

An employer may provide benefits under a plan established by it and administered by it or on its behalf. Employer schemes are known as occupational schemes and are usually established under a trust. Benefits under an occupational scheme may be related to an employee's salary at or near retirement, in which case they are known as final salary or defined benefits. Alternatively, they may depend on the contributions paid to the plan, the investment return achieved and the cost of 'buying' a pension from a provider at retirement. In this case, they are known as money purchase or defined contribution benefits. Occupational schemes are commonly used to contract out of S2P.

An employer may also pay contributions to a personal pension or stakeholder pension established by an employee. Some employers establish group personal pension plans, which are simply personal pensions operated on a collective basis with the employer deducting employees' contributions from salaries and remitting them to the provider. The economies of scale are sometimes reflected in higher investment returns to the employees (because lower charges are levied by the provider).

There is as yet no legal obligation on an employer to contribute to any non-state pension arrangement. However, an employer who has at least five employees in the United Kingdom must, unless it qualifies for an exemption, designate a stakeholder scheme for them. In practice, this means no more than nominating a provider, allowing the provider access to the employees and, if they so request, deducting employees' contributions from salaries and remitting them to the provider. The employer may contribute if it wishes to, but it is not obliged to do so.

All types of non-state pension arrangement are usually designed to take advantage of the reliefs that are available to tax approved schemes. There are sometimes special circumstances in which employers forego the tax reliefs by setting up unapproved occupational schemes. These schemes enable an employer to provide benefits beyond the strict limits that apply to tax approved schemes.

The tax regime that applies to approved schemes has just undergone radical change. This could affect the way in which employers provide benefits through occupational schemes, but it is unlikely to affect how individuals provide for themselves.

Stock options

Tax

The law relating to the implementation and taxation of share options plans and other share or share-related awards is a complex area and legal advice should be taken early in the process. There are tax-efficient methods of granting options to employees but whether it is possible to grant tax-efficient options is dependent on the grantor company or its shares fulfilling certain strict criteria at the time of grant of the option and, in some instances, throughout the life of the option. It is possible to grant tax-efficient options under both discretionary plans and all employee plans. Examples of plans available in the United Kingdom include Inland Revenue-approved stock/share option schemes, unapproved stock/share option schemes and Enterprise Management Incentive plans (EMIs). If it is not possible to grant options under a tax-efficient plan the options will be taxed in the hands of employees as employment income and any gain in the value of the shares over the life of the option will be chargeable to income tax at the date of exercise.

If at the time of exercise of an option the shares are 'readily convertible assets', that is, there are trading arrangements in place or likely to come into existence in respect of the shares, or the shares are in a subsidiary of a non-listed company, the employer company will have an obligation to withhold any income tax due on the exercise via PAYE together with any employee's (primary) Class 1 National Insurance contributions. The employer company will also have a liability to employer's (secondary) Class 1 National Insurance contributions. This is a cash liability for the employer company. It is possible for the employer company to seek an indemnity from the optionholder in respect of this employer's NIC charge. It is also possible for the liability for employer's National Insurance contributions to be transferred to the optionholder by way of an Inland Revenue-approved joint election agreement.

For a parent overseas company that prepares its accounts under US GAAP, seeking an indemnity for employer's National Insurance contributions rather than using a joint election agreement to transfer the liability to the optionholder may have adverse accounting implications as may the timing of the execution of the joint election in respect of the grant of the options. Advice must be taken to ensure that the grantor company and/or the employer company are protected in respect of the tax and accounting implications of granting options or other share awards by using an Inland Revenue approved election agreement.

As a practical point, no inward investor should be seeking to grant options over its UK subsidiary. It should also not be seeking to issue options in itself without considerable thought and legal advice. The issue of stock options and restricted shares are restricted under the Financial Service Act to certain categories of person and the procedure for the grant is highly regulated. Option or share awards granted to consultants, non-executive directors and other advisors should be dealt with separately from those being made to employees.

Employees share plan

In order to comply with UK securities laws and to benefit from the exemption on the prohibition on financial promotion, any options granted to employees in the United Kingdom must be granted under the terms of an 'employees' share scheme'. An employees' share scheme is one that is for the benefit of bona fide employees or former employees of the grantor company or its subsidiaries or holding company or a subsidiary of its holding company, or certain close relatives of those employees or former employees. It is therefore important to ensure that any options or share awards are granted under a plan whose participants are limited to employees or former employees and their close relatives. For this reason, if the grantor company's main stock plan allows the grant of options or stock awards to consultants or advisors as well as employees it will be necessary to establish a new UK plan or a UK sub-plan for grants to UK employees (depending on the rules of the plan).

It is important that participation in a share option or award plan does not form part of the employee's entitlement under the terms of his or her contract of employment but is expressed as being in addition to and separate from those terms. This prevents the employee from claiming damages for unfair or wrongful dismissal for the loss of any gain in respect of the share options.

Immigration into the United Kingdom

Gavin Jones and David Kent, Inward Investment Group, Taylor Wessing

This chapter does not aim to discuss in detail all of the immigration applications available to foreign nationals wishing to visit or transact business in the United Kingdom. It is aimed at senior employees or owners of companies wishing to establish a business presence.

Introduction

As a rule, overseas nationals coming to the United Kingdom to work or to establish themselves in business require permission to do so. For most workers, permission is in the form of a work permit. Permission for those coming to establish a business is in the form of an entry clearance granted specifically for that purpose.

There are exceptions to the rule that every foreign national coming to the United Kingdom for work will need permission. The exceptions apply to EU nationals, EEA nationals, overseas nationals with indefinite leave to remain (settlement) in the United Kingdom, overseas nationals who have subsequently naturalized in the United Kingdom – as well as dependants of those with any of the foregoing or other exemptions to immigration control. Advice should always be sought at the earliest possible stage in order to assess what status and concessions may exist.

Work permits

Work permits are only issued for positions requiring a university degree or three years' work experience. Work permits are not issued for manual or low-level administrative positions. There are, however, concessions within the immigration rules to cater for seasonal agricultural workers (as well as sports persons and entertainers). However, as stated above, this chapter is aimed at senior management/business owners.

The government takes a strict view on employer/employee relationships and therefore will not normally approve a work permit for an employee holding more than 10 per cent of the stock of the UK company – or overseas parent. In most cases, stock options offered to employees will not cause difficulties.

A work permit application is applied for by the UK employing company. The work permit is specific to the employer, their address and a particular position within the organization. Any change of conditions post-issue needs to be notified to the government body – Work Permits UK. Some changes of conditions will need approval before taking effect; other 'technical changes' can be instigated and then notified to Work Permits UK. Where a company is making its first work permit application (or the first for a number of years) it is necessary to show the active trading status of the organization. In the absence of this evidence, a work permit (if approved) may be restricted for an initial permit until further evidence becomes available.

Usually the proposed employee should be outside of the United Kingdom at the time the application is filed (and ideally remain outside until the application is approved). However, there are exceptions. Certain categories of leave to remain in the United Kingdom (for example, student, businessperson, etc) can be transferred to work permit holder. Advice should always be sought as to whether 'in-country' or 'out of country' applications should be made.

A work permit application itself will be made under Tier 1 or Tier 2 of the work permit scheme. Tier 1 applications do not require a resident labour test. Currently the Tier 1 exceptions are for intra-company group transfers, senior (management) level employment, employment to release investment into the company and finally, where the employee possesses 'shortage skills'. The government maintains a list of what they consider to be skills in short supply in the UK workforce. Historically, this list has been made up of medical and teaching roles (in virtually all disciplines) and from time to time includes other industries. It is essential that advice be taken before considering an application under the shortage skills concession (as it changes). As stated, any application that does not fall within the strict parameters of Tier 1 will automatically be considered Tier 2 and therefore require a resident labour test – or a commercial argument why such a test would be pointless.

The resident labour test will usually take the form of advertising in a newspaper available throughout the EU or in a relevant trade journal. The test as to whether adequate efforts have been made is whether the advertisement represents a genuine effort to search the resident labour markets for the position in question. Again, it is important to take advice before advertising to ensure that any advertising does meet the requirements of Work Permits UK.

A work permit application should take between one and three weeks to be considered provided there are no questions asked by Work Permits UK. The application should not be made more than six months before the employee is required in the United Kingdom. In addition it should be noted that if the work permit is approved for more than six months, then the employee will be required to apply for entry clearance (in effect, a visa) in their home country prior to travelling to the United Kingdom – but see 'Visa nationals' below.

Sole representatives

Where an overseas company does not yet have a trading UK business then entry for a senior employee may be considered under the sole representative rules. It is a key element of this application that the company does not have (and has not had) a UK trading presence. However, securing a company name in anticipation of UK entry is permitted.

The application is made to the UK consulate closest to the residential address of the employee (that is, not the address of the overseas company). It is an application, which in effect is an undertaking to establish a taxable UK business (branch office or subsidiary) within three months of arrival. Accordingly, if approved, initial leave to remain is for 12 months. On application, the standard extension period is for a further three years – provided all the requirements of extension have been met. Like the work permit application, there are criteria that both the company and the individual need to meet for a successful sole representative's application:

● The company must be at least one year old – preferably at least two.

● It must not have an existing business, representative or agent already in the United Kingdom.

● The company's principal place of business and headquarters must remain overseas and all revenues earned in the United Kingdom business must be remitted to the parent.

● The sole representative must be a senior employee of at least six months' standing who was recruited overseas.

● The employee cannot be a major shareholder. A shareholding of less than 30 per cent will generally not raise any concerns. A shareholding of over 30 per cent will raise questions. A shareholding of over 50 per cent will mean the application is refused. The transfer of the sole representative is meant to be a benefit to the overseas business, not a transfer of the business.

- The sole representative will be expected to be able to maintain and support him- or herself solely by virtue of this employment.

The application is filed at the UK consulate overseas, which will usually determine the application locally within a matter of days (or in some cases hours). The UK consulate, however, is sometimes required to make enquiries back to the Home Office in the United Kingdom, and this can delay the decision by several weeks. It is therefore advisable to take advice on the preparation and submission of applications in order to ensure that they are approved in the shortest possible time. Notarized statements from the company and the sole representative confirming their compliance with their specific requirements will normally support an application. In addition, it is advisable to present a business plan/feasibility study of the proposed UK venture. It will also be necessary to show the trading status of the parent company by way of trading accounts.

Businesspeople

A further option for entry into the United Kingdom to establish a business is under the provisions relating to persons wishing to establish themselves in business. This is again an entry clearance application. Unlike the sole representative application, no prior service with a company is required. The application is based on two simple requirements: 1) that the person has £200,000 to invest in a UK company and 2) that this investment will create at least two full-time jobs in the UK company. Although the requirements appear basic, there is an underlying series of requirements:

- that the businessperson is bringing money of his or her own to put into the business;
- that the level of financial investment is proportional to his or her interest obtained in the business;
- that the businessperson will be able to bear his or her share of the liabilities;
- that he or she will be occupied full time in the running of the business; and
- that there is a genuine need for the services in the United Kingdom.

Again, an application will ideally be supported by a detailed business plan showing the investment and the UK business to be joined as well as projections for profits and employment to be created.

A key element to this application is the funds to be invested into the UK business. It has been held on judicial review that long-term loans are acceptable evidence of funds being under the sole control of the businessperson but short-term secured loans or any other form of control will not be acceptable. The funds should obviously not be held in an institution – or indeed a country – where their immediate transfer could be delayed.

In the case of an applicant wishing to join an existing business, it will be necessary to produce not only audited accounts from the company showing the previous year's results but also the terms on which the applicant will join the business (for example, a shareholder agreement). In line with the basic provisions of the sole representative scheme, an initial approval at entry is for 12 months. An extension may be necessary to show that the money has been invested and the jobs created. An extension is usually for a further three years.

Business immigrants under EU association agreements

There is a concession within the immigration rules to encourage developing EU nations. Therefore, while applications can be made under the businessperson criteria, the financial investment does not need to be shown. It is therefore important to take advice to see whether these association agreements can be applied where possible.

Investors

The United Kingdom has provision within the immigration rules to allow overseas nationals to come to the United Kingdom so they can invest in the UK economy. The level of investment required has traditionally been set at £1 million. The immigration rules were updated to take into account how other countries operate similar policies to attract investment. The entry requirements now are either that the investor has money under their own control in the United Kingdom amounting to not less than £1 million or they own personal assets which taking into account any liabilities, have a value exceeding £2 million and has at least £1 million under their own control in the United Kingdom which can include money loaned by a Financial Services Authority regulated institution. There are also requirements governing the investment itself. At least £750,000 must be invested in government bonds for share/loan capital in active and trading UK companies (other than those engaged solely or principally in property or banks etc); £250,000 can be used in securing property in which to live. In view of legislation governing money laundering, an investor application will come under very high scrutiny. However, these applications are traditionally dealt with very quickly.

Again, in line with the businessperson application, initial entry clearance is for 12 months and an extension application will need to be supported by evidence of investment. In addition, it is necessary that the applicant is able to maintain him- or herself and any dependants without needing recourse to public funds or employment outside of the investment business.

Highly skilled migrants

In November 2003, the government lowered the criteria for entry/leave to remain in the United Kingdom under the highly skilled migrant programme. Alongside lowering the points required, the government also lowered the qualification threshold for applicants under the age of 28. Unlike other categories discussed above, the highly skilled migrant programme does not require any specific employment or business to be undertaken. The applicant merely undertakes to be 'economically active' in the United Kingdom broadly in line with their previous work experience.

This application can be made either as an entry clearance application or as an in-country change of status application (provided the existing status permits such a switch). The application requires an applicant to score points based on academic background, work experience, previous earnings, achievements and also allows points to be claimed if the applicant has a spouse/partner who holds a university degree or university level work experience. There is, in addition, a separate section for medical doctors.

The application requires a basic number of points to be scored. It is not required to score points in all sections, for example, a research fellow in say, China, may score points in academic qualifications and work experience but not necessarily have earnings set at the minimum level (currently £40,000 for those over 28) to meet the criteria in that individual category. The government has tried to address differentials in the standard of living available worldwide and has grouped countries together in a number of bands.

The application is made to Work Permits UK directly in England whether filed as an in-country or an out-of-country application. If filed as an out-of-country application, the applicant will then take their approval letter to make the entry clearance application. Approval is for an initial 12-month period and on extension it is necessary to show that the broad intentions as stated in the application have been followed. It is important to note that a complete change in direction and intention after approval may cause difficulties with an extension application.

For both an individual entrepreneur and also for an overseas company where the company is unable to use the established methods of immigration into the United Kingdom, the Highly Skilled Migrant Programme is a much better approach, particularly when compared with the constraints on an individual of entry as a businessperson or as an investor.

Business visitors

Not all business conducted in the United Kingdom requires one of the permissions outlined above. Where an overseas company has no trading presence within the United Kingdom then it is possible for employees of that overseas company to come to the United Kingdom and discuss/sign contracts with UK customers, although this may give rise to a taxable presence. The general rule of thumb is that pre-sales work is usually permitted as a business visitor; however, post-sales work will usually cause problems. There is, however, a concession within the immigration rules concerning the erection and construction of machinery and the installation of software where sales contracts provide for this. In the event that a UK subsidiary exists on behalf of the seller, however, it will be presumed that the services are subsequently being carried out on behalf of the UK entity and therefore permission to work will be required. This is an area where caution is wise. If in doubt, obtaining a work permit is sensible and will prevent unnecessary hold-ups and possible deportation where the business visitor is mixing a business visit with work for the UK entity.

Spouses/family members

The UK immigration rules allow for spouses and immediate dependants to transfer when one family member is transferring to the United Kingdom. Generally speaking, spouses and children under 18 at the time of application will be permitted. Their passports will be endorsed with the leave to remain in line with the principal, and dependants will not usually have any prohibition on working. It should be noted that only intra-company work permit applications extend to other family member dependants so entry clearance will be needed for each family member.

Settlement

As with all of the categories discussed above, once an applicant has spent four years in the United Kingdom, they (and their families) are entitled to apply for indefinite leave to remain. This category is also known as permanent leave to remain or settlement. It has the effect of removing the applicant from immigration control and therefore free of any restriction on business/employment. It is also the first step in an application for naturalization – a UK passport. Whereas an application for a passport can change an applicant's domicile for tax purposes, an application for settlement has no such effect. Therefore, it is unlikely that an applicant in the position to apply for settlement will fail to do so.

Visa nationals

Citizens of certain countries are considered to be 'visa nationals'. The effect of this is that they must apply for a visa before entering the United Kingdom irrespective of the purpose of the visit or indeed length of visit. The list of countries that make up the visa nationals list is varied on an irregular basis by the UK government and accordingly advice must be sought in order to check whether certain nationalities require this additional visa.

In the case of a non-visa national coming to work in the United Kingdom for four months, no visa or entry clearance is required, just presenting the original work permit with the passport on entry will suffice. A non-visa national coming to work for 10 months will require the work permit and an entry clearance application. A visa national coming to work for any length of time will require the work permit and the entry clearance application.

5.4

Taxation for Foreign Nationals

Tim Cook, Wilder Coe

Introduction

This chapter deals with the UK taxation implications for a foreign national coming to the United Kingdom to live and work. The UK tax year is very individual; it starts on 6 April and ends on 5 April. There are three personal taxes to which an individual may become liable; income tax, capital gains tax and inheritance tax. Additionally, National Insurance is likely to be due on any salary. In order to determine the UK taxation treatment of an individual it is necessary to consider three basic principals: residence, ordinary residence and domicile. These are discussed in detail below.

Residence

The term residence is not defined in UK tax law despite being the starting point for determining any liability to UK tax. Over the years, the UK Inland Revenue has built up a system based on statute and decisions of the courts (case law). The result of this is that we now have established practice that deals with this. Residence is where you are physically present, at any one time. There are two basic tests for residence from a tax point of view: 1) firstly being present in the United Kingdom for more than 183 days in a tax year (6 April to 5 April); or 2) for those not considered resident under the above rule, there is a second test, which is being present in the United Kingdom for more than 90 days per year on average over a period of four tax years. Those to whom this applies are considered tax resident from the beginning of the fifth tax year.

The UK Inland Revenue has stated that normally it only looks at whole days in the United Kingdom, ignoring days of arrival and departure. However, it would be dangerous to rely on this statement, as the statutory position is that both days of arrival and departure should be counted (*Wilkie v IRC 32 TC 495*).

Dual residence

It is possible to be tax resident in more than one country at a time, looking at the individual residence rules for each country, in which case it is necessary to look to see if there is a double tax treaty between the United Kingdom and the relevant country. This can be a very complex matter and is not dealt with in the chapter; further specific advice should be sought on this.

Ordinary residence

Again, there is no statutory definition of ordinary residence; the UK Inland Revenue looks at a combination of statute and case law. Taking one year with another, ordinary residence is where the individual is usually resident. Normally, the UK Inland Revenue looks at residence in the previous four years, in which case the individual will be regarded as ordinarily resident from the fifth year. However, when coming to the United Kingdom, an individual planning to stay in the United Kingdom for more than three years will be considered ordinarily resident from the outset.

Domicile

This term is also not defined in UK tax law. It takes its meaning from general law. It looks for what is considered the 'mother' country from which the individual hails. There are three types of domicile: origin, dependence and choice.

Domicile of origin
This is the domicile that is acquired at birth, being that of the individual's father, unless their parents were unmarried or divorced during their minority, in which case it is the domicile of the mother or the parent with whom they lived.

Domicile of dependence
During an individual's minority, a domicile of dependence can displace a domicile of origin if the parents adopt a new country as their 'mother' country and settle there; or, as mentioned, if the parents separate or divorce.

Domicile of choice
It is possible to shed domicile of origin in favour of a domicile of choice,

by taking various steps. It is not a straightforward matter to shed domicile of origin, particularly for those trying to shed a UK domicile of origin. This is really a whole subject on its own and is beyond the scope of this chapter. However, specific advice on this issue should be sought.

Deemed domicile
If not actually domiciled in the United Kingdom, see above, an individual may be deemed to be domiciled for inheritance tax purposes only if they have been tax resident in the United Kingdom *at any time* in 17 out of the last 20 tax years. Specific advice should be sought on this aspect.

Inland Revenue formalities

Upon entering the United Kingdom it is necessary for the individual to establish if they have a liability to tax and to notify their existence to the UK Inland Revenue. There are some forms that should be completed:

- Form P86 – if you are entering or returning to the United Kingdom;

- Form DOM1 – if those contending that they are not domiciled in the United Kingdom have income or gains arising abroad;

- Form P46 – for an employee who has just commenced work in the United Kingdom.

It is suggested that professional assistance be obtained when completing these forms; once residence, ordinary residence and domicile position has been established any liability to tax can be calculated.

Income tax

Individuals who are resident, ordinarily resident and domiciled in the United Kingdom are liable to income tax on their worldwide income on an arising basis. However, for those individuals who are considered resident and ordinarily resident but not domiciled in the United Kingdom, they are only taxed on UK source income on an arising basis; income from abroad is taxed on a remittance basis. Careful planning can enable funds to be held offshore and remitted to the United Kingdom without liability to UK tax. It is best to take advice on this before becoming resident in the United Kingdom. Non-UK residents are still liable to income tax on UK source income usually on an arising basis, for example, on rental income from a UK property or a salary from a UK company. Individuals taxable in the United Kingdom will be entitled to a personal allowance of currently £4,745 (2004/05). The tax rates that apply after that are shown in Table 5.4.1.

Table 5.4.1   Income tax rates after the first £4,745

Income	Tax Rate (%)
First £2,020	10
Next £29,380	22
Dividend income above this	32.5
Any other income above this	40

Capital gains tax (CGT)

The charge to capital gains tax relies on individuals being resident and ordinarily resident in the United Kingdom, in which case they are liable to capital gains tax on their UK gains on an arising basis. If an individual is also domiciled in the United Kingdom, they will be liable to CGT on their worldwide gains on an arising basis. However, individuals who are considered resident and ordinarily resident but not domiciled in the United Kingdom are only taxed on UK source gains on an arising basis. Gains from abroad are taxed on a remittance basis. Unfortunately, it is not possible to remit a capital loss to the United Kingdom, only a capital gain, with no set off available against offshore gains, which you may feel is inequitable, but this is unfortunately the law. It is suggested that before coming to the UK, advice is taken on mitigation strategies. There are various exemptions available, the most common ones listed in the following sections.

Annual exemption

Each tax year an individual is entitled to an exempt amount of capital gains, which is not taxable. The current amount is £8,200 (2004/05). Any unused exempt amount cannot be carried forward to any future year.

Spouse exemption

Transfers between spouses are exempt.

Business asset taper relief

This reduces the amount of the capital gain chargeable to tax, dependent on the length of ownership in complete years of qualifying assets as shown in Table 5.4.2.

Table 5.4.2   Reduction of capital gain dependent on years held of business assets

Complete Years Held	Gain Exempt (%)
One	50
More than two years	75

Qualifying business assets

Taper relief was introduced on 6 April 1998. The definition of business assets and the percentage exempt has been changed a number of times since its introduction. The current definition of a business asset is:

- all unincorporated trading businesses whether as a partnership or as a sole trader;

- all unquoted trading companies, which are not subsidiaries of quoted companies;

- unquoted non-trading companies where you own less than 10 per cent;

- quoted trading companies for whom you work full time;

- assets used in a business owned by the individual or an unquoted trading company.

Non-business asset taper relief

Assets that do not qualify as business assets qualify for non-business asset taper relief. This is also dependent on the number of complete years the asset has been held. If the asset concerned has been held since pre-16 March 1998, an extra year is added to the ownership period from 6 April 1998. The relief is calculated by reference to Table 5.4.3.

Tax rate
Any chargeable gains in excess of the annual exemption are added to income and taxed as if they are the top slice of income.

Inheritance tax (IHT)

The charge to inheritance tax is dependent on where the asset is situated and the domicile of the individual or trust concerned; residence or ordinary residence is not relevant. A charge arises on all gifts of UK-sited assets, whether or not the individual is domiciled in the United Kingdom, subject to various exemptions discussed below.

Table 5.4.3   Non-business asset taper relief dependent on years held

Complete Years Held	Gain Exempt (%)
One	0
Two	0
Three	5
Four	10
Five	15
Six	20
Seven	25
Eight	30
Nine	35
Ten	40

Additionally, those individuals and trusts that are either actually domiciled or deemed domiciled in the United Kingdom are liable in respect of gifts of their worldwide assets.

Lifetime gifts to individuals and some trusts are not immediately chargeable to tax, but are considered 'potentially exempt' subject to the transferor surviving for seven years from the date of the gift. If death occurs within the seven-year period following the gift then any tax due (payable by the donee) is reduced using a sliding scale shown in Table 5.4.4.

Any gift made is accumulated with earlier gifts made in the previous seven-year period in order to calculate the tax due. There are a number of specific exemptions available to offset against any gift before charging it to tax. The most common ones are:

Table 5.4.4   Sliding scale of tax reductions of inheritance tax

Death in Year (Following Gift)	Percentage Reduction in Tax Due on Gift
1–3	0
4	20
5	40
6	60
7	80
8	100

- Annual exemption. Total gifts of up to £3,000 annually are exempt. Any unused exemption may be carried forward one year only.

- Small gifts to individuals. Gifts totalling £250 to an individual per year are exempt.

- Spouse exemption. Gifts to a spouse who is domiciled in the United Kingdom are unlimited. However, gifts to spouses who are not domiciled in the United Kingdom are limited to £55,000.

- Regular gifts of income. Taking one year with another, regular gifts made out of excess income are exempt.

- Business assets. Gifts of business assets such as an unincorporated business or shares in a 'family' company are exempt in full. Personally owned assets used in a business may qualify for 50 per cent relief.

- Agricultural property. There is a similar relief to business property relief.

- Gifts in consideration of marriage. Gifts may be made to the bride or groom, the amount that is exempt depends on the relationship to the couple as shown in Table 5.4.5.

Table 5.4.5 Tax exemptions depending on relationship to married couple

Relationship to Couple	Exempt Amount
Parent	£5,000
Grandparent	£2,500
Remoter ancestor and otherwise	£1,000

Tax rate
Lifetime chargeable transfers in excess of any available exemptions and the 'nil rate' band are chargeable at 20 per cent. The rate upon death is 40 per cent. Advice should be sought before making any gifts so that all the taxation consequences may be considered, including capital gains tax and stamp duty (a tax on transactions and documents).

National Insurance

This is a social security tax payable on earnings. Contributions are payable by both employees (primary) and employers (secondary). An individual who is an EEA national and continues to pay social security taxes in another EEA country in respect of earnings, will not be liable to National Insurance in the United Kingdom. However, if the individual ceases to pay contributions in another EEA country he/she will immediately become liable to pay National Insurance in the United Kingdom. Non-EEA nationals will normally have a 12-month period before they have to pay National Insurance contributions in the United Kingdom.

Non-UK employers are not liable to pay secondary National Insurance contributions where they do not have a permanent establishment in the United Kingdom. However, if employees of the non-UK employer are seconded to the United Kingdom to work for a UK company although they are still paid by the non-UK employer, then the UK company may be liable to pay the secondary contributions. Contributions for 2004/05 for employed earnings are shown in Table 5.4.6. Contributions are also payable by self-employed earners.

Table 5.4.6   National Insurance contributions 2004/05

	Employee (%)	Employer (%)
£91.01 to £610 per week	11	12.8
Over £610 per week	1	12.8

UK tax returns

UK tax returns are issued annually, normally on 6 April for filing at the latest by the following 31 January, that is, for the year ended 5 April 2004, the return would have been issued on 6 April 2004 for filing by 31 January 2005. The forms are on a self-assessment basis subject to audit by the Inland Revenue at any time within 12 months of the filing deadline, that is, for the 2004 tax return by 31 January 2006.

Payment of UK tax

Payment of any tax liability calculated to be due is normally made on 31 January following the year of assessment, the same date as the tax return filing deadline (see above). However, in certain circumstances where insufficient tax is payable at source during the tax year the UK Inland Revenue requires that payments on account are made equal to the previous year's liability in two equal instalments on 31 January in the tax year and 31 July following the tax year. For example, for 2003/04 payments on account would have been due on 31 January 2004 and 31 July 2004 with any balance being due on 31 January 2005 together with the first instalment for the following year. Late payment of tax carries interest currently 6.5 per cent per annum and a surcharge of 5 per cent if the final tax due for a year is not paid by 28 February following the filing deadline, in this example, 28 February 2005, with a further 5 per cent surcharge becoming due if the tax remains outstanding by 28 August.

Remuneration packages

The UK Inland Revenue has developed a very wide definition of earnings over the years to include most forms of remuneration and benefit in kind, which are subject to income tax and National Insurance contributions when payment is made. Many benefits such as company cars now carry a charge to National Insurance as if they were salary for earnings purposes (see above). It is still possible, however, to remunerate employees with share options and share incentives tax effectively using:

- approved share options – subject to a maximum value of £30,000;

- approved savings-related share option schemes – subject to a maximum of £250 per month;

- enterprise management incentives – subject to a maximum value of £100,000 available to smaller companies only.

Non-tax effective schemes such as unapproved share options and 'phantom' shares schemes, are both subject to tax and National Insurance.

It is common for employees seconded to the United Kingdom to be provided with rent-free accommodation. This is subject to both tax and National Insurance. The cost in terms of tax and National Insurance can be expensive where the value of the property involved is in excess of £75,000. In this situation the benefit in kind is calculated by taking the value of the property when first provided to the employee and treating the excess over £75,000 as an interest-free loan to the employee. The benefit is calculated as this amount at the official rate of interest, currently 5 per cent (2003/04). Any costs paid by the employer and 20 per cent of the value of any furniture supplied in the house is also considered taxable benefit. This benefit is then added to the employee's salary and taxed at their highest rate. For a higher rate taxpayer they will pay tax of 2 per cent of the value of their house in excess of £75,000; so for a £500,000 property the tax due would amount to £8,500 with £2,720 National Insurance due by the employer, plus any tax and National Insurance contributions due on the running costs of the house paid by the employer.

Dual contracts

It is still possible to have dual contracts for employments where the duties are performed both in the United Kingdom and abroad. One contract should be for the UK duties, which would be taxable in the United Kingdom, and the other contract would be for duties performed abroad. If the employee is domiciled outside the United Kingdom and the contract for the non-UK duties is with a non-UK company with the salary being paid abroad and not remitted to the United Kingdom no UK tax will arise.

Taxation in country of origin

Individuals should always remember that although they have become resident in the United Kingdom and liable to tax here, their country of origin (for example, United States) may still tax them on the same income. It is therefore essential to ensure that any planning takes account of this. It is pointless avoiding tax in the United Kingdom when the same income is taxable in their home country. The most important thing to bear in mind in situations where taxation arises in two countries is to ensure that credit for the tax paid in the United Kingdom can be obtained against the same income taxable in the home country; it is therefore necessary for the individual's UK accountant to liaise with his/her home country accountant.

Employers are required to deduct tax and National Insurance from salary and certain benefits in kind as they arise under what is known as Pay As You Earn (PAYE). These deductions are then paid to the Inland Revenue on a monthly basis by the 19th of the month following payment.

Trips to the home country

Employees working in the United Kingdom, who are not domiciled in the United Kingdom, may for the first five years after arrival be entitled to have trips to their home country paid for by their employer tax-free. Additionally, if the employee is in the United Kingdom for 60 days or more it may also be possible for their spouse and any children under the age of 18 to travel to and from the UK tax-free, but limited to two trips per person in a tax year. There are a number of specific rules that need to be adhered to, to gain this relief.

5.5

Regulation of Financial Services

Richard Millar, Eversheds

Scope of regulation of financial services

Since December 2001, the regulation of financial businesses in the United Kingdom has been consolidated. There is now one single regulator, the Financial Services Authority (FSA), and the scope of its regulation covers the businesses of banks, building societies, insurance companies, investment businesses, friendly societies, credit unions, Lloyd's of London and other financial businesses. This scope of regulation will be further extended on 31 October 2004 when the businesses of mortgage lending and administration, mortgage advice and mortgage arranging will become regulated activities, together with long-term care insurance; and it will be further extended from 14 January 2005, when insurance mediation will become a regulated business. This structure of a single regulator overseeing such a wide range of businesses is probably unique in the world of financial regulation.

The FSA

The role of the FSA as regulator derives from the Financial Services & Markets Act 2000 (the Act) and from numerous government orders made under the Act. The Act establishes the powers and authority of the FSA, setting out regulatory objectives and functions for it. The FSA is not a government department. It is a separately constituted company, limited by guarantee, and its staff are not government employees, although they do enjoy immunity from claims arising from the performance of their duties. The FSA is accountable to parliament through reporting to the Treasury and by the Treasury having the power to appoint and remove its chairman, currently Mr Callum McCarthy, and the members of its governing body, including its Chief Executive, currently Mr John Tiner.

The FSA has a budget for 2004/05 of over £217 million largely raised by fees from authorized firms. It has direct responsibility for monitoring and enforcing the regulation of financial businesses. It currently authorizes over 11,000 firms and 180,000 approved persons and these figures will rise substantially as the scope of regulation expands during 2004 and 2005.

The Regulated Activities Order

The Act (section 19) prohibits any person from carrying on a regulated activity in the United Kingdom, or purporting to do so, unless he or she is an authorized person or an exempt person (referred to as the General Prohibition). Contravention of this is an offence, with penalties of fine or imprisonment. A contract made by a person carrying on a regulated activity in contravention of the General Prohibition is unenforceable against the other party, with compensation payable for loss.

The Act does not set out the detail of what activities constitute ones that are covered by the General Prohibition. This detail is contained in the Regulated Activities Order 2001 (No 544), which sets out the specific activities that, when carried on in or from the United Kingdom, constitute regulated activities.

Among the activities that are regulated are: accepting deposits (essentially banking); acting as principal as an insurer; dealing in securities or contractually-based investments as principal or agent; managing investments; acting as custodian of securities or contractually-based investments; managing a collective investment scheme; and giving investment advice relating to securities or contractually-based investments. Acting as lender of a mortgage, the terms of which qualify it as a regulated mortgage contract, will apply from 31 October 2004, as will other mortgage-related activities. General insurance mediation will become a regulated activity from 14 January 2005.

The Regulated Activities Order also states the kinds of investment that are covered in the above, including deposits, insurance contracts, shares, debentures, loan stocks, bonds, government securities, units and certain options and futures.

Financial promotion

Alongside the General Prohibition, the Act contains a Financial Promotion Restriction (Section 21). This forbids a person, in the course of business, from communicating an invitation or inducement to engage in investment activity unless the person is an authorized person or the content of the communication is approved for the purposes of the Act by an authorized person. Where a communication originates outside the United Kingdom, this applies only if the communication is capable of having an effect in the United Kingdom. An agreement entered into in breach of the Financial Promotion Restriction is unenforceable and allows the other party to recover money paid and to receive compensation for loss.

As with Regulated Activities, the Act does not describe the investment activities, or exemptions from the restriction, which apply. The Financial Promotion Order 2001 (No 1335) delineates the scope of the Financial Promotion Restriction, by identifying what are controlled activities, by listing controlled investments and by setting out three categories of communication that are exempt from the Restriction. The Restriction applies to communications to a particular person, for instance, in a telephone call or letter or e-mail, or to persons generally, for instance, in a television broadcast or a website. There are different exemptions depending on whether the communication is a real time communication or is a solicited real time communication. The exemptions contain the territorial limits on the scope of the Financial Promotion Restriction. There are also exemptions regarding communications directed at identified recipients, including investment professionals, high net worth companies and certified sophisticated investors.

Financial businesses

A person, which includes a company or partnership, wishing to carry on one or more of the regulated activities within or from the United Kingdom is required to obtain authorization from the FSA (see Authorization, below) and that authorization will contain one or more permissions, specifically identifying the category or categories of regulated activity that the authorized firm is permitted to carry on.

Collective investment schemes

Separate regulations apply to the promotion of collective investment schemes, which for historic reasons, enjoy a separate regime of regulation under the Act. The retail forms of UK collective investment scheme, which are open-ended, are either constituted under trust as unit trusts or are formed as open-ended investment companies under separate regulations; these are not companies formed under the Companies Acts like other UK companies. These forms of UK collective investment scheme may only be promoted by an authorized person generally to the public in the United Kingdom if they are authorized schemes, that is, they comply with and receive authorization from the FSA. Non-UK schemes may be so promoted if they qualify as recognized schemes, that is, certain schemes set up in other EU member states and qualifying as UCITS schemes under the UCITS Directives, schemes set up in certain offshore jurisdictions (currently Bermuda, Guernsey, the Isle of Man and Jersey), and overseas schemes that are individually authorized. The above restriction on promotion, referred to as the Scheme Promotion Restriction, is subject to a separate regime of exemption, in the Promotion of Collective Investment Schemes (Exemptions) Order, No 1060, which follows some of the exemptions contained in the Financial Promotion Order. Investment trust companies, the most common form of closed-ended scheme, are formed as companies and are listed on a recognized exchange.

FSA's *Handbook* of Rules and Guidance

The procedure for becoming an authorized person and the regulations that apply to all authorized persons, including enforcement and disciplinary procedures, are contained in the FSA's *Handbook*, which runs to 27 volumes. It is accessible on the FSA's website (www.fsa.gov.uk) and is available from the FSA by subscription in hard copy and on CD ROM. The *Handbook* is divided into five separate 'Blocks', and the following summary of these gives an indication of the breadth of regulatory power of the FSA:

- Block 1, described as containing High Level Standards. This sets out the FSA's principles for regulated businesses, its requirements for senior management arrangements, systems and controls, threshold conditions (containing the minimum conditions a firm is required to satisfy to have a permission, including useful flow charts) and provisions relating to approved persons (the individuals who work within an authorized firm on its regulated activities) including fit and proper tests that apply for such persons.

- Block 2 contains specific business standards, covering the prudential requirements of banks, building societies, friendly societies, insurers and investment businesses, the Conduct of Business Sourcebook, which contains the day-to-day regulations affecting all businesses other than those that have their own sourcebook, the client asset sourcebook, mortgage and insurance sourcebooks (effective from the dates when they become regulated activities as above), the market conduct sourcebook relating to listed securities, training and competence and money laundering sourcebooks.

- Block 3 deals with the regulatory processes of authorization, supervision, enforcement and decision-making.

- Block 4 provides for redress in the form of dispute resolution and the handling of complaints through the Financial Ombudsman Service, operation of the Financial Services Compensation Scheme where an authorized firm is insolvent, and the conduct of complaints against the FSA.

- In Block 5 are specialist sourcebooks covering authorized collective investment schemes, credit unions, Lloyd's, professional firms and others and also dealing with the regulation of UK recognized investment exchanges and clearing houses. The FSA is the United Kingdom Listing Authority for the purpose of various EU directives and the Listing Rules now appear in this Block 5. There are also special guides relating to specific businesses.

The *Handbook* includes both the FSA's rules and its guidance in connection with those rules, the distinction being that the rules are directly enforceable, whereas the guidance is only an indication of the interpretation that the FSA would expect to be placed upon the rule concerned; non-compliance with a guidance is not in itself a breach of the *Handbook*.

Authorization

A person, including company or partnership, wishing to conduct a regulated activity in or from the United Kingdom must apply to the FSA, providing all the required information, when its application will be considered and a decision made. An aggrieved applicant may appeal to a separately constituted Financial Services and Markets Tribunal. The *Authorization Manual* sets out the procedures for obtaining authorization and the information to be supplied and is very detailed in its scope. Capital adequacy requirements are set out in the interim prudential sourcebook for the relevant type of business.

In most cases it is advisable for a potential applicant for authorization to make contact with the Corporate Authorization Department of the FSA to discuss the nature of the application, which will include the potential regulated activities, the corporate structures in place, control through share ownership and other consideration of the applicant, and what approvals are required by individuals under the Approved Person Regime for all the persons who will be carrying on functions at the authorized firm, which may only be conducted by such an approved person.

An authorized firm is subject to ongoing supervision by the FSA, which is described by the FSA as being a risk assessment approach.

This includes: assessment by the FSA that the authorized firm can satisfy the threshold conditions; base line monitoring that is designed to ensure that an authorized firm complies on a continuing basis with the regulatory requirements that apply to them, using data supplied by the firm and by third parties; sectoral reviews and thematic work; programmes designed to mitigate specific risks in individual authorized firms; and work undertaken when a particular risk has escalated or crystallized. The FSA has wide-reaching powers relating both to its supervision of authorized firms and to its ability to withdraw authorization and require a firm to cease to carry on any regulated activity.

Control

Of particular interest to investors in United Kingdom financial businesses may be the extent to which the FSA is concerned with vetting controllers of such businesses. Control means the holding of 10 per cent or more of the share capital of the authorized firm or of a parent undertaking, or 10 per cent or more of the voting power in either, or of being able to exercise significant influence over the management by virtue of shareholding. Above 10 per cent, the notifiable levels are: from below 10 per cent to between 10 per cent and 20 per cent; from below 20 per cent to between 20 per cent and 33 per cent; from below 33 per cent to between 33 per cent and 50 per cent; and from below 50 per cent to 50 per cent or more, or where control reduces within these notifiable limits.

Notice must be given to the FSA of a proposal to take or reduce control, within each of such levels. The FSA has three months in which to decide whether to approve the proposal, or to serve a warning notice of objection, and may impose conditions. The FSA has various powers to impose restrictions on the power of a controller. In relation to an insurance intermediary, separate levels apply at 20 per cent. The parent undertaking test includes an undertaking with a 20 per cent or more interest and so is wider than the usual parent/subsidiary test.

EU directives

Finally, any consideration of the regulation of financial services in the United Kingdom should recognize the passporting conferred on areas of financial business under various EU directives. Thus, a business established in the United Kingdom and authorized to carry on banking, life insurance or investment services (or UCITS management under the recent UCITS Directive) may be passported to offer such services in the other member states of the EU, and businesses set up in those other member states may be passported into the United Kingdom. In setting up a business that may wish to offer its passported services in member states other than that in which it is formed, the promoter will want, in choosing the domicile for such business, to consider a range of factors, including the effectiveness of regulation, levels of taxation and business efficiencies, such as communications, staffing and premises. The United Kingdom is often seen as the location of choice for such a business.

5.6

Money Laundering Regulations

Mark Saunders, Wilder Coe

Introduction

In accordance with the requirements of the Second European Community Money Laundering Directive of 2001 the UK government has introduced the Money Laundering Regulations 2003, which came into force largely with effect from 1 March 2004. The purpose of the regulations is to implement a regime whereby those businesses and individuals operating within the 'regulated sector' will report any knowledge or suspicions of money laundering they might have to the National Criminal Intelligence Service (NCIS).

What is money laundering?

Money laundering legislation in the past has primarily concerned itself with identifying funds that are the result of terrorist activities or illegal drug trafficking. However, the scope of the legislation has been widened and it now encompasses the possession, dealing with, or concealing the proceeds of any crime. This obviously still includes terrorist funds, funds that may be used for terrorist purposes or the proceeds of terrorism or illegal drug trafficking.

Money laundering involves the hiding, converting, transferring or taking out of the country of any criminal proceeds. It covers anyone who agrees to or is involved in helping, or suspects they are involved in helping another person to acquire, keep or use criminal property. It also includes anyone who acquires, uses or possesses any criminal property. Criminal property in this case includes anything, whether it is money or property, by which a person or company gains, either directly or indirectly, as a result of criminal activity. It is worth clarifying that this definition of criminal property also covers the proceeds of tax evasion, bribery or corruption.

Which businesses have to comply with money laundering regulations?

The regulations define relevant businesses – being those businesses that have to comply with the money laundering regulations – as including:

- banking generally;
- any business that accepts deposits;
- the effecting or carrying out of long-term insurance;
- dealing in investments either as principal or as an agent;
- arranging deals and investments;
- managing, safeguarding or administering investments;
- advising on investments;
- the operation of a Bureau de Change;
- transmitting money by any means or cashing cheques, which are made payable to customers;
- estate agency;
- casino operation;
- insolvency practitioners;
- those who offer tax advice;
- those who offer accountancy services;
- those who offer auditing services;
- those who offer legal services;
- those who offer services in relation to the formation, operation or management of a company or trust;
- those dealing in goods of any description where a transaction will involve the acceptance of a cash payment of 15,000 euros or more – including acting as an auctioneer.

It can be seen from the above list that this largely involves those individuals and businesses that are involved in financial transactions. It significantly includes banks, accountants, solicitors and estate agents, at least one of whom is likely to be involved in assisting any proposed new business within the United Kingdom.

Requirements for businesses in the regulated sectors

Businesses and individuals within these regulated sectors need to do the following:

- Appoint a representative who will be the money laundering reporting officer.

- Train all employees in relevant positions in recognizing and reporting money laundering. Those employees will be responsible for reporting to the money laundering reporting officer.

- The money laundering reporting officer has a responsibility to report any knowledge or suspicion that a money laundering offence has been committed to the NCIS. This report has to be made no matter how small the amounts involved or how serious the offence appears to be.

- In a situation where a report has been made the persons making the report must do nothing to help the suspected money launderer for a period of seven days unless told to do so by the NCIS. This may result in any work on a particular transaction being suspended during this period. If nothing is heard from the NCIS at the conclusion of that period of seven days then the reporting business can continue to deal with the respective transaction. If the reporting business is in itself not involved in the transaction but has become aware of its suspicious nature and has reported it then they do not need to await any consent from the NCIS to continue working.

- Maintain identification procedures in respect of every business and individual with whom they do business (see below).

'Tipping off' and failure to make report

The law makes it an offence to 'tip off' a suspected money launderer that a report has been made or is contemplated to the NCIS. It is also an offence to fail to make a suspicious transaction report. Further, it is an offence for any person who receives information in the course of their business within the regulated sector to fail to inform NCIS or their businesses money laundering reporting officer of that knowledge or suspicion that another person is engaged in money laundering. The penalties for failure to report or tipping off can lead to prison sentences of up to five years and monetary fines.

Identification procedures

Every business within the regulated sector will be required to maintain identification procedures with regard to every person and business with which they do business. This means that, as soon as is reasonably practicable after contact is first made with a business or individual, that this business or individual must produce satisfactory evidence of their identity and their residential or business address. This would usually require the provision of at least two documents. For an individual the documents would include in order to confirm identity – a current signed passport, a UK photo card driving licence or a home office residency permit; in order to confirm address – a recent utility bill, local authority tax bill or bank or building society or mortgage statement. In some cases a visit to the person's home may establish proof of address.

With regard to a corporation, a copy of the deed of incorporation would confirm identity and, if the entity is within the United Kingdom, this can be checked with details held at Companies House. For other nationalities, if there are similar public registers then this information can be checked independently.

In order to obtain proof of address of a company then similar evidence to that above including utility bills or rent statements would suffice, or once again a visit to the company's premises. In the case of unincorporated organizations such as trusts or partnerships then a copy of the trust or partnership deed would be obtained and similar identification procedures to those relating to individuals carried out in respect of each trustee or partner. Businesses within the regulated sector are required to maintain evidence of the identity checks they have made.

Practical considerations for those considering doing business within the United Kingdom

For anyone considering doing business within the United Kingdom it is almost inevitable that they will have contact and carry out business with one or more organization within the regulated sectors. Under such circumstances, therefore, each such business should be prepared to provide the identification evidence indicated above. Having such evidence readily available and having anticipated a need to provide it will greatly facilitate commencing business within the United Kingdom.

Secondly, in order not to arouse suspicion that any transaction taking place could conceivably be construed as money laundering it would be wise to be as frank and open as possible in relation to any business carried out. Details of the source of all funds being used should be freely shared and at no point in time should any doubt be allowed to enter into the details of any transaction. Most business and trading activities will be of a relatively routine and repetitive nature and should never cause a problem. It is likely to be the unusual or large transactions that might arouse doubt or suspicion.

A ready compliance with all United Kingdom taxation requirements would also be recommended, particularly those relating to employment – Pay as You Earn, which should be administered by all employers, and VAT.

Trading in the regulated sectors

For those who are considering commencing a business within the United Kingdom that falls within one of the regulated sectors there is a clear need to comply with the requirements of the money laundering regulations. Many of the regulated sectors have their own professional bodies or trade associations who will be able to advise on the specific requirements of the business sector in which the operations are planned to take place. In the case of any doubt then advice should be sought at the earliest possible opportunity. In such cases professional advisors such as accountants or solicitors, who should all be well versed in the obligations of the money laundering regulations as they relate to their own activities, should be able to advise on how to proceed.

Conclusion

Similar regulations to those being applied in the United Kingdom are being enacted throughout the European Community and throughout much of the rest of the world. The international fight against terrorism and drug trafficking, which has provided the impetus for this kind of legislation, has caused it to be expanded to include all areas of crime, in particular the areas of tax evasion and the 'cash' economy. However, compliance with these regulations should hold no fears for those involved in honest business activity and, although the cost of compliance in terms of time and money may initially be great, the erad-ication of crime from business should result in a level playing field for all and greater integrity within the business environment worldwide.

5.7

Environmental Issues

Alison Askwith and David Kent, Inward Investment Group, Taylor Wessing

Introduction

The risk of environmental liability must be considered when purchasing or occupying potentially contaminated land or when purchasing or operating a potentially contaminative process. Liability arises either under UK statute enforced by a regulator or under English common law claimed by a third party. The regulatory regime, and to some extent the environmental legislation, varies between Scotland, England, Wales and Northern Ireland. This chapter deals only with the liability arising on the purchase of assets in England and Wales. However, the regime in Scotland is very similar.

The United Kingdom has had a long industrial history, which has meant that environmental liability arises from principles established through case law (known as common law), statute, as well as more recently through European legislation adopted in the United Kingdom. Environmental issues are slightly different depending on whether an investor is acquiring shares or assets and the differences are set out in the text below.

This chapter sets out a brief synopsis of the relevant environmental legislation and then deals with the relevant issues when acquiring land and the additional issues that need to be considered if acquiring an operational business on that land.

The law

Contaminated land

Regulatory liability
The Environmental Protection Act 1990 Part II(A) sets out the structure of the contaminated land liability regime. Local authorities

are required to investigate their area for contaminated land. Where they believe land to be contaminated, the local authority must investigate and consider remediation. The local authority is obliged to serve notices ('remediation notice') on those they believe to be liable, requiring them to investigate, provide site assessments and remediate and conduct post-remediation monitoring as appropriate. It is a criminal offence not to comply with the remediation notice. If the works are not carried out, the local authority may carry them out and charge the costs of so doing. This cost can be a registered charge against the interest in the land. In respect of heavily contaminated sites ('Special Sites') the local authority hands over its duties in respect of requiring remediation to the Environment Agency.

Once the site has been identified as potentially contaminated and prior to the service of a remediation notice, the local authority must enter into a process of consultation with site owners, occupiers and any other 'appropriate persons' (see below). This consultation period lasts for a period of three months. The local authority discusses with the site owners occupiers, etc, what should be included in any remediation notice. This will include the extent to which the land is contaminated (if at all), who is the appropriate person (see below), whether or not there are any reasons why somebody should not be liable, what type of remediation is necessary and whether or not that can be carried out at a reasonable cost. If the appropriate person undertakes voluntary remediation then the local authority will publish a remediation statement recording what steps are to be undertaken and by whom. Both the remediation notice and the remediation statement are placed on the Contaminated Land Register, which is a public document (see reference below to obtaining information).

An understanding of the above process requires an understanding of the terminology used. One of the most important definitions is that of 'contaminated land'. Land is only contaminated where significant harm is being caused or where there is significant possibility of significant harm being caused or where pollution of controlled waters is being or is likely to be caused. Harm is defined as harm to the health of living organisms, other interference with ecological systems or harm to owned property. There is no requirement to clean up contaminated land therefore, unless at the very least there is significant possibility of significant harm or pollution of controlled waters likely to be caused. Each of the following must be present:

- A source of contamination.
- A sensitive receptor, that is, something that can be harmed by the contamination.

- A pathway along which the contamination travels to the receptor. This is commonly known as a pollutant linkage.

In addition to a pollution linkage, the harm must be significant. There is guidance setting out what constitutes significant harm. Some of the more obvious is set out below:

- death, disease or serious injury;

- substantial damage or failure of buildings, plant or equipment;

- disease or other physical damage or death to livestock, or crops where there is a substantial loss in their value.

The standard of remediation required will depend on the current use of the property. If the use is industrial usually the remediation will be less stringent than if the use is residential.

The second important definition is 'an appropriate person' for the purposes of identifying who is liable for the cost of remediation. The local authority must identify the appropriate person or people in the process of consultation for a remediation notice/remediation statement. The local authority is required to first try to identify the original polluter. If the original polluter cannot be identified after reasonable enquiry then the local authority is entitled to look to the owner or occupier of the land for the time being as the appropriate person.

An original polluter is someone who either caused or knowingly permitted the contamination. If there are several different types of contamination in the ground then there may be several people responsible within that liability group. Whether or not a person has caused pollution is a factual position and does not require fault. 'Causing' can include simply creating a situation that in the ordinary course of events has led to pollution or contamination. Employers are responsible for the actions of their employees.

'Knowingly permit' includes actual knowledge and wilful blindness, that is, deliberately ignoring the obvious. 'Permitting' probably requires the ability to control the situation. In addition, government guidance indicates that a person would only be regarded as having knowingly permitted if they had the knowledge at the time when they was able to do something about the contamination, not subsequently.

It is possible to pass on liability as original polluter to a purchaser. The legislation allows a seller to sell with information. If the contract for sale includes clauses indicating that the buyer has been given an opportunity to find out about the condition of the property and the seller has passed on all information, the buyer will, so far as the regulator is concerned, become responsible for the seller's liability.

Liability under common law

When investing in real estate in the United Kingdom it is important to understand the risk of liability to third parties including neighbours. Claims most commonly brought are claims in respect of negligence, nuisance, the rule in *Rylands* v *Fletcher* and trespass.

In order to sue in negligence, there must be an existing duty of care that has been breached and damage to the third party resulting from that breach. In addition, any third party must demonstrate that the breach of the duty of care caused the damage and that it was foreseeable. In environmental issues, to be able to show causation is quite frequently difficult. Where the land is owned by the claimant and there has been interference with rights, the claimant will have a claim under the law of nuisance. However, there is still an issue of proving foreseeability.

The rule in *Rylands* v *Fletcher* imposes strict liability for substances that have been brought onto land and which have escaped, causing damage. There is no need to prove foreseeability or fault. However, the possible problem of demonstrating causation still exists.

Trespass to land may also be used where matters or substances have been placed on another person's land. The advantage of trespass is that the third party does not have to establish loss or that the trespass was intentional or negligent. An investor must be aware that if a claimant is successful under common law he or she will be entitled to either damages or an injunction or both. This will be of particular concern where acquiring an ongoing operation.

EU Directive on Environmental Civil Liability

At the time of writing this chapter the European Commission had announced that after 15 years of negotiation, a directive on liability for damage resulting from activities dangerous to the environment, had been agreed. The main negotiations had faltered on the question of whether firms engaged in high-risk activities should be required to take out insurance or other types of financial guarantees to fund a pool for environmental clean-up. The Commission is to review the need for financial guarantees six years after the directive enters into force.

Integrated pollution prevention control

The Environmental Protection Act 1990 introduced a regime for regulating emissions to the environment. The intention of the regulatory regime is that emissions from the affected industries will be reduced and that industry will invest in technology to achieve this end.

Qualifying processes have to obtain an integrated pollution control permit in order to operate lawfully. Some processes were regulated in relation to all their emissions and some to air only. Those processes where all emissions were affected were regulated by the Environment Agency and those where only emissions to air were affected were regulated by the local authority. Each industry that had a qualifying process had to apply to either the Environment Agency or the local authority (as relevant) for the permit. In the application they had to describe the process and the techniques they were using to stop or, where that wasn't possible, minimize emissions. The industries were obliged to demonstrate that they were using the best available techniques not entailing excessive cost in order to either stop or minimize these emissions. The permits were given with conditions that had to be complied with. The relevant regulatory body reviewed these conditions at least every four years to ensure that techniques had not changed that would reduce the current level of emissions in relation to each of the processes. Failure to obtain the permit or to comply with any of the conditions resulted in prosecution.

The relevant regime is now that of integrated pollution prevention control (IPPC). This is a similar process to that described above. The new regime of IPPC has been introduced throughout Europe and requires a phased compliance so that some industries are already operating under an IPPC permit while others have yet to apply for one and in England and Wales are still governed by the old IPC regime.

The IPPC regime requires qualifying processes to have a permit that has conditions. The applicants must demonstrate that they are using the best available techniques that are available at reasonable cost. The permits are reviewable every four years with the view to ensuring that emissions are gradually reduced as technology is introduced to achieve this.

There are two significant differences between the old regime of IPC and the new one of IPPC. IPPC requires many more processes to have consents. This has particularly impacted the waste industry. In addition, the application for a permit must include a survey of the current state of the condition of the soil and groundwater of the property on which the relevant process is located. To be allowed to surrender the permit (when the operation ceases) the permit holder must return the land and water to the state it was in at the time of obtaining the permit.

Transaction solutions

Availability of information

In assessing the risk arising from the acquisition of land or an operational facility, the first step is to obtain as much information as possible. The risk of liability arises from both historic activities on the site and any ongoing operation.

A certain amount of information will be available from standard property searches carried out with the local authority for the relevant area. Standard enquiries of the local authority will include questions concerning whether or not the site is on the local authority's Contaminated Land Register. At the time of writing this article only about a third of local authorities have set up Contaminated Land Registers and most have not completed the process of identifying land to be placed on that register. Therefore, it is sensible not only to ask whether or not a piece of land has been placed on the register but also, in case the process has not gone that far, whether or not the authority has any information that would mean that it would be placed on the register in the future. If the land to be acquired is leasehold, then further information as to historic use may be available in the property documentation.

Desktop environmental studies (referred to as Phase 1 studies) may be commissioned from an environmental consultant. These studies will report on historic ordinance survey maps of the area, which will show the historic uses of the site, and will raise enquiries of all regulatory agencies including the Environment Agency. There are two types of Phase 1 studies available in the market. The cheaper option is one that simply reports the information with no comment. The second will be an evaluation carried out by an environmental consultant who will also visit the site. The latter, although more expensive, is more effective in analysing the risk. Commonly, an environmental consultant will take five to 10 working days to produce a Phase 1 report.

If such a study reveals that there is a risk it may be sensible to commission a Phase 2 study. This is an intrusive investigation of the site that will confirm whether or not the risk analysis is correct and identifies areas of contamination. It will also comment on the like-lihood of whether the contamination has travelled off-site. This will provide an indication of the extent of liability. Many reports will also include an estimate of costs for remediation. The Phase 2 study will take between three to five weeks and will cost several thousand pounds depending on the size of the site investigated.

Both Phase 1 and Phase 2 studies, depending on the scope of work, should include comment on the current operations at the property and the risk associated with those operations. A comprehensive Phase 1 will include cost estimates for any works to be carried out to rectify any breach of the regulatory regime. In addition, it will point out any defi-ciency in data that stops the study being complete. It is increasingly common for sellers to have already carried out either a Phase 1 or Phase 2 study. When acquiring property the enquiry should always be raised of the seller whether or not such studies have been carried out.

The studies are commonly addressed to the person commissioning the report and therefore, if the buyer wishes to rely on these reports, the reports will have to either be readdressed or a warranty obtained from the consultant. It is important to understand the terms and conditions of any such warranty including the level of insurance provided by the environmental consultant.

What happens if an issue is revealed?

In respect of historically contaminated land, that is, land that was contaminated prior to current ownership, the extent of the issue will depend on whether shares or assets were purchased. If purchasing the shares, then clearly any liability of the company will become the new owner's. If purchasing the land in normal circumstances liability arises in the first instance only with the original polluter. However, if the original polluter cannot be identified then the new owner/occupier may well become liable for contamination that is not theirs. The following are options to consider depending on the circumstances of each transaction:

- remediation;
- indemnity;
- insurance.

Remediation
It is possible to negotiate contractual terms that allow for the purchaser either to have the area remediated prior to purchase or for the area to be remediated post-purchase. The usual contractual terms will involve the joint appointment of an environmental consultant to carry out the works so that the consultant's duty of care is owed both to the buyer and the seller. Although the environment agency will not 'sign off' remediation as being all that is required, it is possible to obtain approval to the remediation as being satisfactory for the current purposes.

Indemnity
Where there is significant contamination it may not be appropriate to remediate. If the purchaser is confident with the covenant strength of the seller, then an indemnity may be considered. The weakness of an indemnity is that it quite often restricts ongoing operations. It will be limited in time and probably have a cap or other devices to restrict the amount of liability. The indemnity will commonly not cover contamination arising from change of use, redevelopment, construction on the site, extension of the site. Frequently, contamination becomes an issue when there is development; therefore these restrictions are an

important consideration when looking at an indemnity. In addition, it is quite common for a seller's liability to decrease over the period of the indemnity.

Insurance
At the time of writing this chapter the insurance industry is reviewing the terms upon which it wishes to offer environmental insurance. Insurance has been an expensive option and has other shortcomings. It will quite often require some element of remediation prior to activation of the insurance and will deal with off site liability associated with historic contamination only. It is commonly not available for change of use or development. In addition, it has not been possible to obtain insurance for longer than a 10-year period.

In transactions that may involve the purchase of several sites, if insurance is a possibility, then information between the site occupiers and the purchaser should be monitored closely. Insurance policies are vitiated if the insurer has not been provided with all relevant information. Such relevant information can be passed informally between the site occupier and consultant, for instance, and if this is not then passed on to the insurers, the policy will be worthless.

In addition, the insurance will very rarely cover indemnities given by the buyer to a third party. It is quite common if there is a 'sold with information' clause in the sale contract for there also to be an indemnity by the buyer to the seller. Therefore, if insurance is an option this should be considered at an early stage when reviewing the provisions of the contract.

In respect of operational breaches an assessment will need to be made of the cost to obtain regulatory compliance and an assessment of the liability for historic breach. If the covenant strength is satisfactory, an indemnity in respect of the breach can be requested. It is likely that any such indemnity will be of shorter duration than for contaminated land.

Director's liability

It is still relatively unusual for an individual director or manager to be prosecuted for environmental liability. However, all environmental legislation allows for prosecution of directors, managers and company secretaries if there has been connivance or negligence.

Part 6

UK Regional Options

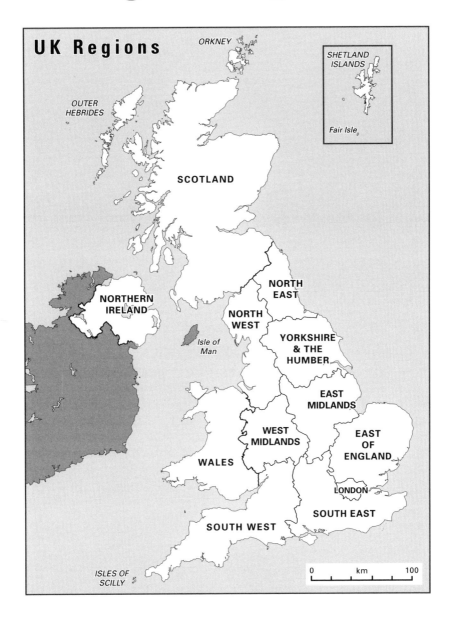

6.1

North East England

One North East

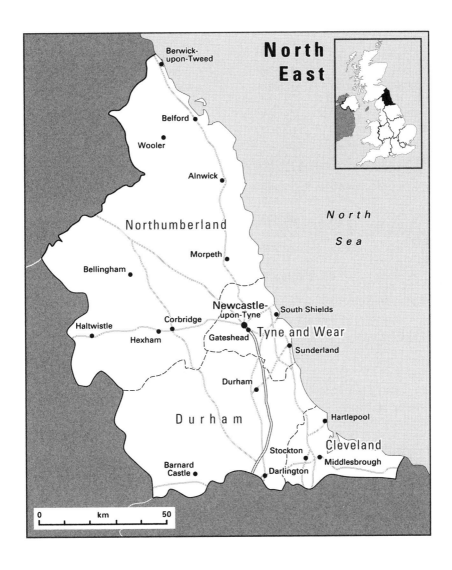

Berwick-upon-Tweed

North East

Belford

Wooler

Alnwick

North

Northumberland

Sea

Morpeth

Bellingham

Newcastle-upon-Tyne

South Shields

Haltwistle

Corbridge

Tyne and Wear

Hexham

Gateshead

Sunderland

Durham

D u r h a m

Hartlepool

Cleveland

Stockton

Middlesbrough

Barnard
Castle

Darlington

0   km   50

Demographics

Tables 6.1.1 and 6.1.2 show the population by age in the region and also the number of people employed in each of the main sectors.

Table 6.1.1   Population by age in the North East

Age Range	Total	Males	Females
0–4	138,441	70,909	67,532
5–9	157,444	80,961	76,483
10–14	167,435	85,484	81,951
15–19	164,054	82,620	81,434
20–24	14,9847	74,823	75,024
25–29	148,190	72,134	76,056
30–34	178,238	86,282	91,956
35–39	195,130	95,570	99,560
40–44	183,057	89,869	93,188
45–49	167,262	83,467	83,795
50–54	177,788	88,725	89,063
55–59	140,950	70,049	70,901
60–64	131,328	63,761	67,567
65–69	121,206	57,786	63,420
70–74	100,037	40,400	59,000
75–79	88,599	36,536	52,063
80–84	55,430	19,853	35,577
85–89	28,946	8,388	20,558
90 and over	13,797	2,916	10,881
Totals	2,515,479	1,218,602	1,296,877

Source: ONS Census 200

Table 6.1.2   People employed by sector

	Persons Employed
Agriculture and Fishing	5,369
Energy and Water	9,977
Manufacturing	158,873
Construction	53,558
Distribution, Hotels and Restaurants	228,114
Transport and Communications	53,519
Banking, Finance and Insurance, etc	132,658
Public Administration, Education & Health	304,294
Other Services	53,597
Total	999,959

Source: ONS Annual Business Inquiry 2002, North East

Did you know the North East of England has...?

Life Sciences
- The Institute of Ageing & Health, the largest of its kind in the UK
- The Institute for Genetics, the largest in Europe - 150 research staff
- University of Newcastle, one of only 3 areas tasked by the UK government to take forward stem cell research

Digital Technology and Media
- One of the largest clusters of games companies in the UK
- One of only 3 areas recognised as a Centre of Excellence in the area of Virtual Reality
- The University of Sunderland supplies more graduates to Microsoft than any other University in the UK

New and Renewable Energy
- The only UK region to have its own energy strategy
- The New and Renewable Energy Centre (NaREC) to lead Europe in developing new technologies
- The world's first tidal stream generator was developed in the North East

Chemicals
- The largest Chemicals industry in the UK contributing 20% of the UK's entire Chemical production
- Pioneering work in Fuel Cells/ Alternative Fuels
- Strong in petrochemicals, fine chemicals, polymers

Nanotechnology
- One of only 3 hotbeds of Nanotechnology in UK, and one of only 12 centres in Europe
- Best equipped facility in Europe for R&D work at the nano-scale
- Strengths are in Sensors, Materials, LEDs, Bio-Nano
- Major manufacturers of microsystems, Filtronic and Atmel, have research and manufacturing bases in the region

Automotive
- Nissan - most productive car plant in Europe
- 25,000 people employed in the Industry
- Pioneering industry-led initiatives to improve lean manufacturing resulting in greater productivity - £10m investment

Pharmaceuticals
- Over 70 of the world's largest manufacturers based in the region including Avecia, GlaxoSmithKline; Procter & Gamble and Merck, Sharpe and Dohme with a combined annual turnover of £1 billion
- 7,000 employed in the pharmaceutical sector
- The School of Pharmacy at the University of Sunderland is the largest of its kind in the UK

What One NorthEast can do for you:
- Provide a single point of contact for developing plans for the European markets
- Help bridge the gap between industry and academia
- Provide a free and confidential service in the identification of a suitable greenfield site location, joint venture company or partner for collaboration on new research and development
- Access to financial assistance for the creation and development of new business ventures in the North East
- Organisation of structured inward visits to the region

For further information about the North East's successful sectors please contact:
Paul Taylor
Inward Investment Manager
Tel: +44 (191) 229 6325
Email: paul.taylor@onenortheast.co.uk

www.onenortheast.co.uk

Local economy

Structure of GDP

The North East economy generated a GDP of £25.9 billion in 1999, representing a GDP of £10,024 per head and 77.3 per cent of the UK average. In 1998, the main sectors contributing to it were manufacturing with 27 per cent, business services, 15 per cent, wholesale and retail trade,10 per cent and health and social work, 9.5 per cent. Table 6.1.3 shows GDP for the period 1995–99.

Table 6.1.3   NE GDP 1995–99

1995	1996	1997	1998	1999
82.8	81.5	78.4	77.6	77.3

Note: £ per head index.
Source: ONS Regional Trends 2002

The importance of manufacturing in the region remains significantly greater than in the United Kingdom overall (United Kingdom, 20 per cent of GDP) while financial services contribute under half as much to GDP (3 per cent) as in the United Kingdom (6.2 per cent). Business services has grown in the North East in recent years, rising from 14.1

Table 6.1.4   Sectoral contributions to GDP

Economic Structure North East, 1998		
	North East	Percentage
Agriculture, Hunting, Forestry & Fishing	188	0.9
Mining, Quarrying of Energy Producing Materials	144	1
Manufacturing	6,904	28.7
Electricity, Gas & Water Supply	645	2.6
Construction	1,474	5.2
Wholesale & Retail Trade (including Motor Trade)	2,632	10.3
Hotels & Restaurants	707	2.4
Transport, Storage & Communication	1,804	6.8
Financial intermediation	762	3.7
Real Estate, Renting & Business Activities	3,856	14.1
Public Administration & Defence	1,394	6.7
Education	1,688	7.1
Health & Social Work	2,394	9
Other Services	1,154	3.9
Adjustment for Financial Services (FISIM)	−453	−2.5
Total	25,294	100

per cent of the region's GDP in 1994 to 15.2 per cent in 1998. This is still substantially less than the United Kingdom as a whole (over 21 per cent of GDP). Health and social work has grown since 1994 (9 per cent) to 9.5 per cent in 1998, nearly three percentage points above the UK average. Table 6.1.4 shows the sectoral contributions to GDP in the region.

Between 1994 and 1998 the share of GDP attributed to manufacturing fell slightly from 28.7 per cent to 27.3 per cent. This decline in manufacturing follows the trend evident over the last decade. In 1989, manufacturing made up 31.9 per cent of the North East GDP before declining in the 1990s. Financial and business services as a proportion of North East GDP increased from 16.2 per cent in 1989 to 18.2 per cent in 1998. Over this period, six out of the nine service industries increased their proportion of the region's GDP. Table 6.1.5 shows the employment figures for the region.

Table 6.1.5   Employment

Employees	1,060,000 (2003)
New Graduates	14,000
Unemployment	6.1% (Apr–Jun 2003)
Economic Activity	72.9% (Feb–Apr 2003)

Factory and office accommodation

Factory purchase
Tables 6.1.6 to 6.1.9 indicate rental and capital values for five typical classes of industrial buildings. The first four types are assumed to be on an industrial estate and let on Full Repair and Insure (FRI) terms. They are of modern construction but not of high-tech design and are heated by free-standing heaters.

Type 1. Small starter units, 25 square metres–75 square metres. Steel framed, concrete block or brick construction, often built in terrace layout and let on weekly terms.

Type 2. Nursery units, 150 square metres–200 square metres. Steel framed on concrete base, concrete block or brickwork to 2 metres with metal PVC covered cladding above. Eaves height 4.3 metres to 5.5 metres with lined roof. Ten per cent to 15 per cent office content. Detached on own site with private parking and loading facilities.

Type 3. Industrial/warehouse units circa 500 square metres. Steel framed on concrete base, concrete block or brickwork to 2 metres with metal PVC covered cladding above. Eaves height 4.3 metres to 5.5

metres with lined roof. Ten per cent to 15 per cent office content. Detached on own site with private parking and loading facilities.

Type 4. Industrial/warehouse units, circa 1,000 square metres. Steel framed on concrete base, concrete block or brickwork to 2 metres with metal PVC covered cladding above. Eaves height up to 7.6 metres with lined roof. Ten per cent to 15 per cent office content. Detached on own site with private parking and loading facilities.

Type 5. Converted ex-mill units. Ground floor unit converted from 19th-century multifloor ex-mill or similar building of four to five storeys. Brick construction with tile or slate roof. Unit of circa 150 square metres with heating from central piped water system. Electric goods lift to upper floors and sprinklers to all levels. Tenant responsible for internal repairs and insurance. This type is only found in certain areas of the country.

Table 6.1.6   Factory capital values

Type 1 25–75m²	Type 2 150–200m²	Type 3 Circa 500m²	Type 4 Circa 1,000m²	Location
520	380	320	290	North Tyneside
425	350	315	270	Cramlington Northumberland
540	450	425	400	Team Valley
315	375	400	375	Middlesbrough
400	320	260	240	Durham

Note: Capital values £/m².

Table 6.1.7   Factory rental values

Type 1 25–5m²	Type 2 150–200m²	Type 3 Circa 500m²	Type 4 Circa 1000m²	Location
65	48	40	36	North Tyneside
47	40	35	30	Cramlington, Northumberland
60	53	45	43	Team Valley
40	45	40	38	Middlesbrough
50	40	40	30	Durham

Note: Rental values £/m².

Table 6.1.8 Northern enterprise zone – factory capital values

Type 1 25–75m²	Type 2 150–200m²	Type 3 Circa 500m²	Type 4 Circa 1,000m²	Location
300	260	250	220	East Durham
–	–	675	600	Tyne Riverside, Newcastle

Note: Capital values £/m².

Table 6.1.9 Northern enterprise zone – factory rental values

Type 1 25–75m²	Type 2 150–200m²	Type 3 Circa 500m²	Type 4 Circa 1,000m²	Location
38	38	31	27	East Durham
–	–	60	55	Tyne Riverside, Newcastle

Note: Rental values £/m².
Source: Property Market Report, Spring 2003

Uniform business rates
The rating system imposed by local authorities has been revised for businesses in the light of the implementation of the Council Tax for domestic property owners. To calculate the uniform business rate for a non-domestic property the current national rate (poundage) is multiplied by the rateable value of the property. Rateable values are based on rental values and take into account things such as square footage and area in which the property is situated. Properties are revalued every five years to provide a fair and up-to-date base for the system.

The poundage for 1998/99 (from 1 April 1998) is 0.465 (or 46.5 pence) in the pound for property with a rateable value under £10,000 and 0.474 in the pound for properties valued over £10,000. On the last revaluation of properties used for business purposes measures were introduced to limit the increase in rate bills. For large properties the limit was 10 per cent per annum in real terms, 7.5 per cent for small properties and 5 per cent for composite properties.

Office and rental costs
The North East of England's office rents are appreciably lower than in the London area and in most other provincial centres elsewhere in the United Kingdom, as Table 6.1.10 indicates.

Type 1. Town centre location. Self-contained suite over 1,000 square metres in office block erected in last 10 years, good standard of finish with a lift and good quality fittings to common parts. Limited car parking available.

Type 2. As Type 1 but suite size in range of 150 square metres to 400 square metres.

Type 3. Converted former house usually just off town centre. Good-quality conversion of Georgian/Victorian or similar house of character. Best-quality fittings throughout. Approximately 150 square metres with central heating and limited car parking. Denotes accommodation with air-conditioning

Table 6.1.10   Office rental costs

Location	Type 1	Type 2	Type 3
Newcastle upon Tyne	* 200	* 200	75
Morpeth, Northumberland	–	–	53
Sunderland	80	80	55
Middlesbrough	–	75	58
Durham	95	125	100
Teesdale (see below)	**135	140	

Note: £/m²/ann; *Accommodation with air-conditioning; ** Type 1 and 2 are out of town at Thornaby, Middlesbrough.
Source: Property Market Report, Spring 2003

Transport and communications

The North East of England has a first-class industrial and commercial infrastructure and excellent communication links. The region offers:

- readily available industrial sites, both brown- and greenfield, at costs appreciably lower than London and most provincial centres;

- Enterprise Zones and sites for industry ranging from 50 hectares down – gives the region one of the best property profiles in the country;

- two international airports – less than one hour to London;

- excellent road and rail links – two and a half hours by rail and under five hours by road to London;

- freight to major European destinations within 48 hours, many within 24 hours;

- six major ports serving Europe and the rest of the world including the all-weather Port of Tyne, with roll on/roll off capabilities handling up to 400-tonne loads;

- deep docking facilities for tankers, bulk and chemical carriers at Teesport;

- a series of reservoirs guaranteeing undisrupted water supplies for the region and electricity, gas and effluent services, among the most competitive in Europe;

- fully integrated public transport system, the Tyne & Wear Metro links rail, car parking, bus and ferry services and accesses 1.6 million people (see Table 6.1.11 for distribution times).

Table 6.1.11   Distribution times from Newcastle

London	Within 4–6 hours
Berlin	Within 24 hours
Cologne	Within 24 hours
Hamburg	Within 24 hours
Hannover	Within 24 hours
Amsterdam	Within 24 hours
Munich	Within 48 hours

There are direct flights from Newcastle and/or Teesside airports to the following European destinations:

Alicante	Amsterdam	Brussels
Dublin	Düsseldorf	Geneva
Malaga	Paris	Prague
Stavanger		

FDI

The North East of England has key industrial clusters and sectors that have helped to regenerate the region's economy. Its reputation for innovation and industrial change is well documented. The following list shows the main areas of strength and some of the major company investments:

- **automotive** – led by Nissan, supported by a wide range of component companies, and other manufacturers such as Komatsu and Caterpillar;

- **consumer electronics and microelectronics** – major investments by Philips, Samsung, LG, Filtronics, Lite-On and Atmel;

- **life sciences** – International Centre for Life including the Human Genetics Institute and Bioscience Centre and the Institute for the Health of the Elderly;

- **chemicals** – investors include Huntsman, DuPont, BASF and ChiRex;

- **pharmaceuticals** – supported by Merck, Sharpe & Dohme (MSD), Monsanto, Searle, Sanofi Winthrop and GlaxoSmithKline;

- **engineering** – major international companies, with expertise in offshore and sub-sea technology as well as a long-established tradition of precision and high-quality engineering;

- **call centres and shared services** – growing service sector of over 30 call centres representing household names such as AA Services, British Airways, BT, One 2 One, Orange, Abbey National, Convergys and SITEL;

- **software development** – increasing reputation for high-quality bespoke software from companies such as Sage and Verisign.

In addition to these sector strengths, the region is supported by a number of renowned Centres of Excellence, which assist the growth and development of the sectors. These include digital technology and digital media, life sciences, nanotechnology, new and renewable energy, and process industries. Table 6.1.12 shows the foreign direct investors in the region.

Table 6.1.12   Foreign direct investors in the North East

Sector	Financial Year	No of Investors	Origin	Capex (£m)	Jobs Created/ Safeguarded
Automotive	2000/01	3	USA × 2, Japan	166	1951
	2001/02	7	USA × 2, France × 2, Japan, Canada, Spain	39.85	589
	2002/03	10	Japan × 4, Germany × 2, USA × 2, Spain, France	28.28	814
Call Centres	2000/01	5	USA, China, Germany × 2, France	18.03	2803
	2001/02	3	USA, France, South Africa	3.2	940
	2002/03	–	–	–	–
Chemicals	2000/01	–	–	–	–
	2001/02	2	USA, Holland	7.9	111
	2002/03	2	Australia, USA	29.8	203
Clothing & Textiles	2000/01	-	–	–	–
	2001/02	2	USA, China	0.05	25
	2002/03	1	China	N/A	5
Electronics	2000/01	3	USA, Korea, Holland	557.91	1792
	2001/02	4	China, Sweden, USA, Taiwan	22.94	273
	2002/03	6	China × 4, Japan, Sweden	0.1	100

continued overleaf

Sector	Financial Year	No of Investors	Origin	Capex (£m)	Jobs Created/ Safeguarded
Engineering	2000/01	2	Japan, China	2.7	129
	2001/02	5	Belgium × 2, Japan × 2, Australia	11.33	572
	2002/03	7	China × 2, USA × 2, UAE, Japan, Canada	8.71	600
Food & Drink	2000/01	1	China	0.5	5
	2001/02	1	China	0.2	25
	2002/03	2	China, Taiwan	1.27	32
Life Sciences	2000/01	6	Italy × 3, India, Japan, New Zealand	21.1	265
	2001/02	3	USA, China, Australia	1.55	76
	2002/2003	1	Spain	0.64	26
Logistics	2000/01	1	USA	3	60
	2001/02	1	USA	0.1	40
	2002/03	–	–	–	–
Offshore & Marine	2000/01	–	–	–	–
	2001/02	1	Holland	2.9	25
	2002/03	1	Denmark	0.75	22
Plastics & Packaging	2000/01	-	–	–	–
	2001/02	1	USA	0.84	45
	2002/03	4	USA, China, Israel, Norway	6.06	284
Software/IT	2000/01	1	USA	4.1	386
	2001/02	2	China, Germany	0.1	15
	2002/03	2	China, USA	N/A	18
Other	2000/01	6	China × 6	0.02	11
	2001/02	1	China	N/A	5
	2002/03	5	China × 4, USA	N/A	32

Availability of EU Structural Funds

Assistance from Europe typically originates from the European Social Fund, European Regional Development Fund or the European Investment Bank. The European Structural Funds provide grants to support projects throughout the United Kingdom to promote social and economic regeneration and competitiveness, although most of the funding is concentrated on areas of greatest need – so-called Objective 1 and 2 areas (the North East region has no Objective 1 areas). The funds contribute towards infrastructure, supporting existing and start-up businesses, research and development and training, as well as other specific areas such as rural and environmental development, all of which provide new employment.

Information on the European Regional Development Fund can be obtained from the following website: http://www.europa.eu.int/comm/

regional_policy/funds/prord/prord_en.htm. Information on the European Social Fund can be obtained by clicking from: http://www.europa.eu.int/comm/employment_social/esf2000/index-en.htm. Information on the European Investment Bank for loans to finance capital investment can be obtained from: http://www.eib.org/.

Infrastructure

Telecoms

The North East of England has the finest urban telecommunications infrastructure in the United Kingdom outside of London. Although rural and remote areas are less well connected, the RDA has recently awarded a contract to enable all rural and remote areas to receive broadband. Additional features of the region include large-scale call centre capacity, large-scale data storage capacity, both with direct links to continental and transatlantic internet highways. The rate of broadband growth and the take up of internet-related application and services is currently the fastest in the United Kingdom. The North East is truly becoming an eRegion.

Business parks

Co Durham
Belmont Business Park
Bracken Hill Business Park
Durham University Science Park
Ponds Court Business Park
Abbey Woods Business Park

Northumberland
Northumberland Business Park, South Cramlington
Regents Drive Business Park, Prudhoe
Wansbeck Business Park, Ashington

Tyne & Wear
Balliol Business Park
Baltic Business Park
Boldon Business Park
Cobalt Business Park
Doxford International
Metro Riverside
Newburn Riverside Industry Park
Newcastle Business Park
Newcastle Great Park
Sunderland Enterprise Park

Tees Valley
Kirkleatham Business Park
Queens Business Park
Belasis Hall Technology Park
Teesside Business Park
Wynyard Business Park

Utilities

Water
Water supplies are deregulated, but the major company within the North East Region is Northumbrian Water. Northumbrian Water's Kielder Reservoir, situated in the North Tyne valley, is the largest man-made lake in Europe, with a usable storage capacity of over 44,000 million gallons (nearly 200,000 million litres). The reservoir is able to yield up to 200 million gallons per day, thereby ensuring that the region's domestic and industrial supply can be met well into the next century.

Electricity
Electricity generation in the United Kingdom is carried out by power stations owned by a number of generating companies, of which the main three are National Power, Powergen and Nuclear Electric. The operation of the transmission system is the responsibility of the National Grid Company. There are 12 regional electricity companies (RECs) whose core business is the distribution and supply of electricity. Distribution is the operation of the distribution networks. The supply business covers the purchase of electricity in bulk through the wholesale market and its sale to customers. All the major generating companies are required to sell the electricity they produce into an open commodity market known as the 'pool'. To ensure competition in the supply business, RECs are required to provide open access to their distribution networks on a non-discriminatory basis. As a result, not all customers to whom an REC distributes electricity are necessarily supply customers of that company. Only companies holding electricity supply licences can sell electricity and everybody can choose from companies who hold a supply licence.

Gas
In 1997 British Gas de-merged into two entirely separate companies. The supply business is now part of the holding company, Centrica plc, while the pipeline and storage businesses, most exploration and production and research and development have been retained within British Gas plc, renamed BG plc. Business users buy their gas from a number of licensed competing suppliers including Business Gas, a

subsidiary of BG plc, Enron Direct, Kinetica and SWALEC. A full list of these is available from Ofgas, the gas industry regulatory body that issues gas supply licences.

Education and training

Universities

There are five universities (see Table 6.1.13) in the region, all of which offer excellent degree courses and carry out research in relevant disciplines.

Table 6.1.13   Universities of the North East – number of graduates in the North East of England 2002

University of Durham	2,863
University of Newcastle upon Tyne	2,695
University of Northumbria at Newcastle	3,977
University of Sunderland	3,744
University of Teesside	1,988
Graduate Total	14,094

Colleges of further and higher education

The region has 23 colleges of further and higher education offering a full range of vocational education and technical training, ranging from diplomas to degree standard courses. The colleges also support industry through offering services including product and materials testing, consultancy and a broad range of general support services. The colleges run a diverse range of training courses in conjunction with the Department for Education and Skills, allowing for the customizing of courses to meet a company's specific needs. For example, Nissan established a customized training programme with Wearside College, which enables their employees to undertake a four-year training scheme in automotive construction and engineering skills.

Vocational training

North East CourseFinder
The CourseFinder database, holds information on full- and part-time courses in North East England. Note that Tees Valley information is no longer available on this site. Please call Jenny Dobinson on +44 (0) 1642   743077.   This   website   lists   course   providers: http://www.tap.co.uk/html3/providera.php?providera.php?pr=A.

Research

Science and Industry Council

Under the leadership of Sir Ian Gibson, the Science and Industry Council, founded in December 2001, has established an authoritative position as the appropriate forum for policy matters relating to the science and industry agenda, bringing together the worlds of academia and business to ensure North East companies secure a competitive advantage in the global market place. The Council is promoting the North East internationally as the premier location to conduct scientific research and enterprise, and members use their knowledge and reputations to act as influential voices for the region. The government is now encouraging all RDAs to establish such councils capable of developing regional knowledge economic strategies.

Centres of Excellence

Five Centres of Excellence have been set up:

nanotechnology, photonics and microsystems (CENAMPS)
life sciences (CELS)
digital technology and media (Codeworks)
new and renewable energy (NaREC)
process industries (CPI)

These areas have been identified on the basis of their potential to achieve world-class competitive excellence through technology transfer to business from the research base. In addition, a regional exploitation company, NSTAR, exists to provide commercial and intellectual property management resources.

The Centres of Excellence initiative is a critical investment in research and development aimed at creating wealth in the region, attracting inward investment and a home for world-class businesses and the finest intellectual capital. The principal function of the Centres of Excellence is to 'condition' technologies arising from the regional research base to a form where they can be utilized for commercial purposes. The Centres will achieve the goal of long-term structural change and sustainable development directly through their own development and particularly by linking with and becoming central elements of mainstream regional programmes, physical regeneration and inward investment. This initiative is a cornerstone of the Strategy for Success and the regional economic strategy.

Public sector business support organizations

Acas
www.acas.org.uk

Building up Business (North Tyneside Council)
www.buildingupbusiness.com

County Durham Business Link
www.blcd.co.uk

County Durham Development Company
www.cddc.co.uk

Northumberland Business Link
www.n-bs.co.uk

Northumberland County Council Economic Development Unit
www.northumberland.gov.uk

Tees Valley Business Link
www.tees.businesslink.co.uk

Tyne & Wear Business Link
www.businesslinktw.co.uk

County Durham Development Company
www.durham4business.com

Entrust
www.entrust.co.uk

European Information Centre
www.northeasteic.com

Government Office for the North East
www.go-ne.gov.uk

North East Chamber of Commerce
http://www.ne-chamber.co.uk/

The North East Chamber of Commerce is owned by its members. It exists to serve their interests locally and throughout the region. With over 200 staff, NECC is the largest Chamber of Commerce in the United Kingdom and represents the independent voice of North East business. It provides a comprehensive range of business services, products and expert training to help businesses realize their potential. It keeps members informed, increases their business prospects and saves them money. Its resource and influence, as the largest, most proactive business organization in the North East, makes membership of the Chamber an essential business tool.

Small Business Service
www.sbs.gov.uk

TEDCO
www.tedco.org

Tees Valley Regeneration Company
www.teesvalleyregeneration.co.uk

Planning is the responsibility of the planning offices at the individual local authority:

County Durham
Chester-le-Street District Council
http://www.chester-le-street.gov.uk/

Derwentside District Council
http://www.derwentside.gov.uk/

Durham City District Council
http://www.durhamcity.gov.uk

Durham County Council
http://www.durham.gov.uk/

Easington District Council
http://www.easington.com

Sedgefield District Council
http://www.sedgefield.gov.uk

Teesdale District Council
http://www.teesdale.gov.uk

Wear Valley District Council
http://www.wearvalley.gov.uk

Northumberland
Alnwick District Council
http://www.alnwick.gov.uk

Berwick-upon-Tweed Borough Council
http://www.berwick-upon-tweed.gov.uk

Blyth Valley Borough Council
http://www.blythvalley.gov.uk

Castle Morpeth Borough Council
http://www.castlemorpeth.gov.uk

Northumberland County Council
http://www.northumberland.gov.uk

Tynedale Council
http://www.tynedale.gov.uk

Wansbeck District Council
http://www.wansbeck.gov.uk

Tees Valley
Darlington Borough Council
http://www.darlington.gov.uk

Hartlepool Borough Council
http://www.hartlepool.gov.uk

Middlesbrough Council
http://www.middlesbrough.gov.uk

Redcar and Cleveland Borough Council
http://www.redcar-cleveland.gov.uk

Stockton on Tees Borough Council
http://www.stockton.gov.uk

Tyne & Wear
Gateshead Metropolitan Borough Council
http://www.gateshead.gov.uk

Newcastle upon Tyne City Council
http://www.newcastle.gov.uk

North Tyneside Council
http://www.northtyneside.gov.uk

South Tyneside Metropolitan Borough Council
http://www.southtyneside.info

Sunderland City Council
http://www.sunderland.gov.uk

6.1.1 GATESHEAD

If you are interested in exploring European markets, take your business to Gateshead in the North East of England. Undergoing dramatic regeneration, Gateshead is known around the world for its cultural renaissance and iconic structures following the recent development of BALTIC, a Centre for Contemporary Art, Gateshead Millennium Bridge, the Angel of the North and the Sage Gateshead.

At the heart of the region's capital, Gateshead is perfectly placed to help businesses to work with international markets, with low-cost, low-risk opportunities to test the market. Underpinned by a range of

Economic Development Service

Gateshead Council
www.gateshead.gov.uk

Think Business
Think Gateshead

IF YOU ARE THINKING OF TAPPING INTO NEW MARKETS IN THE UK & EUROPE - TALK TO US.

Gateshead Council's Economic Development Service has been helping businesses like yours for many years. Its proven track record is based on sound business advice, expertise and a knowledge of the region that can help open doors to new markets and business opportunities.

The North East is experiencing a cultural and economic renaissance. It leads the way with its exciting approach to regeneration. Here in Gateshead, the Angel of the North and Gateshead Millennium Bridge are symbolic of the optimism and innovation found in the rest of the region.

Gateshead's new International Business Centre with its high-tech accommodation will bring another dimension to the reputation of our region to inspire and support businesses.

BUSINESSES CAN DO WELL HERE - AND WITH OUR HELP AND SUPPORT YOU COULD BE ONE OF THEM.

To find out how we can help you, contact:
+44 (0)191 433 2084 or email:
economicdevelopment@gateshead.gov.uk
for our information pack.

one
NorthEast

EUROPEAN COMMUNITY
European Social Fund

PEOPLE   BUSINESS   SUPPORT

business support services, Gateshead has a great reputation for innovation and technology, the availability of a skilled workforce and a great quality of life.

Excellent transport links

Including:

- fully integrated public transport system with a Metro service linking air, rail, car and ferry services, serving 1.6 million people;
- two international airports;
- excellent road and rail links with access to London in two and a half hours by rail and under five hours by road;
- freight to major European destinations within 48 hours, many within 24 hours;
- six major ports serving Europe and the rest of the world.

Support for your business

Including:

- dedicated and committed business support network;
- low operating costs;
- flexible, skilled and readily available pool of labour;
- fast and efficient logistics network;
- strong academic support – five universities and 24 colleges;
- excellent communications infrastructure;
- a first-class range of property solutions.

Innovation/technology

The North East of England has a strong reputation for innovation and industrial change. The region has world-class strengths in digital technology and digital media, life sciences, nanotechnology, new and renewable energy and process industries, supported by specialisms within local universities and Centres of Excellence.

People

With a population of 2.5 million, the region has a workforce of 1.06 million and 14,000 new graduates. The workforce in the North East has a reputation for being hard working and flexible in its working practices. There is a readily available supply of labour, much of which is skilled or has been retrained. There are also a wide range of agencies and organizations offering extensive training facilities and support to investors.

Supporting investors

To support businesses working in international markets, Gateshead has a range of prestigious accommodation and managed workspaces. Gateshead International Business Centre, situated at the heart of the North East of England, is a key development of the Gateshead Quays regeneration. The Centre provides investors with a unique package of assistance to make exploring European markets and joint ventures with local businesses as easy as possible. An innovative four-storey building comprising 51 offices, meeting rooms, a reception, utility rooms and informal meeting places with high-tech ICT facilities, benefits include:

- high-profile town centre site;

- competitively priced business accommodation with flexible monthly licence agreements;

- friendly, experienced and efficient staff to help with day-to-day issues and provide services such as telephone answering, reception, hospitality for customers and visitors and administrative support;

- a wide range of rented living accommodation options;

- access to a well-developed network of business support providers to help investors do business and explore markets in the United Kingdom and Europe.

Baltic Business Quarter will create 1,500 square metres of office space and 5,000 jobs. The £250 million high-quality urban development is a unique scheme, which includes Knowledge Campus, a design and development community that harnesses emerging collaborative working practices in global product development. It will include 40 buildings ranging in size from just over 1,000 square metres up to almost 10,000 square metres.

To take your business to Gateshead, contact Gateshead Council on Tel: +44 (0)191 433 2084.

6.1.2 NEWCASTLE

Providing the competitive edge to your business model

As a fast-growing location for new business projects, Newcastle owes much of its recent success to its ability to demonstrate that it can add significant value to an investor's global business model: it can leverage innovative suppliers, designers and intermediaries and has the proven ability to accelerate the introduction of product/service sets to new and existing markets. This is completed by a richness of talent and human capital, effective knowledge and financial networks and a world-class connectivity and logistics infrastructure.

Newcastle is an energetic, ambitious and attractive European city. As the region's business services centre it drives the rapidly diversifying economy of the North East of England. New technologies, entrepreneurship and creativity meet here to create a dynamic, focused and knowledge-centric business culture in a vibrant cosmopolitan city rich in talent and ideas.

Effective partnerships for project development

Newcastle has a strong track record in creating the partnerships necessary for the efficient delivery of business projects at all stages of development. Consequently, Newcastle supports the region's long-term strategy to exploit its strengths in technology and build capacity for innovation with a focus on advanced design, technical creativity and knowledge transfer. International companies like SAGE plc, Procter & Gamble, British Airways, AMEC, Wellstream and DUCO have developed successfully here because of this approach. This is underpinned by a unique academic–industry support structure available within a 45 minutes' drive of the city centre. Several networks link client businesses, universities, research and technology organizations and professional and financial intermediaries.

An integrated business support infrastructure provides access to regionwide knowledge transfer networks, regional exporting partnerships, access to portal sites for global promotion and investment support such as Proof of Concept funding, equity funds, venture capital/financial assistance. An extensive aftercare scheme for newly located companies also operates in Newcastle.

Newcastle has a wide range of world-class business locations offering tailored, sector-specific strategic environments able to fit any business model:

Advanced engineering: 180,000 square metres at Newburn Riverside
ICT/knowledge-based: 185,000 square metres at Newcastle Great Park
Marine and offshore engineering: 10,000 square metres at Walker Riverside including 14-acre development site with quay frontage
Creative and media: 28,000 square metres at Ouseburn/city centre
Investment and corporate: 128,000 square metres in new developments city centre
46,000 square metres existing and over 1,700 listed buildings

Newcastle is now the most wired city in the region in terms of broadband network coverage enabling large-scale data processing and access to broadband hubs in order to meet the demands of international and knowledge-based markets.

Speed of turnaround in new product development

Newcastle excels in its engineering and technology design capability, which, when utilized through partnering and the specialist support organizations based in or near to the city, produces faster new product development cycles and reduced time to market.

Partner organizations such as the five regional Centres of Excellence in Advanced Technologies, the Resource Centre for Innovation and Design, the Knowledge House brokerage service, the NaREC renewables testing facility, the School of Marine Engineering and Knowledge Campus work with client business to make the development and funding of new products, processes and the transfer of technologies quicker and more efficient in Newcastle compared with its European competitors. Strengths include:

- the commercialization of intellectual property;
- leaders in innovation through design solutions;
- advanced prototype design manufacture and testing;
- pioneering work in virtual prototyping and 3D modelling in design;
- sophisticated and wide-ranging test facilities;
- partnering at all levels of project development.

Newcastle hosts many of the regional Centres of Excellence, which its partner, One North East, the regional development agency, is using to channel investment into commercial R&D and market-ready academic intellectual property:

Centre of Excellence in Life Sciences (CELS)
stem cell research (University of Newcastle upon Tyne)
Institute of Aging and Health (largest in United Kingdom), Institute for Genetics

NaREC – New and Renewable Energy
leading on development of new energy-based technologies
development of first tidal stream generator

Codeworks – (Digital Technology and Media)
global reputation in game design and virtual reality
strong supply base of graduates in digital technology and media

Nanotechnology, Photonics and Microsystems (CENAMPS)
£25-million development based at Newcastle University
best-equipped facilities in Europe
one of only three hotbeds in United Kingdom

Process Industries (CPI)
over 70 of world's largest manufactures based in region
including: Procter & Gamble and GlaxoSmithKilne
NStar Finance
early stage technology venturing
investing between £20,000 and £1 million

Speed and connectivity of access of goods and services to market

It is undoubtedly a major benefit to any business to access the fastest routes to market. Newcastle sits at the centre of a high-quality, uncongested transport infrastructure that provides the connectivity needed to get products and services to market quickly and efficiently. This includes:

- two regional airports;

- Newcastle – 30+ destinations/one-hour flight time from seven European/transatlantic hub airports;

- Teesside – freight capacity one hour from the city centre;

- fast and efficient logistics/national freight network – rail and motorway;

- two sea ports: Tyne and Blyth 30 minutes from the city centre;

- fully integrated public transport system linking 1.5 million people (Metro subway, rail links, bus and ferry services).

For global production and service businesses, Newcastle's geography and transport links make the city an excellent marketing and distribution platform providing an added-value gateway into the European market place.

Fast supply chain access

A proven reputation for the availability and ease in sourcing supply chain partners is a further indicator of the added value Newcastle can bring to your business model. Newcastle has significant strengths in robust, diverse and integrated supply chains serving key sectors such as offshore, renewables, high-value engineering, process industries, life sciences and digital technology. This is supported by a growing sector of financial and professional firms.

Sector-specific partner trade organizations and portals provide a fast and integrated source of supply chain partnership and information. For instance, NorthHUB a web-based engineering firm resource in the city, provides efficient electronic communication with 2,500 local suppliers.

The right people to operate the business

Newcastle offers the investor access to a large pool of talent and ideas. The regional skills partnership it works within can supply the human capital to drive, deliver and develop your business model augmented by a wealth of students in higher education, delivering a versatile, motivated and skilled workforce of 400,000 within its travel to work area:

- excellent academic support: two city universities with strong international linkages to academic and corporate communities;
- 24 regional colleges with a student population of 200,000;
- over 70,000 students in graduate-level higher education;
- universities that excel in engineering, medicine, IT, mathematics, design and research;
- three other regional universities operating within one hour of city centre: Durham, Sunderland, Teesside;
- targeted student placements, tailored skills programmes accessing talent/people/availability of labour.

Newcastle is building on its ability to successfully provide added value to the global business models of companies located here. The magnificent quality of life, the wide diversity of countryside and cosmopolitan environments just minutes from the city centre, only complement a commercial location that will provide your business with a truly competitive edge.

6.2

North West Region

Northwest Development Agency

North West

Carlisle

Keswick

C u m b r i a

Kendal

Barrow in Furness

Lancaster

Irish Sea

Lancashire

Blackpool

Preston

Burnley

Blackburn

Wigan

Greater Manchester

Oldham

Merseyside

Liverpool

Manchester

Birkenhead

Stockport

Macclesfield

C h e s h i r e

Chester

Crewe

0   km   50

England's North West is one of the powerhouses of the UK economy. With a population of over 7 million and a bigger economy than Denmark or Finland, it would have the potential to be the twelfth biggest state in the United States. The region is the largest in the United Kingdom outside London and the South East, comprising five counties: Cheshire, Cumbria, Greater Manchester, Lancashire and Merseyside.

Inward investment and key industries

The North West Development Agency (NWDA) was established in 1999 to drive forward the economic growth of the North West and build on the region's reputation as a leading location for inward investment. With a budget of £1.4 billion over the next three years, the NWDA is now well positioned to provide the leadership to bring about sustainable economic development and prosperity throughout the North West.

The region is already home to over 350,000 companies, of which 1,700 are overseas-owned organizations. Three-quarters of the United Kingdom's top 100 companies have operations in the region including the Bank of New York, MBNA, Jaguar, General Motors, Siemens, Fujitsu, and Kellogg's. A major new investment was also recently announced by Irish company, Quinn Glass, to build a £120 million factory at Ince in Cheshire. The NWDA provided £4.9 million to establish this comprehensive glass packaging, filling and distribution service for the drinks industry.

The attraction of such high-quality foreign direct investment is a crucial economic driver for England's North West and an important element of the regional economic strategy. It delivers employment, higher salaries, advanced skills, new technologies and a positive image of the region, helping to strengthen the regional supply chain and maximize the opportunities arising from the North West's science and technology base.

Scientific research and development

The region is already an international leader in scientific research and development, and a premier location for biomanufacturing in Europe. The life sciences sector is supported by the presence of leading international pharmaceutical companies, including Avecia, Aventis, Eli Lilly, Unilever and GlaxoSmithKline. AstraZeneca is to build a new £61 million cancer research centre at its Alderley Park site, and Chiron Vaccines, the United Kingdom's leading vaccine manufacturer, is investing £85 million to expand its manufacturing capacity and development capabilities. The NWDA provided funding support of £20 million to enable this to happen.

The Agency has also allocated £30 million for the creation of a National Biomanufacturing Centre to focus on biotechnology business development. The facility will support university start-ups and provide a crucial bridge between academic innovation and commercial bioman-ufacture development. Lilly will further strengthen this biomanufac-turing capacity, investing £45 million in its manufacturing centre at Speke, to expand capability for its growth hormone product.

Support services for this sector, including technical consulting, analytical service providers, patents and licensing, distribution, waste disposal, recruitment and full-service marketing, are also very well established. The Northwest Science Council, and the NWDA's industry development group, Bionow, both provide a range of support. The region also has the capacity to accommodate companies at all stages of their development, with two specialist incubators in Liverpool and Manchester.

Aerospace

The North West is the largest single centre of aerospace manufacturing and production in the United Kingdom and a leading centre of excel-lence in Europe. Over 60,000 people work in the sector, contributing £7 billion to the regional economy through companies such as BAE Systems, Airbus and TRW-Lucas.

The North West Aerospace Alliance was formed 10 years ago to maintain the region as a global leader within the aerospace economy, and is dedicated to championing the North West's knowledge, expe-rience and competitiveness in this vibrant sector. Funded by the NWDA, the Alliance is working to facilitate activity in the region to enable North West companies to successfully bid for aerospace contracts and last year the two organizations combined their expertise to profile the North West at the prestigious International Air Show in Paris.

Automotive industry

Home to vehicle manufacturers such as Jaguar, General Motors and Bentley, England's North West has the third largest automotive output in the country and employs over 15,000 people. The Ford Halewood, Merseyside plant produces the Jaguar X Type and is one of Ford's most advanced plants. General Motors' Vauxhall plant is based at Ellesmere Port, Cheshire, and is investing a further £80 million on upgrading to enable the assembly of both Astra and Vectra models.

Digital industries

Over 60,000 people are employed in digital industries in the North West, with leading technology companies including IBM, Hewlett-Packard, Brother, Sharp, ICL, Siemens, Philips and Photronics. As the second biggest digital cluster in Europe, the region also has a proven track record as a winning location for leading software projects.

The North West's eight universities have a strong technology base, providing over 15,000 science and technology graduates. The National Advanced Robotics Research Centre is based at Salford; the National Computing Centre is in Manchester, and Liverpool Digital, an ICT centre of excellence and major knowledge-based centre, is currently being developed to accommodate ICT companies in a dynamic environment. Digital Industries Northwest, supported by the NWDA, was established in 2002 to promote the region's outstanding capability in the digital sector, providing information on the skills of companies, research and sources of financial assistance found in the region.

Service sectors

England's North West is a leading region for business excellence, being particularly successful in attracting and retaining contact centres and shared service centres. These cover a diverse range of sectors, including banking and financial services, technical support, mail order, product fulfilment and distribution. The region's people are key to its success – offering a large pool of skilled people, above-average staff retention, a multilingual society and excellent ITC literacy. An advanced telecoms environment offers contact centres the dual benefits of high bandwidth and low costs.

High-quality workforce

Market leading companies such as MBNA International, IBM, Shell, US Airways and Arvato Services have all cited the quality of the local workforce as a key factor in their choice of location. JT International, the world's third largest international tobacco company, opened a new European Business Services Centre for large volume financial transaction processing in Manchester recently, following regional selective assistance funding from the NWDA.

Transport communications

The region's first-class travel links also place the North West as a leading business location. Manchester International Airport is the

United Kingdom's largest airport outside London. It serves over 19 million passengers a year, with flights to over 170 destinations worldwide, and 103 European cities. Liverpool John Lennon Airport is also Britain's fastest-growing regional airport handling 2 million passengers a year. With such a network, the region can ensure first-class global access for businesses, people and goods.

The region is also exceptionally well served with 10 ports, including a deep-sea port and free port. These handle a total of 42 million tonnes of freight every year. Liverpool Docks handle over 28 million tonnes alone and have daily ferry services to Northern Ireland and the Irish Republic.

England's North West also has the highest concentration of motorways in the country. The United Kingdom's main North–South and East–West routes both run through the region, linking companies quickly to the rest of the United Kingdom and Europe.

Real estate

Fundamental to the prosperity of the North West is the ability to offer a high-quality portfolio of sites to potential investors and firms, and the NWDA has designated a list of strategic regional sites, which will act as a key resource for attracting inward investment. These include the 558-acre Omega site near Warrington and a new science park at Daresbury.

Incentives and financial assistance

There is a wide range of financial assistance available for companies locating in the North West. The NWDA alone is responsible for business finance worth £80 million to the region's businesses. This includes the North West Business Investment Scheme, a £17.5 million initiative to enhance the growth of the region's small businesses. The newly launched North West Seed Fund will also invest £4.5 million to help the region's entrepreneurs take ideas from the drawing board to achieving their first sales.

Work environment

The North West's offer to international businesses is compelling and highly competitive. The region is home to a highly skilled and productive workforce and its centres of academic excellence and strength in innovation makes it the perfect location for dynamic businesses. The planned merger of the University of Manchester and

UMIST into a single, world-class institution will attract the best students and academics from across the world, reinforcing the already excellent research and development facilities and support.

Quality of life

The North West is also one of the most vibrant regions in Europe. The region's sports teams and musicians are renowned throughout the world and the North West boasts some of the best arts and sports facilities, with shopping and nightlife second to none.

The region offers one of the highest qualities of life anywhere in the United Kingdom, providing an excellent balance between the metropolitan and the rural, between affordable housing and easy commuting, between high technology and traditional values. The North West is a region that offers something for everyone; from the exquisite beauty of the Lake District to the cosmopolitan life of Manchester; and from the ancient Roman heritage of Chester to the maritime history of Liverpool. The people in the region are renowned for their friendliness and hospitality, and the multicultural society offers a range of cultures and traditions to inspire and educate.

Forward strategy

In 2003, the Northwest Development Agency launched the Regional Economic Strategy, a blueprint for the region's future, building on all of the region's outstanding qualities, and providing the economic development framework for the whole of the North West. In delivering the strategy, the NWDA is working hard to transform the region through sustainable economic development, improving competitiveness, while at the same time protecting and enhancing its diverse environment, tackling the causes of social exclusion, and recognizing the needs and contribution of everyone.

Historically, the North West has been the engine of the United Kingdom's growth, having led the world in the industrial revolution to being a significant contributor in the development of the information and knowledge revolution. Today the region is home to a wealth of talent and an innovative and entrepreneurial spirit continues to thrive.

England's North West is a region on the move and the NWDA is firmly committed to maintaining that momentum. For further information please visit www.englandsnorthwest.com or www.nwda.co.uk.

6.3

Yorkshire and Humber

Yorkshire Forward

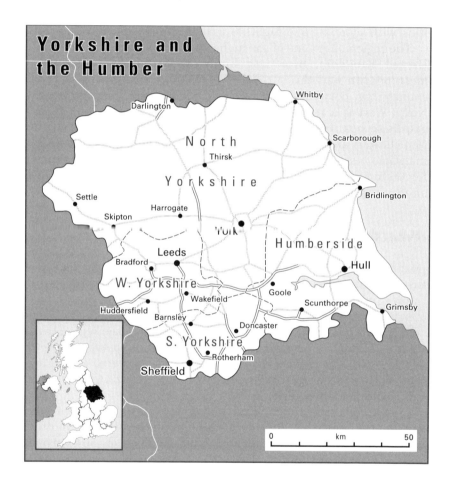

Need to expand?

Need the right property?
Need the right people?

Need to ask your questions once,
not a thousand times?

Need quick, honest answers?

You need Invest in Bradford

**Talk to us. Contact Stuart Byrnes
and tell us what you need**

Tel: 01274 437727
www.investinbradford.com

Supported by the European Union

investinbradford

New figures show that Yorkshire and Humber is now the United Kingdom's most profitable region with companies generating returns of nearly 12 per cent on their capital – more than twice the national average – and excellent news for the region's 1,100 foreign-owned companies already located in the region. The findings, by Experian, show that Yorkshire and Humber is bucking the national trend of a decline in profitability, with companies making increasing returns on their investments in each of the last four quarters. These findings follow the latest regional survey of economic trends carried out by Yorkshire Forward and the Confederation of British Industry (CBI), which shows that business confidence levels in the region are at their highest for three years – with domestic orders improving and employment levels at a 30-year high.

In fact, overall, Yorkshire and Humber's £65 billion economy is growing faster than the European average, with some of its fastest growth in the future expected to come from a number of key clusters such as digital industries and chemicals. Since 1989, GDP has increased by 75 per cent and GDP per head is now £12,648. By 2009, the regional economy is forecast to grow by 18 per cent. Distribution, hotels and catering and financial services are two of the largest contributors to the economy, while outside of London, the region has the third highest number of plc headquarters, with 101 companies.

Table 6.3.1 Output by sector (£ billion)

Sector	2002	2009
Agriculture Forestry & Fishing	0.933	0.923
Extraction of Oil & Gas	0.027	0.027
Mining & Utilities	1.572	1.314
Metals, Minerals & Chemicals	4.019	4.222
Engineering & Vehicles	2.701	3.251
Other Manufacturing	6.223	6.654
Construction	4.085	4.779
Distribution, Hotels & Catering	10.527	12.503
Transport & Communications	5.236	6.822
Financial & Business Services	8.896	12.124
Other services	15.110	17.246
TOTAL	59.329	69.865

Source: Experian Business Strategies, Regional Planning Service, 2003

The region's population of 5 million, equivalent to that of Scotland or Denmark, enjoys a quality of life unrivalled in the country, with three National Parks, a stunning coastline and the mix of modern, cosmopolitan cities and historic market towns with easy access to the rest of the United Kingdom. On a day-to-day basis, travel to work times are among the lowest in the country, investment incentives are among

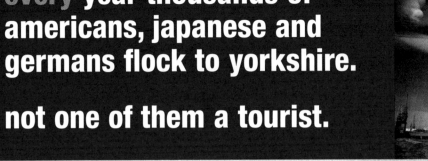

every year thousands of americans, japanese and germans flock to yorkshire.

not one of them a tourist.

These days the business world is beating a path to Yorkshire and the Humber's door.

A strong skills base, superb transport network and an economy growing faster than the European average have turned the region into one of the best possible locations for any business looking to relocate or expand.

Add to that Yorkshire's eight world-class universities spending twice the national average on R&D – over £284 million – and a regional venture capital market worth over £500 million and it's easy to see how much support businesses enjoy in the region.

And when you consider that Yorkshire and the Humber currently offers one of the best financial assistance packages in Europe, it's hardly surprising that the region has already attracted over 1100 overseas businesses – including half of the world's ten most respected companies.

To find out more about the opportunities in Yorkshire & the Humber, call +44 (0)113 394 9708, email marketing@yorkshire-forward.com or visit www.yorkshire-forward.com to request your free Business Guide to Yorkshire.

It could be the best move you ever make.

YORKSHIRE FORWARD

Yorkshire *Alive with Opportunity!*

www.yorkshire-forward.com

the most generous in the United Kingdom and with space to develop and grow the region offers the perfect environment for potential investors. Industrial rents measured against the United Kingdom average are some of the lowest of any region and office costs begin as low as £9 per square metre.

The region's geographical position, equidistant between London and Edinburgh, has proved to be a successful strategic location for many companies with the East Coast mainline putting London within two hours' reach, while a catchment market of more than 25 million people is available within a three-hour drive.

Finningley Airport near Doncaster is set to become the country's first new international airport in more than 20 years when it opens in 2007 while the government has just announced plans for the expansion of Leeds/Bradford and Humberside airports. The region also benefits from direct rail access to Manchester Airport while North Sea Ferries offers daily overnight sailings to mainland Europe.

In 2002, against a national decline, Yorkshire and Humber accounted for around 4 per cent of total foreign direct investment projects. New investors to the region over recent years include Guardian Glass, which has invested £115 million in a new plant at Goole, and Nippon Gohsei, which has developed a new chemical production plant on the Humber to supply its European markets with a now environmentally friendly synthetic packaging material.

Yorkshire and Humber has one of the best financial packages available for business anywhere in Europe including the £1.8 billion Objective 1 programme in South Yorkshire. Leeds, the region's capital, is BT's second city in the United Kingdom after London and has the largest internet server in Europe, with a third of all the United Kingdom's internet traffic passing through the city. The region also has one of the highest levels of broadband penetration with all its major cities enabled while Hull, home to Kingston Communications, boasts the most advanced telecoms system in Europe in terms of transmitting video over digital subscriber lines (DSL).

The region boasts nine universities, producing 45,000 highly skilled graduates a year with business studies, medicine and engineering among the leading qualifications. The region's universities invest more than twice the national average on research and development, equivalent to more than Oxford and Cambridge combined. Strengths include biomaterials and tissue engineering, stem cell biology, polymers, particle science and materials analysis.

Yorkshire Forward has pioneered a number of initiatives to help exploit this research strength to benefit businesses through a network of Centres of Industrial Collaboration, helping firms to innovate their products and processes to stay ahead of their competitors. Yorkshire Forward's team of professional advisors around the globe provide a

a brighter
business future...

SPACE & SUCCESS
Sites and premises readily available
More than four out of five businesses operating profitably

SUPERB TRANSPORT LINKS
At the heart of the UK, with comprehensive road, rail and air networks

COMMITMENT
Hard work and quality production

QUALITY OF LIFE
70% rural, with a quality of life that is hard to beat

space

prosperity

industry

...in

ROTHERHAM
UK

Locate in a place that matches your ambitions

RELOCATING companies need partners whose ambitions can match and support their own, especially if the project is in a new location, possibly in a foreign land.

The track record of the metropolitan borough of Rotherham, at the heart of the UK, shows that it not only has big ideas but that it makes them work, to the benefit of its people and its business sector.

Future prospect? Express Park's proposals for Rotherham's Manvers Lakeside.

Rotherham is passionate about progress and committed to business, which helps explain why almost 90 overseas companies, including 20 from the USA, have chosen this 110-square-mile (285km²) borough. They achieve handsome payback on investment, and independent surveys have consistently shown that about four out of five companies operate profitably in the borough.

Business people testify to the quality of the workforce and the support they get from Rotherham Borough Council and its regeneration arm, Rotherham Investment & Development Office.

Among others on hand to help companies are South Yorkshire Investment Fund, Business Link South Yorkshire, Renaissance South Yorkshire and Yorkshire Forward, and the EU's Rotherham-based Objective 1 office for South Yorkshire.

Business benefits include the highest level of financial support in Europe and excellent interstate and rail links that mean cities such as London, Manchester, Liverpool and Sheffield are anything from a few minutes to two hours away.

Other important benefits include quality of life, a pleasant environment – the borough is 70% rural and highly attractive prices on land, premises and homes. Research in early 2004 showed it to be one of the top four safest places in Yorkshire and Humber, a region of some five million people.

The head of Toyoda Gosei, part of the Toyota group, Mr Tokio Horigome, summed up the attractions when the company chose Rotherham for its first European car-components plant:

> **"We decided to build in Rotherham because the total evaluation is the best. We are deeply beholden to the Government and Rotherham Borough in particular for their tremendous support and unfailing co-operation every step of the way."**

Toyoda Gosei forecast 300 jobs by the end of 2004. It is now approaching 700.

Latest ambitious projects include Rotherham Renaissance, a 20-year regeneration of its town centre. It is already under way and is expected to attract many hundreds of thousands of pounds' worth of investment . It has just won support from legendary England goalkeeper David Seaman – a native of the borough.

Two £100m ($184m) developments are under way, both at Manvers, in the north of the borough. Just announced is a project to create a business park, leisure complex, golf course and homes on 280 acres (113 hectares) around Manvers Lake. At the time of going to press, Anglo-Dutch company Express Park Developments is preparing to submit its planning application to Rotherham Council. And South Yorkshire company St Paul's Developments is well into preparing an 84-acre (34ha) near-neighbour site for a variety of business uses.

Ready and waiting: new high-spec space at Rotherham's Manvers Enterprise Zone, which offers special business incentives.

Such projects symbolise how Rotherham's public-private

partnership approach has transformed the economic landscape across the borough. Manufacturing,

Into the future: illustration of planned keystone building on the Advanced Manufacturing Park, Rotherham.

including steel and engineering, is still a major feature, and is increasingly being joined by advanced manufacturing, high-tech and IT.

The Advanced Manufacturing Park is already being developed jointly by regional development agency Yorkshire Forward and site-owner UK Coal. The Park has already attracted a joint Boeing-Sheffield University Advanced Manufacturing Research Centre – one of only about 12 worldwide – Britain's National Metals Technology Centre, and TWI, The Welding Institute, from Cambridge.

Entrepreneurs with ambitions to start their own businesses are also greatly supported, with special full-service business centres to nurture them.

Rotherham Investment & Development Office is dedicated to inward investment and support for companies, whether new or already in the borough, helping them find the right sites and premises, the right workforce, financial support, customers…and easing them through planning and other issues.

Virginia KMP, part of the worldwide Kenmore International Group, chose Rotherham for the manufacture of refrigeration components and supplies a comprehensive range of chemicals and components to European commercial refrigeration and air-conditioning markets.

Going up: Newburgh's key account director David Greenan, left, and joint MD Vincent Middleton, centre, hitch a lift for an overview of their £5.5m new Rotherham factory.

"Everyone involved with the area seemed really to have their act together," said finance director Phil Brooke."

A leading engineering company, Newburgh, is investing £5.5m to set up a manufacturing operation in Rotherham that will employ more than 40 people.

It makes and supplies components for industries ranging from aerospace to deep-sea oil extraction. It is based in Bradwell, North Derbyshire, but its Rotherham plant, at Templeborough, is now completed.

Joint managing director Vincent Middleton said: "RiDO has been brilliant. Yorkshire Forward and Objective 1 have also been excellent. They are all enthusiastic about manufacturing and engineering."

Riverside regeneration: the Rotherham Renaissance project focuses on the River Don, flowing through the town centre.

Entrepreneur Gordon Styles chose Rotherham for his Springer Rapid Industries because of the partnership approach and that same enthusiasm.

"All the agencies have been incredibly helpful including Yorkshire Forward, Renaissance and RiDO," he said.

To join the success story, contact RiDO at:
Reresby House, Bow Bridge Close, Templeborough, Rotherham S60 1YR
Tel: +44 (0)1709 372099   Fax: +44 (0)1709 837953
Email: info@rido.org.uk   www.rido.org.uk
www.dearnevalley.org   www.buy-local.co.uk

RiDO
Rotherham Investment
& Development Office

single point of contact for any company looking to expand or relocate into the United Kingdom. Its services are free and cover everything from guidance on financial incentives and access to its world-class research and development expertise, to information on recruitment and training. For more information visit www.yorkshire-forward.com.

6.3.1 BARNSLEY

Easily accessed via the main UK road network and surrounded by rolling countryside, Barnsley offers an excellent location for business and an unrivalled quality of life.

Barnsley is located in the centre of the United Kingdom and within two hours' drive there is access to a market of 21 million people; within 24 hours goods can reach a market of 170 million across Europe. Four international airports, at Manchester, Leeds-Bradford, East Midlands and Humberside, all lie within an hour's drive of Barnsley.

The traditional industries of mining and engineering in Barnsley have provided investors with a legacy of high-tech skills, which have proved easily transferable, offering companies a highly skilled workforce to meet their business requirements. In addition, young people coming into the workforce benefit from extensive education and training facilities in the area.

To ensure that Barnsley becomes an even more desirable place to live, work, shop and to visit, a major urban renaissance programme named 'Remaking Barnsley' is under way. The programme has a long-term vision of 30 years, with projects in the first five years providing the catalyst for change, bringing improved confidence and new investment into the town.

Two of the first major transformational projects are 'The Barnsley Market Project' and the redevelopment of the transport interchange. The market project is now well under way, with more than £30 million invested to acquire the site. The project will bring extensive retail and leisure facilities to drive the local economy, providing new employment and attracting more shoppers and visitors. The £23 million redevelopment of the interchange, planned to start in 2004, will see existing bus and rail facilities brought together through a ground-breaking design, unique to Barnsley.

Barnsley Development Agency (BDA) is home to Barnsley Metropolitan Borough Council's Inward Investment and Development Team, which offers potential inward investors a friendly and professional service, free of charge. Services provided by this team include land and property information and advice; planning information and advice; financial assistance and grant availability; recruitment and training support; business advice; ongoing project support and an aftercare programme second to none.

The team at BDA has been working hard, with property developers on the preparation of business plans, site investigations and feasibility studies for a number of employment sites across Barnsley. This partnership approach to working with the private sector will result in the availability of new high-quality developments becoming available during 2004 and the provision of additional strategically located, serviced employment land. Major business parks are being developed adjacent to the M1 motorway at J36, M1 J37 and in the Dearne Valley, providing hundreds of acres of serviced employment land with speculative high-quality business units planned for 2004.

The highest level of government and EU financial support is available to companies locating in Barnsley. With excellent access to the whole of the UK transport network, attractive land values, a skilled and loyal workforce and ongoing support from the BDA, Barnsley has many incentives to offer inward investors.

Many companies have seen the advantages of locating in Barnsley. True Manufacturing, a US world leader in the development and manufacture of commercial refrigeration products for the food and beverage industry, located its European headquarters in Barnsley. Steve Young, General Manager commented: 'We located our new facility in Barnsley because of its central location and availability of quality personnel. Moreover, we found the help and advice of BDA in finding our way through UK regulations invaluable.'

For further information please contact Barnsley Development Agency, Beevor Court, Pontefract Road, Barnsley, S71 1HG. Tel: +44 (0) 1226 784451; e-mail: equiries@barnsleydevelopmentagency.co.uk.

Demographics

Barnsley has a population of 218,000 of which 132,000 (61%) are of working age.

Table 6.3.1.1 Population and age distribution

Age Range	Total	% Total
0–4	12,498	5.7
5–9	14,570	6.7
10–14	14,544	6.7
15–24	23,840	10.9
25–39	47,678	21.9
40–59	58,352	26.8
60–74	30,417	13.9
75+	16,163	7.4
Total	**218062**	**100**

Source: National Census, 2001

There are 1.3 million people of working age within a 30 minute driving radius of Barnsley and nearly 4.5 million people within a 60 minute radius.

The key employers in Barnsley are manufacturing industries, specifically food manufacturing (employs over 2,000 people), glass products (employs over 2,000 people), and window and doors (employs around 1,650 people). The service industry has grown significantly accounting for 73 per cent of jobs in Barnsley. The largest employers are healthcare, retail and business services.

Table 6.3.1.2   Workforce and distribution by industry

Industry	Workforce	%
Primary Industries	152	0.2
Manufacturing	13977	19.1
Construction and Utilities	5767	7.9
Wholesale/retail trade; repair, etc	11048	15.1
Hotels and restaurants	4201	5.7
Transport, storage and communication	4901	6.7
Financial intermediation	1349	1.8
Real estate,renting,business activities	6239	8.5
Public admin/defence; social security	4060	5.5
Education	7717	10.5
Health and social work	9815	13.4
Other community, social/personal service	3969	5.4
Total	**73196**	**100**

Source: Annual Business Inquiry, 2002

Local economy

Table 6.3.1.3   Structure of Business Numbers by main industry sector/activity

Industry	%
Primary Industries	0.2
Manufacturing	8.7
Construction and Utilities	11.4
Wholesale/retail trade; repair, etc	27.3
Hotels and restaurants	8.1
Transport, storage and communication	6.2
Financial intermediation	2.1
Real estate, renting, business activities	17.6
Public admin/defence; social security	1.8
Education	3
Health and social work	5.9
Other community, social/personal service	7.6

Source: Annual Business Inquiry, 2002

Table 6.3.1.4   Structure of Value Added by Sector 2001

	% Total Value Added
Primary Industries	2%
Manufacturing	27%
Construction & Utilities	11%
Retail & Distribution	27%
Business Services	9%
Public Services	20%
Other Services	3%

Source: Yorkshire Forward/Business Strategies Regional Econometric Model 2003 (2001 Baseline data)

Employment statistics

Approximately 89,000 people aged 16–74 are in employment. Barnsley has a workforce with a diverse range of skills. There is a large labour pool of skilled manual workers as well as people with professional, technical and managerial skills.

Table 6.3.1.5   Occupation breakdown

Occupation	%
Managers and senior officials	11.2
Professional occupations	7.0
Associate professional and technical occupations	10.6
Administrative and secretarial occupations	10.8
Skilled trades occupations	14.5
Personal service occupations	7.8
Sales and customer service occupations	8.6
Process; plant and machine operatives	13.7
Elementary occupations	15.7

Source: National Census 2001

Table 6.3.1.6   Full-, Part-time and self-employment

	Part-time	Full-time	Self-employed
% of those employed	22.5	66.1	11.4

Source: National Census, 2001

Factory and office rentals and local taxes

Quality industrial premises are very competitively priced.

Table 6.3.1.7   Rental rates by type of premises

Type	Rent per sq.ft
Standard industrial	£3 – 4.50
High quality industrial	£5 – 6
Office rental (urban centre)	£12 – 13
Technology incubation units	£11 – 12
Retail (Prime Zone A)	£110–120

Source: Barnsley Development Agency. NB these are approximate rents

Transport and Communications

Barnsley is well served by air, road, rail and waterways transport links.

By road

The town has excellent access to the national motorway network with Junction 37 of the M1 only 1.5 miles to the west of the town centre.

By rail

Barnsley has excellent regional passenger rail routes to London. Operators provide frequent services with journey times of 90 minutes on certain routes.

Regional Rail Ports provide flexible overnight freight rail access to the Channel Tunnel and the Humberside Sea Ports in the East giving access to Koln (Germany) and Lille (France). Rail freight hubs can be reached within 36 hours.

At the end of these road and rail routes lay the UK's gateways to the world: airports, seaports and the direct route to the European mainland – the Channel Tunnel.

By air

There are four international airports within a 60 minute drive of Barnsley. Manchester International Airport serves over 150 international destinations, including daily flights to North America, Europe, Asia and the Middle East. Major airlines serving Manchester International Airport include: British Airways, Virgin Atlantic, US Airways, Singapore Airlines, and BMI. Leeds Bradford, East Midlands, and Humberside Airports have direct daily flights within the British Isles, and to many European destinations and connections worldwide.

By sea

The excellent Humberside International Ports are within 60 minutes drive from Barnsley. They are accessible 24 hours a day and the new deepwater international cargo terminal makes worldwide port sailings possible. From the Humberside ports some 170 million European customers are accessible within 24 hours through ports in Germany, the Netherlands, Scandinavia, and the Baltic Sea Region.

Foreign Direct Investment

Value of current and accumulated inward investment by country of origin and industry sector

BDA has supported 54 inward investments into Barnsley, which have created 2,200 jobs since 1997. Inward investment projects have mainly come from within the UK, with the second largest source of investment being the United States.

Table 6.3.1.8   Sources of inward investment

Country of Origin	% of projects	% of jobs created
France	2	1
Germany	4	2
Italy	2	1
Japan	2	8
Norway	2	0
USA	13	31
UK	76	57

Source: BDA Database 1997–2003

Availability of EU structural funds and investment incentives

Barnsley is in the highest tier for UK assistance, which means businesses can receive the highest levels of support from Regional Selective Assistance and Regional Enterprise Grants. As part of South Yorkshire it also benefits from the £700 million EU Objective 1 Programme providing support for economic development in South Yorkshire. BDA also offers financial support for workforce training, product feasibility studies and exhibitions.

Infrastructure

Telecommunications (including broadband availability)

The main regional operators are BT, ntl and Telewest. Broadband is now available in most areas.

Business parks

Barnsley is home to BBIC – the UK's largest business innovation centre, which has helped over 70 small high-tech businesses to grow and flourish.

Education, research and development

Universities and technical colleges

Barnsley's neighbouring cities – Sheffield and Leeds – each have two top-class universities: Leeds Metropolitan University, Leeds University, Sheffield University and Sheffield Hallam University. The Universities have strengths in: Biosciences and Biomedical sciences; Material, Mechanical, Electrical and Electronics Engineering; Food Sciences; Environmental and Earth Sciences; Information Studies; Computing; Art and Industrial Design; and Languages.

Vocational training centres

Barnsley College offers a diverse training programme in a wide range of vocations and subjects. Courses are offered at levels to suit all needs from basic skills levels to professional accreditation to degree-level qualifications (from Sheffield and Leeds Universities).

Dearne Valley College is a short travelling distance from Barnsley and offers customized courses to meet the needs of businesses. Short courses provided range from Windows software training (Word, Excel, PowerPoint etc) to business related courses.

Local service providers

Public sector support agencies

BDA works closely with Yorkshire Forward – The Regional Development Agency for Yorkshire and the Humber, Jobcentre Plus Teams offering recruitment advice and assistance and Business Link South Yorkshire for business support provision.

Local authority planning services – Barnsley Metropolitan Borough Council

Barnsley Chamber of Commerce is a partner in the BDA.

For further information please contact Barnsley Chamber of Commerce and Industry, Innovation Way, Wilthorpe, Barnsley, S75 1JL. Tel: +44 (0) 1226 217770; Fax: +44 (0) 1226 215729; e-mail: info@barnsleychamber.co.uk.

6.3.2 DONCASTER
A new outlook

Doncaster covers an area of 57,000 hectares, with a population of approximately 286,866 people. In the heart of the town, regeneration plans are under way for some of the most exciting projects Yorkshire has ever seen. These plans will produce many commercial developments, all of which will be contemporary yet functional and will offer something for everyone. With so many projects currently being built or at an advanced planning stage it is exciting to envisage what the town will look like in five years' time. It appears that no other town or city in the country is currently immersing itself in so many large-scale projects within such a small time scale.

A brand new urban infrastructure

So, what are these projects? With £700 million pounds of European funding being used to restructure the economy of the Doncaster area there are some action-packed plans to create a number of innovative developments.

One of the furthest developed and most dramatic projects to appear in Doncaster is Lakeside, located just outside the town centre. Lakeside has become one of the leading business parks in the North of England. The centrepiece of the site is a 52-acre man-made lake, which will provide visitors with the use of water sports.

Another exciting prospect for Doncaster, and indeed the region, is the development of an international airport at Finningley, which will hold 2.3 million passengers. The airport will create 7,300 jobs for the region by 2014; there will be 5,600 onsite and 1,700 outside the airport in surrounding communities.

There are a number of widespread regeneration projects across Doncaster at the moment, all of them offering an imaginative host of investment opportunities as well as increasing employment.

Doncaster
discover the spirit

ready to fly?

Spread your wings in Doncaster and experience the thrill of success in this unique, entrepreneurial environment.

With its strategic location, a motivated and flexible workforce, unparalleled choice of sites and properties and commitment to success, Doncaster can offer you and your business unlimited opportunities.

For professional and friendly advice on the right location, financial support and recruitment and training assistance, contact the Investment Team on 01302 736975.

The Investment Team
Doncaster Metropolitan Borough Council
Enterprise House
White Rose Way, Hyde Park
Doncaster DN4 5ND
T · 01302 736975

THE **DONCASTER**
DYNAMIC >>

Frenchgate Interchange

The town centre is now well under way with work on the new retail and transport development, Frenchgate Interchange. The new centre will be twice as big and most importantly will create a 21st-century shopping experience overtaking many areas of the region. The project will incorporate:

- an integrated transport interchange combining the existing bus and railway station;
- high-quality passenger facilities;
- upgraded Frenchgate Shopping Centre with many additional stores;
- 20,000 square feet of refurbished office space.

Education City

A major part of Doncaster's vision is the creation of the new Doncaster Education City. Valued at £250 million, this project is the largest education development in the country. It will provide:

- an integrated approach to learning;
- learning through state-of-the-art teaching methods;
- Doncaster with a proposed university;
- Doncaster's people with better skills, better qualifications and in the long term more opportunities.

Doncaster Waterfront

Doncaster's Waterfront provides a unique and significant development opportunity and offers one of the largest and most exciting opportunities in the sub-region to create a high-quality waterfront destination. The proposed plans are to:

- redevelop the traditional markets area into a fully serviced prime development site, which maximizes its water-based location;
- deliver a new marina with residential units;
- build development platforms to accommodate a range of mixed uses.

There is much happening in Doncaster at the moment; it is definitely a great place to be in business. Doncaster constantly attracts both visitors as well as capital investors. Many new investors choose Doncaster due to its site locations, excellent transport links and a dynamism, which is making people sit up and take notice.

With its town centre awarded as 'the best-performing town centre in 2003', along with some of the most exciting development opportunities in Yorkshire, Doncaster looks set to hold a dynamic future.

6.4

West Midlands

West Midlands Development Agency

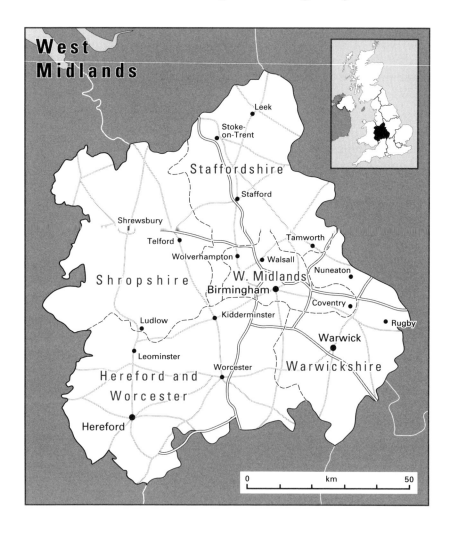

The West Midlands is one the United Kingdom's primary regions for commerce and industry with 180,000 companies accounting for 9 per cent of UK GDP and 10 per cent of the UK workforce. Situated 110 miles northwest of London with a population of 5.3 million the West Midlands is home to the United Kingdom's 'Second City' – Birmingham. Please see 'Key statistics for the West Midlands', Table 6.4.1, at the end of this chapter.

Universities

The West Midlands is a large academic centre with 64 centres of further education and nine universities producing over 35,000 graduates per year. Some of the key universities in the region are listed below:

Aston University	www.aston.ac.uk
Birmingham College of Food, Tourism and Creative Studies	www.bcftcs.ac.uk
Birmingham School of Speech and Drama	www.bssd.ac.uk
The University of Birmingham	www.bham.ac.uk
University of Central England in Birmingham	www.uce.ac.uk
Coventry University	www.coventry.ac.uk
Harper Adams University College	www.harper-adams.ac.uk
Keele University	www.keele.ac.uk
Newman College of Higher Education	www.newman.ac.uk
Open University	www.open.ac.uk
Staffordshire University	www.staffs.ac.uk
University of Warwick	www.warwick.ac.uk
University of Wolverhampton	www.wlv.ac.uk
University College Worcester	www.worc.ac.uk

Source: Higher Education Research Opportunities

Science/business parks

The region has eight science parks located in Warwick, Coventry, Birmingham, Aston, Keele, Stafford, Wolverhampton and Malvern:

University of Warwick Science Park	www.uwsp.co.uk
Coventry University Technology Park	www.cutp.co.uk
Birmingham Research Park	www.bham.ac.uk/BRPL
Aston Science Park	www.astonsciencepark.co.uk
Keele University Science Park	www.keele.ac.uk/depts/uso/scipark.htm

Why West Midlands?

1 Unique Central Location

The West Midlands Region is uniquely situated at the heart of the UK's road and rail network. 75% of the UK's population are closer than a 5 hours' truck drive away. Birmingham New

Street station offers more passenger services to more locations than any other station in the UK. Birmingham International Airport is the second largest airport in the UK outside London and offers scheduled and charter flights to over 100 destinations worldwide.

This offers your business the unrivalled ability to reach customers, suppliers and partners throughout the Region, the UK and the world rapidly and easily. It also provides your staff with a superb transportation infrastructure – enabling them to get to work and conduct your business smoothly and efficiently.

2 Established and Competitive Business base

There are more than 180,000 companies here – including the presence of over 2,000 non-UK companies from some 40 countries who employ more than 10% of the Region's workforce. The regional strengths include Manufacturing, IT, Food & Drink, Distribution & Logistics, and Professional Services. Birmingham, the second largest city in the UK, is independently rated as a leading major European city for high value and cost effective Shared Service Center operations. For instance PWC has 1400 employees based in Birmingham of which 300 professionals work in either the Human Resources or Tax Compliance Shared Service Centers.

3 The Place to Live and Work

The region is renowned for its rural setting amongst its thriving cities and towns. Property prices in the Region are significantly below the national average; we have one of Europe's largest, cost effective and skilled labour pools; personal and corporate taxes which are among the lowest in the European Union; 10 renowned universities and other centres of excellence work with businesses to extend the technological and commercial excellence of the Region.

Your Gateway to the Region

Advantage West Midlands is the Government Agency dedicated to driving the economic development of the West Midlands Region. Whether you need information on properties, financial incentives, statistics on economics, demographics or supply chains, and our **free and confidential** investment advice service will give you a head start.

Please contact us at **+44 (0)121 380 3500** to find out how we can help you share in the success of our Region.

Staffordshire Technology Park	www.staffstechpark.org.uk
Wolverhampton Science Park	www.wolverhamptonsp.co.uk
Malvern Hills Science Park	www.mhsp.co.uk

Source: UK Trade and Investment

Research infrastructure

There are a number of high-profile research organizations based in the West Midlands that specialize in connecting research, education and industry:

Polymer Training	www.polymertraining.co.uk
Motor Industry Research Association	www.mira.co.uk
QinetiQ	www.qinetiq.com
Rubber & Plastics Research Association	www.rapra.net
British Ceramics Research Association	www.ceram.co.uk
Warwick Manufacturing Group	www.wmg.warwick.ac.uk

Source: UK Trade & Investment

Transport links

Roads

Main roads in the region:

M6 (inc. Toll)	A38M
M42	M69
M54	M40
M5	M50

Distances by road from London (City):

Birmingham – 120 miles
Coventry – 99 miles
Dudley – 132 miles
Sandwell – 126 miles
Solihull – 113 miles
Walsall – 125 miles
Wolverhampton – 132 miles

Airports

Birmingham International Airport	www.bhx.co.uk
Coventry-Baginton Airport	www.coventryairport.co.uk

Rail

Centro is the corporate name of the West Midlands Passenger Transport Executive. This body is responsible for promoting and developing public transport across the West Midlands metropolitan area. There are eight local rail lines in the West Midlands, providing links to the rest of the United Kingdom. The region also has a new light rail system, known as the Midland Metro. The first line of the service, Line One, provides a fast link between Snow Hill Station in Birmingham City Centre and Wolverhampton via West Bromwich and Wednesbury.

Inward investment

One of the key aims of inward investment strategies in the region is to ensure that the West Midlands maintains and increases its share of inward investment. This is done through the implementation of a cluster-focused inward investment strategy, which principally entails inward investment being prioritized towards five key areas:

- transport technologies;
- food and drink;
- ICT;
- business and professional services;
- medical technologies.

There are two additional clusters that form a secondary focus for inward investment into the region: environmental technologies and building technologies. These activities are supported by a network of overseas support in the Americas, Europe and Asia (*source: Advantage West Midlands*).

Table 6.4.1 Key statistics for the West Midlands

	West Midlands	United Kingdom
Population, 2001[1] (thousands)	5,267.1	58,836.7
Percentage aged under 16[1]	20.8	20.1
Percentage pension age and over[1]	18.5	18.4
Standardised mortality ratio (UK=100), 2000	102	100
Infant mortality rate,[2] 1999–2001	6.8	5.6
Percentage of pupils achieving [5] or more grades A*–C at GCSE level or equivalent, 2000/01	47.4	51.0

continued overleaf

	West Midlands	United Kingdom
Economic activity rate,[6]		
Spring 2002 (percentages)	78.6	78.5
Employment rate,6 Spring 2002 (percentages)	74.3	74.4
ILO unemployment rate,6 Spring 2002		
(percentages)	5.5	5.2
Average gross weekly earnings: males in		
full-time employment, April 2001 (£)	462.1	488.2
Average gross weekly earnings: females in		
full-time employment, April 2001 (£)	340.9	365.5
Gross domestic product, 1999 (£ million)	63,495	771,849
Gross domestic product per head index,		
1999 (UK=100)	91.7	100.0
Total business sites, 2001 (thousands)	208.1	2,527.2
Average dwelling price, 2001 (£)[3]	97,542	119,982
Motor cars currently licensed,[4] 2001		
(thousands)	2,479	25,340
Fatal and serious accidents on roads,[5] 2000		
(rates per 100,000 population)	59	61
Recorded crime rate, 2001/02 (notifiable		
offences per 100,000 population)[3]	11,881	10,440
Average gross weekly household income,		
1998–2001[7] (£)	462	480
Average weekly household expenditure,		
1998–2001[7] (£)	353.20	365.80
Households in receipt of Income		
Support/WFTC,[5, 8] 2000/01 (percentages)	18	16

1 Population figures for 2001 are the first in a new series that are based on the 2001 Census (see also tables in chapter 1, 3.1, 3.2, 3.3, 3.4, 3.5, 14.1, 15.1, 16.1 and 17.1). The figures for earlier years from 1991 shown in the rest of Regional Trends 37 are unrevised and are not consistent with them. Pension age is men aged 65 and over and women aged 60 and over.
2 Population figures for 2001 are the first in a new series that are based on the 2001 Census (see also tables in chapter 1, 3.1, 3.2, 3.3, 3.4, 3.5, 14.1, 15.1, 16.1 and 17.1). The figures for earlier years from 1991 shown in the rest of Regional Trends 37 are unrevised and are not consistent with them. Pension age is men aged 65 and over and women aged 60 and over.
3 Deaths of infants under 1 year of age per 1,000 live births.
4 Figure for the United Kingdom relates to England and Wales.
5 Totals for the United Kingdom include vehicles where the country of the registered vehicle is unknown, that are under disposal or from counties unknown within Great Britain.
6 Figure for the United Kingdom relates to Great Britain.
7 For people of working age, men aged 16 to 64 and women aged 16 to 59.
8 Combined years 1998–99, 1999–2000 and 2000–01.
9 In October 1999 Family Credit was replaced by Working Families Tax Credit.

6.5

East Midlands

East Midlands Development Agency

The East Midlands is the fourth largest region in the United Kingdom and is truly unique, both geographically and economically. Its central location and five major urban conurbations provide endless advantages to organizations choosing to settle in the area.

Businesses looking for a flexible and highly skilled workforce, a wide spread of industry sectors, excellent communications, cultural diversity and a high quality of life will find that the East Midlands has all these to offer. The six counties – Nottinghamshire, Derbyshire, Leicestershire, Northamptonshire, Lincolnshire and Rutland – all with their individual appeal, can provide a suitable location for everything from growing organic food to programming microchips, and the range of business premises is endless.

An outstanding place to live and work

The East Midlands is home to over 4 million people, over 70 per cent of whom are of working age and nearly 80 per cent economically active in an extensive range of industry sectors. The highly skilled, well-educated and flexible workforce ensures a high level of employment, and companies moving to or expanding in the region enjoy successful recruitment. Patrick Nelson, Director of Corporate Communications for Capital One – which recently established its European Headquarters in Nottingham – said: 'We have been overwhelmed by the response to our job advertisements. We are really encouraged in terms of both the quantity and quality of applications.'

The region's outstanding quality of life, beautiful countryside, vibrant cities and cost-effective living, all encourage people to stay in and return to the East Midlands to live and work. Over 10 per cent of the region has been declared an area of outstanding natural beauty and England's first National Park, the Peak District in Derbyshire, is among over a 100 parks and woodlands open to the public. The three premier cities, Nottingham, Leicester and Derby, provide outstanding shopping, entertainment and culture. The region also boasts fantastic sporting venues including Trent Bridge cricket ground, Walker's Stadium (home to football team Leicester City), Silverstone – the UK's premier international racing circuit – and the National Ice Arena. Simon Proffitt, Research and Development and Site General Manager for Astra Zeneca in Charnwood, Loughborough, said: 'England's East Midlands is an extremely attractive area which has a lot going for it. It has financial advantages over other regions, and there is also a very good quality of life.'

By choosing the region as home for your business you would be joining companies like Rolls Royce, JCB, Capital One, AstraZeneca,

British American Racing, Carlsberg Tetley, Nestlé UK, Boots, Toyota and many more.

A location for business success

The East Midlands' central location and comprehensive network of road, rail, air and sea links means that over 99 per cent of the UK market is within one day's journey by road and major European cities can be reached within hours. The region's airport, Nottingham East Midlands, runs domestic and international flights for passengers and freight. Three major train lines, East Coast, West Coast and Midland Mainline, provide fast rail links throughout the country. Northamptonshire contains two dedicated rail freight terminals and from 2007, the region will connect to Paris and Brussels via the Channel Tunnel. Two motorways, the M1 and the A1 (M), provide fast road links to the North and South. London is only an hour and a half drive from the south of the region and a comprehensive improvement scheme will ensure that the region's roads continue to meet its transport needs. The UK's main northern ports, Felixstowe and Harwich, as well as the Eastern ports, Hull, Immingham and Grimsby are also all in easy reach. Panasonic General Manager Don Gilbert says: 'It was decided that Northampton was ideal in terms of its proximity to our customer base and its central location. Northampton is also ideally placed for all major transport routes; our vehicles can leave the distribution centre up to 10.00pm in the evening and still achieve next day delivery anywhere in the United Kingdom.'

Home to a vast range of businesses, the East Midlands has a GVA (gross value-added) of £55.4 billion and the highest GVA per head outside London and the South East. During 2002–03, over 30 overseas companies chose to invest in the region to join this vibrant and buoyant economy. Originating from Europe, North America and Asia Pacific and covering biotechnology, electronics, automotive, ICT, pharmaceuticals and the food and drink industry, the investment created 1,314 new jobs and safeguarded a further 1,875. The region is the most favoured inward investment region in Europe, attracting over 40 per cent of all European investment from the United States.

Developing the future

The East Midlands Development Agency (emda) is among the most proactive of the UK's regional development agencies, with a distinctive private sector approach. Its goal is for the East Midlands to be among the top 20 regions in Europe by 2010 and inward investment is key to its strategy. emda is therefore working hard to make the East Midlands one of the most attractive areas in the United Kingdom in which to invest.

Dr Bryan Jackson OBE, Senior Director of Toyota Manufacturing UK, which has a site in Burnaston, near Derby, said: 'My advice to any potential inward investor is to talk to the East Midlands Development Agency team. Our experience has been positive and they are prepared to listen. It would have been difficult to achieve all that we have so far without their support.'

emda's role is to help your company with relocation, expansion or collaboration, and offers a number of free and confidential services. These include property and site searches, regional tours and visits, links to research centres and experts in your field, introductions to government and private sector companies and access to financial assistance and grants.

The East Midlands is continuing to develop its business infrastructure. Due to its central position, the region straddles the networks of all the United Kingdom's telecommunications companies, it has the second highest business connectivity to the internet in the United Kingdom and over 70 per cent of the population already have access to broadband. There are dedicated business parks throughout the six counties including three BTelocations – premier business, technology and science parks, which have the most advanced telecommunications infrastructures – and a dedicated health care and bioscience innovation centre, BioCity Nottingham.

Key facts about the East Midlands

Over 1000 overseas companies already here
Fourth largest region in the UK
Population over 4 million
4.5 per cent unemployment rate
GVA of £55.4 billion

North/South motorway links – M1 A1 (M)
London only an hour and a half by car
Over 99 per cent of the UK market within a day's journey by road
Nottingham East Midlands Airport flies direct to 19 destination per day
Five ports to the North and East
Three major rail operators
Channel Tunnel link to Europe by 2007

Eight world-class universities
36,000 graduates each year
4,510 language students
570 research groups

Supporting the region's economic prowess are its eight universities, producing high-quality graduates for the workforce, carrying out research projects and proving to be Centres of Excellence in their own right. Offering a range of courses from law and medicine to fashion design they include established institutions such as the University of Nottingham, generally accepted as one of the top five universities in the country. Between them they contain over 570 research groups and produce over 36,000 graduates a year.

The East Midlands is a region of diversity and versatility and offers the ideal location and workforce to ensure the future success of your business. To find out more please contact the Inward Investment Team at emda on +44 (0) 115 988 8521, e-mail: locate@englandseastmidlands.com or visit www.englandseastmidlands.com.

6.5.1 LEICESTER AND LEICESTERSHIRE

Leicester is a dynamic and forward-looking city for the 21st century, surrounded by a prosperous and attractive county providing the ideal location and environment to allow every type of business to prosper. Its cost-effective workforce, diverse economy and major regeneration plans make it an excellent choice for business relocation.

Centrally located, Leicestershire has excellent road, rail and air links. Leicester is only an hour away from London by train, and many major motorways go through the county. With its international airport (Nottingham East Midlands), Leicestershire is one of the most accessible parts of the United Kingdom.

A recently published review of public sector relocation showed Leicester as an ideal base for key civil service functions. The research assessed major English cities for their suitability to support government functions, from administration and call centres to scientific research and policy-making. The review gives Leicester an excellent opportunity to expand the extensive work already being done to promote investment in the area.

Leicester's regeneration is continuing to build on the strengths of an already vibrant commercial capital. The Leicester Regeneration Company's 10-year master plan is set to introduce new forms of employment while improving the city's image and quality of life. The plan includes proposals for a 500,000 square foot office district, new housing, improved retail facilities, a science park and redevelopment of Leicester's waterfront areas.

Outside the city, Leicestershire boasts over 20 quality business parks capable of accommodating a range of requirements. Distribution hubs such as Interlink and Magna Park are at the heart of the motorway network, providing unrivalled access to domestic and

European markets. Further developments – including Carlton Park on the outskirts of the city and Pegasus Business Park next to the airport – have been designated BTelocations and provide premises with high-speed broadband connections.

Major international companies have already chosen Leicestershire. They cite a skilled workforce, relatively low wage costs, a central location and excellent university links as some of the reasons behind their continued success. Pharmaceutical company AstraZeneca, heavy equipment and engine producer Caterpillar, HSBC bank and Disney Stores all have large facilities in the county.

Leicestershire's strong industrial heritage has created an enviable level of manufacturing expertise. New technology has brought training and development in many areas, resulting in the multi-skilled work-force of today. Key sectors for the development of business in the county are the food and drink industries, creative industries (specifi-cally new media, marketing, public relations and advertising agencies, design companies and the film industry), call centres, financial services, logistics and the life science and biotech sector.

Leicestershire boasts three major universities, De Montfort University and the University of Leicester in the city and Loughborough University. All three institutions have centres of research excellence and innovation centres to nurture spin-out companies. They enjoy strong relationships with local, national and international companies. The UK government also acknowledges the achievements of the county's universities. In a series of exercises conducted nationally to assess the quality of research in the United Kingdom, all three scored very highly.

The two city universities are also playing a central role in the regen-eration of the city. Between them they are planning to inject £400 million into building developments to modernize large areas of the city centre. Although the prime beneficiaries of this investment will be the universities themselves, the planned developments will also help persuade a larger proportion of students to stay on in the area after graduation, thus improving the quality of the workforce.

The county is also home to a number of thriving market towns such as Loughborough, Market Harborough, Melton Mowbray and Hinckley. The towns have proved popular with residents and busi-nesses alike, offering some of the best homes, transport links and business parks in the county.

Ethnic diversity has always been important to Leicester. Forty per cent of people living in the city belong to an ethnic community other than white British, the majority of them being from Asian or Afro-Caribbean groups.

Leicester was recently voted joint second-most Bohemian city in the United Kingdom. The city tied with London and was beaten only by

invest! Le!cestershire

Leicestershire is the **perfect business location** for many reasons: **excellent access** to the rest of UK and Europe, a **flexible workforce, cost effective property** and a truly **enviable quality of life**, to name a few.

With a major regeneration masterplan now in place, the city of Leicester is primed for significant redevelopment, including office, science park, retail and waterfront projects.

Glasgow

Edinburgh

Newcastle-Upon-Tyne

Leeds Hull

Manchester

Liverpool Sheffield

Birmingham

London

Southampton Dover

Plymouth

Le!cestershire

M1

M69

M1

To find out why global businesses succeed in Leicestershire contact:

Leicester Shire Promotions
7-9 Every Street, Town Hall Square,
Leicester LE1 6AG United Kingdom

T: +44 (0) 116 225 4071 **E:** invest@l-p-l.com

www.investleicestershire.com

Manchester. The Boho Britain index is based on a US model of measuring economic regeneration, the three key indicators being ethnic diversity, the proportion of gay residents and the number of patent applications made per head. Creativity is thought more likely to exist in an environment where minority cultures feel welcome.

Investors are also attracted to the area by Leicestershire's quality of life. Leicester offers excellent shops, restaurants and sporting and cultural facilities. Minutes away you can discover beautiful countryside, historic market towns and picturesque English villages, making the county an ideal location in which to live as well as invest.

6.5.2 NOTTINGHAM
Quality of life

Nottingham offers an extremely high quality of life. The city centre is well established as the region's premier retail, leisure and office location. People want to live here. It is no wonder that many of the 100,000 students that study at its universities and colleges want to work here too. One in 12 Nottingham residents is a university student, keeping the city young at heart and providing industries and inward investors with a constant diverse supply of educated workers.

The city's population currently stands at 267,100, although this is not a fair reflection of the labour market, with Greater Nottingham having a population of 625,400, there being a travel to work area population of 737,400 (460,000 of which are of working age) and 3 million people living within an hour's drive. Nottingham is a highly accessible city with an excellent communications network. Its central location places it within two hours' travelling time of most of the country.

Transport

Greater Nottingham has been rated the best area in the country for its visionary and ambitious Transport Masterplan. Over the next few years, £300 million will be spent on transport, including the development of the Nottingham Express Transit (NET) and the Nottingham railway station.

Nottingham has an excellent communications network. The A1 is close by as well as the M1 motorway with three junctions within easy reach (10 miles) of the city, which links the area to the rest of the United Kingdom's motorway network. The transport network and infrastructure within the city is also excellent. The recently opened NET – a high-speed modern tram, the £200 million supertram project and 8-mile route (linked to 3,000 places on the city's Park & Ride

Experience the 'WOW' Factor in Nottingham

Nottingham has the 'wow factor'. It excites and inspires. And it's not just us who say so.

Deputy Prime Minister John Prescott, speaking recently, praised achievements in Nottingham as giving a sense of pride. Nottingham, he argues, has undergone a "quiet revolution" in achieving demonstrable success. We agree - of course we would! - but we also firmly believe that now is the time to move Nottingham to the top of the location wish list…

Why locate in Nottingham? Well, we believe that the main factors that sway the relocation decision can be summed up simply - availability of qualified people to help you staff up; the chance of career development for you and your colleagues; and a choice of premium sites from which you can be based. Nottingham has all this and more.

In terms of land and sites, take your pick from any of the developments which form part of a £7 billion project to transform Nottingham city centre. It's one of the largest build programmes in the country, which means there will be something to meet your needs. It's exciting too - with your location decision you have the opportunity to shape the future of the capital of the East Midlands.

Turning to careers, the opportunities are outstanding, whether in the private or public sector.

Taking the former, Nottingham is home to major blue-chip companies including Boots, Experian, Speedo, Raleigh, Northern Foods, the BBC, Siemens and Powergen. Capital One has made Nottingham the location for its European headquarters. Each has made a long-term commitment to the city and are set to offer career opportunities to qualified people for a long time to come.

In the public sector, the Inland Revenue, the Government Office for the East Midlands, and the East Midlands Development Agency are all based here. And Sir Michael Lyons' review rated Nottingham highly for its potential to accommodate policy workers.

As for a local labour force, the numbers speak for themselves. A doubling of the city centre population in the past seven years and no fewer than 3 million people living within an hour of the Nottingham give a ready pool of labour worthy of one of Britain's leading cities.

In addition, our two leading universities - Nottingham and Nottingham Trent - focus on equipping students for the world of work, with Nottingham Trent topping national league tables for graduate employment levels.

It's a powerful combination. So if you want to find out more, who can help?

A new inward investment service has been created which brings together specialist staff from the City, County and District Councils in and around the Greater Nottingham area. The new initiative, based in the heart of Nottingham city - is designed to be the single point of contact for investors looking to establish their operation in the Nottingham conurbation.

We offer a free service and design bespoke information packages tailored to the specific needs of each client. What we think makes us different is that not only will we do our best to deliver what you need, if we can't we'll find someone who can. We'll go the extra mile to help.

We will be led by you and your needs as a relocating organisation. We understand that relocation can be a complex and painful process and our team is here to work with you in any way feasibly possible to remove the burden.

So how does it work in more detail?

Once you have made an enquiry you will be appointed an account manager that will provide all the information you need to build a business case for Nottingham.

We will co-ordinate city visits for your board, introduce you to partnerships and people and - so important in the relocation process - we will look after you.

We will provide you with a wide choice of potential business accommodation, and work with you and the local planning authority to resolve any possible issues.

A new Nottingham website **www.innottingham.info** that is due to be launched by Summer 2004 will provide users with the ability to access information online and undertake their own interactive commercial property search.

We will connect you to a quality labour pool and specialised training services through our new one stop recruitment shop.

Once a decision has been made we will provide the assistance you need to organise reconnaissance tours for your staff, and bespoke information packs including jobs for spouses, schools for children and a new home.

We passionately want your organisation to be a success in Nottingham. So the service won't end once you move. We can offer introductions into business networks and events, connections to local strategic partnerships, companies and people, and aftercare to ensure that you stay happy.

Nottingham is a great city with a friendly Inward Investment team. All of us appreciate that the relocation process needs to be dealt with the utmost sensitivity. So for an initial conversation in confidence, please call **Gerry Emmerson** on 0115 915 5381 or email **gerry@innottingham.info**.

SUMMARY OF SERVICES
WAYS WE CAN HELP YOU

- Brokering and project management
- Making connections
- Nottingham city visits
- Site selection
- Property planning issues
- Access to qualified labour
- Design of bespoke training programmes
- Introduction to strategic business partnerships / networking events
- Aftercare and business support

Wake up to Nottingham

system) will be integrated into the rail network, transforming the way people travel into and around Nottingham. This forms part of Nottingham Development Enterprise's Big Wheel scheme, encouraging the use of public transport as part of Nottingham's commitment to reducing pollution and congestion, and improving the environment its residents live and work in.

Nottingham East Midlands Airport is only 12 miles from the city centre (30 minutes' drive), and is one of the United Kingdom's largest air cargo gateways with excellent airfreight facilities. In 2003, passenger figures topped 4.3 million – a 32 per cent rise from 2002.

Local economy

Nottingham is one of the fastest-developing economic centres in the United Kingdom. In the last five years, unemployment has halved and the GVA per capita for the City of Nottingham is £20,782, which is 40 per cent above the UK average.

Choosing to invest or locate your business in Nottingham you can be sure that you will be in good company. Nottingham is home to over 50 regional and national headquarters including Boots, Experian, Capital One (European headquarters) and the Inland Revenue.

The future

Further major developments are currently underway that will dramatically transform the city, creating additional wealth and enhanced opportunities for investors. There are three designated regeneration zones – the Eastside, the Waterside and the Southside:

- the Eastside:
  - consists of 56 hectares of land alongside Nottingham's vibrant Lace Market and retail core;
  - contains a number of significant projects combined to deliver in excess of 4,000,000 square feet of mixed-use development;
  - a focus on a new city centre office quarter to the south with retail and leisure to the north, in addition to at least 1,600 new apartments;
  - the Island Business Quarter – Nottingham's biggest office development, carefully master-planned to provide 450,000 square feet of high-quality office accommodation at the heart of the city's bright and lively waterside crescent and part of the Eastside Regeneration Zone.

- the Waterside:
  - 10-year plan to create an attractive location for new homes, work-places and leisure facilities;
  - promoting major new housing developments in a series of new waterside communities that will house up to 4,000 new homes together with local facilities;
  - employment uses, leisure, retail and local services focused in a central neighbourhood development.

- the Southside:
  - Nottingham station and the Southside Regeneration Zone, the key gateways into the City of Nottingham;
  - focused on the expansion of the city centre southwards for mixed use – capturing the benefits of major retail development at Broadmarsh;
  - £400 million redevelopment of the Broadmarsh Shopping Centre, doubling its size to nearly 1.3 million square feet to regenerate the southern gateway to the city.

Nottingham is one of the most successful cities in the United Kingdom. With the world-class BioCity science park and over 1,000,000 square feet of quality office space at the ng^2 mixed-use business campus, Nottingham is a city that has a lot to offer to both people and businesses. The existing developments and planned regeneration places Nottingham on the threshold of establishing itself as an important and inspiring European city.

6.6

East of England

Invest East of England

Inward investment

Invest East of England has had an overall total of 106 inward investment successes in its six years of operation. In terms of origin, Europe provided the highest percentage of new project enquiries (43 per cent), with North America second (35 per cent) and companies in Asia Pacific accounting for 20 per cent of overall enquiries. By sector, business and financial services led the way with 31 per cent, followed by manufacturing and engineering (27 per cent) and ICT (24 per cent). Other sectors represented were electronics (7 per cent), life sciences (6 per cent) and automotive (3 per cent).

Universities

The seven are listed below:
Cambridge University – www.cam.ac.uk
Anglia Polytechnic University – www.anglia.ac.uk
University of Hertfordshire – www.herts.ac.uk
Essex University – www.essex.ac.uk
Cranfield University – www.cranfield.ac.uk
University of Luton – www.luton.ac.uk
University of East Anglia at Norwich – www.uea.ac.uk

Science and business parks

Not an exhaustive list but the main ones are listed below:

Cambridge Science Park – www.cambridgesciencepark.co.uk
Cambridge Research Park – www.cambridgeresearchpark.com
Adastral Park – www.adastral-hub.com
St John's Innovation Centre – www.stjohns.co.uk
Norwich Research Park – www.nrp.org.uk

A detailed description of the Cambridge science and research parks and the high technology industry clustered around Cambridge is given in Chapter 2.8.

Transport links

Roads

The main roads in the region are:
A1 (M); M1; A10; M11; A12; A14. Distances by road from London (City) to:

Hertford = 30 miles
Bedford = 58 miles
Cambridge = 62 miles
Colchester = 65 miles
Ipswich = 80 miles
Norwich = 113 miles

Airports

Stansted Airport – www.stansted.co.uk
Luton Airport – www.london-luton.co.uk
Norwich Airport – www.norwichairport.co.uk

Rail

There are five main lines providing rail links to the region leaving from Moorgate, King's Cross, St Pancras, Liverpool Street and King's Cross Thameslink. Timetable information can be accessed from www.nationalrail.co.uk. Length of journey from London to:

Hertford = 47 minutes (Moorgate)
Bedford = 33 minutes (King's Cross Thameslink)
Cambridge = 46 minutes (King's Cross or Liverpool Street)
Colchester = 49 minutes (Liverpool Street)
Ipswich = 59 minutes (Liverpool Street)
Norwich = 1 hr 38 minutes (Liverpool Street)

Ports

Felixstowe
Harwich
Ipswich
Great Yarmouth
Lowestoft

6.7

London

London First Centre (LFC)

London's population is set to grow by 800,000 in the next 15 years. This growth will present London with enormous challenges, and an enormous opportunity to improve the quality of life for everyone who lives and works in our city.

Our major regeneration initiatives help to ensure that London can meet the demand, unlocking the potential for new homes, space for businesses, new jobs and community facilities.

We work to create strong long-term economic growth, supporting business growth and development, promoting equality and combating poverty, so that all London's residents can contribute to, and share in, the prosperity of their city.

CAPITAL GROWTH.

We co-ordinate support for areas in need of renewal right across London, improving infrastructure and the environment and clearing barriers to development such as contaminated or derelict land and lack of access.

Our work in east London's Thames Gateway will help to create at least 91,000 new homes and our support for London's 2012 Olympic bid will accelerate our plans to transform the neglected Lower Lea Valley.

To find out more how we are driving major transformations of the Royal Docks, the Royal Arsenal development at Woolwich, Fresh Wharf Estate Business Park, the new National Stadium at Wembley, Crystal Palace National Sports Centre and the White Hart Triangle Business Park, visit our website, or contact us for a copy of our information leaflet 'Making a Difference':

E: info@lda.gov.uk
T: 020 7954 4500

The LDA: the Mayor's agency for business and jobs.

LONDON
DEVELOPMENT
A G E N C Y

www.lda.gov.uk
Devon House, 58-60 St Katharine's Way, London E1W 1JX

MAYOR OF LONDON

This statistical summary and commentaries are prepared by the London First Centre.

Demographics

Population in London

London's population rose 8 per cent over the 10 years to 2002 with Inner London rising by 10 per cent, as Table 6.7.1 demonstrates.

Table 6.7.1   Changes in London's population

	All London				All Ages	
						Thousands
	0–14	15–64	65 and over	All Ages	Inner London	Outer London
Estimates						
2001	1,366	5,050	892	7,308	2,838	4,470
2002	1,354	5,112	889	7,355	2,867	4,488
Percentage Change						
2001–02	−1	1	0	1	1	0

Source: London Travel Report 2003 (GLA, ONS)

The disposition of London's workforce by sector of activity is detailed in Table 6.7.2.

Table 6.7.2   Workforce distribution in London by industry

Percentages & Thousands	2001
Agriculture, Hunting, Forestry & Fishing	0.1
Mining & Quarrying; Electricity, Gas & Water	0.3
Manufacturing	6.5
Construction	3.3
Distribution, Hotels & Catering, Repairs	22.2
Transport, Storage & Communication	8.0
Financial & Business Services	33.0
Public Administration & Defence	5.1
Education, Social Work & Health Services	14.4
Other	7.1
Whole Economy (=100%) (thousands)	4,015

Source: Table 6.4, p 63, *Focus on London* 2003 (LDA, GLA, ONS, GOL)

Local economy

See Tables 6.7.3 to 6.7.7. Please note that GVA growth rate and level are used instead of output/GDP; GVA is a term introduced by 1995 revision of the European System of Accounts (ESA95); GDP estimates can differ slightly from GVA.

Table 6.7.3   GVA annual percentage growth rate projection 2003

	2003 (%)
Average	1.8
Lowest	0.7
Highest	2.3

Table 6.7.4   GVA level projection 2003

	2003 (Constant Year 2000 £bn)
Average	158.7
Lowest	157.1
Highest	159.7

Source: Greater London Authority

Table 6.7.5   Residence-based GVA in London 2000–01

	2000	2001
Headline residence-based GVA at current basic prices (£ million)	133,179	140,354
GVA per head (£)	18,746	19,526

Source: ONS (2003) *Economic Trends*, Table 1, p 40, October 2003

Table 6.7.6   Workplace-based GVA 2000–01

	2000	2001
Workplace-based GVA at current basic prices (£ million)	154,465	163,099
GVA per head (£)	21,742	22,690

Source: ONS (2003) *Economic Trends*, Table 12, p 60, October 2003

Table 6.7.7   Residence-based headline GVA by industry: accumulated and 2002 statistics

	£m 1999	£m 2000
Agriculture, Hunting, Forestry & Fishing	6	17
Mining and Quarrying of Energy Producing Materials	180	199
Other Mining and Quarrying	49	48
Manufacturing	14,297	14,750
Electricity, Gas and Water Supply	1,474	1,512
Construction	5,007	5,345
Wholesale and Retail Trade (Including Motor Trade)	15,393	16,036
Hotels and Restaurants	4,870	5,364
Transport, Storage and Communication	13,987	14,847
Financial Intermediation	14,042	14,964
Real Estate, Renting and Business Activities	42,952	47,287
Public Administration and Defence	4,178	4,309
Education	6,782	7,215
Health and Social Work	7,087	7,560
Other Services	10,331	11,030
FISIM	−13,512	−17,303
Total	127,124	133,179

Source: ONS (2003) *Economic Trends*, Table 3, p 43, October 2003

Employment in the Greater London Area

Employment in London has increased by over 15 per cent during the last 10 years but, as Table 6.7.8 shows, fell very slightly in 2002.

Table 6.7.8   Jobs in the Greater London Area 2001/02

Year	Employee Jobs in Greater London (000s)
2001	4,040
2002	3,970

Note: Greater London is the area of the combined London boroughs.
Source: ONS (2003) *London Travel Report* 2003

In spring 2002, 71 per cent of the working-age population in London were in employment. The number of people of all ages who were in employment in London stood at 3.4 million (*source: Focus on London 2003* (LDA, GLA, GOL, ONS).

Projections of employment growth in London

Employment in London is likely to grow at a faster rate than in the United Kingdom as a whole. Table 6.7.9 below summarizes projected employment growth in London (both on a residential and workplace basis) for various time periods between now and 2041.

Table 6.7.9 Projected employment growth in London

Time Period	Annual Average Growth in London (%)
2003–08	1
2008–13	0.75
2013–22	0.75
2022–32	0.25
2032–41	0.50

Source: GLA Economics, TfL, LDA, Mayor of London (2003) Working Paper 4: 'Long-term employment projections for London', Table 3, September 2003

Real estate – London office rentals

Tables 6.7.10 and 6.7.11 give some key market statistics.

Table 6.7.10 Key London office market statistics for Q4 2003

Area	Availability (millions sq ft)	Vacancy Rate (%)	Take-up (millions sq ft)	Investment (£m)
West End	10.28	11.6	1.22	531.7
City	15.07	13.7	1.01	2,017.2
Docklands	2.21	12.1	0.13	22.5
Central London	27.56	12.7	2.36	2,548.9

Source: Central London Quarterly – Quarter 4 2003, Knight Frank

West End

Prime West End headline rental values remain unchanged quarter-on-quarter at £62.50 per square foot, down from £70 per square foot at the end of 2002.

City

City rental values have softened by £10 per square foot during the course of the year to stand at £45 per square foot.

Docklands

Canary Wharf Group formally announced quoting rents of £42.50 per square foot on new space within the estate during quarter 4. Outside this area, headline rental values are now estimated to be in the region of £17.50 per square foot, a 30 per cent annual decline and a notable quarterly adjustment of 12.5 per cent.

Table 6.7.11   M25 office market key statistics for Q4 2003

Area	Stock	Availability (sq m)	Vacancy rate (%)	Total take-up (sq m)
M25	11,859,560	1,156,743	9.8	56,454

Source: M25 Offices – Quarter 4 2003, Knight Frank

Transport and communications

London's transport connections

London is the best city in terms of transport links with other cities and internationally, according to the Cushman & Wakefield Healey & Baker *European Cities Monitor 2003*. London also has the best internal transport links of any city in Europe. Its public transport system is composed of an extensive, radial regional rail network (with 570 railway stations), 12 underground lines (with 275 stations) and 649 bus routes that operate at high frequency.

Air

London's five international airports, Heathrow, Gatwick, Stansted, London City and Luton are the world's busiest, handling some 88 million international airline passengers a year. From London you can fly to 277 destinations and all of Europe's principal business centres are within a two-hour flight time (*source: OAG World Flight Guide*).

Heathrow, Gatwick and Stansted have trains or London Underground (Metro) stations within the airports. London Underground trains operate every four to six minutes direct from Heathrow's four terminals to central London and link with the citywide Metro network. In addition, the Docklands Light Railway (DLR) now carries 45 million passengers a year.

Rail

London is the main hub of the national inter-city rail system and the 12 national rail terminals in London provide direct access to all parts of the United Kingdom, as well as the rest of Europe via the Eurostar from Waterloo. The Eurostar offers rail services to mainland Europe through the Channel Tunnel. There are 15 trains a day to Paris (two hours 35 minutes) and an average of 10 trains every day to Brussels (two hours 20 minutes).

A massive programme of investment is transforming connections within London, with the new Thames Gateway Bridge set to open in 2013. The new Channel Tunnel Rail Link at Stratford and King's Cross will also connect travellers from Paris and Brussels directly to rail networks serving the Midlands, the North and Scotland.

Road

London is at the hub of the United Kingdom's national road and rail freight network. London also has a radial motorway system and its orbital motorway – the M25 – provides easy access to the rest of the United Kingdom and the Channel ports. A third of the EU's economy and population can be reached in 10 hours by road and the London's orbital motorway has numerous modern distribution facilities.

Waterways

London River Services (LRS) is responsible for the management and the operation of eight piers on the River Thames, and provides licences to the riverboat services that serve those piers. The years 2002/03 marked the installation of the Millbank Millennium pier near to Tate Britain and the completion of the Thames 2000 Project, which included the replacement of Tower and Westminster piers and the construction of new piers at Blackfriars and Waterloo (close to the BA London Eye) in 2000. In the three years to 2002/03 there was a nearly 10 per cent increase in use of London River Services (*source: London Travel Report 2003*).

Infrastructure

London is ranked as the best city in Europe for the 'quality of its telecoms' in the Cushman & Wakefield Healey & Baker *European Cities Monitor 2003*. London's state-of-the-art telecommunication networks means fast, reliable contacts to the rest of the world 24 hours a day.

London has the most advanced telecoms knowledge base in the United Kingdom and is the centre of telecoms regulation. ADSL broadband is already available to virtually all of London's population and businesses (BT internal information indicated 99.7 per cent of Londoners were served by ADSL, June 2002). BT works closely with the Greater London Authority, the London Development Agency and other public bodies to support the GLA's digital inclusion programme, driving up the use of broadband by businesses and individuals (*source:* 'Broadband connecting to London's future', BT and the GLA).

London also has the highest level of internet use and e-commerce adoption in the United Kingdom and is regarded by businesses as the most favourable location in Europe for conducting e-business (*source: European e-Locations Monitor*, Healey & Baker, June 2001). E-business adoption in London is among the highest in the world, with 96 per cent of London companies having internet access, 88 per cent having a company website and 33 per cent actively trading online. Internet usage among people living in London is the highest in the United Kingdom at 58 per cent (source: 'The internet user profile survey', *NOP World*, June 2002, www.nop.co.uk).

WLAN and public Wi-Fi are new market opportunities, with London seen as a leading-edge location. The UK government is encouraging the use of Wi-Fi via deregulation, resulting in the creation of several hundred 'hotspots' in coffee shops, transport hubs and hotels in London. One thousand locations had commercial Wi-Fi services by June 2003, expected to be 3,000 sites by the end of 2003.

Foreign direct investment

Foreign direct investment in London increased by one-third in 2002. London remains by far the most popular business destination in Europe with 125 new investments in 2002, an increase of 33 per cent on the previous year, according to the Ernst & Young *European Investment Monitor*. London accounted for 7 per cent of all investment projects in Europe, up from 5 per cent last year. These figures have remained constant over the past few years and, increasingly, foreign companies have chosen London to move to or locate their regional headquarters, research, development and design centres and sales and marketing operations.

Over the past eight years LFC, working in conjunction with its partners, has provided a wide range of services that have assisted 680 companies from 35 countries to either locate or expand their businesses in the capital. These 680 projects have directly led to the creation of, or safeguarding of, nearly 32,000 jobs. Tables 6.7.12 and 6.7.13 show investment projects in Greater London by country of origin and by industry.

Table 6.7.12   Greater London Inward Investment projects by country of origin: accumulated and 2002 statistics

Country of Origin	Accumulated Projects from 1997–March 2003 (%)	Projects for 2002 (%)
Australia	1.9	1.6
Canada	3.6	4.8
China	0.9	4.8
France	3.7	0.8
Germany	5.5	3.2
India	3.4	10.4
Italy	1.2	1.6
Japan	6.3	4.8
Netherlands	1.3	0.8
Russian Federation	0.9	1.6
South Korea	1.5	3.2
Sweden	2.0	3.2
Switzerland	1.3	1.6
USA	57.5	50.4

Source: European Investment Monitor Base Data (1997–2002)

Table 6.7.13   Greater London Inward Investment projects by industry: accumulated and 2002 statistics

Industry	Accumulated Projects from 1997–March 2003 (%)	Projects for 2002 (%)
Energy	0.7	0.8
Financial & Business Services	56.8	73.6
Manufacturing	20.2	20.0
Retail & Hospitality	1.5	2.4
Transport & Communications	7.7	3.2

Source: European Investment Monitor Base Data (1997–2002)

Regional Selective Assistance*

The British government, through the Department of Trade and Industry, provides financial assistance to UK and overseas companies through the Regional Selective Assistance (RSA) scheme. RSA may be available for projects over £500,000. It is a discretionary grant scheme enabling a project to proceed where it would not otherwise. The grant is negotiated on the basis of need, investment and jobs created/safe-guarded, subject to European ceilings. RSA is available to eligible

---

*In England, RSA has recently been substituted by the Selective Finance for Investment (SFi) scheme (see page 258).

projects in most manufacturing and certain service industries. Eligible investment costs include the acquisition of land, buildings, plant and machinery but exclude normal overhead costs. Grant is taxable and paid in arrears of agreed milestones such as capital expenditure or job targets.

EU Structural Funds for 2000–06

The EU supports economic regeneration through the Structural Funds, which are targeted at the lesser-developed areas of the EU. Parts of North and East London contain deprived areas with high levels of unemployment. During the next period of Structural Funds programmes (2000–06), funding is available under three objectives. Objective 2 aims to support the economic and social conversion of areas facing structural difficulties. It is the second highest level of funding available from the EU. Areas qualifying for Objective 2 fall under four strands – industrial, rural, urban and fisheries. London wards qualifying for Objective 2 Structural Funds are: Hackney, Hammersmith & Fulham, Haringey, Newham, Tower Hamlets, Barking & Dagenham, Bexley, Brent, Ealing, Enfield, Greenwich, Havering, Waltham Forest.

Education, research and development

London is a recognized world Centre of Excellence for research and education with one of the largest critical masses of educational and academic facilities and diverse stores of knowledge anywhere in the world. With 28 universities, 12 colleges of higher education and over 300,000 higher education students, London is the centre of higher education in the United Kingdom. Of the 300,000+ students there are 53,740 overseas nationals studying at London's universities. In addition, London has the most graduates in the United Kingdom – one-third of the working population hold a degree – and over 300 languages are spoken due to large immigrant communities.

London Universities

Birkbeck College
Brunel University
City University
Goldsmiths College
Imperial College London
King's College London
Kingston University
London Guildhall University
London Metropolitan University

London School of Economics
London South Bank University
Middlesex University
Queen Mary and Westfield College
Royal Holloway and Bedford New College
Thames Valley University
University College London
University of East London
University of Greenwich
University of Westminster

Science parks

There are seven science and technology parks in London that serve to facilitate the transfer of academic expertise and research to business, as well as offering accommodation for high-tech companies. These are:

Brunel Science Park
Cleveland Road
Uxbridge
Middlesex
UB8 3PH
Tel: +44 (0) 1895 272192
Website: www.brunel.ac.uk/scipark

Kingston Innovation Centre
Unit 3
Kingsmill Business Park
Chapel Mill Road
Kingston-upon-Thames
KT1 3GZ
Tel: +44 (0) 28545 2875
Website: www.kingstoninnovation.com

Lee Valley Technopark
Ashley Road
London
N17 9LN
Tel: +44 (0) 20 8880 3636
Website: www.leevalley.co.uk

The London Bioscience Innovation Centre
Royal College Street
London
NW1 0TU
Tel: +44 (0) 20 7691 1122
Website: www.rvc.ac.uk/LBIC/Index.htm

The London Science Park
Regeneration Team
c/o London Borough of Enfield
Civic Centre
Silver Street
Enfield
Middlesex
EN1 3XY
Tel: +44 (0) 20 8379 3155
Website: www.thelondonofficeandsciencepark.com

South Bank Technopark
90 London Road
London
SE1 6LN
Tel: +44 (0) 20 7928 2900

Thames Gateway Technology Centre
University of East London
Docklands Campus
4 University Way
London
E16 2RD
Tel: +44 (0) 20 8223 3388
Website: www.uel.ac.uk/tgtc/contact.htm

Business parks

Business Parks within the Greater London area include:

Bedfont Lakes (including New Square Business Park)
Feltham
Middlesex
TW14

Birchmere Business Park
Eastern Way
Thamesmead
London
SE28 8BF
Website: www.birchmerebusinesspark.co.uk

Centaurs Business Park
Grant Way
Isleworth
Middlesex
TW7 5QD

Charlton Gate Business Park
Anchor & Hope Lane
Greenwich
London
SE7

Chiswick Park
Pinn Lane
London
W4
Tel: +44 (0) 20 8636 8080
Website: www.enjoy-work.com

Cowley Business Park
High Street
Cowley
Uxbridge
Middlesex
UB8

Electra Business Park
160 Bidder Street
Canning Town
London
E16

FirstCentral (Guinness Brewery Site)
Park Royal Road
Park Royal
London
NW10
Website: www.firstcentral.co.uk

London Science Park
Mollison Avenue
Enfield
EN3

Optima Park
Thames Road
Crayford
Kent
DA1

Royal Arsenal Development (iO Centre)
Gunnery Terrace
Woolwich
London
SE18 6SW
Tel: +44 (0) 20 7344 6610

Royal Docks Business Park
Dockside Road
London
E16

Stockley Park
Heathrow
Middlesex
UB11

Sunbury International Business Centre
Broadlands Close
Windmill Road
Sunbury-On-Thames
TW16 7DX

Uxbridge Business Park
Uxbridge
Middlesex

West Thamesmead Business Park
Nathan Way/Boughton Road
Thamesmead
London
SE28

Utilities

The United Kingdom is self-sufficient in energy and is one of only five OECD countries to produce more energy than it consumes. Gas and electricity prices in the United Kingdom are the most competitive in Europe (*source:* UK Trade & Investment website, NUS Consulting). Due to deregulation of the market, competition has increased, leading to a reduction in prices and an increase in service and efficiency for both gas and electricity.

Water, gas and electricity services can be obtained from a number of private utility companies. The business customer has, therefore, a choice of supplier and services, and a range of very competitive prices. Online channels exist that allow businesses to select the best option for their energy needs. The customer can compare over 1,340 gas tariffs, 2,970 electricity tariffs and many dual fuel tariffs, and in some instances you can apply online (*source:* http://www.top-creditcards. com/utilities.htm).

Vocational training centres

City & Guilds is the leading provider of vocational qualifications in the United Kingdom. The 500 qualifications available assess skills that are of practical value in the workplace. They are recognized for their quality and are valued by employers in every sector of business:

City & Guilds
1 Giltspur St
London
EC1A 9DD
Tel: +44 (0) 207 294 2468
Website: www.city-and-guilds.co.uk

Edexcel is the United Kingdom's largest awarding body to offer a range of both general and specialist qualifications, for UK and international markets:

Edexcel
Stewart House
32 Russell Square
London
WC1B 5DN
Tel: +44 (0) 870 240 9800
Website: www.edexcel.org.uk

OCR is responsible to the government as one of the United Kingdom's leading awarding bodies, providing qualifications to students at school, college, in work or through part-time learning programmes. OCR provides a range of specialist support services to customers in the South East of England, including London. These services include advice, quality assurance support and training.

OCR
Veritas House
125 Finsbury Pavement
London
EC2A 1NQ
Tel: +44 (0) 20 7256 7819
Website: www.ocr.org.uk

TECs

The following London-based Training and Enterprise Councils encourage local economic growth and regeneration through training and enterprise:

AZTEC
Manorgate House
Manorgate Road
Kingston-upon-Thames
KT2 7AL
Tel: +44 (0) 20 8547 3934
Website: www.londonlearningzone.co.uk

Focus Central London
103 New Oxford Street
London
WC1A 1DR
Tel: +44 (0) 20 7 896 8484

London East TEC
Boardman House
64 Broadway
Stratford
London E15 1NT
Tel: +44 (0) 20 8432 0000

North West London TEC
Kirkfield House
118–120 Station Rd
Harrow
Middlesex HA1 2RL
Tel: +44 (0) 20 8901 5000

North London TEC
Dumayne House
1 Fox Lane
Palmers Green
N13 4AB
Tel: +44 (0) 20 8447 9422

SOLOTEC
Lancaster House
7 Elmfield Rd
Bromley
Kent
BR1 1LT
Tel: +44 (0) 20 8313 9232

West London TEC
West London Centre
15–21 Staines Road
Hounslow
Middlesex
TW3 3HA
Tel: +44 (0) 20 8577 1010
(*source:* http://www.linklondon.co.uk/guides/tec/)

Research institutes

Together, the London universities have many research institutes pursuing thematically related academic and policy research in their chosen area. Several of the institutes are multidisciplinary, related disciplines being brought together to address major social, scientific, technological or policy-related issues in a vibrant and challenging intellectual environment. In addition, London has a number of 'Think Tank' research institutes, including:

Adam Smith Institute (ASI)
Centre for Economic Policy Research (CEPR)
The Centre for European Reform (CER)
Centre for Policy Studies (CPS)
Demos
Fabian Society
Institute for Public Policy Research (IPPR)
Institute of Economic Affairs (IEA)
International Institute for Environment and Development (IIED)
International Institute for Strategic Studies (IISS)
National Institute of Economic and Social Research (NIESR)
New Policy Institute
Overseas Development Institute (ODI)
The Policy Studies Institute (PSI)
Royal Institute of International Affairs
Social Market Foundation (SMF)

Local service providers listing

Public sector support agencies

Business Link 4 London
Centre Point
103 New Oxford Street
London
WC1A 1DP
Tel: +44 (0) 845 6000 787
Website: www.businesslink4london.com

English Partnerships
110 Buckingham Palace Road
London
SW1W 9SA
Tel: +44 (0) 20 7881 1600
Website: www.englishpartnerships.co.uk

Greater London Authority
City Hall
The Queen's Walk
London
SE1 2AA
Tel: +44 (0) 20 7983 4000
Website: www.london.gov.uk/gla/city-hall

London Development Agency
Devon House
58–60 St Katharine's Way
London
E1W 1JX
Tel: +44 (0) 20 7680 2000
Website: www.lda.gov.uk

London First Centre
1 Hobhouse Court
Suffolk Street
London
SW1Y 4HH
Tel: +44 (0) 20 7925 2000
Website: www.lfc.co.uk

Local authority planning services

Each London borough has its own local authority planning department. In addition, the RIBA London Planning Group was formed to address planning issues that directly affect London:

Royal Institute of British Architects
66 Portland Place
London
W1B 1AD
Website: www.riba.org

Chambers of Commerce

The following Chambers of Commerce are located in London:

London Chamber of Commerce and Industry
33 Queen Street
London
EC4R 1AP
Tel: +44 (0) 20 7248 4444
Website: www. londonchamber.co.uk

Barking & Dagenham Chamber of Commerce
Roycraft House
15 Linton Rd
Barking IG11
Tel: Tel: +44 (0) 20 8591 6966
Website: www.barking-dagenham.gov.uk

Barnet Chamber of Commerce
23–35 Hendon Lane
Finchley
London N3
Tel: +44 (0) 20 8343 3833
Website: www.nlcc.co.uk

Enfield Chamber of Commerce
Enfield Business Centre
201 Hertford Rd
Enfield EN3
Tel: +44 (0) 20 8443 4464
Website: www.nlcc.co.uk

Haringey Chamber of Commerce
Sentinel House
Ashley Rd
Tottenham
London N17
Tel: +44 (0) 20 8365 1958
Website: www.nlcc.co.uk

International Chamber of Commerce
14–15 Belgrave Square
London
SW1X 8PS
Tel: +44 (0) 20 7823 2811
Website: www.iccuk.net

Islington Chamber of Commerce
64 Essex Road
London N1 8LR
Tel: +44 (0) 20 7226 1593
Website: www.islchamber.org

6.7.1 THAMES GATEWAY LONDON

Gateway to London

Overview

Thames Gateway London has a population of 2.8 million, constituting nearly 40 per cent of London's total population. The most populous city in the European Union, London is one of the largest cities in the developed world in terms of its built-up area. Recent projections identify Thames Gateway London to have the fastest-growing population in the London area with an 11 per cent increase forecast between 2001 and 2016. Some 65 per cent of residents are of working age. This, combined with a total workforce catchment area covering the majority of Greater London as well as suburban areas of South Essex, North Kent and Surrey, all within one hour's travel, offers an unparalleled labour pool.

London is one of the strongest and most diverse market economies in the world. In recent years, its economy has remained resilient to the pressures present in the global economy, allowing continued growth. There are more than 674,000 businesses in London, of which 255,000 are registered for VAT (source: Office of National Statistics, *Focus on London*); 28 per cent of these are located in Thames Gateway London. The scale of opportunity and diversity offered to investors is reflected in the range of business sectors already thriving here. The top four sectors in the sub-region (measured by number of VAT-registered businesses) are real estate, wholesale and retail, construction and manufacturing, with logistics and financial services also featuring strongly.

The economy

Gross value-added (GVA) per head on a workplace basis in Inner London is the highest not only in the United Kingdom but also in the European Union. GVA per head for London as a whole on a residence basis was £17,000 in 1999, compared with under £13,000 for the United Kingdom. The real estate, financial services, manufacturing and wholesale and retail sectors provide the highest GVA.

Employment within Thames Gateway London is predominately within service-based industries, employing over 1 million people and reflecting the success of areas such as City of London and City Fringe, Greenwich, Canary Wharf and Stratford. More than 250,000 people are employed in banking and financial services. Manufacturing and logistics are also important areas, both sectors having higher rates of

Onwards and upwards

GATEWAY TO
LONDON
OPPORTUNITIES
IN THE THAMES
GATEWAY

> Welcome to the land
of unlimited opportunity.
Thames Gateway
London is Europe's
fastest growing and
most dynamic business
region. Buy, build or
lease premises and
you'll be close to City
Airport, minutes from
the City and right at
the heart of London's
most flexible business
environment.

If you prefer to set
your sights high,
move onwards and
upwards to Thames
Gateway London.

Secure a prime
location and an
excellent package
of incentives by
calling Gateway
to London on
020 7540 5560
or visit
www.gtlon.co.uk

employment in Thames Gateway London than in other parts of London. Manufacturing accounts for 40 per cent of employment in the heart of the sub-region and 11 per cent in the outer areas. Logistics accounts for about 20 per cent of employment with an even spread of density across the whole of Thames Gateway London, demonstrating the sub-region's excellent regional and international connections. Thames Gateway London has the lowest overall employment costs of anywhere in London and one of the lowest in Southern England. These low employment costs coupled with the United Kingdom's low overall business costs make Thames Gateway London a successful and popular business location.

The area has been shaped by the Thames, with Canary Wharf, the Royal Docks, Woolwich Arsenal and Dagenham being long-standing commercial centres established around river uses. As the commercial role of the river has declined, many of the old bankside buildings are being given a new lease of life as apartments, offices and industrial space. Docklands has been transformed, with Canary Wharf and The Royals providing high-quality growth space for the business and financial services sectors as they expand east from the City.

Thames Gateway London's vibrant town centres offer a variety of inexpensive office accommodation. Hubs such as Stratford, Lewisham and Sidcup are successful secondary office locations accommodating back-office service centres.

The industrial heart of the area running along the north side of the Thames is still a preferred location for high-end manufacturing. New industrial developments based around the Centre for Engineering and Manufacturing Excellence (CEME) and Ford's new diesel engine plant offer a wide range of premises from incubators to large-scale design-build opportunities.

Distribution and logistics have become major sectors in Thames Gateway London thanks to the ever-improving transport infrastructure providing fast access to London, national and European markets. Established freight-forwarding hubs such as Thamesmead, Dagenham and Thurrock offer large-scale sites for warehousing and easy motorway access to Europe and the rest of the United Kingdom. The international container ports at Tilbury, Purfleet and the proposed Shellhaven development, along with major rail freight routes, provide efficient networks for the transport of bulk goods.

Thames Gateway London-offers the most competitive property cost in Greater London and rental prices are typically 15–20 per cent less than those of Central and West London. Business rates are payable on most commercial property, such as shops, offices, warehouses and factories and are the means by which businesses make a contribution towards the cost of local services. Properties are given a value based on market rental value in 1998 and businesses pay a yearly national rate, which is currently 43.7 per cent of its value.

Transport communications

The area has the fastest-improving transport infrastructure in the United Kingdom. London City Airport is just six miles from the City centre and three miles from Canary Wharf, connecting London to 24 European cities, including all major capitals. There is no better business airport in the United Kingdom.

The Channel Tunnel Rail Link is the United Kingdom's first major new railway for over a century and will provide a new transport hub in Thames Gateway London at Stratford. The new high-speed line between London's St Pancras and the Channel Tunnel will slash journey times to Paris and Brussels and double the number of Eurostar trains that can run at peak time. Section 1 between the Channel Tunnel and Fawkham Junction in north Kent opened in October 2003 and section 2 into London's St Pancras is scheduled to complete by the end of 2006.

Crossrail will create a brand new network of services linking East and West London, significantly reducing travel congestion and disruption by enabling existing suburban services to run through London. The preferred route for Crossrail is currently undergoing consultation and features a tunnelled route across London, with new stations at Paddington, Bond Street, Tottenham Court Road, Farringdon, Liverpool Street/Moorgate, Whitechapel and Isle of Dogs (Canary Wharf).

The Docklands Light Railway (DLR), providing fast, frequent passenger services linking the City of London and Canary Wharf with the many residential areas, already services much of Thames Gateway London. DLR extensions to City Airport and across the river to Woolwich are currently under construction and further extensions are planned extending the network to Dagenham. Regional transport initiatives include the Thames Gateway Transit, which will connect town centres, interchanges and development sites, for example, in North Greenwich, London Riverside, Redbridge and Havering. Phase 1 of East London Transit (Ilford–Dagenham Dock) is due for completion in 2006.

Inward investment

The United Kingdom is the leading inward investment destination in Europe and London is the largest beneficiary of inward investment into the United Kingdom, reflecting the leading position London has in the world economy. In the past 18 months, 12 inward investors have chosen Thames Gateway London, creating more than 650 jobs. The investors have come from a range of ICT, business services and logistics operations from North America, South East Asia and India.

There are a wide range of financial assistance and incentive packages available to businesses looking to move into Thames Gateway London or already in the area and wanting to grow. The majority of business locations in Thames Gateway London are eligible for Regional Selective Assistance, which offers grants for business investments more than £500,000*. For companies investing less than £500,000 Enterprise Grants are often available.

Telecommunications

London is one of the best-wired global cities. It was recently ranked as the best city in Europe for the 'quality of its telecoms' in the Cushman & Wakefield Healey & Baker *European Cities Monitor, 2003*. Companies have multiple choices in their telecom service provision and broadband access is a standard feature. Thames Gateway London offers an advantage to companies requiring reliability and speed for their internet and data hosting services, as it is home to the London Internet Exchange (LINX) carrying 90 per cent of the United Kingdom's internet traffic.

Education and research

Companies wishing to efficiently develop and commercialize technology can take advantage of any of London's nine research and technology organizations (RTOs), which offer strong business and research links. Five of the United Kingdom's top 10 research-led universities are in London. And in the latest Research Assessment Exercise, London had 180 departments that were awarded the top 5* or 5 rating. A unique aspect of London universities is their multidisciplinary research, with key strengths in art and design; bioscience; IT/telecoms; digital media; materials; business/finance/economics; and engineering. Much new research is conducted at the boundaries of the traditional subject areas.

The Centre for Engineering and Manufacturing Excellence – the first of its kind in Europe – provides a range of seamless education opportunities from basic skills and apprenticeship training to higher

---

*In England, RSA has recently been substituted by the Selective Finance for Investment (SFi) Scheme (see page 258).

and further education, including undergraduate and post-graduate research in association with established academic institutions. Businesses in Thames Gateway London are benefiting from cutting-edge facilities, easy access to leading research and development and training courses.

Business support agencies, including chambers of commerce, are very active and highly regarded and their networks are second to none, providing unrivalled support to investors. Gateway to London works closely with local, regional and national organizations, acting as a single point of contact for the sub-region and ensuring that the best information and support is available to existing and prospective investors. The area's local planning authorities are among Gateway to London's partners and it has extensive experience in assisting business through the planning process.

6.8

South East England

*South East England Development Agency
(SEEDA)*

Overview of the economy

The South East of England is the economic powerhouse of the United Kingdom with its GVA (economy) currently estimated to be £147 billion per annum for 2003. Not only does it have the largest population and workforce, but also the highest R&D spend in the country. Located between the nation's capital and Europe, the region has attracted many of the world's leading global businesses.

Industry sectors

Although financial and service sector industries dominate the economy of the region, there is a strong and diverse manufacturing base – in GVA terms, manufacturing in the South East is the highest in the country. Key industry sectors include electronics, high-tech engineering, computer hardware and software, telecommunications, e-commerce, pharmaceuticals, biotechnology, marine technologies, automotive and avionics sectors.

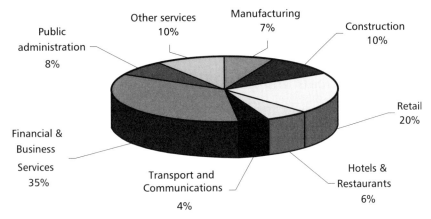

Figure 6.8.1   Classification of business types in the South East, 2002
Source: ONS 2003

Inward investment

A large number of overseas companies have invested in the region, accounting for around 7,000 foreign-owned business operations, which include many UK or European headquarter corporate functions. Some examples are Dun & Bradstreet, Veritas, Siebel Systems, Honda, HP, Silicon Graphics, Motorola, Nortel, Panasonic, Siemens, Hitachi, Sony and Electronic Arts.

Research and development

Businesses in the South East spend more on R&D than in any other part of the United Kingdom, supported by access to numerous centres of academic, technical and scientific excellence. The region's 26 universities and higher education colleges and 71 further education colleges produce approximately 60,000 graduates annually. There is a network of regional technology centres and extensive R&D consultancy and facilities available from academic institutions. Research centres established in the South East cover fields ranging from electronics to software and molecular sciences to pharmaceuticals. For example, Philips Semiconductors has a facility in Southampton and Samsung Electronics Research Institute is based in Surrey.

Among the region's world-class universities, Oxford is the most renowned and its science park is host to firms specializing in computer software, pharmaceutical, biosciences and optoelectronics, including Sharp, which has a major R&D facility on the park.

ICT

The United Kingdom's 'Silicon Valley' runs west from London along the M4 corridor and is the location for high-profile names such as Cisco, Oracle, Computer Associates, Microsoft and Novell.

Pharmaceuticals and health care

The pharmaceutical and health care industries are very well represented in the region by companies such as Johnson & Johnson, Eli Lilly, Pfizer, Procter & Gamble, GlaxoSmithKline and Aventis Pharma. Anglo-Swiss company Syngenta, a world-leading agribusiness, has located its European regional centre in Guildford. In Kent, Pfizer is a long-standing investor, recipient of the Queen's Award for Innovation 2001 and is expanding its R&D facility in Sandwich – where the drug Viagra was developed and more than 5,000 people are employed.

Automotive

The automotive sector is also strong in the South East. BMW built the new Mini in Oxford and the new £60 million Rolls-Royce head office and manufacturing plant is now complete at Goodwood in West Sussex. German company Nord has expanded its factory on the Abingdon Science Park, where it manufactures high-performance gearboxes. The majority of the world's Formula 1 and Indy cars are designed and developed in South East England, with clusters in the north of the region around Banbury and Milton Keynes and in Surrey. McLaren has a £200 million complex in Woking, for the production of the new Mercedes SLR sports car.

Call centres

Nineteen per cent of call centres in the United Kingdom are based in the South East. IBM has its national call management centre in Portsmouth, while Global Home Loans is based on the Crossways Business Park near Dartford, Kent. Winterthur Life is based in Basingstoke and American Express has its European operating headquarters in Brighton and Hove, which is also the location of the Kimberly-Clark European Shared Service Centre.

Infrastructure

The South East has an excellent transportation infrastructure, with 20 per cent of the United Kingdom's motorway network serving the region. Links to the rest of the United Kingdom are via the M25 motorway; and to Europe via the Channel Tunnel, which has a Eurostar passenger station and its international freight and vehicle terminus in Kent.

London Heathrow and Gatwick Airports, two of the busiest international airports in the world, are in the region. Smaller airports such as Southampton are becoming increasingly important for domestic and European connections. Some of the United Kingdom's most important ports are in the South East, including Southampton, Portsmouth and Dover. There are many smaller ports, such as Sheerness, Newhaven and Ramsgate serving the roll-on roll-off trade.

Premises

The range and size of premises in the South East is very wide with many business parks, industrial premises and development sites throughout the region that can accommodate a full variety of office, manufacturing, warehouse and distribution activities. SEEDA is taking a lead role in providing business incubator space for high-tech companies on flexible terms through its Enterprise Hub initiative, which is already attracting interest from potential foreign inward investors. The cost of business space and land in the South East is competitive compared with the rest of the United Kingdom. The cost does vary across the region and it can compete favourably with all UK regions.

Employment

The South East offers an accommodating, highly skilled and flexible workforce, with a history of stable employer–employee relations. Over

4.3 million people make up the South East's labour force, which is greater than any other region and represents over 14 per cent of the UK total employed workforce. A greater than average proportion of the workforce is employed in jobs requiring high qualifications. This reflects the extensive skill levels, the flexibility, adaptability and high level of motivation of the local workforce, a key factor in attracting successful firms to the region.

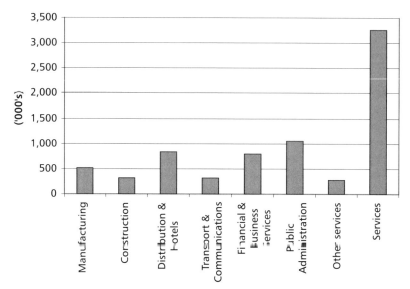

Figure 6.8.2   Employmnent by sector 2003
Source: Labour force Survey 2003

Leisure

An attractive lifestyle is essential for enticing and retaining the right people for business. In South East England, key personnel and their families can live in a first-class environment with a rich mix of cultural heritage and outstanding natural beauty.

The South East offers an excellent living environment with easy access both to the benefits of the United Kingdom's capital city, London, many major towns, and a significant rural environment, with many well-preserved historic buildings and other tourist attractions. The South East is surrounded by coastline, cliffs and beaches, most of which are specially protected. The region has some of the best golf courses in the country, including the world-renowned venues of Wentworth in Surrey, Sunningdale in Berkshire and Sandwich in Kent. There is a choice of ultra-modern shopping malls and town centres that cater for all household or consumer items. Many of the region's historic towns have attractive speciality shopping precincts, for example The Lanes in Brighton catering for antique collectors. The South East has a wonderful variety of cultural facilities with the largest number of museums in England and numerous art galleries.

Education

The South East has an excellent range of international schools including American, international and Japanese schools. The American Community Schools (ACS) have three campuses in the South East region, which have evolved to serve both American and international families with dynamic, friendly campuses and small classes. The diplomas available include the traditional American Diploma for acceptance into American colleges and universities or the International Baccalaureate Diploma for worldwide university access. Day schools and boarding programmes are also available.

Professional support

The South East England Development Agency (SEEDA) is responsible for promoting the South East as the premier business location and assisting companies in establishing their presence in the region. The International Business Development Team at SEEDA is able to offer a free and highly professional consultancy service to companies wishing to expand existing businesses or invest in the region for the first time. This will include advice on skills, available premises, sites, subcontractors, component suppliers and a wide range of other issues. Its aim is to save your company valuable management time and speed up your decision-making process. For more information visit www.seeda.co.uk.

6.9

South West England

South West England Development Agency

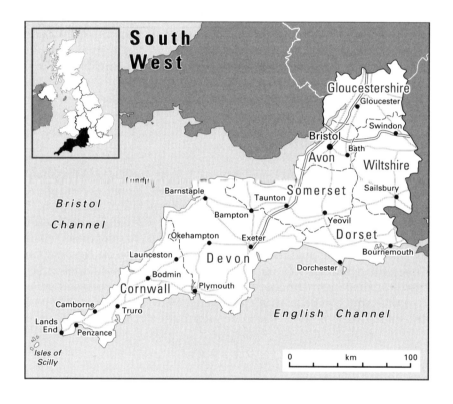

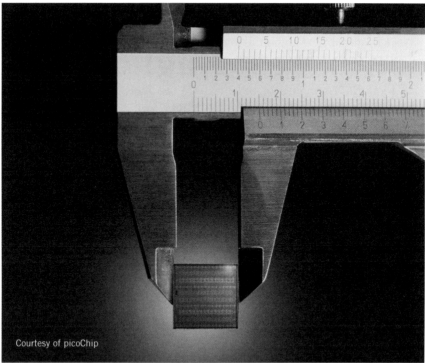

Courtesy of picoChip

According to a survey by *Country Life* magazine, among the top six counties in the United Kingdom to live and work, four are in South West England. The region also continues to attract more tourists and visitors than any other region outside London. Yet, at the same time, South West England, which stretches from Gloucestershire in the north to Bournemouth in the east and the Isles of Scilly in the west, has become one of the United Kingdom's fastest-growing economies. Clearly, there is more than meets the eye to one of the most attractive locations in the United Kingdom. So what is behind the success of South West England? Here are a few factors:

- strong clusters of economic activity in the following sectors: information and communication technology (ICT), biotechnology, marine, creative industry, tourism, financial and food and drink;

- easy access to the rest of the United Kingdom and Europe via major and minor roads, rail links, key airports at Bristol and Plymouth and a number of major ports;

- a workforce of 2.4 million with a record of loyalty and low absenteeism;

- highly skilled and educated workers;

- low-cost offices in many parts of the region;

- very strong research and academic resources and infrastructure;

- an outstanding quality of life.

Business environment

South West England's economy was worth £63.6 billion in 2001, and generates 9 per cent of the total output in England. The region is one of the United Kingdom's fastest growing, with GDP growth outstripping the national average.

The region's unemployment rate has remained consistently below that of the United Kingdom and EU average. In 2002, the region's unemployment rate stood at 3.8 per cent compared with the UK average of 5.6 per cent. One of the region's key strengths is that its workforce has the labour market skills to match the growth in technology and service sectors, underpinned by a strong education and training sector. The workforce is among the most highly qualified in the United Kingdom with 18.8 per cent of the region's population qualified at degree level or higher.

South West England also has well-established sector clusters in many traditional as well as emerging technologies, all backed by strong links to Centres of Excellence. The ICT sector is large and diverse in South West England, comprising hardware manufacture, computer and related activities and telecommunications. According to recent research, South West England and its surrounding area hosts the largest UK and European semiconductor design cluster with 500 pure silicon design engineers.

The marine sector comprises of approximately 2,700 marine industry businesses and an estimated workforce of 30,000. Ship building and repair in the region accounts for 18 per cent of the United Kingdom's marine industry and building and repair.

Biotechnology and environmental technology businesses are fast establishing themselves within the region and investment is under way to extend the resources and support the infrastructure. There are 35–40 core biotech companies in research and development and the region has the first university in Europe, Exeter University, with a biocatalysis centre. There are now between 90 and 100 biotech manufacturers and suppliers and several thousand more researchers based in the region.

The creative sector has grown rapidly in the last decade with the sector now employing over 16,000 people. Much of the activity is concentrated in and around Bristol where there is a strong presence of multimedia and television. Examples of the region's creativity include the Oscar-winning Aardman Animation's *Wallace and Gromit* and *Chicken Run* films, which have become world famous.

Food and drink employs around 44,000 people. The gross value-added output of the food and drink industry in South West England amounts to more than £3 billion, with more than 200 specialist producers.

South West England is also regarded as a world-class centre for advanced engineering, home to big names in the aerospace sector such as BAE and Rolls Royce. In fact, the region has the largest concentration of aerospace-related companies in Europe. The region has also played a key part in the history of the UK space industry. The British Aeroplane Company launched the 44-foot Skylark rocket in 1957, eight months before the Russians launched Sputnik, and currently Chippenham-based CodaScisys is working on software for the European Space Agency's Cryosat spacecraft.

In the financial sector a large number of international financial players have developed businesses here. Services range from global transaction processing to the retail corporate headquarters of the United Kingdom's biggest banking group, LloydsTSB.

Tourism – South West England is steeped in natural beauty and with attractions such as Bath, Stonehenge, the Jurassic Coast and the Eden Project. Within the United Kingdom, the region attracts more visitors than any other outside London, with over 21 million visitors each year. In addition, 72 per cent of the United Kingdom's ancient monuments and 25 per cent of historic buildings are to be found in South West England.

Environmental technologies – South West England's natural environment is a significant economic advantage. Businesses linked to the land and the wider environment (agriculture, forestry, tourism, land management, environmental technology, waste treatment and energy) contribute over £656 million to the region's GDP and sustain thousands of jobs. South West England also offers extensive coastline with opportunities for offshore energy from wind, tidal barges, tidal current and wave energy technologies.

Working environment

The options for business space are exceptional. Premises and development space are readily available on modern business parks in strategic locations, many of them regenerated, such as Temple Quarter and Harbourside in Bristol and Royal William Yard and Plymouth International Business Park in Plymouth. There are also a number of high-quality incubation centres providing workshops, resources and business networks. Many of the region's incubation centres and science parks are closely linked to research and academic institutions.

International investment

There are over 1,200 non-UK-owned companies in the South West of England. Global blue chip players such as JP Morgan Chase, Honda, Intel, Orange, Toshiba, Hewlett Packard and Siemens have established operations here. The region is attracting increasingly more inward investment projects, taking 7 per cent of UK investment projects in 2002. Major inward investors include Airbus SAS, Honda Motor Co, Halliburton Company and Tyco International Ltd.

Research and development

The ability to develop next-generation products is one of the key criteria for businesses choosing to locate in the region. For example, Hewlett Packard, Lucent Technologies, Motorola and Toshiba have all based some of their most important R&D facilities in the region, knowing they can benefit from the research resources available at some of the United Kingdom's leading universities. South West England's academic institutions have extremely strong links with business. This fosters a culture of cooperation leading directly to research and development programmes that generate income for institutions and new products and services for the private sector.

Beyond the beaches

South West England is a region of Europe with an unparalleled track record for innovation, where businesses of all sizes can tap into the key resources needed to succeed. Beyond the traditional image of sun-soaked beaches and breathtaking countryside lies the region's best-kept secret – a thriving economy and a dynamic business location. Twelve hundred of the world's leading foreign-owned companies can't be wrong!

The South West of England Regional Development Agency (South West RDA), a single point of contact for overseas companies, provides a comprehensive service for any company interested in locating their business in the region. It will help you make the right decisions for your business and will ensure your move to the South West of England is successful.

For more information please contact Tim Bagshaw, Head of Sector Development of South West Regional Development Agency on Tel: +44 (0) 1752 251071, e-mail: enquiries@southwestrda.org.uk, or visit www.southwestengland.co.uk.

6.9.1 SWINDON
Major growth is forecast in Swindon

If you think that there is not much more to Swindon than a convenient stop between London and Bristol – think again. Swindon is already the location of choice for major leading high technology companies such as Honda, Intel, Motorola and Lucent Technologies and now is the time to take a look at all the potential development opportunities that Swindon has to offer.

The New Swindon Company (Swindon's Urban Regeneration Company) is tasked with ensuring that the town centre fulfils its role as an important commercial centre. That means making sure that the town delivers everything one would expect – a thriving retail hub, leisure, cultural and education facilities and attractive town centre living and working.

The aim of the regeneration work is to ensure that Swindon plays a leading role in the regional economy and this will be achieved through:

- building a stronger local economy, which recognizes the need to accommodate the growth of existing businesses, as well as encouraging new enterprises;

- improving the retail, leisure and cultural offers;
- more town centre living;
- better transport with safe and accessible parking;
- pleasant and safe public spaces surrounded by quality design and architecture.

Ideas to achieve these aims were communicated as part of an extensive consultation programme in the summer and included four broad zones. Examples of these are:

- retail core – major new retail development to include a new department store, multiplex cinema and broader range of shops; more cafes and restaurants;
- commercial and cultural quarter – new library; office and residential development;
- the Station Gateway – improvements to the railway station with new entrances and squares; a new pedestrian bridge over the railway;
- Heritage Quarter – development of vacant land for uses such as leisure, residential and business.

The good news is that there are already a number of projects coming forward to address some of these ideas. Westfield Shoppingtowns is planning a major redevelopment that will include a new department store and multiplex cinema; the National Trust is moving its headquarters to an area adjacent to the Outlet Centre; and Swindon Borough Council has just recently announced its intention to develop a new library, art gallery and museum in the Theatre Square area. Whether it is a commercial scheme, a new residential development, leisure or retail complex, there's never been a better time to 'invest in the west'.

Population growth

The population of Swindon Borough is about 180,600, of which about 150,000 live in the main urban area. The population of Swindon Borough has doubled in the last 50 years. This compares to a 20 per cent increase in the population of England. Swindon is a major centre of employment, shopping, leisure and community facilities. A population of approximately 300,000 live within 20 miles of the town centre. The population of Swindon is slightly younger than the national

focus on Swindon

The Economic Development Team, dedicated to promoting and encouraging the economic wellbeing of Swindon, creating a great place to do business.

Telephone: 01793 466421
internet: www.investinswindon.co.uk
email: invest@swindon.gov.uk

business friendly

free information on the local economy

impartial advice

focus on
Swindon
economy

SWINDON
BOROUGH COUNCIL

average. Fifty-six per cent of the borough population is aged under 40, compared with 53 per cent for the whole of England.

Communications

Swindon's communications are excellent. The town is situated at the centre of the M4 corridor between the important commercial cities of London and Bristol. In addition, the M5 is easily accessible via the A419 to the north of the town. This strategic location offers business unrivalled access to UK and overseas markets.

Travel to Heathrow Airport is quicker than from Central London by road. The M4 and two motorway junctions provide rapid access to the town centre and business parks. There is also good access to the M5 via the improved A419. The town has a modern road network and extensive parking facilities.

Swindon is situated on the main London rail line to Wales and the West Country. Rail connections to other parts of the United Kingdom are first class. London is 58 minutes by high-speed train and Bristol is just 40 minutes. A daily direct connection to the Eurostar service from Waterloo International is operational

Freight transport

The docks at Bristol, Southampton and Cardiff are also within easy reach. Bristol Airport is the main air cargo centre for the South West region. Swindon has a well-developed orbital route for the transport of freight by road, providing good access to business parks. Keypoint, an intermodal rail terminal close to the A419 and adjacent to the main London/Bristol railway line, provides facilities for the direct transfer of freight from road to rail. Several advanced distribution and warehousing operations are also located in the town, including WH Smith, Book Club Associates and Tibbett and Britten. In addition, serviced warehouse facilities are available that provide a full range of contract packing, warehousing and distribution services.

Telecommunications

Swindon is a modern, developing centre for industry and commerce and has the benefit of a large investment in telecommunications infrastructure. There is an established cable network in the town and new wireless facilities are now available. Additionally, Swindon is one of only seven areas in the country selected to be included in BT's Smartplace programme, which will accelerate the delivery and take-up of broadband in the area.

Swindon's labour market

There are approximately 102,000 people in Swindon's workforce, 56,000 men and 46,000 women. The economic activity rate for all people aged 16 plus in Swindon in 2001/02 was 71.1 per cent compared with a regional and national average of 64 per cent. Average gross earnings in Swindon in 2002 were £417 per week, 6.5 per cent higher than the national average.

The knowledge-based economy in Swindon is strong compared with the national picture. Employment in the local high-tech and medium high-tech manufacturing sectors is well above the national average.

Employment land and commercial property

Swindon has 40 industrial estates and business parks. Many have been constructed in recent years and are therefore well equipped for the needs of modern industry. Employment land for industrial, office and mixed-use development is available at a wide range of sites and two new major greenfield employment sites will become available in the next few years. Services and utilities are readily available on all of the major employment sites. Land for employment uses, including office, leisure and retail developments is also available in the town centre. Commercial rents and the price of employment land in Swindon are consistently lower than in most competitive locations in the M4 corridor.

Education and training

The Learning and Skills Council (LSC) for Wiltshire and Swindon assists companies with their training requirements. The LSC will assist companies wishing to achieve 'Investors in People' status and promotes the use and development of National Vocational Qualifications (NVQs) and Modern Apprenticeships.

Swindon has two further education colleges offering a comprehensive further education service. New College caters for 16–19 year-olds, offering a wide range of academic courses up to 'A' and 'AS' levels, as well as GCSE and pre-vocational courses leading into employment.

The University of Bath in Swindon is located at the Oakfield campus close to the town centre. The university provides a range of undergraduate and postgraduate programmes as well as continuing professional development. The University Business Services Centre offers a wide range of services to support businesses in the Swindon area and the new Oakfield Innovation Centre supports the development of new high-growth technology businesses.

Housing

A substantial programme of house building has accompanied Swindon's rapid expansion over the past four decades and a further area of town expansion is currently under development at the northern edge of the town. There are also a number of small developments under way on sites within the urban area of Swindon and in the surrounding villages. Executive housing is available in a number of the surrounding towns and villages, notably Chiseldon, Wanborough, Highworth, Shrivenham, Cirencester, Marlborough and Cricklade, all of which are within easy commuting distance of Swindon.

The business community in Swindon

Famous names in Swindon
The breadth of the economic base of Swindon is considered to be one of its greatest advantages. The main industries are electronics and telecommunications, car manufacturing, financial services, business services and distribution. Famous names with headquarters or major manufacturing facilities in Swindon include Honda, Intel, Motorola, Lucent Technologies, RWE Innogy, Zurich IFA and the Nationwide Building Society. Swindon is also the home of four government research councils and the National Monuments Record Centre. In 2003, the National Trust announced plans to build a new headquarters in Swindon on the historic site of the former railway works.

Business and professional services in Swindon
The rapid growth of industry and commerce in Swindon has stimulated the development of an extensive business and professional services sector offering a comprehensive range of services to new and established companies in the town. Local companies have grown to meet the demands of incoming organizations and national business services companies have set up local branches to serve the market in Swindon.

There is a wide range of foreign-owned companies located in Swindon from the United States, Europe and the Far East and Swindon's business and professional services sector has considerable experience in meeting the needs of overseas as well as UK companies.

Leisure and lifestyle

Swindon's top attractions
STEAM – Museum of the Great Western Railway – offers a great day out for the whole family. Young and old will find plenty to enjoy at STEAM, which celebrates 'God's Wonderful Railway'. STEAM has

entertained thousands of visitors with the remarkable human stories behind the magnificent locomotives on display.

The National Monuments Record Centre is the public archive of English Heritage. The magnificent collection holds over 10 million historic and modern photographs, texts and documents – the national record of England's built heritage.

The Swindon Art Gallery has a reputation as one of the best collections of modern British art outside London. The collection includes works by Henry Moore, Graham Sutherland, L. S. Lowry, Paul Nash, Steven Pippin and many more.

The Science Museum in Wroughton houses the National Science Museum's larger objects including aircraft, vintage cars, motorbikes, buses and agricultural machinery. The extensive collections can be viewed on special open days that are held by the museum.

Shoppers' delight

The Great Western Designer Outlet Centre is Europe's largest covered designer outlet centre with over 100 designer label shops and enjoys discounts between 30 per cent and 50 per cent off top brands. What makes the Outlet Centre unique is its setting in the splendidly restored Victorian buildings of the Great Western Railway Works, where original architectural features have been restored. Swindon's old town offers a more traditional shopping environment, where you will find several long-established family businesses selling antiques, jewellery, unusual home furnishings, books and art.

Country life

Swindon is surrounded by picturesque villages, miles of countryside, sweeping woodlands and country parks. Thousands of trees are being planted around Swindon in the Great Western Community Forest to enhance the landscape and enrich its wildlife. Lydiard House, set in 250 acres of parkland, is a delightful place to explore at any time of year and Stanton Park with a large lake and semi-natural woodland is also well worth a visit.

Further afield

Travel just a short distance from Swindon and discover some of the most breathtaking scenery to be found in England. Just 10 miles from Swindon is the largest henge monument in the United Kingdom at Avebury. Between Avebury and Marlborough you will find the most enigmatic monument in the area at Silbury Hill. Wiltshire is famous for White Horses figures carved in the chalk of the Wiltshire downs, most dating back to the 18th and 19th centuries. Wiltshire also has its fair share of historic houses: choose between Bowood House, Corsham Court, Longleat, Wilton and Stourhead.

Hotels and conference centres
Swindon offers a superb selection of international hotels, elegant country houses, family-run guesthouses, conference venues and non-residential corporate training facilities. The town's good communications, attractive environment and proximity to London and the South East, have created an excellent location for business meetings and events. Corporate hospitality and incentive ideas include karting, shooting, jet skiing and some of the best golf courses in the region.

The Economic Strategy and Promotion Team

The Economic Strategy and Promotion Team provides a wide range of services to industry and commerce. The team promotes Swindon as an excellent location for industry and commerce in the United Kingdom and as a centre for tourism. The team has substantial experience of relocating companies and their staff into the area. The services provided can be tailor-made to suit the needs of individual companies and include all or some of the following:

● information packs on Swindon and local facilities;

● presentations to staff and their families;

● guided tours of the town and surrounding countryside;

● information on land, business premises and the local economy;

● contacts with business support organizations and the business community;

● advice on accessing the UK and European market;

● tourist information and a conference venue location service.

For information on any of the above services, please contact: Economic Strategy and Promotion Team, Swindon Borough Council, Premier House, Station Road, Swindon SN1 1TZ. E-mail: focus@swindon.gov.uk. Tel: +44 (0) 1793 466421. Fax: +44 (0) 1793 466442. websites: www.focusonswindon.com; www.visitswindon.co.uk.

6.10

Northern Ireland

Invest Northern Ireland

Demographics

Northern Ireland has one of Europe's youngest populations; nearly 60 per cent of the region's 1.69 million residents are under the age of 40. The United Kingdom's National Statistics Regional Trends for 2002 forecasts a higher population growth for Northern Ireland of more than 4.5 per cent from 2000 to 2011, compared with less than 3 per cent for England, under 2 per cent for Wales and a population decline in Scotland.

The economy

Northern Ireland is the fastest-growing regional economy in the United Kingdom and has performed well, with unemployment levels at a 25-year low and strong growth in manufacturing output, well above the UK level. Gross Domestic Product of £17,003 million was registered for 1999. Northern Ireland's GDP had the largest increase between 1990 and 1999 of all the UK regions during this period. It is estimated to have grown by 2.5 per cent in 2003, accelerating to 3 per cent for 2004.

Origins of gross value-added (GVA) by industrial sector

As Table 6.10.1 indicates, Northern Ireland's flourishing services sector contributes almost 70 per cent to GDP, reflecting the growth of its knowledge-led economy. Over the past five years, the output growth of Northern Ireland has outstripped the other UK regions, increasing by 11.0 per cent compared with a corresponding fall of 4.1 per cent in the United Kingdom overall.

Table 6.10.1   GDP by industrial sector

Sector	%
Services	68.0
Manufacturing	20.5
Construction	7.0
Agriculture	2.0
Electricity, Gas & Water	2.0
Mining and Quarrying	0.5
TOTAL	100.0

Source: Northern Ireland Annual Abstract of Statistics 2003

Aligned to this excellent output performance, there has been a significant growth in manufacturing labour productivity, which has been

A QUALIFIED WORKFORCE YOU DON'T HAVE TO GO TO THE ENDS OF THE EARTH FOR

DEPARTURES

Northern Ireland offers
many things to business
investors - low property prices,
state-of-the-art communications,
world-class facilities, competitive
operating costs and a quality
workforce. And it is this workforce
that we are extremely proud of.
Highly motivated, well educated,
determined to succeed and closer
to you in terms of location
and aspirations.

To find out more about what
Northern Ireland can offer your
business contact
Kyra Morrison
t. 020 7222 0599
email: kyra.morrison@investni.com
www.investni.com/invest

Look no further.

Northern Ireland
fresh talent at work

increasing in Northern Ireland since the mid-1990s at almost twice the UK average rate.

Inflation

Northern Ireland benefits from the strength of the UK economy and its low interest rate, low inflation climate. Until recently, the current interest rate stood near a 40-year low while inflation remains below many other European countries.

Labour

The disposition of the Northern Ireland workforce is summarized in Table 6.10.2.

Table 6.10.2   Distribution of the Northern Ireland workforce by activity

Activity	No of Employed	%
Agriculture	14,240	2.0
Industry	132,980	20.0
Services	520,390	78.0
Total	655,800	100.0

Source: Northern Ireland Annual Abstract of Statistics 2003

Unemployment, currently running at its lowest level since records began, has fallen steadily from a peak of 17.2 per cent in 1986 to 5.6 per cent in October 2003, compared with the current EU15 average of 8.1 per cent. Between 1998 and 2003, employee jobs in Northern Ireland increased by 8.9 per cent compared with an increase of 5.7 per cent in the United Kingdom as a whole. Total employment in Northern Ireland is expected to continue growing faster from 2001 to 2010 than in the United Kingdom as a whole in each year of the forecast period, resulting in an extra 40,000 jobs by the end of the decade.

In the manufacturing sector, wages and salaries are highly competitive and up to 32 per cent lower than in the United States and 25 per cent lower than the EU15 average. The US Bureau of Labor Statistics and NI New Earnings Survey cites Northern Ireland hourly compensation costs as the lowest among North America, Japan, Germany, the United Kingdom, France and the Republic of Ireland.

Northern Ireland also enjoys an excellent industrial relations record, with the number of labour disputes in the period 1996 to 2000 well below the European average and the United States'. In addition, levels of staff absenteeism due to sickness are the lowest in the United Kingdom.

Foreign direct investment

Over the past six years Northern Ireland has become increasingly successful in attracting foreign investors, and foreign direct investment (FDI) has increased by 45 per cent. The success of these investments is evidenced by the fact that nearly three-quarters of foreign investors in Northern Ireland have already re-invested or are gearing up to invest more. Investments in ICT, service and technology sectors have increased from 22 per cent of the total in 1993 to account for 90 per cent of all FDI into Northern Ireland in 2002/03, again reflecting the growth of Northern Ireland's knowledge-led economy.

Exports

On average, more than £20 million worth of manufactured goods are sold outside Northern Ireland every day of the year. In the manufacturing sector, 70 per cent of all sales are made to customers outside Northern Ireland. External sales by product group are analysed in Table 6.10.3.

Table 6.10.3 Manufacturing exports 2001/02 by product group

Product	£m	%
Transport Equipment	785	10.9
Electrical & Optical Equipment	1,369	19.0
Chemicals & Man-made Fibres	404	5.6
Food, Drink & Tobacco	2,055	28.5
Non-metallic Manufacturing Products	159	2.2
Other Machinery & Equipment	562	7.8
Textiles	680	9.4
Basic Metals/Fabricated Metal Products	324	4.5
Rubber & Plastics	421	5.8
Paper & Printing	193	2.7
Other Manufacturing	163	2.3
Wood & Wood Products	105	1.5
Total	7,220	100.0

Source: NIERC, DETI (2003) *Sales and Exports* 2001/02, June 2003

The latest export survey, published in June 2003, shows that in 2001/02 export sales accounted for almost 40 per cent of total sales, an increase of 36 per cent over the previous five years. The same survey identifies the principal destinations of manufacturing sales more closely as: the home market: 30 per cent, Great Britain: 31 per cent,

Republic of Ireland: 10 per cent, the rest of the EU: 12 per cent and the rest of the world: 17 per cent.

Education

In 2001–02 there were 346,500 pupils in Northern Ireland schools, accounting for some 3.5 per cent of the UK pupil population. With nearly 21,000 teachers, the pupil/teacher ratio is 19.7 in primary schools and 14.4 in secondary schools. Public expenditure on education is almost double the UK average spend and one-third higher than the Republic of Ireland, accounting for 22 per cent of total public expenditure.

Northern Ireland's educational achievements are high, with more students consistently gaining top grades in school exams than the UK average. In a UK comparison of research work, Northern Ireland's two universities have had major successes. The Research Assessment Exercise 2001, verified by international academics, showed that 53 per cent of the courses assessed at the University of Ulster and 82 per cent of those at the Queen's University of Belfast were carrying out research of national and international excellence.

Infrastructure

Northern Ireland's exceptional transportation and communications network makes it fast and easy to connect to the rest of the world, either face to face or electronically.

Telecommunications

Northern Ireland has an advanced resilient, digital telecommunications network that provides high-speed voice and data connections. It was the first region in the United Kingdom to develop a fully fibre-optic infrastructure, and is part of a UK network that supplies greater bandwidth than the rest of Europe combined.

Northern Ireland is the leading UK region in terms of broadband exploitation. By 2005 broadband coverage will be 100 per cent. The government in Northern Ireland is committed to technology exploitation and adoption for the benefit of investors and local businesses and are in the process of appointing a service provider to accelerate the roll-out of broadband services across Northern Ireland. The cost of a three-minute telephone call from Northern Ireland to mainland Europe is on average 48 per cent cheaper than other EU tariffs, while contacting the United States is nearly 40 per cent less expensive.

Utilities

Electricity

The electric power system is 3-phase AC operating at 50 hertz with transmission systems of 275 kilovolts and 110 kilovolts serving a wide distribution network of 33 kilovolts and 11 kilovolts. Low voltage supplies are 230/400 volts, although many large factories take supply at 11 kilovolts or 33 kilovolts. A range of tariffs is available with rates varying according to the pattern of usage and voltage of supply. As a guide, most large companies pay on average a price between 3.3 pence and 9.2 pence per kilowatt hour.

Gas

To date there are over 3,000 industrial and commercial customers using natural gas supplied by Phoenix Natural Gas, which commenced operations in Belfast in 1997. Customer savings on energy costs in 2003 against their previous fuels amounted to £6 million. Contract customers, using above 25,000 terms (72,000 kilowatt hours) per annum can expect to pay up to 1.65 pence per kilowatt hour depending on the size of load, load factor, contract duration, etc. For large customers with equipment capable of firing on alternative fuels, 'interruptible supply' contracts are available at prices below the 1.4 pence per kilowatt hour level.

Office space

New, purpose-built and fitted out office space is available throughout Northern Ireland and for as little as £12 per square foot in the greater Belfast area. Belfast currently maintains the lowest net rent in the United Kingdom and compares with prime office rents of £22 per square foot and more in other major cities in the EU15.

Invest Northern Ireland's Property Services Unit can advise on design, build and finance provisions managed either by the company or by a property developer. Invest Northern Ireland's online database contains an extensive range of properties and serviced sites available throughout Northern Ireland.

Logistics

Roads

There are 21,636 miles of public roads in Northern Ireland. Traffic congestion is minimal, especially when compared with main trunk routes in England. The well-developed road infrastructure links all major commercial and industrial areas with seaports and airports.

Over 48 million tonnes of freight were transported via the road network in 2002.

Seaports

Over 80 international shipping lines operate out of Northern Ireland's five commercial seaports, which handle 90 per cent of Northern Ireland's total trade and almost 50 per cent of the Republic of Ireland's freight traffic with an average of 150 sailings a week to destinations in Great Britain and throughout the world.

The busiest port in Ireland is Belfast, through which 60 per cent of Northern Ireland's sea-borne trade is shipped. A total of 8,800 ships carrying 17 million tonnes leave the Port of Belfast each year. The Port of Londonderry is the United Kingdom's most westerly port and has a capacity for 30,000 tonne vessels.

Airports

Belfast International Airport serves over 3.7 million passengers a year and is the closest all-weather airport in Europe to the United States. It is the most technically advanced airport in Ireland and the fifth largest regional air cargo centre in the United Kingdom. In addition to regular scheduled passenger aircraft providing airfreight services, the airport handles an increasing traffic in dedicated freighter aircraft, including the Antonov 124. Leading airfreight operators using the 24-hour Belfast service are DHL and TNT; Royal Mail has a large presence there.

Direct flight times to London and Amsterdam are one hour 20 minutes and two hours 35 minutes respectively. Flights to New York via Manchester take eight hours 50 minutes and to Tokyo 13 hours 30 minutes.

Belfast City Airport has opened a new terminal as a result of rapidly growing passenger traffic, which now exceeds 1.3 million passengers each year. The City of Derry Airport serves the North East Region of Ireland and is located seven miles northeast of Londonderry.

Crime

Northern Ireland has emerged from its troubled past and is now among the countries with the lowest rate of violent deaths, being well below the UK average. It is a safe place to live and, according to the 2000 International Crime Victim Survey (ICVS) compiled every four years by the United Nations Interregional Crime and Justice Research Institute, has the lowest crime victim rate in the world.

Contacts

Invest Northern Ireland Headquarters
66 Chichester Street
Belfast BT1 4JX
Tel: +44 (0) 28 9023 9090
Fax: +44 (0) 28 9054 5000

Chicago
2201 Waukegan Road, Suite South 150
Bannockburn IL 60015
Tel: +1 (847) 945 2908
Fax: +1 (847) 945 2900
E-mail: info@investni.com

San Jose
226 Airport Parkway, Suite 310
San Jose, CA 95110
Tel: +1 (408) 441 0544
Fax: +1 (408) 441 0547
E-mail: info@investni.com

Atlanta
2905 Piedmont Road
Atlanta, GA 30305
Tel: +1 (404) 238 9345
Fax: +1 (404) 238 9347
E-mail: infor@invstni.com

Boston
545 Boylston Street, 8th Floor
Boston, MA 02116
Tel: +1 (617) 266 8839
Fax +1 (617) 8914
E-mail: info@investni.com

6.11

Scotland

Scottish Enterprise

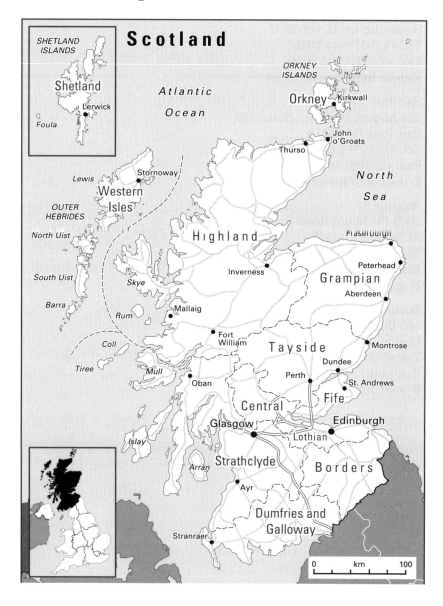

IF YOU WERE SURROUNDED BY MAJESTIC GLENS, PICTURESQUE GOLF AND THE WORLD'S FINEST WHISKY, YOU'D BE WORKING DAY AND NIGHT TO EXTEND LIFE TOO.

Not every scientific discovery is made in a completely sterile environment. Surrounded by breathtaking glens and vistas, Scottish scientists performed many medical miracles. We introduced surgery and anesthesia and developed CAT scans, MRIs and penicillin.

Today, our scientists are making history in drug discovery and development, bioelectronics, genomics, neuroscience and cardiovascular research. Dr. Ian Wilmut cloned the first mammal. Sir Philip Cohen is breaking ground in signal

transduction and cancer treatment. Sir David Lane is also working to cure cancer with the p53 gene. And at Edinburgh University, we're conducting stem cell research. This, coupled with a prosperous biomanufacturing centre, makes ours the fastest-growing biotech community in all of Europe.

We're proud. We

admit it. But we judge our own success based on the impact we make on the world. That's why we collaborate with biotech companies everywhere — and why we established Scottish Development International.

Visit us on the Web to find out how you can capitalise on the products of Scotland's environment: a history of invention, a culture of determination and a destination for renowned scientists.

www.scotsinnovate.com/lifescience

Overview

Scotland has long enjoyed a reputation for being one of the most ingenious, forward-looking and industrious nations in the world. Indeed, Scotland has given rise to many more famous people, notable in the arts, literature, the sciences and as inventors, philosophers, architects and so on, than would be expected for a country of such modest size and population.

The Scottish people and workforce are famous for their integrity, inventiveness, tenacity and spirit – a fact supported by recent research. This, when partnered with Scotland's economic opportunities, means Scotland is a key destination for businesses seeking to expand and develop their commercial activities.

While Scotland has a rich manufacturing and engineering past, its economy has changed beyond all recognition in recent years. Today, Scotland leads the world in modern, knowledge-driven sectors including electronics, education, biotechnology and optoelectronics.

Scotland's political life has also undergone change with the establishment of Scotland's first parliament in 300 years in 1998. The Scottish Executive is a coalition between the Labour and Liberal Democrat parties, under the leadership of First Minister Jack McConnell. The parliament, founded on principles of openness, accountability and equal opportunities, has quickly established its own identity and personality.

Rated among the world's top economic development agencies, **Scottish En**terprise is the main economic development **agency for** Scotland, covering 93 per cent of the population from Grampian to **the** Border. The other 17 per cent is covered by Highlands and Islands Enterprise. Working in partnership with the private and public sectors, they aim to secure the long-term future of the Scottish economy by making its industries more competitive. They are involved in:

- helping business start-ups and existing companies to grow;
- promoting and encouraging export activity;
- attracting inward investment; and
- developing skills.

Priorities include the commercialization of academic ideas into good business opportunities, e-business, globalization and economic inclusion. They are funded by the Scottish Executive and are headquartered in Glasgow and Inverness. The Scottish Executive has set out its strategic vision to guide the strategies and operations of Scottish Enterprise and Highlands and Islands Enterprise.

The vision

The vision is for 'A Smart, Successful Scotland', a Scotland where creating, learning and connecting faster is the basis for sustained productivity growth, competitiveness and prosperity. The role of the Enterprise Networks is central to delivering this vision. The action needed to achieve a Smarter Scotland translates into three key organizing themes for the activities of the Enterprise Networks:

- growing business;

- global connections;

- skills and learning.

The economy

Despite the downturn in the global electronics market, recent figures have shown that Scotland has weathered the storm and its economy is growing. Globally, Scotland's key trade partners such as the United States and the Eurozone countries are experiencing growth, which means businesses from these countries are starting to invest overseas again. Scotland is well placed to reap the benefits of these conditions. Prospects for manufacturing are also improving, and independent economic forecasters are predicting that the sector will return to growth, given the favourable conditions apparent in Scotland – low inflation, low interest rates, low unemployment and strong domestic demand.

Demographics

The resident population of Scotland on 29 April 2001 (Census Day) was 5,062,011, of which 52 per cent were female and 48 per cent were male. Children aged 15 and under accounted for 19 per cent of the population, while people of working age accounted for 62 per cent. People of retirement age accounted for the remaining 19 per cent. There are approximately 90 people for every square mile of land, and the majority of the population are concentrated in the central area around Glasgow and Edinburgh. The Highlands and Islands have the largest area but the fewest people. Scotland has six cities with the following populations:

Glasgow	578,710
Edinburgh	449,020
Aberdeen	211,910
Dundee	145,460
Inverness	50,920
Stirling	86,200

Potential inward investors should be aware that Scotland has a skilled and dynamic workforce, totalling 2,387,000 people. Scotland has a diverse, thriving economy. By sector, Scotland's workforce is employed in the sectors shown in Table 6.11.1.

Table 6.11.1   Percentage workforce per sector

Industry	Scotland (2000) (%)
Agriculture & Fishing	2
Energy & Water	2
Manufacturing	14
Construction	6
Distribution, Hotels & Restaurants	23
Transport and Communications	5
Banking, Finance & Insurance, etc	17
Public Administration, Education & Health	26
Other Services	5

Key industry sectors

The new technology sectors, together with education, tourism, financial and business services and health, account for 70 per cent of Scotland's gross domestic product. Thousands of people are employed in these key industries. Scotland has made a marked transition from the old to the new economy and has based this on a foundation of knowledge, cutting-edge technology and enterprise. Its biotechnology industry, for example, is one of the most successful in Europe, with over 20,000 people currently employed. The industry is growing at an astonishing 30 per cent a year.

Optoelectronics – the use of light to process and transmit data – is another fast-growing sector in Scotland. Although optoelectronics has become an increasingly familiar part of everyday life through the use of devices such as compact disc players, supermarket barcode scanners and mobile phones, Scotland has an impressive track record of innovative academic research in the field. Currently, the sector in Scotland is valued at £600 million and supports around 60 companies, employing 5,000 people with a high percentage of PhDs, product design physicists and engineers.

Some of the largest names in the industry have bases in the country, such as BAE SYSTEMS, Semple Cochrane and Polaroid UK. Meanwhile, progressive Scottish companies such as Photonic Materials, which recently secured £10.5 million of new funding, and Printable Field Emitters, which is part of a European consortium developing large flat panel TV screens less than a third of an inch thick, are at the cutting edge of worldwide optoelectronic research and design.

In semiconductors, Scotland has become a world leader in their development and manufacture, with companies such as Motorola and National Semiconductor located here. Furthermore, the world's premier location for the design of advanced system-on-chip semiconductor devices, the Alba Centre, is based in the heart of Scotland's Silicon Glen near Livingston. Electronics also remains a key sector for Scotland, despite the global downturn in the industry. Scotland is home to a number of the world's biggest companies.

Financial services too is one of the most successful industries in Scotland. With £351 billion in funds managed, Scotland is the sixth biggest financial centre in Europe. Scotland is home to four clearing banks, eight major insurance companies and dozens of world-class investment managers, venture capitalists, accountants, corporate lawyers and stockbrokers. Financial heavyweight JP Morgan is among the companies recognizing Scotland's strengths in the field. The company has announced that it is to expand its Glasgow-based European Technology Centre, creating up to 150 new jobs for highly skilled software engineers. Over 106,000 people in Scotland – and a further 289,000 support/backup staff – are employed in the financial services industry. The sector is experiencing much faster growth in Scotland than in the rest of the United Kingdom, and currently generates almost £8 billion in sales and turnover for the economy.

The energy sector continues to be a major source of employment in Scotland, with around 37,000 people involved in the oil and gas extraction industries based around the North Sea. This is a major growth industry in Scotland: it is calculated that the sector will require an additional 5,650 employees between 2001 and 2006 – a sharp contrast with the rest of the United Kingdom, which has seen the industry wane.

Meanwhile, tourism remains an important industry, employing an impressive 8 per cent of the total Scottish workforce. Tourism injects £2.47 billion into the Scottish economy each year.

Foreign direct investment

Scottish Development International is a government-funded organization that can help overseas businesses tap into Scotland's strengths in knowledge, high-level skills, technology and innovation. Established as a joint venture between Scottish Enterprise and the Scottish Executive, the aim of Scottish Development International is to broaden Scotland's international appeal as a first choice source of knowledge from which to develop and exploit innovative technologies and ideas.

Scottish Development International aims to show how Scotland can match its expertise to modern global business needs. During 2001/02, Scottish Development International and its partners helped attract 59 inward investment projects to Scotland, involving a planned investment of £271 million. This investment is expected to lead to the creation and safeguarding of over 6,000 jobs.

Scotland has much to offer potential inward investors, including a competitive cost base for investment, attractive salary and operating costs, together with one of the lowest standard rates of corporate tax in the European Union. In addition, there is a range of public sector financial incentives to help offset the costs of relocation or expansion in Scotland.

Incentives for investors

Support programmes are listed in the following sections.

*Regional Selective Assistance**

Regional Selective Assistance (RSA) is a national grant scheme, aimed at encouraging investment and job creation in areas considered suitable for development under European guidelines. Businesses of all sizes can apply for RSA, whether they are Scottish-owned or not. It is administered by RSA Scotland, part of the Scottish Executive. In the five years to the end of March 2002, businesses in Scotland have accepted over 1,000 RSA offers of grant, totalling £550 million. These offers relate to projects with planned investment of over £4 billion, with the aim of creating or safeguarding over 70,000 jobs. In order to qualify for RSA, projects must:

- take place in an Assisted Area;
- directly create or safeguard jobs;
- not be simply offset by job losses in other Assisted Areas;
- involve an element of capital investment;
- be financially viable;
- be mainly funded from the private sector.

Research and development tax credits

Companies of all sizes can claim these tax credits, although there are two different schemes – one for large companies, and another for small

---

*In England, RSA has recently been substituted by the Selective Finance for Investment (SFi) Scheme (see page 258). However, the original RSA scheme still applies in Scotland.

and medium-sized companies (SMEs). The SME scheme encourages small and medium businesses to carry out R&D for the first time, or to increase their level of R&D. It works by giving companies tax credits on the money they spend on R&D by increasing the tax relief they can claim from 100 per cent to 150 per cent on their qualifying R&D spend if the business is in profit. Companies in the red receive a cash payment of £24 for every £100 they spend on R&D. Meanwhile, large companies can claim an additional tax deductible allowance of 25 per cent on top of the existing 100 per cent first year allowances on qualifying R&D spend.

Training assistance

This is available towards eligible training costs, regardless of whether the training takes place in Scotland or overseas. Assistance is available for up to 25 per cent of approved eligible costs for specific training and 50 per cent for general training. This funding is available throughout Scotland and not just in Assisted Areas.

Property

Scotland has a number of specialized, custom-built properties tailored to particular key industry sectors or areas of expertise. These include the following.

The Alba Centre

This is a world-leading centre for the electronic and related design industries of the future. It provides a unique infrastructure for electronic design and is actively overcoming the challenges associated with the rapid implementation of system-on-chip designs. The Centre has a number of elements – the Alba Campus, the Institute for System Level Integration, the Virtual Component Exchange, the Microelectronics Test Centre, the Talent Scotland recruitment programme, the Scottish Embedded Software Centre and the Alba Associates programme.

Hillington Park Innovation Centre's Wireless Development Centre

The Centre provides a showcase for Scotland's wireless technology. Future and existing clients at the Centre enjoy facilities including mixed technology wireless infrastructure, support and consultancy from technology and business advisors onsite and state-of-the-art development tools and system hardware.

Other modern, prestige property is available at a number of sites across Scotland including Edinburgh Park, Edinburgh, West of

Scotland Science Park, Glasgow, Luna Place Technology Park, Dundee and the Scottish Enterprise Technology Park, East Kilbride.

Transport and communications

Scotland has one of the best working travel infrastructures in the United Kingdom. Glasgow, for example, has the largest suburban rail network outside of London, an uncomplicated underground rail system and a modern overground bus system. Edinburgh and Glasgow are linked by the M8, ensuring there is no more than an hour's journey between the two cities. This allows access to the Central Belt population of over 2.4 million. Both cities are at the centre of Scotland's motorway network, providing fast links to the rest of the United Kingdom. Scotland's road network is also significantly less congested than other parts of the United Kingdom.

There are four major airports in Scotland – Glasgow International, Glasgow Prestwick, Edinburgh International and Aberdeen. A network of regional airports also link cities such as Dundee, Inverness and the Scottish islands. Flights are plentiful, with over 60 flights per day from both Glasgow and Edinburgh Airports to London. More and more international flights are being added on a regular basis, providing greater communication than ever before with mainland Europe and the rest of the world.

A modern rail network allows the majority of Scotland's population to use public transport to travel to work. Trains depart every 15 minutes between Glasgow and Edinburgh, and Glasgow has been voted the United Kingdom's Best City for Transport to Work (Healy & Baker, 2000).

Education, research and development

In December 2002, Scottish First Minister Jack McConnell unveiled ambitious plans to create thousands of high-quality job opportunities by making Scotland a world leader in three of the global economy's major growth sectors – energy, life sciences and communications technology/digital media. Scottish Enterprise is committing £450 million to the three flagship Intermediary Technology Institutes (ITIs), each specializing in one of these three fields of scientific research. These sectors of research were chosen on the basis of Scotland's acknowledged and proven strength in global terms. The Institutes – based in Aberdeen, Dundee and Glasgow – will create a climate of innovation and are expected to create at least 75 spin-out companies in the first 10 years, and around 170 after 20. The ITIs are unique to Scotland, and seek to address the strengths and weaknesses of the country's economy. The institutes aim to:

- create and expand the number of high-growth, high-value technology companies in Scotland;

- attract and expand foreign direct investment that is linked to knowledge and retained skills;

- nurture strong technical, entrepreneurial and flexible skills to create a fertile environment for growth;

- increase both the technology research and commercial reputation of Scotland;

- build significant, sustainable economic impact for Scotland in these key global market areas.

The three institutes will act as centres for identifying, commissioning and supporting the diffusion of market-focused pre-competitive technology. Existing and new high-growth companies will be able to access and build on the technology platforms developed by this process, helping them meet the challenges of rapidly evolving global markets. These facilities build on Scotland's already well-established reputation for excellence in education.

In addition to 13 universities, the country also supports six specialist higher education institutions and 37 further education colleges. It is this reputation for quality that persuades thousands of students from all over the world to complete their education in Scotland.

The number of students in further education has doubled in less than 10 years, with almost half the young people in Scotland going on to further education, compared with the UK average of 32 per cent. Scottish universities produce 17 per cent of the United Kingdom's graduates with first degrees in medicine and dentistry, despite Scotland having less than 9 per cent of the UK population. Scotland also produces nearly 11 per cent of the United Kingdom's engineering and technology first degrees. Listed here are some of the jewels in Scotland's research and development crown:

- Edinburgh University's Artificial Intelligence Applications Institute is one of the world's top three research centres into the subject. The institute has pioneered artificial intelligence applications to the aerospace, manufacturing, finance and engineering sectors.

- The Parallel Computing Centre at the University of Edinburgh has state-of-the-art computing facilities, including a Cray T3E – the most powerful supercomputer in Europe.

- The Wellcome Trust has invested £12 million in a new biomedical sciences research centre at Dundee University, where more than 200 scientists research the fundamental causes of diseases such as cancers, diabetes and arthritis. A recent survey has placed three of its scientists in the United Kingdom top 20 for medical research.

- Research and Enterprise is the research development and commercialization arm of the University of Glasgow. Since it was established in 1997, it has worked to make the university the enterprise and research capital of the world. In 1999/2000, its research sales were worth £110 million, and it has identified areas such as clinical, biomedical, veterinary and life sciences, arts, humanities, computing, engineering and physics and key research priorities.

- Glasgow University has recently received an exclusive five-star rating for research in computing science – the highest honour.

- The Yashitomi Research Institute of Neuroscience is a multi-million pound collaborative venture between Yashitomi Pharmaceuticals Industries of Japan and the Universities of Strathclyde and Glasgow. The institute's mission is to discover, study and evaluate new antipsychotic drugs.

Public sector support agencies

Scottish Enterprise
5 Atlantic Quay
150 Broomielaw
Glasgow
G2 8LU
Tel: +44 (0) 141 248 2700
Fax: +44 (0) 141 221 3217
E-mail: network.helpline@scotent.co.uk
Website: www.scottish-enterprise.com

Scottish Development International
Based at the address above
Tel: +44 (0) 141 228 2828
Fax: +44 (0) 141 228 2089
E-mail: investment@scotent.co.uk
Website: www.scottishdevelopmentinternational.com

Highlands and Islands Enterprise
Cowan House
Inverness Retail and Business Park
Inverness IV2 7GF
Tel: +44(0) 1463 234171
Fax: +44 (0) 1463 244469
E-mail: hie.general@hient.co.uk
Website: www.hie.co.uk

Scottish Executive
St Andrew's House
Regent Road
Edinburgh
EH1 3DG
Tel: +44 (0) 131 556 8400
Fax: +44 (0) 131 244 8240
E-mail: ceu@scotland.gov.uk
Website: www.scotland.gov.uk

6.12

Wales

Welsh Development Agency

Overview

Over the past 20 years, more than 1,500 companies have invested some £13 billion in Wales – over 40 per cent of which was reinvestment by enterprises that had decided to devote additional resources to their successful Welsh-based operations. Wales is now a major base for a large number of world-leading companies including Airbus, British Airways, Ford, Bosch, Sony, Dow Corning, 3M and GE.

Since 1999, Wales has enjoyed devolved government by the National Assembly for Wales based in Cardiff and led by a First Minister. Over the next 10 years, the Assembly's 'Winning Wales' strategic plan has identified some £15 billion that will be invested to promote economic development. The Assembly's main economic development arm is the Welsh Development Agency, which is responsible for attracting new investment into Wales and assisting the growth of existing businesses. The WDA emphasizes, among key reasons for investing in Wales:

- an educated and dedicated workforce;
- an academic structure of international excellence;
- a culture of innovation and technological advancement;
- connections to the rest of the United Kingdom and Europe by an excellent transport infrastructure;
- a state-of-the-art telecommunications infrastructure;
- competitive property prices and ready availability of land for development;
- attractive levels of incentives;
- one of the United Kingdom's lowest costs of living;
- an excellent quality of life, with stunning countryside and a diversity of cultural and leisure pursuits.

Demographics

Wales has a population of some 2.9 million people with the greatest concentration being found in the southeast and northeast. Overall, population density is 367 people per square mile, just over half of the UK average. The largest city in Wales is the capital, Cardiff, which has a population of 305,000. Other major centres are Swansea, Newport and Wrexham. In 2001, the median age of the population of Wales was 38 years, up from 36 in 1991.Three in five people living in Wales were of working age.

Wales offers investors an extremely attractive labour environment. It possesses an educated and motivated workforce of more than 1 million people. In terms of occupation profile, the active workforce in Wales can be compared to the UK average as follows in Table 6.12.1.

Table 6.12.1   Employment pattern – Wales vs United Kingdom

	% of Wales's Employment	% of UK Employment
Agriculture, Forestry & Fishing	1.3	1.3
Manufacturing & Construction	23.4	19.5
Services	75.3	79.2

Source: UK government

A more detailed breakdown of Welsh employment pattern is shown in Table 6.12.2.

Table 6.12.2   Welsh employment profile

Industry	Wales 2001
All Industries	1,090,700
Agriculture & Fishing	13,700
All Production & Construction Industries	249,500
Energy & Water	9,900
Manufacturing	189,000
Construction	50,700
All Service Industries	827,400
Distribution, Hotels & Restaurants	259,400
Transport & Communication	49,400
Banking, Finance & Insurance	123,600
Public Administration, Education & Health	341,800
Other Services	53,200

Source: National Assembly for Wales, StatsWales, 2004

The Welsh economy and foreign direct investment

There are now some 500 overseas-owned companies operating in Wales, employing more than 73, 000 people. During 2001/02, companies from the United States were the largest investors in Wales with 33 per cent. Other major sources of investment were Japan (13 per cent), Ireland (10 per cent) and France (10 per cent).

The Welsh economy now has special strengths in a number of key sectors, including aerospace, automotive components, financial services, customer relationship management and contact centres, life sciences, information technology, software and multimedia. For example, there are now more than 100 aerospace and related companies in Wales employing over 20,000 people. More than 30 per cent of the United Kingdom's aircraft maintenance repair and overhaul business by value and 25 per cent by employment are located within 30 miles of Cardiff International Airport – and WDA is developing a major new aerospace business park at St Athan, just outside Cardiff.

Wales is also one of the most advanced automotive supply regions in the United Kingdom. Ford, Toyota, Calsonic and Bosch are among 150 sectoral companies employing some 25,000 people. Ford recently decided to centre European production of its new i6 engine at the company's new Bridgend plant – which is already its main European supplier of petrol engines. Similarly, other key sectors have outstanding, world-class operations in Wales.

Wales has a strong, diverse and vibrant financial community. Welsh financial services now directly employ over 28,000 people and have outstanding capacity for growth. The insurance sector is particularly strong and includes leaders such as Admiral Insurance, Legal and General, AA Insurance and Gerling NCM.

The life sciences sector includes operations by 4 of the world's top 10 medical devices companies – Johnson & Johnson, Bayer, 3M and Bristol Myers Squibb. ConvaTec, a subsidiary of Bristol Myers Squibb specializing in wound and skin care, has chosen North Wales as a location for a global development centre.

The software sector in Wales has an estimated turnover of some £750 million and includes activities in areas ranging from R&D to software design and testing. Companies with operations in Wales include Mitel, BT, Logica CMG and General Dynamics. General Dynamics recently won a £1.6 billion contract from the UK Ministry of Defence to build a digital communications system for the British armed forces. As a result, the company has opened a new R&D centre in Wales.

Optoelectronics companies employ some 3,500 people in Wales, with an important cluster in North Wales. Companies with operations in Wales include Alcatel and Cogent Defence systems, which is creating a new corporate headquarters and research and development facility at Newport

Incentives for investors

Significant financial incentives and other forms of support can be obtained by businesses seeking to establish or develop operations in many parts of Wales. Support programmes include, among others, those listed in the following sections.

Regional Selective Assistance (RSA)*

RSA is the main instrument of government financial aid to industry and commerce. It is a discretionary grant administered by the Welsh Assembly government that provides a contribution towards a project. The grant may be assessed on the fixed capital costs of the project or alternatively, the value of the jobs capitalized over a two-year period. The grant is directed towards businesses making investments that create or safeguard jobs in the Assisted Areas of Wales. Assisted Areas offer a wide range of opportunities including an available workforce, competitive labour costs and high labour flexibility.

The amount of grant that is available for a project is that considered the minimum necessary to allow the project to go ahead. Each case is taken on its merits. There are, however, EC restrictions placed on the total level of public assistance that can be given towards a project.

Property Development Grants

Property Development Grants can be used to support new buildings or extensions to existing premises. Grants are negotiable and are normally awarded based on the minimum amount of funding required to secure the project.

Technology Exploitation Programme (TEP)

Managed by the WDA, this European-funded programme provides practical help to enable businesses to take full advantage of technology to improve their processes and products. An important aspect is the provision of funding to subsidize the costs of accessing facilities or expertise from universities. TEP aims to encourage more companies to use university expertise and facilities. This is achieved 1) via free guidance from WDA in identifying the most relevant source of expertise for a company; 2) for eligible companies, via financial support up to 50 per cent or a maximum of £10,000 towards the cost of a collaborative project with a university. Typical projects include technical problem-solving; design and testing; product development (including rapid prototyping); evaluation and help with the introduction of new materials, processes or techniques.

Regional Innovation Grant (RIN)

RIN is designed to assist projects that involve the development and introduction of new or improved products or processes. Work can range

---

*In England, RSA has recently been substituted by the Selective Finance for Investment (SFi) Scheme (see page 258). However, the original RSA scheme still applies in Wales.

from feasibility studies, development of technical specifications, to design and manufacture of prototypes. Part of the development can be subcontracted where appropriate. There is no maximum limit on the size of projects that can be considered and the scheme can potentially pay up to 50 per cent of eligible costs up to a maximum grant of £25,000. It must be noted that RIN is a discretionary scheme and subject to stringent criteria.

The Wales Innovation Relay Centre (IRC)

Wales IRC is part of a network that provides Welsh organizations with direct links to technology and innovation from the European Union and beyond. Hosted and part-funded by the WDA, the Wales IRC receives the balance of its funding from the European Union's Innovation Programme and has a team of case officers with industrial and R&D experience in various fields. The Wales IRC has had considerable success in helping Welsh organizations develop consortia and apply for EC R&D funding (CRAFT).

SmartWales and SPUR

The SmartWales initiative, Business Services Division, is able to offer a range of assistance for projects that help individuals and companies to develop and introduce new products and processes. SmartWales provides R&D grants on a competitive or selective basis. SPUR offers support for development up to the pre-production proto stage of a new product or process that involves a significant technological advance for the industry sector.

Property

Wales can offer an extensive range of high-quality sites and buildings at very competitive rates when compared to many other locations throughout the United Kingdom. From modern, prestige space and refurbished accommodation to prime development sites, there are opportunities across a variety of locations suitable for all types of businesses, ranging from multinational corporate bodies to small and medium-sized enterprises. The WDA offers a development service aimed at bringing forward sites and property to suit market requirements. Property costs in Wales compare well with other regions. Prime industrial rents currently range between £4 and £6 per square foot depending on location, while prime office rents range between £9 and £19 per square foot.

Transport and communications

Rail services

Wales is ideally situated for fast and efficient access to London and the rest of the United Kingdom. Cardiff is only 150 miles from the centre of London. London can be reached in under two hours by rail from Cardiff with over 20 train services running to London daily.

Road networks

Key UK and European cities can be reached in a matter of hours by road from Wales: the M4 provides a direct route to central London with a drive time of two hours 30 minutes. The M4 motorway also connects with the M50 and the M5 motorways, making for easy access to the Midlands, the North and South West of England. From South Wales to:

London	140 miles	2 hours 15 minutes
Dover	220 miles	3 hours 10 minutes
Southampton	125miles	2 hours 10 minutes
Reading	100miles	1 hour 30 minutes

Source: Autoroute

Sea ports

Around 60 million tonnes a year are moved through Wales's nine main ports – between 10 and 12 per cent of the UK total. The six ports handling over 2 million tonnes each are Holyhead, Milford Haven, Swansea, Port Talbot, Cardiff and Newport. Holyhead has easy access via the A55 (E22) to major road arteries to the rest of the Wales. All South Wales ports have excellent inland transport links: they are located close to the M4 and linked to the motorway via dual carriageways (*source:* ABP, 2002).

By air

Business travellers in Wales are well served for international, European and domestic connections. Cardiff International Airport, just 20 minutes' drive from Cardiff City Centre, provides a wide and rapidly expanding range of domestic, European and worldwide services. From Cardiff International Airport all major international destinations can be reached via Schipol Airport in Amsterdam, an alternative hub to Heathrow. In addition, there are three further major international airports that are easily accessible from South Wales: Birmingham, Bristol and Heathrow. The latter can be reached in approximately two hours by road from Cardiff. Manchester Airport, one of the fastest-growing airports in Europe, is easily reached from North Wales.

Telecommunications

Wales is now among world leaders in communications infrastructure – and provides an ideal environment for e-business with a comprehensive range of services available. There are two main telecommunications providers – BT and NTL – offering a choice of provider and competitive rates. BT has its main site for Internet hosting in Cardiff and NTL has its Internet centre in Newport. Wales can offer:

- virtually unlimited bandwidth;

- 341,754miles of fibre optic network of which 60 per cent remains unutilized;

- deregulated and competitive telecommunications market;

- wide choice of suppliers including BT and NTL;

- high resilience against loss of service;

- ADSL available in major towns and cities.

In addition to the already comprehensive network installed across the country, the Intelligent City project will supply data speeds of up to 256 megabits to broadcasters and new media companies throughout Cardiff. This will give companies access to one of the fastest broadband subscriber access networks currently available globally.

The network throughout Wales is 100 per cent digital, and linked via fibre optic technology. This results in virtually unlimited bandwidth availability and the ability to access all fibre-based digital services across Wales. In addition to this, ADSL is currently being made available across Wales as part of the UK programme to deliver broadband services directly to the home and business. A satellite uplink based at the Celtic Gateway site in Cardiff provides an alternative for companies locating in the area, offering a claimed 25 per cent saving on typical circuits between North America and Europe.

A new BT flagship centre was launched in Cardiff Bay during spring 2003. This new facility represents an investment of over £90 million and builds on BT's hosting strategy, providing customers with a range of advanced and secure services, enabling them to ensure business continuity and derive maximum value from their online operations. The new 60,000 square foot facility occupied by 250 staff, and managing requirements to BT customers worldwide, will provide a range of services from the site including hosting on a dedicated and shared basis, Web design and development, managed services such as data storage, security solutions from online trading and ICT consultancy. The Cardiff Bay data centre is support by the highest levels of security and resilience and is assured by two independent National Grid power supplies.

Education, research and development

The education system in Wales is traditionally among the United Kingdom's best, offering quality education at all levels through first-class public and private facilities. Higher education is a top priority in Wales and a key factor in attracting inward investors. There are over 250,000 students in further and higher education in Wales, with over 100,000 attending higher education courses, which include the University of Wales, which is the United Kingdom's second largest with over 60,000 students (*source*: Digest of Welsh Local Area Statistics, 2002).

The graduate pool is supplemented by technician training programmes organized by colleges of higher and further education. Many of these courses can be tailored to meet the specific requirements of local employers, thus providing total flexibility.

University links with industry

Welsh higher education institutions have forged strong links with industry and a wealth of schemes and networks already in place. They include:

- Aberystwyth University's Research, Innovation and Business Services which provides a gateway for businesses and organizations of all sizes, advice and support to staff seeking to exploit their expertise.

- There are a range of opportunities for businesses to benefit from the transfer of technology and know-how from Bangor University – with grants and subsidized programmes, such as TCS and HELP Wales, to support partnerships between business and Bangor University.

- University of Wales College, Newport, has a wide range of expertise and facilities available to meet the needs of companies and other organizations. ACES can help industry to locate the resources relevant to the organization and manage the provision of services such as training, consultancy, research and graduate placements.

- IT Network Wales is an innovative programme linking the skills and technical requirements of industry to the expertise and resources of the computer science department at University College Swansea.

- The Business School at the University of Glamorgan has developed close relationships with a number of public and private organizations such as Hyder, Bridgend County Council, and Parcelforce.

- Cardiff University Innovation Network – which forges contacts between industry and the university.

All degree and diploma courses at the North East Wales Institute of Higher Education (NEWI) are linked to the needs of industry and graduates enjoy excellent employment prospects. The graduate pool is supplemented by technician training programmes organized by colleges of higher and further education and government-supported Council for Education and Training in Wales (CETW).

Research institutes

The Centres of Excellence for Technology and Industrial Collaboration are 20 industrially focused research groups that have been supported to enhance their delivery of technology transfer activities in support of industry. Each centre has received financial support to fund the recruitment of staff dedicated to helping industry. The centres can also purchase equipment to update their capabilities.

The Technium concept seeks to provide the optimum environment to enable innovative companies to reach their potential while also providing world-class facilities and expertise to attract world-class companies. Inside the eight Technium centres, companies have access to Welsh university colleges and associated Centres of Excellence via high-speed broadband links. They can also benefit from both public and private sector business support and advice ranging from training to intellectual property rights.

Public sector support agencies

Welsh Development Agency
Plas Glyndŷÿur
Kingsway,
Cardiff CF10 3AH
Tel: +44 (0) 1443 845500
Fax: +44 (0) 1443 845589
E-mail: enquiries@wda.co.uk
Websites: www.wda.co.uk and www.locate-in-wales.com

National Assembly for Wales
Cardiff Bay
Cardiff CF99 1NA
Tel: +44 (0) 29 20 825111
Website: www.wales.gov.uk (e-mail link available at this address)

Wales Trade International
(A division of the Welsh Assembly government assisting international trade by companies based in Wales at above address)
Tel: +44 (0) 2920 80 1046
Fax: +44 (0) 29 2082 3964
E-mail: exports@wales.gsi.gov.uk
Websites: www.walestrade.com and www.swansea.gov.uk

Appendices

Appendix 1

Contributors' Contact Details

Artaius Limited
12th Floor, Southgate House
St George's Way
Stevenage
Hertfordshire SG1 1HG
Contact: Alfred Levy
Tel: +44 (0) 1438 847101
E-mail: Alfred@artaius.com

AWS Structured Finance Ltd
Copperfield House
Harlequin Lane
Crowborough
East Sussex TN6 1HU
Contact: Kevin Smith
Tel: +44 (0) 1892 667891
E-mail: kevin.r.smith@awsconsult.co.uk

BTelocations
BT Centre
81 Newgate Street
London EC1A 7AJ
Contact: Kim Hackett, VP New Business
Tel: +44 (0) 01977 591886
E-mail: kim.hackett@bt.com
Website: www.bt.com/btelocations

Chemical Industries Association (CIA)
King's Building
Smith Square
London SW1P 3JJ
Contact: Neil Harvey
Tel: +44 (0) 20 7834 3399
E-mail: harveyn@cia.org.uk

EBRI
St John's Innovation Centre
Cowley Road
Cambridge CB4 0WS
Contact: Jeanette Walker
Tel: +44 (0) 1223 421974
E-mail: jeanettewalker@erbi.co.uk

Eversheds LLP
Senator House
85 Queen Victoria Street
London EC4V 4JL
Contact: Richard Millar
Tel: +44 (0) 20 7919 0596
E-mail: richardmillar@eversheds.com

James Goodwin, MA, MBA
Street Farm, Newbourne
Woodbridge
Suffolk IP12 4PX
Tel: +44 (0) 20 794 7073939
E-mail: jamesdgoodwin@hotmail.com

Neil Harvey
International Trade & Sector Groups
Chemical Industries Association (CIA)
King's Building
Smith Square
London SW1P 3JJ
Tel: +44 (0) 20 7834 3399
E-mail: harveyn@cia.org.uk

HSBC plc
8 Canada Square
London E14 5HQ
Contact: Nick Stephens, Trade Services
Tel: +44 (0) 20 79910538
E-mail: nickstephens@hsbc.com

Hunter School of Entrepreneurship
University of Strathclyde
Glasgow G1 1XQ
Contact: Professor Colin Mason
Tel: +44 (0) 141 548 4259
E-mail: colin.mason@strath.ac.uk

Intellect UK
20 Red Lion Street
London WC1R 4QN
Contact: Charles Ward
Tel: +44 (0) 20 7395 6736
E-mail: Charles.Ward@intellectuk.org

Jones Lang LaSalle
22 Hanover Square
London W1A 2BN
Tel: +44 (0) 20 7399 5750
Fax: +44 (0) 20 7399 5103
E-mail: sotiris.tsolacos@eu.joneslanglasalle.com

Library House
Kett House
Station Road
Cambridge CB1 2JX
Contact: Mark Littlewood
Tel: +44 (0) 1223 500550
E-mail: mark.littlewood@libraryhouse.net

Eli Lilly and Company Limited
Lilly House
Priestley Road
Basingstoke
Hampshire RG24 9NL
Contact: Communications Administrator
Tel: +44 (0) 1256 775412
Fax: +44 (0) 1256 775412
Website: www.lilly.co.uk

London Stock Exchange plc
Old Broad Street
London EC2N 1HP
Contact: Margarita Ledochowski
Tel: +44 (0) 20 7797 1454
E-mail: mledochowski@londonstockexchange.com

Powergen
Wyvern House
Colliers Way
Nottingham NG8 6AT
Contact: Jag Kahlon
Tel: +44 (0) 870 419 1531
E-mail: jag.kahlon@pgen.com

PNO-j4b Consulting Ltd.
51 Water Lane
Wilmslow
Cheshire SK9 5BQ
Contact: Siegfried Doetjes
Tel: +44 (0) 1625 628089
E-mail: info@pnoj4b.com

Renewables UK
Department of Trade and Industry
Atholl House
86/88 Guild Street
Aberdeen AB11 6AR
Contact: Allan Taylor
Tel: +44 (0) 1224 254128
E-mail: Allan.Taylor@dti.gsi.gov.uk

Jonathan Reuvid
Little Manor
Wroxton
Banbury
Oxfordshire OX15 6QE
Tel: +44 (0) 1295 738070
E-mail: jrwroxton@aol.com

FPD Savills
(Residential)
20 Grosvenor Hill
London W1K 3HQ
Contact: Richard Donnell
Tel: +44 (0) 20 7499 8644
E-mail: rdonnell@fpdsavills.co.uk

FPD Savills
(Agricultural)
Wytham Court
11 Wytham Way

Oxford OX2 0QL
Contact: Richard Binning
Tel: +44 (0) 1865 269000
E-mail: rbinning@fpdsavills.co.uk

Snapshots International

5 Dryden Street
London WC2E 9NB
Contact: Debra Curtis
Tel: +44 (0) 20 7829 8408
E-mail: debra.curtis@snapdata.com

Society of Motor Manufacturers and Traders (SMMT)

Forbes House
Halkin Street
London SW1X 7DS
Contact: Mark Norcliffe
Tel: +44 (0) 20 7344 9238
E-mail: mnorcliffe@smmt.co.uk

SPB3

70 Charlotte Street
London W1T 4QG
Contact: Johan Taft
Tel: +44 (0) 20 7419 7400
E-mail: johan@spb3.c.uk

Taylor Wessing

Carmelite
50 Victoria Embankment
Blackfriars
London EC4Y 0DX
Contact: David Kent
Tel: +44 (0) 20 7300 7000
E-mail: d.kent@taylorwessing.com

Wilder Coe Chartered Accountants

233–237 Old Marylebone Road
London NW1 5QT
Contact: Bob Tranter
Tel: +44 (0) 20 724 6060
E-mail: bobt@wildercoe.co.uk

Wilder Coe Business Recovery
Southgate House
St George's Way
Stevenage
Hertfordshire SG1 1HT
Contact: Norman Cowan
Tel: +44 (0) 1438 847101
E-mail: normanc@wildercoe.co.uk

Appendix 2

Industry Sector Web sites

Biotechnology

The Biotechnology and Biological Sciences Research Council (BBSRC)
www.bbsrc.ac.uk

BioIndustry Association
www.bioindustry.org

Bio-Wise
www.dtit.gov.uk/biowise

Medical Reseach Council (MRC) Technology Transfer Group
www.mrc.ac.uk

Natural Environment Research Council (NERC)
www.nerc.ac.uk

Chemical industry

Chemical Industries Association
www.cia.org.uk

The European Chemical Industry Council
www.cefic.org

Process Industries Centre for Manufacturing Excellence (PICME)
www.picme.org

Creative Industries

Architecture

Commission for Architecture and the Built Environment (CABE)
www.cabe.org.uk

Royal Institute of British Architects (RIBA)
www.riba.org.uk and www.architecture.com

Advertising

Institute of Practitioners in Advertising (IPA)
www.ipa.co.uk

The Advertising Association
ww.adassoc.org.uk

Film

UK Film Council
www.filmcouncil.org.uk

UK Film Council International
www.britfilmcom.co.uk

Producers Alliance for Film & Television (PACT)
www.pact.co.uk

Broadcasting, Entertainment, Cinematograph & Theatre Union (BECTU)
www.bectu.org.uk

Interactive leisure software

The Independent Games Developers Trade Association (TIGA)
www.tiga.org.uk/

The Entertainment & Leisure Software Publishers Association
www.elspa.com

Music

National Music Council (NMC)
www.musiccouncil.org

British Phonograph Industry
www.bpi.co.uk

Publishing
The Publishers Association
www.publishers.org.uk

The Periodical Publishers Association (PPA)
www.ppa.co.uk

The Newspaper Society
www.newspapersoc.org.uk

Newspaper Publishers Association
Tel: +44 (0) 20 7207 2200

Television and radio

Independent Television Commission (ITC)
www.itc.ork.uk

Digital Radio Development Bureau (DRDB)
www.drdb.org

Radio Authority
www.radioauthority.org.uk

The arts

The British Council
www.britishcouncil.org

Arts Council of England
www.artscouncil.org.uk

Design Council
www.design-council.org.uk

Crafts Council
www.craftscouncil.org.uk

Independent Theatres Council
www:itc-arts.org.uk

British Fashion Council
www.londonfashionweek.co.uk

British Design Initiative (BDI)
www.britishdesign.co.uk

Visiting Arts
www.visitingarts.org.uk

Food and drink

Campden and Chorleywood Food Research Association (CCFRA)
www.campden.co.uk

The Food and Drink Federation (FDF)
www.fdf.org.uk

Food and Drink National Training Organisation (F&DNTO)
www.foodanddrinknto.org.uk

Institute of Food Research (IFR) – Norwich
www.ifr.bsrc.ac.uk/

Institute of Food Science & Technology (IFST)
www.ifst.org.uk

Institute of Grocery Distribution (IGD)
www.igd.com

Leatherhead Food Research Association (LFRA)
www.leatherheadfood.com/lfi/index.htm

University of Reading – School of Food Biosciences
www.food.rdg.ac.uk

E-commerce

Innovator Scheme
www.homeoffice.gov.uk

Internet First Tuesday
www.firsttuesday.com

Electronics

Intellect
www.intellectuk.org.

Joint Equipment and Materials Initiative (JEMI UK)
www.jemiuk.com

Institute of Electrical Engineers (IEE)
www.iee.org

National Microelectronics Institute (NMI)
www.nmi.org.uk

Financial services

Association of British Insurers
www.abi.org.uk

British Bankers Association
www.bba.org.uk

The British Venture Capital Association (BVCA)
www.bvca.co.uk

Economic Development Unit, Corporation of London
www.cityoflondon.gov.uk

European Banking Federation
www.fbe.be

International Financial Services, London (IFSL)
www.ifsl.org.uk

International Swaps and Derivatives Association (ISDA)
www.isda.org

International Underwriting Association of London
www.iua.co.uk

Nanotechnology

Centre for Molecular and Biomolecular Electronics – Coventry University
www.nes.coventry.ac.uk/research/cmbe

Centre for Nano-Device Modelling – University of Leeds
www.amsta.leeds.ac.uk/cndm

Industrial Research Laboratories – University of Durham (UDIRL)
www.dur.ac.uk/molecular.electronics

Institute for Nanoscale Science and Technology (INSAT)
www.inex.org.uk

Institute of Nanotechnology (ION)
www.nano.org.uk

Mechanical Engineering – University of Strathclyde
www.mecheng.strath.ac.uk

The Nanoscale Physics Research Laboratory – University of Birmingham
www.nprl.bham.a.uk

The North East Centre for Scientific Enterprise
www.dur.ac.uk/scientific.enterprise

The School of Informatics – University of Wales
www.informatics.bangor.ac.uk

Renewables

Association of Electricity Producers (AEP)
www.aepuk.com

Association of UK Energy Agencies (AUKEA)
www.natenergy.org.uk/akea

British Association for Bio Fuels and Oils
www.biodiesel.co.uk

British Biogen
www.britishbiogen.co.uk

British Hydropower Association
www.british-hydro.org

British Photovoltaic Association
www.pv-uk.org.uk

British Wind Energy Association
www.bwea.com
www.offshorewindfarms.co.uk

The Climate Change Projects Office (CCPO)
www.dti.gov.uk/ccpo

The International Technology Promoters
www.globalwatchonline.com

Marine Renewable Energy Association
www.marine-renewables.com

Offshore Wind Energy Network (OWEN)
www.owen.org.uk

Renewable Power Association
www.r-p-a.org.uk/home.asp

Solar Energy Society
www.brookes.ac.uk/other/uk-ises/home.html

Solar Trade Association
www.greenenergy.org.uk/sta

Software

British Computer Society (BCS)
www.bcs.org.uk

International Multimedia Association
www.bima.co.uk

Telecommunications

Federation of Communications Services
www.fcs.org.uk

Intellect UK
www.intellectuk.org

Telecommunications Industry Association
www.tia.org.uk

Appendix 3

Key Government Agencies

UK Trade & Investment
66–74 Victoria Street
Kingsgate House
London SW1E 6SW
E-mail: inward.investment@uktradeinvest.gov.uk
Website: www.uktradeinvest.gov.uk

Department for Environment, Food and Rural Affairs
Nobel House
17 Smith Square
London SW1P3JR
Tel: +44 (0) 20 7238 6951
Website: www.defra.gov.uk

Office of Science and Technology
Albany House
Petty France
London SW1H 9ST
Tel: +44 (0) 20 7271 2000
Website: www.dti.gov.uk/ost/

Small Business Service (SBS)
Kingsgate House
66–74 Victoria Street
London SW1E 6SW
Tel: +44 (0) 845 001 0031
Website: www.sbs.gov.uk

HM Treasury
1 Horse Guards Road
London SW1A 2HQ
Tel: +44 (0) 20 7270 5000
Website: www.hm-treasury.gov.uk

Biotechnology

Bioscience Unit
Department of Trade and Industry
151 Buckingham Palace Road
London SW1W 9SS
Tel: +44 (0) 20 7215 5000
Website: www.dti.gov.uk

The Scottish Executive and Lifelong Learning Department
Meridian Court
5 Cadogan Street
Glasgow G2 6AT
Tel: +44 (0) 141 248 4774
Website: www.scotland.gov.uk/who/dept_enterprise.asp

Scottish Enterprise
Biotechnology Group
120 Bothwell Street
Glasgow G2 7JP
Tel: +44 (0) 141 228 2384
Website: www.biotech-scotland.org

Welsh Development Agency
Technology and Innovation
Principality House
The Friary
Cardiff CF10 3FE
Tel: +44 (0) 29 2082 8712
Website: www.invest-in-wales.com

Industrial Research and Technology Agency
(N. Ireland)
Innovation Services
17 Antrim Road
Lisburn BT28 3AL
Tel: +44 (0) 1846 623144
Website: www.irtu-ni.gov.uk

Creative industries

Department for Culture, Media and Sport
2–4 Cockspur Street
London SW1Y 5DH
Tel: +44 (0) 7211 6200
Website: www.culture.gov.uk

Financial services

Bank of England
Threadneedle Street
London EC2R 8AH
Tel: +44 (0) 20 7601 4444
Website: www.bankofengland.co.uk

The Financial Services Authority (FSA)
25, Canary Wharf
London E14 5HS
Tel: +44 (0) 20 7066 1000
Website: www.fsa.gov.uk

Food and drink

Food Standards Agency
Aviation House
125 Kingsway
London WC2B 6NH
Tel: +44 (0) 20 7276 8000
Website: www.foodstandards.gov.uk

Food from Britain (FFB)
4th Floor, Manning House
22 Carlisle Place
London SW1P 1JA
Tel: +44 (0) 20 7233 5111
E-mail: info@foodfrombritain.com

Renewables

Renewable Energy Industry Development (REID)
1 Victoria Street
London SW1H 0ET
Tel: +44 (0) 20 7215 2501
Website: www.dti.gov.uk/energy/renewables

Telecommunications

Office of Communications (Ofcom)
Riverside House
2A Southwark Bridge Road
London SE1 9HA
Tel: +44 (0) 7297 2076
Website: www.ofcom.org.uk

Index

NB: page numbers in *italic* indicate figures and tables

acquisitions, private company   71–75, 76 *see also* Acts of Parliament (UK)
  competition/anti-trust   74
  disclosure   73
  English law   71–72, 73 *see also* English law/common law
  financial assistance   74–75
  restrictive covenants   73
  stamp duty/stamp duty land tax (SDLT)   74
  warranties and indemnities   72–73
acquisitions, public company   75–81
  acceptance condition   79
  buying target shares   79
  Code (City Code on Takeovers and Mergers) and timetable   76–77
  confidentiality   77
  de-listing   79
  irrevocable undertakings   78
  making the Offer   78
  Offeror's approach to Target   77–78
  Schemes of Arrangement: advantages/disadvantages and procedure   79–81
  squeeze-out procedure   79
  structures   76
Acts of Parliament (UK)   9
  Betting, Gaming and Lotteries (1963)   194
  Companies   243, 245, 247, 248, 252, 306
  Companies (1985)   74–75, 79, 242, 280, 285, 303, 304, 309–10, 311
  Companies (1989)   242, 303
  Data Protection (1998)   335, 356–57
  Employment Rights (1996)   361, 363
  Environmental Protection (1990)   404, 407
  Equal Pay (1970)   368
  Fair Trading (1973)   74, 372
  Finance (2003)   313
  Financial Services   250
  Financial Services and Markets (2000)   19, 392–94
  Landlord and Tenant (Covenants) (1995)   34
  Limited Liability Partnerships (2000)   311
  Limited Partnerships (1907)   280
  Lotteries and Amusements (1976)   194
  Partnership (1890)   279
  Sex Discrimination (1975)   368
  Taxes   316
  Trade Mark (1994)   344, 345
agricultural property   62–66 *see also* residential property
  development   65
  residential and amenity value   64–65
  tax   65–66
  tenure   65
  timing   62, 64
Alternative Investment Market (AIM)   16, 19, 22–29, 76, 117, 302
  admission requirements and rules   23–24
  designated markets   24, 26
  flotation: benefits and key considerations   26–27
  investor attitudes   28
  nominated advisers (Nomads)/brokers   23–26, 28
  outlook   29
  recent new issues   28, *28–29*
art and collectibles   119–30, 161
  art and antiques indexes   127, *128*, 129
  art and antiques market (UK): exports, imports and structure   119–20, 125
  buying and selling: dealers, auctions and auctioneers   120–23, *123*, 124, 129
  company performances   123–24, *123*, 124
  investment value/market research   126–27
  supply and demand   124–25
  taxation   125
automotive industry   133–41 *see also* automotive investment: attraction of UK
  as global business   133–34
  automotive investment: changing pattern in Europe   136–37
  key areas of expertise   140–41
  investing in the future   141
  investment in UK: history   134–35
  UK industry today   135–36
automotive investment: attraction of UK   137–39
  Automotive Academy/Foresight Vehicle/SMMT Industry Forum   138–39
  government–industry partnership   138

open business environment   137
positive economic indicators   137
R&D centres and initiatives   138, 139
skilled and professional workforce   137–38

Barnsley   456–64
demographics   458, *458*, 459, *459*
education, research and development   463
foreign direct investment (FDI)   462
infrastructure   463
local economy *459*,   *460*, 460, *461*
local service providers   463–64
transport and communications   461–62
biotechnology   111, 114, 142–52
access to continental Europe   149
advantages of East of England location
143
advice and support: ERBI   150
bioscience research institutes   143–44, *144*
biotech companies   146, *146*, *147*
Cambridge Nobel Laureates   150–51
international partnering opportunities
150
local universities   144–45, *145*
mature business infrastructure   149
proximity to significant UK biotech clusters
149
research hospitals   145–46
science and research parks   147, *147*, *148*
venture capital, access to   149–50
brand protection *see* intellectual property
business angels and syndicates   102–04, 119
networks (BANs)/National Business Angel
Network   103, 149
tax incentives/Enterprise Investment
Scheme (EIS)   103
business risk   275–78
change and awareness   276
crisis management strategies   277–78
identifying and ranking risks   275–76
insurances and protection   277
monitoring continuous risks/ key
performance indicators   276–77
business taxation   312–23 *see also* business
taxation: business formations (UK)
capital allowances   320, *320*, 321
income *see* business taxation: income
individuals and partnerships   317–18
losses   321
payment of tax   318–20
rollover relief   321–22
stamp duty land tax/stamp duty
(SDLT)/rates   322–23, *323*
thin capitalization   322
business taxation: business formations (UK)
312–14
branch vs subsidiary   313
direct investment vs holding company
structure   314
representative office vs permanent
establishment (PE)   312–13
residence   314
value-added tax (VAT)   314

business taxation: income   314–17
capital gains   316–17
companies and branches   314–16
dividends   317
interest   316
land and property   316
business taxation: individuals and
partnerships   317–18
capital gains/taper relief   317–18
dividends   318
income   317
interest   317
land and property   318

Cambridge   171 *see also* biotechnology *and*
technology and innovation
Chartered Surveyors, Royal Institution of
(RICS)   31, 46–47, 48, 54, 61
chemical industries   153–59
chemical technology (UK) and the business
environment   156–57
Europe: the outlook for UK chemical
industry   157–59
geographical dispersion within UK
153–54, *154–55*
meeting needs and expectations   153
product diversity of UK sector   155, *156*
commercial banking   288–94
cash management, physical   294
cash management: payment
collection/credit management   294
Eurozone countries   291
making payments overseas   291–92
multiple normal payments in UK   289
multiple payments overseas   292
multiple urgent payments in UK   289–90
receiving payments from abroad *see*
commercial banking: payments from
abroad
receiving payments within UK   292
Worldpay   291
commercial banking: payments from abroad
292–94
cheque collections   293
cheque negotiations   293
Euro bulk payment clearing   292
inward payment   292
US dollar and European lockboxes   293–94
commercial property investment (UK)   46–61
economy and the property market   48–49,
49, 50, *50*, 51, *51*, 52–53, *53*, 54, *54–55*
future performance and forecasts   55, *55*,
56, *56*, 57, *57*, 58–59, *59*, 60
research   59–60
occupier markets   46, *46*, 47, *47*, 48, *48*
commercial property market (UK)   30–45
key players *32–33*
leasing structure   33–34, *34*, 35–36
investor categories   37–38, *38*, 39, *39*, 40
market size   30–31, *31*
performance indicators and market
transparency   43, *43–44*
property investment products   41, *41–42*

property lending   40, *40*
real estate investment trust (REIT)   42–43
taxation, management and transaction
    costs   36. *36*, 37, *37*
Companies, Registrar of   73, 242, 243, 244,
    246, 248, 249, 251, 303
Companies House   73, 246, 281, 283–84, 285,
    303, 402
    Articles of Association   283
    Certificate of Incorporation   284
    Companies House Form   10 283
    Statutory Declaration (Form   12) 284
company formation – methods and legal
    implications   279–86
    private company limited by shares
        281–84
    public company limited by shares   284
    registration: incorporated vehicles   280–81
    registration: unincorporated vehicles
        279–80
    review of company law   286
    statutory requirements: accounts, annual
        return and other documents   285
contracting with customers, suppliers and
    partners   353–56
    customer overrides: local law   353–54
    English common law   353
    EU competition rules   355
    law, choice of   353
    liability clauses, exclusion and limitation of
        354
    overseas company, trading methods of   354
    sales representatives, agents and
        distributors   355–56
    shrink-wrap licences   354
Corporate Governance   17, 23
creative industries   160–69 *see also* software
    advertising   161, 164, *164*
    architecture   164
    crafts   164–65
    DCMS   160–61, 167
    definitions   160
    design   165
    designer fashion/fashion designers   165
    economic contribution   161
    film   166
    interactive leisure software   166, *166*, 167
    music/Royal Opera House   167, 169
    performing arts   167
    publishing   167
    television and radio   168

data protection/privacy in UK   356–59
    Data Protection Act (1998)   356–57 *see
        also* Acts of Parliament (UK)
    data protection principles   357–58
    direct marketing rules   359
    notification obligation   357
    rights of data subjects   358
    transfers of personal data outside EEA
        358–59
development and business support agencies

    262–74 *see also* development: R&D
        Assistance
    Enterprise Zones (Ezs)   265–67 *see also
        main entry*
    Global Partnerships and Global
        Entrepreneurs' programme   274
    Regional Selective Assistance   263–65 *see
        also main entry*
    Small Business Service (SBS)   272–74 *see
        also main entry*
    UK Trade & Investment   5, 160, 201,
        262–63, 274
development: R&D Assistance   268–72
    EU Sixth Framework Programme
        (2002–06)   261, 270, *271*
    EUREKA   268
    Foresight   270
    Grant for Investigating an Innovative Idea
        272
    Grant for Research and Development (DTI)
        271–72
    LINK programmes   268–69
    R&D tax credits   267–68
Doncaster   464–47
    Education City   466@Index1:
    new urban infrastructure   464
    regeneration projects   464
    retail and transport development   466
    waterfront   466–67

East Midlands Development Agency   475–85
    see also Leicester *and* Nottingham
    developing the future   477–79
    location for business   476–77
East of England: Invest East of England
    486–89@Index1:
    inward investment   488
    science and business parks   488
    transport links   488–89
    universities   488
Economic Co-operation and Development,
    Organisation for (OECD)   3, 4
    guidelines   178
    Security and Authentication Unit   178
economy and investment environment (UK)
    3–7
    inward investment environment   5–6, *6*, 7
    statistics *3*,   4–5
    UK Inward Investment (2003–04)   7
electronic commerce   175–80
    business property   177
    case studies   179–80
    government support   175
    online annual report (UK)   176
    outsourcing   178
    sector approaches   177–78
    secure environments   178
    telecommunications   176–77
    UK as electronic business capital of Europe
        179
electronics sector (UK)   170–74
    electronic strengths/areas of excellence
        (UK)   172

electronics industry/regional dispersion
170–71
government support   173
major investors   173
trade and professional associations
173–74
employment, pensions and stock options
360–73
discrimination   363–64
employment contracts   361
employment protection and Employment
Rights Act   363–64
European Works Council Directive (EWCD)
367
fixed-term employees   369
health and safety at work   369
maximum working hours/holiday
entitlement   362
National Minimum Wage (NMW)   362
non-competition clauses   361–62
part-time workers   369
pensions   370–71
redundancy and dismissal   365–66
statutory sick pay   362–63
stock options: tax and employees share
plan   371–73
trade union activities, collective bargaining,
employee representation   366–67
transfers of undertaking (TUPE
regulations)   369–70
unfair dismissal   365–66, 373
Working Time Regulations (1998)   362
English law/common law   71–72, 73, 81, 82,
247, 251, 253–54, 322, 349, 353
passing off   282, 349–50
Enterprise Zones (EZs)   265–67
benefits and exemptions   266–67
EU restrictions   266
environmental issues: the law   404–08
contaminated land/ Contaminated Land
Register   404–06, 409
EU Directive on Environmental Civil
Liability   407
integrated pollution prevention control
(IPPC)   407–08
liability under common law   407
environmental issues: transaction solutions
408–11
availability of information   408–10
desktop studies   409–10
director's liability   411
insurances   411
options for revealed issues   410–11
European Economic Area (EEA)   269, 282,
347, 358–59, 374, 388–89
European Union (EU)   3, 9–10, 136, 137, 248,
266, 344, 348, 374, 375, 395, 397–98
competition rules   231, 355
constitution   10–11
Directive on Environmental Civil Liability
407
Enterprise Commissioner   176
EUREKA   173, 268

Eurozone   5, 10, 5, 10, 182, 291
Framework Programme (FP6)   173, 261,
270, *271*
grants, incentives and business support
10, 259–60, *260*, 261
GUIDE project   261
labour legislation   178
law, forms of   9–10
legislation on VAT   125, 314
LINK programmes   173, 268–69
member countries/states   345, 358
parent companies   324
Phoenix Fund   274
state approval rules   101
tax harmonisation   322
Trade Mark Directive   344

finance for companies: acquiring fixed assets
295, 299–301
property and property-associated purchases
299–300
vehicle and equipment acquisitions
300–01
finance for companies: assisting cashflow
295, 296–97
business card   296
invoice finance   296–97
overdraft   296
finance for companies: business growth   296,
301–02 *see also* venture capital
finance for companies: international trade
295, 297–99
Documentary Collections   299
Export Documentary Credits   297
export loans for manufacture   298
export sales, financing   298–99
import loans for traders   298
Import Usance Documentary Credit   298
loans and overdrafts   297
financial reporting and accounting   303–11
accounting basis by lessors   311
accounting concepts   306–07
accounting policies   308
assets leased   310–11
audit, basic definition of   305
audit requirement   304, *304*, 305
distribution of profits/restriction of
distributions   310
partnerships and sole traders   311
provisions   307–08
true and fair concept   306
Urgent Issues Task Force (UITF)/true and
fair override   309–10
valuation of assets/current assets   308–09
financial services   181–85 *see also* regulation
of financial services
background   181–82
banks   182–83
capital markets   183
insurance/Lloyd's of London   184
other markets   184–85
Financial Services Authority   15, 17, 19,
20–21, 185, 225, 396

food and drink   186–92
  attitudes and tastes, change in   186
  exports   189–90, *190*
  household expenditure   188, *188*
  major UK food and drink manufacturers
    190, *191*
  market trends and outlook   191–92
  regional branding   186@Index1:
  restaurant industry   187@Index1:
  retail sales *187,*   188, *188*
  value-added food and drink   189, *189*

gaming   177, 193–98
  Budd Report   194
  divide between USA and UK   193–94
  Gambling Bill proposals/Gambling
    Commission   194–97
  Gambling Industry Charitable Trust   197
  gaming opportunity in the UK   197–98
  moral/religious views: helping the addict
    197
  timetable for the Bill   197
Gateshead   432–36
  business support   434
  innovation/technology   434
  population and workforce   435
  supporting investors   435–36
  transport links   434
government agencies   581–83
grants and incentives within EU parameters
    255–61
  applications, information required for   255
  assistance with applications   256–57
  EU: availability of funds and objective
    areas   258–60, *260*
  EU: direct applications and GUIDE project
    261
  factors to consider   255–56
  funding: useful websites   257
  location, importance of   258, *259*
  regional selective assistance (RSA) grant
    schemes   258
  selective finance for investment (Sfi)
    scheme   258
grants consultants   256–57
gross domestic product (GDP)   4, 30, 50, *51*,
    52, 109, 153, 161

immigration into the UK   374–81
  business immigrants under EU association
    agreements   378
  business visitors   380
  businesspeople   377–78
  exceptions to permission rule   374
  highly skilled migrants   379–80
  investors   378–79
  settlement   381
  sole representatives   376–77
  spouses/family members   380
  visa nationals   381
  work permits/Work Permits UK   374–76,
    379
initial public offering (IPO)   22, 29, 92, 117

Inland Revenue   72, 243, 245, 249, 252, 253,
    311, 328, 382, 384 *see also* taxation
intellectual property   343–59
  contracting with customers, suppliers and
    partners *see main entry*
  copyright   351–52
  data protection/privacy in UK *see main
    entry*
  employee inventions   351–52
  patents   350–51
  registered trademarks *see* trademarks,
    registered
  technology, protection of   352
  trademark law   343–44 *see also* Acts of
    Parliament (UK)

joint ventures   81–85
  confidentiality and non-compete provisions
    84
  contributions of parties   81–82
  decision-making   82
  dispute resolution   84
  duration and termination   85
  English law   81–82
  management   82
  succession   83

leases   251 *see also* commercial property
    market (UK): future trends
  full repairing and insuring (FRI)   35
  internal repairing and insuring (IRI)   35
Leicester   479–82
  industrial heritage   480
  regeneration projects   479–80
  universities   480
legal overview: branches of overseas
    corporations   247–49
  Companies Act: registration regimes   247
  disclosure of annual reports and accounts
    249
  letterhead   248–49
  procedure for branch registration   248
legal overview: inward investors   241–54 *see
    also* Acts of Parliament (UK)
  consultants: view of UK Inland Revenue
    253
  European holding companies   250
  filing requirements   242–43
  issues and choice of entity   243–44
  key legal aspects   253–54
  legal personality   242
  overseas corporations *see* legal overview:
    branches of overseas corporations
  place of business registration   251
  principal UK entities   241–42
  real estate   251
  regulatory permissions and licences   250
  subsidiary company *see* legal overview:
    subsidiary company
  taxable branches or subsidiaries   244
  transfer between UK entities   251–52
  transfer pricing   249–50
  UK entity, reasons for setting up a   252

legal overview: subsidiary company   244–47
  annual return   246
  auditors   245
  directors   246–47
  funding   245
  statutory registers   246
London First Centre (LFC)   490–515 *see also*
    London: Thames Gateway
  demographics   492, *492*
  education, research and development
    500–07
  foreign direct investment   498, *499*,
    499–500
  infrastructure   497–98
  local economy   493, *493, 494*, 494–95, *495*
  local service providers   507–10
  real estate – London office rentals *495*,
    495–96, *496*
  transport and communication   496–97
London: Thames Gateway   510–15
  economy   510, 512–13
  education and research   514–15
  inward investment   513–14
  telecommunications   514
  transport communications   513

mergers, acquisitions and joint ventures *see*
    acquisitions, private company;
    acquisitions,
  public company *and* joint ventures
money laundering regulations   399–403
  businesses required to comply   400–01
  identification procedures   402
  Money Laundering Regulations (2003)
    399
  National Criminal Intelligence Service
    (NICS)   399, 401
  practical considerations   402–03
  requirements for businesses in regulated
    sectors   401
  scope of legislation   399–400
  tipping off/failure to report   401
  trading in regulated sectors   403

Newcastle   436–41
  competitive edge   436
  partnerships for project development   436,
    438
  product development turnaround   438–39
  supply chain access   440
  transport infrastructure   439–40
  workforce   440
North East England: One North East
    415–41 *see also* Gateshead *and*
    Newcastle
  availability of EU structural funds
    425–26
  demographics   416, *416*
  education and training   428
  factory and office accommodation   419–20,
    420, 421, 421–22, *422*
  foreign direct investment (FDI)   423–24,
    424–25

  infrastructure   426–28
  local economy   418, *418*, 419, *419*
  public sector business support
    organizations   430–31
  research   429
  transport and communications   422–23,
    423
Northern Ireland   535–43
  contacts   543
  crime   542
  demographics   536
  economy   536, *536*, 538, *538*
  education   540
  exports   539, *539*, 540
  foreign direct investment   539
  infrastructure   540–41
  logistics   541–42
Northwest Development Agency   442–47
  forward strategy   447
  incentives and financial assistance   446
  inward investment and key industries
    443–45
  quality of life   447
  real estate   446
  transport communications   445–46
  work environment   446–47
  workforce   445
Nottingham   482–85
  future developments   484–85
  local economy   484
  quality of life   482
  transport   482, 484

outsourcing   332–35
  benefits   333
  general principles   332
  services available   334–35
  specialist companies/teams   333

pharmaceuticals   199–203
  Clinical Excellence, National Institute of
    (NICE)   203
  Comprehensive Spending Review (CSR)
    199
  Lilly UK   200–02
  National Health Service (NHS)   199, 202,
    203
  Pharmaceutical Industry Competitiveness
    Task Force (PICTF)   202
  Pharmaceutical Price Regulation Scheme
    (PPRS)   202
private equity and venture capital (PE/VC)
    86–106, 119, 183 *see also* venture capital
  business angels *see main entry*
  definitions and key features   86–87
  investment trends   90, *90*, 91–92, *91–92*,
    *93,*94–96
  market size   88, *89*, 90
  notes and references   104–06
  structure   87–88
protection of intellectual property (brand
    protection) *see* intellectual property

references
  commercial property investment (UK)   61
  commercial property market   45
  private equity and venture capital   104–06
Regional Selective Assistance   263–65
  applications   265
  assistance levels   264–65
  elements judged   264
  forms of assistance   264
  Regional Development Agency (RDA)   265
  regional variations   265
regions   413–566 *see also individual entries
    as on contents pages*
regulation of financial services   392–98
  authorization   396
  collective investment schemes   394–95
  control   397
  EU directives   397–98
  financial businesses   394
  financial promotion/Financial Promotion
    Order (2001)   393–94
  Financial Services Authority (FSA)
    392–93, 396–97
  FSA *Handbook*   395–96
  Regulated Activities order (2001)   393
  scope   392
relocation issues   337–40
  case studies   339, 340
  commercial interior design services
    337–39
  one-stop finance solutions   339–340
  Regional Development Agencies   337
renewable energy   204–18 *see also* renewable
    technologies
  eligible renewable/Renewables Obligation
    204–05, *205*, 206
  export and technology programmes
    216–18
  government policy framework (UK)
    204–06
  investors, opportunities for   217–18
  other support mechanisms   206
renewable technologies   206–16
  advanced thermal technologies   210–11
  biomass   208
  combined heat and power (CHP)   208–09
  combustion with energy recovery   209
  dry biomass fuels   208
  hydropower   211–13
  solar power/PV technology   215–16
  tidal power   213
  useful addresses   207, 211, 214–15, 216
  wave power   213–15
  wet wastes   209
  wind power   206–7
research and development (R&D)   135, 136,
    137, 139, 153, 156, 172, 173, 200, 201,
    202, 206, 211, 263
residential property   66–69
  forecasting future hotspots   67
  profitable investment opportunities
    68–69
  winners and comparative losers   66–68

Scotland: Scottish Enterprise   544–55
  overview and vision   546–47
  economy: demographics and key industry
    547–48, *548*, 459
  foreign direct investment   549–550
  incentives for investors: support
    programmes   550–51
  property   551–52
  transport and communications   552
  education, research and development
    552–54
  public sector support agencies   554–55
small and medium-sized businesses (SMEs)
    93, 101, 223, 224, 234, 235–37, 258, 268,
    269
Small Business Service (SBS)   272–74
  building capability for growth   273
  encouraging dynamic start-up market   272
  finance, improving access to   273–74
  Small Business Research Initiative   273
  Small Firms Loan Guarantee (SFLG)
    programme   273
software   111, 114, 115, 219–26
  IT market (UK)   219–20, *220*
  private sector verticals   224–26
  public sector market overview   22–24
  software market (UK) – product perspective
    220–21
  software market (UK) – vertical perspective
    222–26
South East England Development Agency
    (SEEDA)   516–21
  education   521
  employment   519–20, *520*
  industry sectors   517, *517*, 518
  infrastructure   519
  inward investment   517
  leisure   520–21
  premises   519
  professional support   521
South West England Development Agency
    522–34 *see also* Swindon
  business environment and location
    524–26, 527
  international investment   526
  research and development   526–27
  working environment   526
Stock Exchange, London   19, 22–29, 75, 76,
    79, 88, 99, 117, 183
Stock Exchange Main Market   15–21 *see also*
    Alternative Investment Market (AIM)
  admission   15–16
  advantages/disadvantages   16
  directors' responsibilities   18–19
  Financial Services Authority   15, 17
  flotation timetable   18
  listing costs   18
  OFEX market   19–21
  regulatory requirements   16–17
  techMark/techMark Media Science   15
  UK Listing Authority (UKLA): listing rules
    and continuing obligations   15, 16–17, 18
  ways to market   17–18

Swindon   527–34
  business community   532
  communications   530
  Economic Strategy and Promotion Team
    534
  education and training   531
  employment land and commercial property
    531
  freight transport   530
  housing   532
  labour market   531
  leisure and lifestyle   532–34
  major growth forecast   527–28, 530
  telecommunications   530

tax: capital gains (CGT)   66, 99, 316, 382,
    385–86
  annual exemption/spouse exemption
    385
  business asset taper relief   385, *386*
  non-business asset taper relief   386
  qualifying business assets   386
taxation   65–66, 72, 99, 371–72 *see also* tax
    planning *and* value-added tax
  automotive industry – tax incentives
    139
  business angels – tax incentives   103
  capital gains (CGT)
  corporation tax (CT)   252, 324, 332
  inheritance tax (IHT)   65 , 382, 386–87,
    387, 388, 388
  joint ventures: tax issues   83
taxation for foreign nationals   382–91
  capital gains tax (CGT) *see* tax: capital
    gains (CGT)
  dual contracts   391
  income tax   384
  inheritance tax (IHT)   386–87, *387, 388,
    388*
  Inland Revenue formalities   384
  National Insurance   388–89, *389*
  payment of UK tax   389–90
  remuneration packages   390–91
  residence: dual, ordinary and domicile
    382–84
  taxation in country of origin   391
  trips to home country   391
  UK tax returns   389
taxation planning   324–31
  compliance   330
  consequences of operation via UK resident
    company   324–25
  controlled foreign companies (CFC)   327
  investment in UK properties   327
  key issues   325–26 *see also* taxation
    planning: key issues
  repatriation of profits   328
  sale of UK permanent establishment   327
  trade data and information services   331
  transfer of UK permanent establishment to
    UK company   326–27
  transfer pricing   328–29
  value-added tax (VAT)   329–30

taxation planning: key issues   325–26
  assets, purchase of   325
  shares, purchase of   325
  tax grouping   325–26
technology and innovation   107–18 *see also*
    technology and innovation: Cambridge
    cluster
  Cambridge University   108–09
  consultancies and Cambridge Consultants
    Ltd   108–09
  cultural change, economic viability and
    infrastructure   109
  importance of Cambridge/its institutions
    108–09
  institutional research and development
    109
technology and innovation: Cambridge cluster
    110
  application software   111, 114, 115
  biotechnology   111, 114
  companies   110, *110, 112–13*, 114
  electronic equipment and instruments
    111, 114–15
  investment   115–16, *115*, 116–7, *116, 117*,
    118
  IT sector   111, *111*, 114, 115
  wireless telecommunication services   115
telecommunications   115, 227–33
  broadband   228–29
  case study   233
  customer relationship management (CRM)
    231–32
  in-office communications/infrastructure
  investing in UK   227
  market environment   227–28
  mobile working/technologies   230–31
  outsourcing   231
  sector needs   231–32
  security   232
  wireless technology: Bluetooth and   3G
    229
Trade and Industry, Department of   125,
    173, 256, 262, 268, 304
  Automotive Unit   137
  Electronics Industries Directorate   173
  Global Watch Technology Partnering   217
  Grant for Research and Development   271
  Industrial Development Unit   265
  International Technology Partnership (ITP)
    217
  Renewable Energy Industry Directorate
    206
  Renewables UK (RUK)   206, 216–17
  Small Business Service (SBS)   272
Trade Marks Registry   73, 344, 348
Trade Promotion Service   216, 217
trademarks, registered   344–50
  assignment and licensing   348
  Community Trade Mark Office   345, 348
  domain name disputes   350
  duration and renewal   346
  exclusive rights   346
  infringement   346–48

international aspects   349
IR marks/Madrid Protocol   344
marking® and ™   349
passing off   349–50
qualification for registration   345–50
registration applications   344–45
revocation   348
Transfer of Undertakings (Protection of
    Employment) Regulations (1981)   72,
    252, 369–70

UK see United Kingdom (UK)
UK and the European Union see European
    Union (EU)
UK regional options   413–566
    East Midlands   475–85
    East of England   486–89
    London   490–515
    North East England   415–41
    North West England   442–47
    Northern Ireland   535–43
    Scotland   544–55
    South East England   516–21
    South West England   522–34
    Wales   556–66
    West Midlands   468–74
    Yorkshire and Humber   448–67
United Kingdom (UK) see also immigration
    into the UK
and the European Union see European Union
    (EU)
commercial property investment (UK) see
    main entry
commercial property market (UK): future
    trends see main entry
economy and investment environment (UK)
    see main entry
useful addresses/contacts   61, 217, 569–74,
    581–83
utilities   234–38
    energy efficiency: Action Energy
        programme   236–37
    industry changes   234–35
    investing   234
    online services   236
    retail markets, current   235
    tailor-made service   235–36
    wastage   237–38
    White Paper on energy   238

value-added tax (VAT)   36, 125, 251, 329–30,
    332, 334, 335, 403
    harmonization within the EU   314
Valuation Office Agency (VOA)   30, 36
Venture and Development Capital Investment
    Trusts   88
venture capital   96–101, 149–50, 302
    Bridges Community Ventures   100, 101,
        273
    Corporate Venturing Scheme   100
    Early Growth programme   98, 273
    Enterprise Capital Funds (ECFs)   101
    Regional Venture Capital Funds   97–98,
        98, 273
    UK High Technology Fund   98–99
    University Challenge Funds (UCFs)   97
    venture capital trusts (VCTs)   88, 99, 183
    Venture Capital Association, British   87,
        88, 104

Wales: Welsh Development Agency   556–66
    education, research and development
        564–65
    incentives for investors   559–61
    overview and demographics   557–58, 558
    property   561
    public sector support agencies   565–66
    transport and communications   562–63
    Welsh economy and foreign direct
        investment   558–59
websites   7, 29, 36, 43, 61, 118, 121, 122, 123,
    124,125, 126, 127, 129, 139, 141, 144,
    168, 173,   174, 197, 207, 211, 215, 216,
    217, 218, 236, 257, 261, 268, 269, 270,
    271,   282, 430–32, 543, 554–55, 565–66,
    575–80
West Midlands: West Midlands Development
    Agency   468–74
    inward investment   473, 473–74
    research infrastructure   472
    science/business parks   469, 472
    transport links   472–73
    universities   469

Yorkshire Forward   448–50, 450, 452–67 see
    also Barnsley and Doncaster

Index of Advertisers

Artaius Ltd (Business Outsource Solutions) 287
Barnsley Development Agency 457
Doncaster Investment Team 465
English Partnerships (National Regeneration Agency) 63
Gateshead Council 433
Gateway to London 511
Invest in Bradford 449
Inward Investment Nottingham 483
Leicester Shire Promotions Ltd 481
London Development Agency 491
Newcastle City Council 437
Northern Ireland Development Agency 537
One North East 417
RiDO (Rotherham Investment & Development Office) 453–55
Royal Opera House 162–63, 169
Scottish Development International 545
Snapshots International Ltd iv
South West of England Regional Development Board 523
SPB³ 336
Swindon Borough Council 529
Taylor Wessing 70, 342, 487
UK Trade & Investment 8
UKTRADEINFO (HM Customs and Excise) 132, 331
West Midland Development Agency 470–71
Yorkshire Forward 451